Edwards
on the Will

The Reverend Jonathan Edwards. Oil portrait, c. 1750–1755, by Joseph Badger
Yale University Art Gallery. Bequest of Eugene Phelps Edwards, 1938

Edwards on the Will

A Century of American Theological Debate

Allen C. Guelzo

Wesleyan University Press

Middletown, Connecticut

All inquiries and permissions requests should be addressed to the Publisher, Wesleyan University Press, 110 Mt. Vernon Street, Middletown, Connecticut 06457

LIBRARY OF CONGRESS CATALOGING-IN-PUBLICATION DATA

Guelzo, Allen C.
   Edwards on the will: a century of American theological debate/Allen
C. Guelzo.—1st ed.
      p.   cm.
   Bibliography: p.
   Includes index.
   ISBN 0-8195-5193-7
      1. Freedom (Theology)—History of doctrines—18th century.
2. Freedom (Theology)—History of doctrines—19th century.
3. Calvinism—New England—History—18th century.
4. Calvinism—New England—History—19th century.
5. Edwards, Jonathan, 1703–1758—Influence.   I. Title.
BT809.G84   1989
233'.7'0924—dc19   88-19848
                                                            CIP

Manufactured in the United States of America

FIRST EDITION

For Alan Charles Kors
"A friend in need is a friend indeed"

"Croyez-vous, dit *Candide,* que les hommes se soient toujours
mutuellement massacrés comme ils font aujourd'hui? qu'ils ayent toujours été menteurs, fourbes, perfides, ingrats, brigands,
faibles, volages, lâches, envieux, gourmands, yvrognes, avares,
ambitieux, sanguinaires, calomniateurs, débauchés, fanatiques,
hypocrites & sots?—Croyez-vous, dit *Martin,* que les éperviers
ayent toujours mangé des pigeons quand ils en ont trouvé?—
Oui sans doute, dit *Candide.*—Eh bien! dit *Martin,* si les éperviers . . . pourquoi voulez-vous que les hommes ayent changé
le leur?—Oh! dit *Candide,* il y a bien de la différence, car le
libre arbitre . . ." En raisonnant ainsi ils arrivèrent à Bordeaux.

Voltaire, *Candide, ou L'Optimisme*

Contents

Illustrations

Acknowledgments

One is never quite sure whether acknowledgments ought to go at the back or the front of a book. So much self-congratulation goes on in the customary acknowledgments that it often resembles a party the author throws for his friends to celebrate the completion of his opus. In that light, the only proper place for such literary receiving lines is firmly at the end, when the work is over and done and all fear of academic miscarriage is past.

On the other hand, the acknowledgments also function as the outline of the shoulders we have stood upon in glimpsing the procession of historical events. They are, as Jonathan Edwards would be happy to hear us say, a confession of our reliance upon grace, and, as grace precedes all other qualities in the *ordo salutis,* it is just as well that the choir of acknowledgments goes first.

The origins of this book lie principally in the now-famous seminars on American intellectual history run by Bruce Kuklick in his office-garret at the University of Pennsylvania in 1980 and 1984. (I was part of the first of these, in the fall of 1980.) It will not take the reader long to guess that Kuklick's ideas and methods are the models for much of my interpretation of the Edwardsean legacy, although the canvas upon which I have chosen to paint is significantly smaller than his. To him belongs a tremendous measure of thanks, and whatever honors may be due this work.

Another major event in the composition of this book was the conference "Jonathan Edwards and the American Experience" sponsored by The Institute for the Study of American Evangelicals in October 1984 at Wheaton College, Wheaton, Illinois. It was an unusual assemblage in that an evangelical organization brought together a corps of almost exclusively secular scholars to comment on the most consistently unsecular thinker in American history. It was even more unusual that a conference on Edwards, sponsored by evangelicals under the roof of a building named for Billy Graham, could talk for three days about Edwards and never once mention "Sinners In the Hands of An Angry

God." Nevertheless, the papers read at the conference helped stimulate
my thinking on a number of important points, but, even more, the
conference gave me the opportunity to meet many of the major inter-
preters of Edwards at work today. James Hoopes was more help to me
than he probably imagined by clearing up some critical questions on
Edwards's religious psychology, and I would be a poor Calvinist indeed
if I failed to note the special grace with which Hoopes shared not only
the text of his Wheaton paper (which has only just appeared in a
volume of the conference papers, *Jonathan Edwards and the American
Experience,* edited by Nathan O. Hatch and Harry S. Stout) but an
earlier paper he read to an association meeting of the American Society
of Church History. Thomas Shafer gave freely of his time in correspondence and provided access to the Edwards manuscripts at Yale,
and William Breitenbach shared notes and comments on his own work
on the New Divinity. Norman Fiering arrayed before me topics for
further research, and appropriately scolded me for leaning Edwards too
heavily against Locke.

Other encouragements came from rather more unusual quarters. I
owe much to three classes of students in the Theological Seminary of
the Reformed Episcopal Church who agonized with me (or perhaps
because of me) as I labored to make sense of the theological skeins of
Tasters and Exercisers, Tylerites and Taylorites, and Old Calvinists and
New Divinity. The Reverend Dr. James Montgomery Boice of the Tenth
Presbyterian Church in Philadelphia read parts of the manuscript and,
perhaps unknowingly, made one comment to me which kept me buoyed
up in some heavy academic waters. Charles Dennison and Richard
Gamble kindly consented to allow me to shelve their original invitation
for a paper on Anglicanism in the Revolutionary period and agreed to
publish instead an early version of chapters three and four in *Pressing
Toward the Mark: Essays Commemorating Fifty Years of the Orthodox Presbyterian Church* (Philadelphia, 1986). My brother-in-law, The
Reverend Gregory K. Hotchkiss of Emmanuel Reformed Episcopal
Church, Somerville, New Jersey, patiently agreed to being pulled along
in friendly incomprehension on a number of research expeditions, and
never hinted at what must have gone through his mind, that much
learning had made me mad. Peter Potter of Wesleyan University Press,
who first approached me about the publication of the dissertation as
a book, has provided gentle guidance through the editorial process,

and Jeannette Hopkins, also of Wesleyan, has played the stern but skillful role of bringing textual order out of dissertational chaos.

Special words of gratitude need to be uttered about several select libraries, which stand as reminders of the collective as well as the individual aspect of grace. The Speer Library at Princeton Theological Seminary allowed me free access to rare and precious volumes, and much of this book is distilled from hours, days, and weeks spent in the environs of Princeton. Roy Goodwin of the American Philosophical Society in Philadelphia unfailingly made the APS Library a friendly home for research, no matter how outré a dissertation on the extreme bitter ends of Calvinist theology must have seemed under the aegis of Benjamin Franklin.

The librarians of the Case Memorial Library at Hartford Theological Seminary and of the Presbyterian Historical Society in Philadelphia listened patiently to every absurd request I made, and then did more than I could have imagined and desired. Additional work was made lighter by the help of the C. P. Van Pelt Library at the University of Pennsylvania, the Firestone Library of Princeton University, and that sine qua non of all latter-day Edwardseans, the Beinecke Rare Book Library at Yale University.

To Alan Charles Kors, my debts need no explaining, for he knows what they are. For Debra, continuous in season and out of season in the midst of the bottomless sea of Edwardsean divinity, and for Jerusha, Alexandra, and Jonathan, there are other, vaster, sweeter debts which I daily repay in the typically Edwardsean coinage of the true affections of the heart.

Edwards
on the Will

Introduction

"Edwards on the Will"

"Edwards on the Will"—no single title in American literature has ever had quite the ring of finality, of unquestioned settlement of dispute, as this. For Herman Melville, it was the obvious key to unlock the mystery of Bartleby the Scrivener; for Oliver Wendell Holmes, it was the supreme creation of the Puritanism he longed to shed, so maddeningly perfect in all its parts that it was impervious to logical wear and tear; for Harriet Beecher Stowe, it was the touchstone of New England Calvinism and New England identity. One hundred and ten years after the first appearance of "Edwards on the Will," Rowland Hazard, the amateur Quaker-born philosopher, helplessly acknowledged that "by common consent" it was "deemed impregnable." In Scotland, Thomas Chalmers lauded it as that "which has helped me more than any other uninspired book to find my way through all that might otherwise have proved baffling, and transcendental, and mysterious in the peculiarities of Calvinism." In Isaac Taylor's pungent phrase, it taught the world "to be less flippant."[1]

And yet, for all the laurels heaped upon it, Jonathan Edwards's *A Careful and Strict Enquiry into the Modern Prevailing Notions of that Freedom of Will which is supposed to be essential to Moral Agency, Vertue and Vice, Reward and Punishment, Praise and Blame* has proven in modern times an elusive work. Edwards's literary and historical admirers are generally content to let its sleeping dogmas lie, to acknowledge in a breath its genius and then move hurriedly past to other Edwardseana of less forbidding aspect. Perhaps this is because it is in the nature of literary history to confuse the historical and the aesthetic, and to think that an aesthetic appreciation of grandeur is an adequate substitute for historical understanding; perhaps it is because Edwards has fared better at the hands of historians of philosophy since they usually want, for heuristic purposes, an Edwards of paramount genius sufficient to justify the study of American philosophy (and "Edwards on the Will" gives them this beyond question); but they also want a teleology that will guarantee the triumph of a Benjamin Franklin (who, ironically, wrote an early dissertation on freedom of the will himself). No one seems to fail to call *Freedom of the Will* a work of genius; but by acknowledging its genius scholars have apparently assumed that *Freedom of the Will* need no longer be taken seriously as history.

So, for a considerably long period of time, Edwards's massive exposition of "that freedom of will" has been treated as a kind of cultural oxymoron, without father, without mother, without genealogy, a New England Melchizedek greeting a bewildered American Abraham with sacrifices which secretly terrify him. It has been stood off by itself, like a Puritan *doctrine* bereft of any *uses* or *applications,* as though it were feared that the *uses* of such a work might be more (as someone once said of Edwards's personality) than ordinary people could bear. Sometimes, *Freedom of the Will* has been looked upon as the ultimate jeremiad. More often, we have taken Holmes's way out and caricatured it as Holmes did in "The Deacon's Masterpiece," as a sort of "wonderful one-hoss shay," an interesting contraption to be sure, but one which conveniently fell apart on its own in some unexplained fashion, thus eliminating the need to confront either its claims or its consequences. One literary historian cried out in frustration at a 1984 conference on Edwards, "What does this preoccupation with the will mean?" And it was a frustration as much directed at his fellows as at Edwards.

Part of the problem, to be fair, is that our expectations of Edwards may actually be too high. *Freedom of the Will* is a work of philosophical genius, but Edwards was not a consistent philosopher; he considered himself first and foremost a Congregational parson and never thought of himself as a philosopher. Those who expect his *Miscellanies* (when they are finally published in full) to yield a full intellectual crop are in for an unpleasant surprise. Nor is this merely an accident of genre, for no work of Edwards reveals his patchiness and "variousness" as a thinker more than *Freedom of the Will.* For instance it is a book of undisguised theological intentions, put in terms of a "secular" argument. And it is also a book which introduces a powerful and systematic case for Calvinist predestinarianism, but which concludes by asserting that the author, at least on his own terms, really does believe in freedom of the will.

On the other hand, one has to grant at least some of his "various-ness" to genre, if only because the subject of "free will" encompasses so great a stretch of philosophical terrain, and his place as a specifically Christian thinker only made his path through that terrain narrower and more treacherous. The very fact that the concept of "will" has found a place in Western philosophy owes more to Christian theology than a philosophy. The Greeks, for one, never talked about the "will" or "freedom of the will"; the notion is untranslatable into Platonic or Homeric Greek.[2] The vital catalyst in the arrival of the idea of an independent faculty of will was the intermingling of Christian theology, and the psychology it implied, and classical civilization. And no single Christian theologian did more to bring the concept of the will, con-ceived as a separate entity, into common currency than St. Augustine, whose *Confessions* are the first book of Christian spirituality to mark out clearly the full force of the limits of human freedom by "a chain of habit" within with no reference point other than willing itself.[3] "I knew I had a will [*voluntas*]," Augustine wrote, "as surely as I knew I had life in me." He clearly perceived that, within his conscious self, the mind may try to order itself to "make an act of will . . . yet it does not carry out its own command." Hence, this opposition of mind and will is so formidable, and the mind so easily thwarted, that the "will" must surely enjoy a status independent of the understanding or the appetites, and is sufficiently powerful to check the mind: "the mind is not moved until it wills to be moved." Augustine discovered, when he first contemplated making a public confession of Christianity, that his ideas were entirely at the mercy of an obstinate will: "I was held fast, not in fetters clamped upon me by another, but by my own will, which had the strength of iron chains."[4] Augustine's fascinated exploration of the notion of will by no means settled what the nature of that will was.

According to the categories of the Protestant scholastic thought of the seventeenth century, the most critical relationship among the fac-ulties of the mind was considered to be one of intellect and will, both of which were viewed, along with perception and judgment, as sub-departments of the overall phenomenon of mind. Because of the inher-ent bias of Christian theology toward teleological considerations, the Protestant scholastics—Turretin, Burgersdyck, Voetius, de Maastricht, all of whom Jonathan Edwards was to read as a Yale undergraduate—structured these subdepartments, or faculties, as a hierarchy, and graded them from the most important to the least. But there was no agreement, even in Calvinist New England, on whether intellect or will ought to have first place. "Intellectualists," for instance, placed the intellect first, and conceived of thought as a process in which the intellect synthesizes the information provided by perception and judgment and gives the will orders to follow or to flee from the object of thought. The intellect, then, was clearly considered to be superior to the will, which exists primarily to execute the orders of the intellect. While this is certainly not an Augustinian notion, it has strong classical overtones nevertheless and it acquired a strong following in Christian thought, including the moral philosophy presented in textbooks of Edwards's New England.[5] Calvin taught that "the human soul consists of two faculties, understanding and will"; the understanding distinguishes between good and bad, and the will either follows or flees as the understanding dictates. The mind thus judges—and in judging it instructs the will how to respond, so that "the understanding is, as it were, the leader and governor of the soul; and that the will is always mindful of the bidding of the understanding, and its own desires await the judgement of the understanding."[6] The understanding, Calvin concluded, "is our most excellent part; it holds the primacy in the life of man, is the seat of reason, presides over the will, and restrains vicious desires."[7]

Diametrically opposed (at least on paper) to the intellectualist stood the "voluntarist," who awarded the will the supremacy over the intellect in choice, and this, too, had an impressive genealogy, stretching back through Scotus and the Franciscans to Augustine himself. The voluntarist reversed the priority of intellect and will, and viewed the process of knowing as beginning with perception, judgment, and intellect, remaining a potential quality until and unless the will chooses to cooperate.[8] Voluntarists gave the will this veto power over the intellect itself because they observed that people often see, judge, and understand an object to be good and desirable, yet choose evil anyway. They further observed that even the acts of perceiving, judging, and knowing require decisions to look, to reflect, and to acknowledge. The will thus stands at the pinnacle of the hierarchy of faculties; it is essential to each faculty's operation.

Consequently, the stocking up of the understanding with appropriate facts about godliness brings submission, an end to *masterlessness*, and a decisive act of volition. The most radical scholastic statement of this relationship was certainly John Duns Scotus's maxim *nihil aliud a voluntate est causa totalis volitionis in voluntate*[9] (the will alone is the total cause of choice in the will). But the most piquant scholastic illustration of the incapacity of the intellect to choose is "Buridan's ass." An echo of this will turn up in *Freedom of the Will* in Edwards's example of the chess board. Suppose an ass is placed at equal distances between two equal bundles of hay. The ass's intellect perceives that both are good, but because they are equally good, he cannot tell his will which of the two is the greater good to apprehend, and so he dies of starvation in the midst of plenty since his will is compelled to wait upon recognition by the intellect of which bale is the primary good. Obviously, however, asses do not die in this way; any normal ass would have been led to the one or the other by an effort of will. It was not that voluntarists deprecated knowledge per se, but, in the words of the much revered Puritan theologian William Ames, there was no real force in it without an application of the will: "will is the principle and the first cause of all humane operation in regard to the exercise of the act"; thus, "it follows that the first and proper subject of theology is the will.[10]

But this left the voluntarists with the need to explain *how* the will could make all these choices *prior* to the action. The answer supplied by one school of voluntarists, ranging from Augustine to Jonathan Edwards, was to suggest that the will, although a faculty of the mind, was also directly influenced by the other great psychological entity within the human soul, the *affections*. The scholastic psychology, in which both Timothy and Jonathan Edwards were reared, pictured man as a composite of thinking (which included the mental faculties of perceiving, judging, understanding, and willing) and feeling, and they regarded the feelings, or affections, as the other great pillar of human psychology. The intellectualists had little use for the affections in their descriptions of religious psychology; the voluntarists, however, saw that the affections (which they sometimes referred to as "the heart") could often play an important role, and they frequently described conversion and depravity in terms of the affections, or "the heart."

The best example of this is Augustine himself. "In my case," Augustine explained, "love is the weight by which I act. . . . To whatever place I go, I am drawn to it by love." The will is not an independent actor; it is at the mercy of love. Augustine compared his will to a sack, pulled down to various levels according to the amount of love weighing it down. Let the will be filled with the love of God, and the self will be drawn to follow the will to God; on the other hand, let the will be weighted with lust, and the self will be drawn to it by concupiscence.[11] The will could not be mere freedom, for Augustine discovered time and again that his will was not free to countermand what he loved. "Through sin freedom indeed perished," Augustine warned, for men sin, and love sinning, and so make themselves and their wills so weighted with lust that resistance is in vain. "I am better only when in sorrow of heart I detest myself and seek your mercy," Augustine prayed to God, "until what is faulty in me is repaired and made whole and finally I come to that state of peace which the eye of the proud cannot see."[12] All the emphasis here is on the quality of the affections, the purity of heart, and the proper object of love, and that becomes the central factor in choice.

Even though Calvin is usually classed as an intellectualist, he was hesitant to wall off the intellect from the play of the affections, and he occasionally granted a degree of independence to the feeling of *suavitas* ("sweetness") in religious self-knowledge.[13] And as for his Puritan heirs, no matter what the Harvard textbooks dictated, "heart-language" remained one of the most distinguishing traits of Puritanism. John Winthrop knew he could not have been converted at age fourteen, when he had his third great round of spiritual excitements, because he could not say for sure "how my heart was affected." But when he came under the preaching of Ezekiel Culverwell in 1606, he found "the ministry of the word to come to my heart with power," so that at age thirty, God gave to him "enlargement of heart" to "cry, my father, with more confidence."[14] More than Culverwell, however, Winthrop's pastor in the New World Boston, John Cotton, set forth clearly for Winthrop the Augustinian identification of the will with the "heart." "By the heart," Cotton taught, "is here understood, not as sometimes it is taken, for the mind and judgment, for they are no such faculties." Instead, "by the heart . . . is meant the will of a man, which lyes in the heart, for as the understanding lyes in the head or braine, so the will is seated in the heart."[15] And with that, Cotton insisted on the psychological supremacy of this heart-cum-will. "The heart is the principall faculty of the soule, it rules all, it sets hand and tongue all within a-work." Therefore, Cotton made "keeping the heart" the essence, even the synonym, of moral choice:

Keepe the heart well, and you keepe all in a goode frame: all the senses behold not an object so much as the heart doth; Set before a man any pleasant prospect, and if his mind be on another things, all his senses take no notice of it; if the heart be not taken up with a thing, the eye minds it not; present the eare with any sweet melodious sound, and it heares and minds it not, because the heart was otherwise taken up. . . . If you have the whole man, and not the heart, you have but a dead man, get the heart and you have all.[16]

No matter how one chooses to define the will, the question of greatest importance will always be whether, given any of these definitions, the will is free. Unhappily, the three available answers—"sometimes" (soft determinism), "always" (libertarianism), or "never" (hard determinism)—have been applied to each of the basic theories of will, so that within each there can be conflicting answers as to whether the will is free.[17]

"Hard determinism" most often thinks of freedom as self-determination, and, precisely for that reason, hard determinists as a rule deny that the will can be free, simply because they do not believe that "selves" have the capacity to determine their own existence, much less their own choices. Hard determinism, according to the rationalist philosopher Brand Blanshard, is "the view that all events are caused," or "that every event A is so connected with a later event B that, given A, B must occur."[18] Since it is difficult for most people to argue with the apparent obviousness of cause-effect relationships, the "soft determinists," or *reconciliationists*, generally yield ground and then try to argue about what a cause is, rather than deny that things have causes. In some circumstances, reconciliationists agree that "cause" describes something inevitable. With this notion of cause, which reconciliationists associate with objective compulsion, there is usually a struggle or combat in which the loser is necessarily overborne by the cause. There remain occasions, nevertheless, in which causality does not induce combat. Most often, reconciliationists point to events in which a subjective cause necessitates a certain movement of the will but does so in a direction we, in some way, already desire. In this respect, the will is caused but at the same time it apprehends what the self really desires anyway, and hence, there is no sense of struggle. So long as nothing external to the self interferes with such a volition, the reconciliationist demands to know why this cannot be considered a free act.

By "free," the reconciliationist means not noncausal, but simply "the ability to act according to one's choices." It is all the difference between saying "we are free to do what we will" (which is what the hard determinist opposes) and "we are free to do as we will." Thus, the soft determinist will ask only if an act is objectively valid—that the self can perform without physical hindrance—and leave aside the matter of subjective validity (whether the self or the will really is the cause of what the will wants to do).[19]

The great problem with this, respond the critics of reconciliationism, is that it resembles a sort of intellectual shell game in which determinism and free will are alternately hidden or displayed as need arises; or a sleight-of-hand trick that reconciles a contradiction chiefly by changing the meaning of one of the terms. Shell game or not, reconciliationism ironically reflects much of the ordinary patterns of human thought. R. E. Hobart has observed:

In daily life we are all determinists, just as we are all libertarians. We are constantly attributing behavior to the character, the temperament, the peculiarities of the person and expecting him to behave in certain fashions. The very words of our daily conversation . . . are full of determinism. And we see nothing inconsistent in being aware at the same time [of being] free in choosing.[20]

The mention of libertarianism brings us to the third answer to the question of free will. Libertarianism is, essentially, the opposite of determinism, but not the polar opposite, since libertarians will grant that *some* events are caused. In general, the libertarian holds that in every circumstance a spontaneous act may or may not occur that, in turn, completely changes the course of things, and, says the libertarian, the human will is capable of providing such spontaneity.[21] It is, in a word, *uncaused* in all, or at least in some, of its motions.

Straightforward as this sounds, there are ironies in libertarianism no less than in reconciliationism. Obviously, there is vast scope for responsibility here since the soul becomes the only agent of action. But if the will is free and uncaused, it may lead us to free action, but it may also lead us to meaningless action, or acts done wildly at random, and if the will can be free only by acting out of chance, then we are in perhaps a worse position than the hard determinist, who at least is supported by laws.

Perhaps the greatest irony in all of these terms is how little they accomplish in the way of persuasion. In some airy world of abstract theory it may be possible to arrive at an opinion concerning the will simply by examining the alternatives, and then arriving at a serenely objective decision. In fact, for most of the history of controversies over the will, the very opposite procedure has taken place: people begin with the opinion that the will is, or is not, free a priori, and they then work back from there to which theory of will they propose to hold. This occurs chiefly because in Western Christian theology there has always been another, more powerful, Will to take into consideration beyond that of the individual human. Grant the existence of God, as Jonathan Edwards most certainly did, and one at once acknowledges a Being more powerful than oneself, and if more powerful then also able to restrict or even dictate one's choices, regardless of whether one thinks one's will free or not. Add to that the Christian doctrines of the sinful depravity of human beings and the necessity of redemption from sin by the God-Man, Jesus Christ, and it begins to appear that the human will is not only restricted before we can even agree on what it is, but that independent human willing may be downright undesirable, since the human will, being depraved, can only ever will in defiance and rebellion. The most obvious example of the impact of this theological a priori is John Calvin, who held that

> By his providence, God rules not only the whole fabric of the world and its several parts, but also the hearts and even the actions of men. . . . We mean by providence not an idle observation by God in heaven of what goes on in earth, but His rule of the world which He made; for he is not the creator of a moment, but the perpetual governor. . . . So he is said to rule the world in His providence, not only because He watches the order of nature imposed by Himself, but because He has and exercises a particular care of each one of his creatures.[22]

However, mere declarations of divine sovereignty—and one can get them in just as hair-raising a form from St. Thomas Aquinas as from John Calvin—do not automatically settle the matter in everyone's mind, since people are not generally fond of being told that they can't help what they're doing, no matter on whose authority. Calvin's nemesis, the Dutch theologian Jacobus Arminius, rejected Calvin's notions of divine sovereignty on the humanitarian grounds that

> it is scarcely possible for any other result to ensue, than that the individual who cannot even with great difficulty work a persuasion within himself of his being elected should soon consider himself included in the number of the reprobate. From such an apprehension as this must arise a certain despair of performing righteousness and obtaining salvation.[23]

Arminius was perfectly happy to have God rule by "influence and concurrence" in man's salvation, but only so long as this activity amounts to no more than an "influence" on the recipients of it. Certainly Calvin and Luther and Augustine felt the sting of these criticisms, and in their

writings we see some of the finest, as well as most tortured, demonstrations of reconciliationism available, as each rushes to retort that he
is really not denying free will at all. Augustine, in his struggle with the
Pelagians, insisted that we always possessed *liberum arbitrium,* but not
libertas—we have, in other words, freedom to perform the act of choice
in all cases not involving outright physical compulsion, but we do not,
as sinners, have the liberty to choose the objects of choice.[24] Luther
strained in his polemic reply to Erasmus, *De Servo Arbitrio,* to make
it plain that he was preaching "a necessity, not of compulsion, but of
what they call immutability."[25] Even Calvin claimed, "Compulsion I
always exclude," for though "we can do nothing of our own accord
but sin . . . this does not therefore mean . . . a forced restraint but a
voluntary obedience, to which an inborn bondage inclines us."[26] Even
Timothy Edwards's near contemporary, John Norton of Boston, insisted that "Necessity of infallibility doth not prejudice liberty."[27]

But theological reconciliationism, like reconciliationism in general,
always has an air of unreality to it, of talk that somehow masks the
obvious. Calvin recognized this when he pondered the sort of free will
left by the reconciliationist versions of "necessity":

Man will then be spoken of as having this sort of free decision, not because
he has free choice equally of good and evil, but because he acts wickedly by
will, not by compulsion. Well put, indeed, but what purpose is served by
labelling with a proud name such a slight thing? A noble freedom, indeed—
for man not to be forced to serve sin, yet to be such a willing slave that his
will is bound by the fetters of sin.[28]

If we are all that eager to have free will, why not jettison predestination
and save ourselves the grief of logic-chopping? Because, no matter how
badly we desire to avoid holding a "repugnant" opinion, predestination
has been a vital emotional part of Christianity, perhaps even more
important for its aesthetic than for its doctrinal use. Just how much
emotion lay behind the abstractions of "necessity" appears in manifold
places, but never more dramatically than in Luther, who denied not
only that he had free will but that he even wanted it:

I frankly confess that, for myself, even if it could be, I should not want free-
will to be given to me, nor anything to be left in my own hands to enable me
to endeavour after salvation; not merely because in the face of so many dangers,
and adversities, and assaults of devils I could not stand my ground, and hold
fast my "free-will" . . . but because, even were there no dangers, adversities or
devils, I should still be forced to labour with no guarantee of success, and to
beat my fists at the air. If I lived and worked to all eternity, my conscience

would never reach comfortable certainty as to how much it must do to satisfy God. Whatever work I had done, there would still be a nagging doubt as to whether it pleased God, or whether he required something more. The experience of all who seek righteousness by works proves that; and I learned it well enough myself over a period of many years.[29]

In this context, Arminian (or Pelagian or Erasmian) "free-will" became a metaphor for religious indifference. And so, until the seventeenth century, the energies of Protestantism were linked, in various ways, to determinism and predestination, and doctrines of free will were considered at best to be evidence of a half-hearted Erasmianism, and, at worst, downright atheism.

The philosophical revolution of the seventeenth century we sometimes call the "New Philosophy" successfully stood that arrangement on its head, and sent Protestant divines fleeing to free will for protection from a new kind of determinism—an atheistic one. The fundamental cause for this dramatic shift lies in the seventeenth century's daring overthrow of the Aristotelian mechanics, with its conception of matter as something *moving* according to active, "occult" powers, by the new mechanics of Kepler and Galileo, with their notion of an impersonal and indifferent matter *being moved* by other matter. While the purely physical aspects of this revolution had little to do with theology, it quickly became apparent, and not only to Galileo's ecclesiastical inquisitors, that the denial of activity to matter and the exclusion of spiritual causality lay bare a route to denying the activity of God in the universe, and perhaps to atheism as well. An agitated Richard Baxter compared his modern "Epicureans" to "idle boys who tear out all the hard leaves of their books and say they have learned all when they have learned the rest," for "they cut off and deny the noblest parts of nature and then sweep together the dust of agitated atoms and tell us that they have resolved all the phenomena in nature."[30] On those terms, as Baxter well knew, there can be no predestination (in the sense of a divine spiritual cause) but likewise there can be no self-determination either, and humanity would, in that case, turn out to be the plaything of a faceless determinism that makes nonsense of responsibility and moral choice.

The face of this new determinism was limned out with what amounted to intellectual glee by the most notorious of Baxter's "Epicureans," Thomas Hobbes, and though he was almost the only one to put it as bluntly as he did in his *Leviathan* (1651), he still succeeded in scaring the entire English-speaking theological community out of its wits. Hobbes preached a materialism so thoroughgoing as to make seventeenth-century readers wince, but what drove them wild was Hobbes's strategy of presenting a thoroughly materialistic concept of causality in theological terms. After all, to assert that all events happen as a result of God's laws does not seem to be saying anything all that much different from the claim that everything in the universe happens as a result of mechanical laws. This allowed the rankest materialist to denounce free will with all the zeal of the most spiritual Calvinist. "The question," Hobbes began, "is not whether a man be a free agent," since liberty "is the absence of all impediments to action that are not contained in the nature and intrinsical quality of the agent." There is no such thing as a "faculty" of willing, bound or unbound; "will" is merely the product of a chain of purely physical occurrences:

I conceive that in all deliberations, that is to say, in alternate succession of contrary appetites, the last is that which we call the WILL, and is immediately next before the doing of the action, or next before the doing of it becomes impossible. All other appetites to do, and to quit, that come upon a man during his deliberations, are called intentions, and inclinations, but not wills, there being but one will, which also in this case may be called the last will.[31]

Hobbes, in short, simply reduced the elaborate structure of scholastic psychology to a rubble of words, and eliminated any fundamental distinction between active or passive, dominant or subordinate, faculties within the mind. He conceived of volition in terms of a "single-stage" occurrence in which a single volition is merely an extension of an appetite, so that the will is whittled down to nothing more than a name by which we identify the last in a series of appetites. Add to that Hobbes's consideration that the appetites themselves are merely the mechanical by-product of sensation, and then one has but to supply an external cause, and the whole chain of appetites will necessarily and inexorably produce a volition.

I conceive that nothing taketh beginning from itself, but from the actions of some other immediate agent without itself. And that therefore, when first a man hath an appetite or will to something, to which immediately before he had no appetite or will, the cause of his will, is not the will itself, but something else not in his disposing. To that whereas it is out of controversy, that of voluntary actions the will is the necessary cause . . . it followeth that voluntary actions have all of them necessary causes, and therefore are necessitated.[32]

Of course, then, men were free—just as the Calvinists had said, they were free to do what it was decreed they should do, only now material substance was doing the decreeing. This left the Calvinist with the unpleasant alternative of having to assert indeterminism and libertarianism to order to prove that the mechanical clashing of gears was not all there was to the world, or else be tarred with the brush of Hobbes's mechanism. "There is a plain agreement," Daniel Whitby declared, "betwixt the doctrine of Mr. Hobbes, and of these men [Calvinists], concerning this matter, as to the great concernments of religion," and Calvinists, even great and famous ones like Isaac Watts, took appropriate note and abandoned the predestinarian ship.[33]

The only way left to prove the existence of spiritual substance seemed to be to create some room for the free will of intelligent, spiritual creatures, and this is precisely what English-speaking divines, Anglican and Nonconformist alike, rushed, if in a confused and unholy jumble, to do. They did so, as Samuel Clarke and Richard Bentley did, by pushing the question of active and passive powers back to the front and by insisting that volition really comprises a "two-stage" process in which passive desires are carefully distinguished from an active will—"a different Thing from the Act of Volition"—which is exempt from causal necessity and which is empowered to deal rationally and morally with whatever the desires may be.[34] In his Boyle Lectures of 1704 and 1705, Clarke insisted that the will was an active, independent agent, and not subject to simple determination:

intelligent beings are agents; not passive in being moved by motives as a balance is by weights, but they have active powers and do move themselves, sometimes upon weak ones and sometimes where things are absolutely indifferent.[35]

Or they did so, as Thomas Reid and the Scottish "common sense" philosophers did, by appealing to the direct intuition of freedom which all men find when they have "looked into their own breasts," for the common sense of mankind intuitively senses that acts of will occur freely.[36] Together, their endeavor to undercut the threat of materialistic atheism by resorting to hastily fashioned brands of theistic libertarianism raised up and made respectable the old banner of "Arminianism" and threw Calvinism into a disarray from which it has never entirely emerged.

A large part of this book is given over to examining how New England Calvinism, and particularly Jonathan Edwards, responded to this crisis. The "covenant" theology upon which so much of New England's clergy was built was itself a will-oriented theory, as was the word *covenant* itself. Unlike the medieval Church, which inherited from Thomas Aquinas a view of the relationship of God and human as static and naturalistic, the Reformation conceived of that relationship as dynamic—an unnatural, arbitrary relationship between two utterly unlike parties, which can be bridged only by an act of will. The "covenant" theology of the Puritans was simply another way of recognizing that to cross the gap separating the human being and God requires a voluntary, gracious transaction—an effort of will. Similarly, the "covenanted" churches of the New England Puritans were also a recognition that sin divides people from people, as well as people from God. They testified that the comprehensive, parish-type organization of the Church of England was as ineffective in bridging the human gap as Thomism had been in bridging the divine gap. Accordingly, the "covenanted" church embodied the same principle as the covenant theology, that true union could not be had on natural terms but only by a conscious consent—again, an effort of will. Thus, the Puritan Calvinism of New England found itself absorbed in the need to understand and control the activity and freedom of the will. And since the greater part of American intellectual life before the Civil War was in one way or another linked to Trinitarian Calvinism, it is no surprise that any approach to the problem of freedom of the will ends up heavily weighted with the names of New England Calvinists.

But Edwards's name towers above them all, and not just because his *Freedom of the Will* deals with this dilemma in a fashion sophisticated beyond the grasp of any other Calvinists (or perhaps any other Americans), and turned all subsequent discussion of freedom of the will for a century thereafter into a referendum on his ideas. On the broadest level, Edwards aimed to address an international audience, and thus deal with the perplexing reversal of roles in the eighteenth-century free-will debate. But Edwards also intended to speak to a problem in the New England mind, and *Freedom of the Will* is as much directed to weak-kneed Calvinists as it is to hard-core Arminians. *Freedom of the Will* was Edwards's means of reawakening New England to the demands of the will and to the dreadful anger of a God who kept wicked individuals out of hell only by a pure, arbitrary act of mercy. In this respect, *Freedom of the Will* shoots beyond the customary philosophical targets in the free-will debate to strike at the comfortable naturalism into which a century of prosperity had wooed the erstwhile soldiers of the Covenant.

Indeed, Edwards did not really address the problem of free will as a problem, after all. Instead, he used it as a way to speak to the deepest urges of Puritanism and of New England's collective memory of its own uniqueness, for Edwards's elevation of the critical significance of utter individual *choosing* in religion and ethics boded ill for the organic church-and-community relationships that American Calvinists, in New England and elsewhere, had either inherited or copied from Europe. After Edwards's death, his New Divinity disciples, bound together by the cords of *Freedom of the Will*'s logic in the most remarkable speculative coterie even seen in America, launched a savage assault on the comfortable quid pro quo of church and parish under which most Calvinists had become content to live. The questions Edwards taught them to ask, and the answers he taught them in *Freedom of the Will* to give, pricked the very heart of the New England self-conception. Calvinists who might otherwise have welcomed the prospect of such a mind as Edwards's wrestling with the Arminians now found that Edwards's way of talking about free will cut them down as freely as it did the Arminians. For that reason, the real struggle created by *Freedom of the Will* in American thought has next to nothing to do with the Arminians (and so people like the Methodists occupy a space in this work appropriate to that role); instead, it becomes a scramble in which American Calvinists try to find some other way of talking about Calvinism, before the apostles of *Freedom of the Will* destroy them. In the end, they found an answer in Nathaniel William Taylor; but whether his answer satisfied the question, or merely the questioners, remains another subject.

Because he was dealing with the most fundamental idea of his community, Jonathan Edwards used *Freedom of the Will* to give reason to his own ideal of human community. Like so many other New England theologians, he could not escape a measure of ambivalence: the same wills that made an awakened Northampton, Massachusetts, sing in four-part harmony could turn and destroy him in a strident chorus of denunciation, and he had in the end to admit that he could speak of a necessary result to human choice only in a very qualified sense. His was not a complete triumph. But his was not a complete loss, either. *Freedom of the Will,* the deacon's masterpiece of Oliver Wendell Holmes,

the wonderful one-hoss shay,
That was built in such a logical way
It ran a hundred years to a day. . . .

did not fall apart on the anniversary of Lisbon earthquake day, after all. It remains a necessary document of American uniqueness.

Since so much of this discussion occurs in the context of Christian theology, it would be well to clarify here that, in the minds of the participants in this particular discourse, it was human will after the Fall of Adam, *as a sinner,* that was the object of interest. There is, of course, a substantial literature on the nature and function of Adam's will prior to the Fall, but, except where I have specifically indicated it, the subject under examination by Edwards and his followers and his critics is the human will as it now is.

The opening chapters of this book concentrate on Edwards's personal involvement with the question of free will and give a particular analysis of *Freedom of the Will.* This is followed by an overview of how Edwards's disciples, the New Divinity Men, took *Freedom of the Will* as a sort of *cantus firmus* for their Calvinism, and used and applied it against the peculiarities of New England's church-in-society. Attention then turns to the Old Calvinists of New England to discuss their rage and panic when confronted with the challenges of Edwardsean theory and New Divinity practice; and then to the Presbyterians of the Middle Atlantic region, who seemed natural opponents but among whom Edwards's views found some ardent disciples. The last chapters introduce the figure of Nathaniel William Taylor, who laid the troublesome ghost of *Freedom of the Will* to rest, at least as far as the peace of mind of American theology was concerned. That by no means meant the end of the free-will debate in America; but it did signal the end of its importance as a theological question.

CHAPTER I

The New England Dilemma
Willing and Revival

I

In 1694 a sturdy young candidate for the ministry of the Congregational Way rode up from the Puritan hinterlands of the Connecticut River Valley to Cambridge, to the gates of Harvard College to present himself at commencement and receive his degree of *magistri artis*. The thesis Timothy Edwards propounded from the list proffered him by the worthies of Harvard College was *An Indifferentia sit de Essentia liberi Arbitrii?* "Whether or not indifference is of the essence of free will?"[1] Timothy Edwards had a taste for convoluted questions in moral philosophy, and he was probably as well prepared as any other man in New England to answer that question that day. By putting his *responsio* in the negative, he placed himself as close as one could get to the core of Puritanism itself, for no question could be nearer to the heart of what it meant to be a Puritan than the question of freedom of the will.

In large measure, men like Timothy Edwards found their way to Puritanism because so many of them had been in seventeenth-century England what Thomas Hobbes called *masterless men*—individuals adrift in an England that was itself adrift in change and disarray.[2] Timothy Edwards, although born in Connecticut, shared the same angst. Puritanism provided a new order, a world view in which nothing, not even the worst catastrophe, could come to pass except by God's ordering of events. The doctrine of divine predestination signified to Puritans like Oliver Cromwell that "God would, by things that are not, bring to naught things that are."[3] Puritanism offered not merely an alternative vision of the exterior world, but the prospect of an inner order, an inner discipline that could sustain a man in spite of all the vicissitudes of life, and, if necessary, in the face of any government.

This preoccupation with subjugating the inner man and replacing *masterlessness* with order naturally led the Puritan to the inner mystery of the human will as the chief means by which the individual asserts himself against God's will. For Puritan divines like Timothy Edwards, as well as his preceptors at Harvard College, the study of the will overshadowed all their other examinations of the human spirit since understanding the operation of the will offered the key to understanding how disorder and alienation might be replaced by order and godly self-mastery. In that light, to have suggested that indifference was the essential quality of a free will would have appeared to the godly assemblage at Harvard commencement evidence of either witlessness or bad theology. Timothy Edwards did well to answer in the negative.

The governors of the college were not displeased, and Timothy was allowed to bear off his M.A. in triumph to Connecticut. There, he was ordained pastor of the small congregation in Windsor Farms (now East Windsor, Connecticut) and that November married Esther Stoddard, daughter of Solomon Stoddard, the most powerful clergyman in the Connecticut valley. In time he fathered eleven children, ten of them daughters and one very remarkable son named Jonathan, born October 5, 1703, the fifth of the Edwardses' children. And sixty years after Timothy Edwards had defended his claim to the title of master by denying that indifference is the essence of free will, Jonathan Edwards published a massive *Careful and Strict Inquiry into the Modern Prevailing Notions of the Freedom of Will* (1754), which ventured at much greater length into virtually the same question and returned with virtually the same answer.

Except that it was not really the same question, nor really the same answer. In 1694 Timothy Edwards's traditional responsion to the question of free will and indifference would have sufficed for most of his hearers and probably for most of the European academic world. But over the sixty years between his Harvard commencement and the publication of his son's *Inquiry,* the context and structure of the cluster of questions that surround the nature of human volition had radically altered. That revolution forced Jonathan Edwards into a deeper study of the matter than his father had attempted. He produced a dramatic answer, one epochal for the history of American thought.

II

The world of Connecticut Congregationalism presented an apparently unruffled appearance of stable Puritanical piety, a world of devout, industrious people whose fathers or grandfathers had left the corruptions of the Church of England behind to practice the better part of church reformation unhindered in the wilderness of the New World. The "better part" of church reformation revolved around the polity of the church. According to the official ecclesiastical documents of New England, the best notion of a reformed church was the Congregational Way, in which each congregation was composed of demonstrated believers and none others. These "visible saints" brought their congregations into existence by an act of conscious, regenerate willing known as a "covenant," and, at least on paper, governed congregational affairs independently and without interference from bishops, magistrates, and other loathsomely unreformed principalities and powers.

Ironically, the very idea of covenants, which stood as the symbols of the unity of New England churches and towns, suggested relationships based on contract, mutually arrived at—the instrument par excellence of modern voluntarists in a society devoid of Christian interest. Although the "covenant-theology" of William Ames, John Cotton, and a host of others gave little overt thought to politics or economics, the Puritan obsession with the will partly reflected and partly fed the evolution of voluntarist ideas in church and state, and in contractual rather than feudal relationships between governors and governed, employers and employed.

The irony of this lies principally in the fact that nothing could have been farther from the Puritan intention in coming to the New World than to pitch themselves into modernity. Running behind the formal structure of the New England Way as it appeared in New England's confessional documents is an incessant voice urging the maintenance of communities based on subordination and hierarchy rather than will. At the same time that John Winthrop envisioned New England as a city set upon the hill, he warned his colonists that the only way to maintain that city was an abandonment of free will.[4] If the will was indeed the principal part of the soul, then subduing it became the principal labor, not only of the soul, but of society. For just that purpose Winthrop crossed the ocean, leaving an England which to his mind had become too full of freedom of the will—a state in which political centralization was undermining the traditional authority of the squire and lord lieutenant, and a church in which the absence of true discipline allowed sinners freely to enjoy the sacraments and identification with Christ's Body, with a church hierarchy which now made little secret of its affection for Arminianism.[5]

Yet, despite the official determination to build a church purely on the consent of the regenerate, substantial pockets of resistance to the imposition of pure Congregationalism sprang up almost at once, and in places like Hingham, Massachusetts, where the Hobart family ran the church and town as though they were rectors and squires, the old parish system reappeared and flourished. And then, when in the 1670s the available stock of demonstrated saints had dwindled, church after church began to relax its rules on admission and New England dropped by degrees back to the parish system with something close to a graded ecclesiastical hierarchy. No one pushed this development along harder or faster than Timothy Edwards's father-in-law, the mighty Solomon Stoddard, who dismissed pure Congregationalism as "too Lordly a principle." He rocked New England in 1677 by throwing out his lists of true believers and admitting all and sundry (or at least all and sundry who satisfied his own rather lordly principles) in his parish of Northampton to baptism and the Lord's Supper.[6] Stoddard's rationale for this departure rested on two basic principles: the inscrutability of God's decrees, which rendered perfect self-awareness of election to salvation highly unlikely, and God's command that all persons, elect and otherwise, worship him; even those who did not own God as their savior still owed him a proper obeisance as their Creator, offered in a proper ecclesiastical fashion—in church.[7] Eventually almost everyone in Northampton above the age of fourteen ended up on Stoddard's communicant list. In 1690 the Northampton church gave official approval to Stoddard's innovations.[8]

Timothy Edwards dutifully attempted to follow his father-in-law's church principles in East Windsor, encountering no small degree of conflict in the process. Once, for a three-year stretch, he denied communion to the congregation until they buckled under to his clerical authority. But neither Timothy Edwards nor Solomon Stoddard had so signed off their Puritanism as to seriously believe that they could dragoon New England's laity into the churches and leave the matter there. Stoddard's next step after the organization of a kind of semi-

Presbyterian minister's "Association" in Hampshire County was to supplement his parish system in Northampton with a renewed demand for religious conversion by those whom he had admitted into the ordinances of the church. "They need to be told of the terrors of the Lord, that they may flee from the wrath to come," Stoddard declared. "Ministers must give them no rest in such a condition: They must pull them as brands out of the burning."[9] The precise psychology of the preaching of terror never seems to have been prescribed although Stoddard spoke of the will as a "blind faculty" in 1685 in "The Safety of Appearing," his most celebrated sermon, which took a strikingly voluntaristic tack: "indeed the understanding and will in man being faculties of the same soul and really one and the same thing, the same act of God upon the soul that puts light into the understanding, does also suitably incline the will."[10]

East Windsor, Connecticut, was a relatively new parish, and in new parishes revivalistic preaching that drove home the message of sin and salvation without undue doctrinal elaboration was coming to be accepted as the norm.[11] Thus, Jonathan Edwards would remember years afterward how "my honoured father's parish has in times past been a place favored with . . . four or five seasons of the pouring out of the Spirit to the general awakening of the people," and it is worth wondering whether some of Edwards's later affinities for voluntarism were planted in the revivalistic atmosphere with which his East Windsor boyhood was charged, and also in his brief period of associate ministry with his grandfather in Northampton.

The first of these "seasons" of outpouring of the spirit seems to have occurred when Jonathan Edwards "was a boy, some years before I went to College," and it drove him out into the swamp lands behind the parsonage by the Connecticut River to pray alone or with other youths "in a very retired spot."[12] A second wave of revival swept past East Windsor in 1716, "a very remarkable stirring and pouring out of the Spirit of God." It became the occasion of Edwards's earliest surviving letter, to his sister Jerusha.[13] It was also the year when Jonathan Edwards satisfied his father that he was ready for collegiate study, and on September 12, 1716, the thirteen-year-old boy's name was entered as a freshman on the books of Yale College along with nine others.[14]

Jonathan Edwards was probably at that age almost as tall as his father (he would later break the six-foot mark to stand a head above him), but pale and taciturn, with little of his father's robust health and, if we may believe his complaints about his social awkwardness, little of his father's commanding and precise presence. The turmoils of implementing Stoddardean polity in an unwilling parish, along with Timothy Edwards's incessant financial insecurities, and his mother's natural urge to see him outshine his Stoddard cousins, seem to have left their mark, continually reminding him that the ministry was as much a martyrdom as a vocation. His self-humiliations did not, however, always automatically translate into humility. In one of his earliest notes on "Natural Philosophy," Edwards warned himself to maintain a "superabundance of modesty"—not because of the feebleness of his own understanding, but because his brilliance would provoke jealousy in others. "Mankind are by nature proud and exceeding envious and ever jealous of such upstarts," Edwards noted candidly, "and it exceedingly irritates and affronts 'em to see 'em appear in print."[15] He displayed a testy impatience with his fellow students which shows up in his letters home, and an impatience with many other things which would show up later in his notebooks in attempts to impose order even on trees ("the tree most certainly don't keep to its rule . . . wherefore this matter of the growth of trees still remains very difficult").[16] He had his father's intellectual intensity, and, despite the fact that academic politicking compelled him to move his studies back and forth for three years between New Haven and Wethersfield until the college finally settled itself down, he took the highest rank at the commencement of 1720 and gave the valedictory oration.

After a year of study at Yale for his M.A., in the spring of 1721 Jonathan Edwards was overwhelmed by a "sense of divine things" in a way he had never experienced in East Windsor, and he at last entered into the state of spiritual confidence and salvation that had been the unceasing refrain of his father's and grandfather's preaching. Although he confessed that "from my childhood, my mind had been full of objections against the doctrine of God's sovereignty," the "extraordinary influence of God's Spirit" now gave him "quite another kind of sense of God's sovereignty than I had then," so that "the doctrine has very often appeared exceeding pleasant, bright, and sweet." It became "my delight to approach God, and adore him as a Sovereign God, and ask sovereign mercy of him."[17] Thoroughly Calvinized at last, he was settled over his first pastoral charge as the minister of a small dissident Presbyterian church in New York City in August 1722. One month later, Arminianism arrived with a bang in New England.

No one had less reason than Jonathan Edwards to be surprised that the New Arminianism should prove as contagious in New England as in old England. Thomas Hobbes, the determinist, was certainly known and read in New England, if not directly then probably at second hand through hostile commentaries, or through periodical anthologies, or works like the 1735 English edition of Pierre Bayle's *Historical and Critical Dictionary*. Edwards, for one, alluded to some reading of, or perhaps about, Hobbes early on in his *Miscellanies* as well as in his reading *Catalogue*. Nor was Hobbes the only new philosopher being read by alarmed New Englanders: the donation of books made to the Yale library by Jeremiah Dummer, Connecticut's agent with the English government, in 1715 brought the works of Gassendi, Locke, LeClerc, Malebranche, and a copy of the *Principia Mathematica* personally pulled down from a shelf and donated by Isaac Newton himself. All of these turn up in Edwards's *Catalogue* as books he read or wanted to read. Young men at Yale and elsewhere in New England who had begun to entertain quiet doubt about whether Calvinistic determinism really differed from the ethical horrors of Hobbesian determinism had plenty of food available for thought.

At the September 1722 Yale commencement, the rector, Timothy Cutler, a former tutor named Samuel Johnson, and five others staged a sensational "apostasy" from Congregational principles and confessed they had embraced Anglicanism. The "Great Apostasy" has usually been described as springing purely from doubts about the validity of Congregational orders, but New Englanders of the day thought they knew better. The Church of England meant not just "bishops" but also the "Arminianism" of Samuel Clarke, the most famous Church of England divine of the early eighteenth century; Samuel Johnson in particular sloughed off predestination at the same time as he submitted to the Church. Whatever disenchantments Cutler and Johnson felt with the Connecticut Establishment, they were not limited to questions about valid ordinations. Above all the other questions they raised, they rejected the entire Calvinist mentality, predicated on the inability of Calvinism to offer a reliable alternative to Hobbes. In embracing "Arminianism," Cutler and Johnson appropriated, not the tenets of the Dutch heresiarch, but rather the antimaterialist free-willism of Samuel Clarke. But this distinction did nothing to assuage the rage of Connecticut at the apostates, and the catchword of "Arminianism" stuck to anyone in New England who forsook Calvinism for indeterminism as a better protection against the storm of Hobbesian atheistic determinism.[18]

Nor did the lure of "Arminianism" diminish merely because Cutler and Johnson conveniently removed themselves into the ecclesiastical jurisdiction of the Church of England. Jonathan Edwards was called back from New York City in April 1723 to undertake a candidacy in Bolton, Connecticut. He evidently was not happy at leaving New York, and although he signed an agreement to settle at Bolton, he allowed it to lapse and in June 1724 took up duties as one of the two tutors of Yale College replacing the "apostate" Samuel Johnson. Edwards might better have gone to Bolton, for his life as a Yale tutor quickly devolved into a misery of "despondencies, fears, perplexities, multitudes of cares, and distraction of mind," as he wrote in his "Diary."[19] Part of that misery was surely due simply to overwork. Since the Trustees of the College were to spend until 1726 cautiously negotiating for a new rector to succeed the apostate Cutler, many of the administrative tasks which had been the rector's now fell to the tutors, which in Edwards's case meant that, in addition to the daily burdens of recitations and the management of unruly freshmen, he drew the tedious chore of cataloguing the library. But it may also be true that some of his "cares" were a consequence of the influence of Cutler and Johnson on the students: James Pierpont declared in 1730 that Yale had been "corrupted and ruined with Arminianism & Heresy" despite the best efforts of the rector the Trustees had eventually hired, Elisha Williams, a cousin of Edwards.[20] Aaron Burr, Edwards's future son-in-law, was a student at Yale in the early 1730s and "was strongly attached to the Arminian scheme" in the same years in which Samuel Johnson won several Yale graduates over to the Church of England.[21] In that light, Edwards's gloomy diary entry for May 21, 1725—"If ever I am inclined to turn to the opinion of any other Sect: *Resolved,* Beside the most deliberate consideration . . . privately to desire all the help that can possibly be afforded me, however strongly persuaded I may seem to be, that I am in the right"—may have indicated that he too was under intellectual siege.[22]

In the end, Edwards's Calvinism proved sturdier than the blandishments of Arminianism, sturdier even than his health, which collapsed toward the end of the summer of 1725. After a year-long convalescence, Edwards went to Northampton to be assistant to his grandfather Stoddard. Invited to preach there at the end of August 1726, Edwards had eagerly (and perhaps presumptuously) resigned his Yale tutorship and in October presented himself as a candidate. He was duly, on November 21, voted by the congregation to become Solomon Stoddard's assistant. He signed his name in the Northampton Town Book on February 15, 1727, and was ordained a week later. Although he would never actually use the title "pastor" while his grandfather lived, under his grandfather's tutelage he preached and ministered and passed securely into Stoddard's fold with its tenets of the invisibility of grace, the sovereignty of God, the urgent quickening of the will in the hearing of the Gospel. In 1729, after Stoddard's death, Edwards became the sole pastor of the Northampton church and, under the burden of the responsibilities, the entries in his philosophical notebooks slowed to a trickle. He married Sarah Pierrepont in the summer of 1727, and together they set about filling a generous-sized frame house on King Street in Northampton with a family. He had matured out of the awkward boy he had been at Yale, no less stubborn now but without the priggishness; his moral rigorism was built now around principles, aided by a subtle command of dialectical method, Reformed scholastic divinity, and a taste for Cartesian metaphysics. He had become a skillful preacher, not by any means theatrical but capable of making his hearers wonder whether his sermons on the Judgment Day would be followed within the hour by that dread roll call. Gazing westward from Mount Tom, where he often rode with Sarah or his children, across the Connecticut River and over the roofs of Northampton to where, in 1737, the spire of a new church building was going up, he must have seen the specter of Arminianism as distant and inconsequential. "Our distance from the seaports, and being so far within the land, in the corner of the country, has doubtless been one reason why we have not been corrupted with vice, as most other parts," Edwards concluded. "I suppose we have been the freest of any part of the land from unhappy divisions and quarrels in our ecclesiastical and religious affairs."[23]

And yet Arminianism refused to leave Edwards alone. In 1733 a Harvard graduate named Benjamin Kent was charged by the Marlborough Association (Massachusetts) of ministers with being a "profest Arminian," and in 1734 Edwards recorded that "a great noise" went up in the Connecticut Valley "about Arminianism."[24] At stake was the suspected unorthodoxy of William Rand, minister of Sutherland, Massachusetts, and Robert Breck, a candidate for the pulpit of Springfield, Massachusetts, whom Edwards and the other Congregational ministers of Hampshire County had tried to block from accepting the call to that church. Nor was Hampshire County alone in suffering Arminian infection. All over New England, complained John White of Gloucester, younger ministers "are under prejudices against" Calvinism and "argue for, propagate, and preach the Arminian scheme."[25]

The sheer inertia of tradition, however, would preserve New England and Hampshire County Calvinism largely intact until the Great Awakening of the 1740s. That upheaval, which among other things featured the most enthusiastic religious wildfire since the days of Anne Hutchinson, also prominently featured the hottest possible brand of hellfire Calvinism; the conjunction of the two gave sober ministers pause to wonder whether there might be something more than coincidence to it. John Bass, who lost his pulpit in Ashford, Massachusetts, "for dissenting from the Calvinistic sense of the Quinquarticular Points," blamed the Awakening for his troubles and claimed that the behavior of his congregation had revealed to him that the habit of "representing our Nature as exceeding corrupt and wicked . . . has, so far as I can see a natural Tendency to fill the mind with the most gloomy Apprehensions of the Author of our Being, to damp our Spirits, to turn away our Hearts from Him; and, in a Word, to the Destruction of all Religion."[26] Experience Mayhew, who protested that he really possessed a genuine loyalty to Calvinism, also protested that, if God really did arbitrarily decree the salvation or damnation of men, then "they are under an inevitable necessity of doing whatever Actions are done by them, and have no more Liberty than a Clock or Watch has, that is moved by Weights and Springs that are the irresistable Cause of its Motion." If this is the doctrine of the Calvinists, Mayhew concluded, then "*Hobbs,* who asserted the Necessity of all Things, was in the Right."[27]

Edwards did not share the Arminian rush to indeterminism; far from being stampeded by the Great Awakening, Edwards was one of the principal stampeders. Furthermore, he would have been the first, thinking as he did, to acknowledge that it was impossible for him to consider taking intellectual refuge in a flight into "Arminianism." Edwards's Calvinism was now bound too tightly to him by the cords of philosophy, theology, and, above all, his experience of divine grace. It followed, then, that those who relieved God of His sovereignty for the sake of making room for mere human goodness were no better than thieves of the divine glory, and of Edwards's delight. "Some of the ill consequences of the Arminian doctrines," Edwards wrote in his note-books, "are that it robs God of the greater part of the glory of his grace, and takes away a principal motive to love and praise him."[28] Anything that made "men value themselves for their own righteous-ness" invited Edwards's condemnation, and Arminianism did nothing if not that. So, when the Breck affair in Springfield caused "the great noise" in 1734, Edwards mounted his pulpit to preach on the insuf-ficiency of men's works, and on God's justice in damning them for not doing better.

The impulse to strike some sort of blow against the Arminian threat was not unique to Edwards, and New Englanders like Samuel Niles produced spirited, if unimaginative, apologetics for the faith of their fathers. Edwards might have contented himself with producing some-thing of the same genre, and answered the challenge of Hobbes and the new determinism in the same way his father had in his Harvard commencement thesis. But Edwards seems to have realized, perhaps as a result of his studies and struggles as a tutor at Yale, that he could not resolve the challenge of "Arminianism" in the traditional ways. At the same time desiring to have "no other end but religion" and "to shew how all arts and sciences, the more they are perfected, the more they issue in divinity," he saw plainly by 1725 that he was going to have to develop "as clear a knowledge of the manner of God's exerting himself, with respect to Spirits and Mind as I have, of his operations concerning Matter and Bodies."[29] For, in truth, nothing less than that would suffice anymore.

Edwards had begun in the early 1720s the long series of philosophical notes and jottings on that "clear knowledge" that comprise his "Mis-cellanies" and his several notebooks on the mind and natural philos-ophy. A precise list of the authors and the books that went into the making of his speculations is difficult to determine, and even the lengthy *Catalogue* of his reading, which does survive, gives no indi-cation of what he actually read. Citations of names are comparatively rare in his notes; the notebooks were, after all, never intended for scholarly inspection. Also, since Edwards's interests were basically both utilitarian and eclectic, only a rash person would attempt to hang his *pensées* on a single metaphysical peg. Not that some have not tried. Samuel Hopkins recalled in his 1765 biography of Edwards that Ed-wards had remarked that in his student days he had taken more pleasure in discovering a copy of John Locke's *Essay Concerning Human Under-*

standing "than the most greedy miser finds when gathering up handfuls of silver and gold."[30] But Hopkins may have meant to prove no more than that Edwards was a lover of philosophic reading (a fact Hopkins may have thought needed proving, since Edwards's "Miscellanies" and notebooks were not published until the 1830s). A reading of Locke's *Essay* had by that time become the acknowledged entryway into the world of English-speaking philosophy for nearly every mind disposed to genteel speculation.

Certainly Edwards learned a good deal from Locke, and it may well have been the reading of the *Essay* that introduced him to larger problems concerning the method and certainty of knowledge and the relationship of ideas to the objects they represent, and that later provoked his decisive shift from immaterialism toward an idealist phenomenalism. But that does not make Edwards a Lockean, first, because Edwards read others as well, and second, because Locke's principles were shared by other seventeenth-century philosophers—on many other issues that supposedly mark him off from them Locke was ambiguous. Locke's relationship to Descartes, who erected a strongly rationalist scheme of metaphysics to counterbalance the skepticism of the new mechanics, is a case in point. Whatever their other differences, both Locke and Descartes at least agreed on the standards of knowledge, and even on the sources of knowledge, since Locke, for all his stress on experimental deduction, left critical areas open to the operation of intuition.[31] If, as is often said, Descartes's a priori rationalism could only solve the connection of mind and body by referring to intuition, so, too, Locke found such relationship inexplicable.[32] It is more likely that what Edwards learned from Locke was that the *Essay* offered good starting points for debate; Locke's views were well-known enough to be commonly understood as elements of debate. Edwards eventually arrived at conclusions quite antithetical to the spirit of Locke's *Essay*.

Those differences became more apparent as time passed. Locke was reputed to be a materialist and a religious skeptic (he denied both charges); Edwards was neither of these. Locke's status as a thinker rested largely on his important distinctions between perception and knowledge; Edwards differed sharply over what those distinctions told us about the ontological status of the source of those ideas. Locke doubted whether any kind of spiritual substance could be proved to lie behind perception or other mental qualities, although he fell back on the intuition of personal identity to account for such substance;

Edwards at first agreed, but then rejected this reasoning as insufficient. Locke found no role for the affections in knowledge; Edwards found them crucial. Locke, who initially adopted a one-stage theory of volition similar to that of Hobbes, substituted a two-stage theory in the third edition of the *Essay* to placate his critics; Edwards labored to adapt a one-stage theory to Calvinism. And finally, underscoring how little Edwards really did depend on Locke, there is no substantial evidence that Edwards arrived at these conclusions after sustained contemplation of the *Essay* followed by principled rebellion.[33] It is possible to draw a straight line, not from Locke to Edwards, but from Descartes to Edwards via Descartes's immaterialist disciples—Regius, Cordemoy, Fardella, and especially Nicolas Malebranche, whose *The Search After Truth* appears in Edwards's *Catalogue* and with whose occasionalist notion of causality Edwards would display strong affinities—and English "platonists" like Henry More and John Norris of Bemerton, both of whose works were part of the Dummer collection.[34] And the importance attributed by Edwards to the affections, which figures so centrally in almost every important thing he wrote, has a great deal more to do with his reading of Shaftesbury and Hutcheson than of Locke.[35]

Whatever the precise origins of Edwards's philosophical thinking, one thing is absolutely certain: the whole direction of his natural and moral philosophizing, as much as his Calvinist divinity, completely cut off any notion of a retreat to indeterminism or libertarianism. This is obvious as early as in his essay "Of Atoms," begun probably toward the end of 1720, before he had left Yale for New York, and his essay "Of Being," most of which dates from 1723.[36] It is striking that his notion of bodies in the first essay is couched in curiously Newtonian terms, that all material substance was composed of, and could only be reduced to, "atoms," the least divisible constituent of any body.

All bodies whatsoever, except the atoms themselves, must of absolute necessity be composed of atoms, or of bodies that are indiscerpible, that cannot be made less, or whose parts cannot by any finite power whatsoever be separated from one another. . . . Breaking of a body all over, or in every part, is the same as to annihilate it.[37]

It is hard to pin this down as strictly Newtonian. Edwards lacked the mathematical skills to penetrate to the heart of Newton's writings, and he cannot be classified as a "Newtonian" except in the sense that he was acquainted with the conclusions Newton came to concerning natural philosophy, and he would have agreed with few of them anyway.[38] Nor was Newton the only atomist he could have read about. Henry More was also an atomist, and that queer word "indiscerpible" was almost certainly borrowed from More.[39] But whatever the source, this indivisibility did intrigue Edwards. In some way, atoms—in order to demonstrate that they really were atoms—had to resist penetration, or "fracture." Hence, Edwards concluded, the only primary quality of atoms was solidity, for solidity, not extension or mobility or figure, best satisfied the "resistance" which atoms offered to "fracture."[40]

And yet, "resistance" implies activity. Newton had conceived of atoms as passive and inert, but it occurred to Edwards that resistance is an active response, a putting forth of effort. Yet, material substance, by definition, does not "put forth" effort. Moreover, since the resistance, or solidity of the atoms, must successfully overcome "any finite power whatsoever," its resistance must be infinite in nature. Thus Edwards demanded of atoms not only that they resist, but insisted that their resistance by infinite in duration and power in order to avoid annihilation. Whence comes this infinitely active power? Not from material substance, which can be neither active nor infinite. Atoms must therefore be preserved by another sort of energy, and since there was by definition only one sort of infinitely active energy in the universe, only God could actively enable atoms to retain solidity.[41] Edwards concluded, "Solidity is from the immediate exercise of divine power" and "it follows that all body is nothing but what immediately results from the exercise of divine power in such a particular manner."[42]

On one level, this satisfied Edwards's desire to attack materialism at its roots and show that the universe Hobbes had imagined, functioning according to inevitable natural force, was a delusion, and that the true universe functioned according to spiritual power. It followed from Edwards's reasoning that, since the resistance atoms put forth was really the power of God, and since resistance, or solidity, was their essential characteristic, then the atoms themselves were spiritual and the "substance" in which the qualities of bodies inhere was not "substance" at all, but the continuously creative power of God.[43] "No matter is, in the proper sense, matter," Edwards speculated, simply because

the substance of bodies at last becomes either nothing, or nothing but the Deity acting in that particular manner in those parts of space where he thinks fit. So that, speaking most strictly, there is no proper substance but God himself (we speak at present with respect to bodies only). How truly, then is he said to be *ens entium*.[44]

The world must be seen as spiritual rather than material in substance, and dependent on God's power from moment to moment. There is, as Edwards told his fellow ministers in 1731, an "absolute and immediate dependence which men have upon God . . . for all their good," and indeed for all of everything.[45]

Edwards did not rest content with an immaterialism which showed only that matter was not a real substance and that the universe functioned according to spiritual power: by the time he finished composing "Of Being," he was intent on demonstrating that the universe was itself an expression of the divine mind.[46] Since matter was a spiritual substance, it could only be perceived spiritually—or, to put it another way, since all bodies were spiritual, they were ideas only and could be perceived only by minds. For instance, Edwards suggested, suppose that the world was deprived of every ray of light, and "altogether deprived of motion."

The case would stand thus with the world: there would be neither white nor black, neither blue nor brown, bright nor shaded, pellucid nor opaque . . . nor solidity, nor extension, nor figure, nor magnitude nor proportion; nor body, nor spirit. What then is become of the universe?[47]

What indeed? Without a steady source of sensations, the mind would revert to *tabula rasa* and the world might as well cease to exist. But of course it would not, because a mind in such a dilemma would at least have memory, and could go on associating and thinking of color and motion based on prior ideas of such things. But that, for Edwards, only proved that minds form ideas apart from sensation, and that minds are conversant only with their ideas and dependent upon whatever sensations or substances might or might not be behind them.[48] For Edwards, that meant that "nothing has existence anywhere else but in the consciousness"; he drew the dramatic corollary "that those beings which have knowledge and consciousness are the only proper and real and substantial beings."[49] If ideas are not the product of empirical sensation, they must be the creation of something spiritual.[50] And that, as Edwards had demonstrated with the atoms, can only be God. Hence, "all existence is perception," which is "communicated immediately to us by God," and truth is, not our associations of simple ideas from sensation, but rather "the determination, and fixed mode, of God's exciting ideas in us," and exciting them "so that truth in these things is an agreement of our ideas with that series in God."[51]

Predestination had to be the practical outcome of Edwards's im-

materialism. "The existence of things," Edwards wrote in his notebooks sometime in 1725, "consists only in power, or in the determination of God that such and such ideas shall be raised in created minds
upon such conditions."[52] If existence is the perception of ideas created,
ordained, and ordered by God, and all the vast apparatus of the physical world only an idea totally dependent on the power of God, then
the notion of an autonomous human will in the eighteenth century,
captain of its fate and master of its soul, was not only impious but
ludicrous. Our wills, like "our bodies and organs are ideas only," and
"the connection that our ideas have with such and such a mode of our
organs is no other than God's constitution that some of our ideas shall
be connected with others to such a settled law and order, so that some
ideas shall follow from others as their cause."[53]

Yet another, and more original, element in Edwards's thought
worked against libertarian notions of free will. Edwards had observed
a general human trait that the "great part of our thoughts and the
discourse of our mind concerning [things] is without the actual ideas
of those things . . . but the mind makes of signs instead of the ideas
themselves." Reading a page in a book, an individual may notice "such
terms as God, man, angel, people, misery . . ." without stopping or
being struck by all the enormous ramifications of the term "God."
This is because one uses a mental "sign" rather than "an actual idea
of supremacy, of supreme power, of supreme government, of supreme
knowledge, or will, etc."[54] That, to Edwards, was an analogy of how
ungodly men comprehend divine truth: they may hear of God, but "that
understanding . . . consists in mere speculation . . . without any ideal
apprehension or view." Or, to put it another way, the understanding
of ungodly men is "only by signs" and does not "consist in or imply
some motion of the will."[55] But the knowledge the godly obtain
through conversion and sanctification appeared to be of another sort
altogether. Where the ungodly saw only "signs" the godly saw, and
were ravished by, the "spiritual beauty and excellency" of God and
"the ideal apprehension of other things that appertain to the thing
known"—for instance, "in a sense of the terribleness of God's dis-
pleasure there is implied an ideal apprehension of more things than
merely of that pain or misery."[56] And, even more important, where the
ungodly had merely "speculative knowledge" of these things, the godly
had a living and active "sense of them," so that they were struck deeply
in their "heart," or in "the will and affections."[57]

But to call this "ideal apprehension" a *sense* was a misnomer (Edwards admitted that he was speaking in "vulgar speech") since a sense conjured up associations with Locke, and Edwards had something significantly different in mind.[58] Edwards's "sense" differed from the natural senses not as "ideas or perceptions of the same sense may differ from one another but rather as the ideas and sensations of different sense do differ."[59] It was so far from being comparable to the human senses that Edwards could only see it as "a new supernatural sense" that equips the godly with "a certain divine spiritual taste" as diverse from the ideas ungodly men have of religion "as the sweet taste of honey is diverse from the ideas men get of honey by looking on it or feeling of it."[60] And because it was supernatural it could only be obtained by the Spirit of God as God willed to give it:

The spiritual work of the Spirit of God, or that which is peculiar to the saints, consists in giving the sensible knowledge of the things of religion with respect to their spiritual good or evil, which does all originally consist in a sense of the spiritual excellency, beauty, or sweetness of divine things. This is not by assisting natural principles but by infusing something supernatural.[61]

The most significant aspect of this for Edwards in the construction of the arguments in *Freedom of the Will* was that this "sense of the heart" was not merely a matter of something received, and then acted upon as the receiver saw fit. To the contrary, once the godly were equipped with this "taste or relish of the amiableness or beauty" of spiritual things, it at once compelled activity. It might only be the activity that "commands assent to their divine reality." Edwards spoke of experiencing "delights . . . of an exceeding different kind" from his unconverted days, "what I then had no more notion of, than one born blind has of pleasant and beautiful colors."[62] Or it might provide "a new kind of exercises of the same faculty of understanding" which had hitherto had no such "perception or sensation."[63] But what was more, as Edwards discovered, the new sense acted upon all the faculties, not only the understanding directly. This led Edwards to suspect that the traditional psychology of his education, which rigidly parceled the mind into faculties of will, understanding, and passions, and then argued over which was the principal, might be in error. Since the "new sense" acted equally among the faculties, it seemed more likely to Edwards that understanding, passions, and will were much more closely linked, and on a more equal footing, than the scholastic psychology in his Yale textbooks had allowed.[64]

Edwards proposed to treat understanding, perceiving, and willing as aspects, or descriptions, of the mind's unitary operation, not as quarreling subdepartments within it.[65] The mind's activity is a complex at any given moment of intellection, perception, and volition. Accordingly, the understanding is inseparable from the will, and the will from the understanding. The "new sense" allows the understanding to apprehend beauty and excellency, but the apprehension is an act of the will, because volition is an "expression of inclination *through the mind*."[66] Similarly, the affections, or "the heart," are bound up closely with these various operations; conversion itself was most essentially a matter of the heart's being possessed of this "new sense." Edwards had seen that the "new sense" made persons *feel* in new ways in response to grace, and also *think* and *do* as well. Moreover, he could not believe that the "new sense" produced mere heightened affection but rather a grasp of divine truth. Any Quaker or papist could otherwise as easily claim to possess heightened affections in the presence of their errors. Genuinely gracious affections acted on, Edwards claimed, and were in turn acted upon by the understanding, as the "new sense" allowed it to see truths it had never "seen" or loved before. "Gracious affections do arise from the mind's being enlightened, rightly [and] spiritually to understand or apprehend divine things," Edwards explained.[67] Gracious affections were dependent on the motion of the will. Like Augustine, Edwards closely identified affections and volitions, heart and will, loving and acting. "All the acts of the affections of the soul are in some sense acts of the will, and all the acts of the will are acts of the affections," Edwards wrote in 1743.[68] Even more, the "affection of the soul differs nothing from the will."[69]

Edwards was attempting to describe an unusually monolithic notion of the self, compounded of the affections, the will, perception, and understanding. He resisted a rigid hypostatization of the faculties. Edwards would continue to distinguish among the faculties because he found it impossible not to make such distinctions on the verbal level, but he otherwise embraced a strikingly unified image of the mind and heart. Knowing apart from willing was evidence of spiritual deadness— if "our wills and inclinations be not strongly exercised, we are nothing."[70] But knowing, as a compound with willing, under the "sense of the heart," produces "holy affections," and it was a basic principle of Edwards's Calvinism that "true religion, in great part, consists in holy affections."[71] Likewise, if willing is a compound with the understanding, and subservient to the affections and the "sense of the heart" that the Spirit of God implants in human souls, then how can it be imagined that the will has a power on its own to its own self-determination?

Even as his ontology and his psychology pointed away from an autonomous free will, Edwards found the clinching evidence of the will's bondage in the spiritual experience not only of his own soul but also of those of the converts who came under his preaching in Northampton. And he did not lack for them, either. Suddenly, almost without warning, in 1734 and again in the 1740s Northampton was engulfed in a series of revivals. These arousals of the spirit became famed, and notorious, as the Great Awakening. They offered for Edwards a perfect psychological laboratory in which to test his theories. And nothing confirmed his contentions about the sovereignty of God and the weakness of man more than the testimonies of those who, like himself, were suddenly given a "new sense." They confessed, as he expected they would, that "before their own conversion they had very imperfect ideas of what conversion was," but now they saw clearly and Calvinistically "the dreadful corruption of their nature" and "the stubbornness and obstinacy of their wills." He discovered that "no discourses have been more remarkably blessed, than those in which the doctrine of God's absolute sovereignty with regard to the salvation of sinners . . . have been insisted on."[72] Elsewhere in New England, the pattern was repeated: the farmer Nathan Cole, hearing George Whitefield preach, "was convinced of the doctrine of Election."[73] To Edwards and to these others, the Great Awakening was the ultimate justification of the morality and virtue of determinism, and the only real safeguard against infidelity, Samuel Clarke notwithstanding. "Now," Edwards wrote, in 1742, "is a good time for Arminians to change their principles."[74]

III

The Arminians did not change their principles, or at least the important Arminians in Boston did not. The Great Awakening was burned out by 1744, assisted by the onset of fresh conflict in British America between France and England, as well as by the hostility of its critics and the idiocy of some of its friends. Edwards became one of the principal victims of his own movement, for, in 1744, having concluded that there was no point in preaching spiritual awakening and then admitting to church membership those with no profession of such awakening in their lives, Edwards attempted to close off the Northampton church to all but the demonstrably regenerate. His congregation recoiled, and Edwards descended slowly into a several-year pastoral nightmare in which he stubbornly refused to concede membership to any but those who satisfied his definition of visible sainthood, while the leaders of the congregation prevented anyone from joining under those terms. By the spring of 1750 the impasse led to a call by the Northampton church membership for a council of local clergy from the Hampshire Association to obtain the Association's approval of Edwards's dismissal from the Northampton pulpit.

One of the local clergy summoned was Robert Breck. His presence on that fateful council could only have deepened Edwards's propensity to see the black hand of Arminianism at work in all his troubles, especially since Breck's vote turned out to be the swing vote in the 5–4 decision that recommended Edwards's dismissal. But, in fact, Edwards had been in trouble with his congregation for some time over a number of other, more mundane, issues. Although Edwards never openly accused his opponents in the membership controversy of being outright Arminians—his immediate enemy there was the figure of his grandfather Solomon Stoddard, not Arminius—he did insist that the opposition to strict communion had something more behind it than filial allegiance to Stoddard's memory.[75] He privately described his cousin Joseph Hawley, who had led the lay opposition to him in the church, as "a man of lax principles in religion, falling in, in some essential things, with Arminians, and is very open and bold in it."[76] His farewell sermon to the Northampton church warned "young persons" in vague but ominous terms about "Arminianism, and doctrines of like tendency . . . creeping into almost all parts of the land."[77] To John Erskine he was even more oracular: "The longer I live, and the more I have to do with the souls of men, in the work of the ministry, the more I see of this," referring to "the notion of liberty"—"Notions of this sort are one of the main hindrances of the success of the preaching of the word, and other means of grace, in the conversion of sinners."[78]

The most telling evidence that Edwards was seeing the communion controversy as a sort of stalking horse for Arminianism lies in the fact that shortly before the communion controversy had reached its ugly pitch he had begun an elaborate study of the "notion of Free Will." In a letter to his former student Joseph Bellamy in January 1747 he said he had been involved "pretty thoroughly in the study of the Arminian Controversy" and "have got so deep into this Controversy, that I am not willing to dismiss it, till I know the utmost of these matters." Almost as an afterthought, he added, "I don't know but I shall publish something after a while on that Subject." His notebook on "the Mind," to which he had turned only by fits and starts during the long period of his pastorate, was suddenly revived in 1747 with a substantial notation on volition, in which it was evident that he had been paying close and renewed attention to Locke's *Essay*.[79] He asked Bellamy to approach Samuel Johnson for "the best book on the Arminian side," since the only outright Arminian work he had been able to lay hands upon was by the Anglican Daniel Whitby; and in August 1748 we find him beseeching his Scottish correspondent, John Erskine, for "the best Books that have lately been written in defense of Calvinism."[80] His earliest letter to Erskine makes it clear that as early as the summer of 1747 he had definitely resolved on "writing something particularly and largely on the Arminian controversy . . ."

beginning first with a discourse concerning the Freedom of the Will, and Moral Agency; endeavoring fully and thoroughly to state and discuss those points of liberty and necessity, moral and physical inability, efficacious grace, and the ground of virtue and vice, reward and punishment, blame and praise, with regard to the dispositions and actions of reasonable creatures.[81]

What the Great Awakening had failed to do experientially in justifying the ways of Calvinism to men, perhaps close reasoning would.

But the battles Edwards entered after 1747 in Northampton called for tactics, directed against Stoddardeanism, rather than the strategic work against Arminianism he was only now beginning to think was its logical outcome. "An End is put for the Present by these Troubles to the studies I was engaged in, and my Design of writing against Arminianism," he wrote half-apologetically to Erskine in 1750. "I had made considerable Preparation, and was deeply engaged in the Prosecution of this Design, before I was rent off from it by these Difficulties, and if ever God should give me Opportunity, I will again resume that Affair."[82] Instead of further work on freedom of the will, Edwards published *An Humble Inquiry into the Rules of the Word of God concerning the Qualifications requisite to . . . Full Communion* in August 1749, followed by a series of Thursday lectures on the same subject. His defense of his views on visible sainthood precipitated the crisis that resulted in his dismissal ten months later.

Erskine appealed to Edwards to move to Scotland, but there is no evidence he ever gave such a move serious thought. He stayed in Northampton for more than a year after his dismissal until he accepted a position as pastor of the mission station at Stockbridge, twenty-five miles west of Northampton on the frontier of New England. His removal there has sometimes been described as a sort of country idyll, in which he left behind the practical stresses of the pastoral ministry to indulge in hermetic speculations on free will. Nothing could be less true: he carried on his battle with the Northampton opposition through a set of family proxies in Stockbridge, and in November 1752 he published his notes and writings on the communion controversy as *Misrepresentations Corrected and Truth Vindicated*. Only then did he pick up the threads of his study on "free will," not as a break from the communion controversy, but as an extension of it.

Even before *Misrepresentations Corrected* was back from the printer, Edwards spread out before Erskine the plans he had outlined five years before. He declared that he had now at last set to work

to write something on the Arminian controversy . . . endeavouring, with as much exactness as I am able, to consider the nature of that freedom of moral agents which makes them the proper subjects of moral government, moral precepts, councils, calls, motives, persuasions, promises and threatenings, praise and blame, rewards and punishments; strictly examining the modern notions of these things, endeavouring to demonstrate their most palpable inconsistency and absurdity; endeavouring also to bring the late great objections and outcries against Calvinistic divinity, from these topics to the test of strictest reasoning; and particularly that great objection, in which the modern writers have so much gloried . . . *viz*. That the Calvinistic notions of God's moral government are contrary to the common sense of mankind. In this Essay, I propose to take particular notice of Dr. [Daniel] Whitby, and Mr. [Thomas] Chubb, and the writings of some others, who, though not properly Pelagians, nor Arminians, yet in their notions of the freedom of the will, have, in the main, gone into the same scheme.[83]

By mid-April 1753 he could speak of the first draft as "almost finished."[84] Ill health delayed its completion, and on March 14, 1754, he made out a will, "having much in the infirmity of my constitution to put me in mind of death and make me sensible of the great uncertainty of my life."[85] Malarial fevers wasted him in July, "followed with fits of ague" and shivering until September. He was left "like a skeleton."[86] But somehow the work on his book went forward. When it was completed to his satisfaction, he took it himself from Stockbridge intending to deliver it to his printer in Boston. It is not clear whether he was actually able to deliver it: he traveled by fits and starts as the malaria and his use of the "Peruvian bark" permitted, spending a week or more with Bellamy when he was unable to ride or to write.[87] In any case the manuscript was in the hands of his printer soon thereafter, and on October 17, 1754, it was published under the title *A Careful and Strict Enquiry into the Modern Prevailing Notions of that Freedom of Will, which is supposed to be essential to Moral Agency, Vertue and Vice, Reward and Punishment, Praise and Blame.* Of its 298 subscribers, forty-two were Scottish.[88] Only seven subscribers appear as residents of Northampton.

Edwards published his noted *Freedom of the Will* in full knowledge that many people in New England, like Charles Chauncy, were still denying the presence of any real Arminians in New England; they saw Edwards as off on an enthusiast's goose chase. Chauncy was particularly aggrieved at the insinuation that often came to his ears that those who opposed the Awakening were trying to sell Calvinism down the Charles River. "As for PELAGIANISM, 'tis a base slander, to publish it to the World, as if any Minister in this Country entertain'd a favourable Opinion of it," Chauncy objected, "Nor can I suppose, there are so many as some suggest, who think with Arminius."[89] But Chauncy really knew better: what he meant was that there was no Pelagianism or Arminianism in the strict historical sense in New England, and in that sense he may well have been statistically correct. Both Edwards and Chauncy surely understood that New England freewillers were motivated to a rejection of Calvinism by a different sort of intellectual circumstance than that created by Jacobus Arminius, and that it involved a different set of ecclesiastical corollaries, the import of which Edwards had learned the hard way in the Awakening and in the communion controversy. But that did not mean that the term *Arminian,* with all its attached opprobrium, was undeserved. "I will not deny, that there are some unhappy consequences of this distinction of names," Edwards conceded, but "the difference is such as we find we have often occasion to take notice of, and make mention of," and that sufficed as the reason "I have so freely used the term 'Arminian.' "[90] If Edwards was stretching the term *Arminian* to make it fit certain New Englanders, Chauncy was at least guilty of trying to shrink it so that it fit none.

Perhaps for that reason little of *Freedom of Will* is devoted to his-

torical or even theological Arminianism, but is instead constructed as
a secular argument based on demonstrably psychological premises. Admittedly, the "secularism" of Edwards's argument is really only a
means of justifying the theological a priori of Calvinism, and anyone
who misses either the textual invocation of St. Paul on the title page
("It is not of him that willeth—") or the satisfaction Edwards takes in
having justified Calvinistic divinity in the "Conclusion" in the interests
of savoring Edwards's "modernity" can honestly be said to have missed
the whole point of his enterprise. But it is true all the same that Edwards
has surprised many a commentator, hostile and friendly alike, with a
"secular" discussion rather than a strictly theological discussion of the
will.[91] And it would appear that he did so because it was a kind of
argument he plainly felt himself forced to explore because the eighteenth-century debate over the will had become impervious to Scrip-
ture-proofing. The Brecks, the Briants, and the Basses who were
converting to "Arminianism" were doing so for philosophical reasons
rather than theological ones to avoid being tarred with the brush of
Hobbesian determinism, and so Edwards's most immediate task was
to cut the ground out from under the Arminian by showing on the
Arminian's own "secular" terms that, in his haste to escape materialism and atheism, he had actually worsened the case for theism. Edwards never doubted that "of all kinds of knowledge that we can ever
obtain, the knowledge of God, and the knowledge of ourselves, are the
most important." But in the particular instance of "the knowledge of
ourselves," it was necessary to delineate "right apprehensions concerning those two chief faculties of our nature, the *understanding* and *will*,"
and for that the eighteenth century would force Edwards to define
volition on its ground if he wanted to be heard at all.[92]

Consequently, what Edwards produced turned out to be more than
just a critique of Arminius or a justification of the Westminster Confession. He began with an act of definitional aggression, carefully defining
will so as to make Arminianism a theological improbability, and also
a secular and psychological impossibility. "The will . . . is plainly, that
by which the mind chooses anything . . . that faculty or power or
principle of mind by which it is capable of choosing."[93] The emphasis
here is on *that by which*—the will, according to Edwards, is a *means*,
and only a means, by which an action flows immediately from the
understanding to actual apprehension. It is, therefore, a slip of language
to attribute to the will an independent power of choosing, as Clarke

and Locke had done in breaking volition down into a two-stage process that allowed the will a freedom to pause and consider what the other faculties had proposed. The mind (or the individual faculties of understanding or perception) does not first choose and then cajole or order the will to will its choice; the will *is* the mind *choosing*. Or, as Edwards had written in a preliminary note, "The will is the mind's inclination."[94]

So then, the will is determined. But what is it determined by?—"to talk of the determination of the will, supposes an effect, which must have a cause."[95] In one sense, Edwards seemed to have supplied the answer when he said that the will is that by which the mind chooses. But the mind does not *cause* the will to choose (as in, for instance, the intellectualist notion of the relation between mind and will), since any effort of the mind to cause something is itself an operation of the will. The idea that the will is, in Edwards's sense, an instrument, or aspect of, the mind is part of his overall attempt to reduce *all* the mind's faculties to instrumental aspects of the whole mind, so that intellection and volition are but names applied to a larger whole. Hence, one cannot simply say that the will is determined by the mind, since the mind cannot move to its perceiving or intellecting without willing to do so. There must be a cause that, "in the view of the mind," pulls on the understanding and the affections and, at the same time, attracts the choice of the unified self and moves the will.[96]

This, Edwards called a "motive"; or rather, the "strongest motive," for he defined the real determiner of the will as that which was the greatest "good" apparent to perception. Hence, the will "is as the greatest apparent good is." Furthermore, perceiving the apparentness of a good, understanding that it is apparently the greatest good, and willing to do or possess it, cannot be diced up as separate operations or even laid out in a neat, sequential order. Let there be a motive of surpassing agreeableness, and the movement from the motive to the action will be so swift and interrelated that the middle terms can virtually be dropped out, and a direct line drawn from the motive itself to the willing of it. "It appears from these things, that in some sense, the will always follows the last dictate of the understanding," Edwards concluded, provided of course that "the understanding must be taken in a large sense, as including the whole faculty of perception or apprehension, and not merely what is called the reason or judgement."[97]

The next question is one Edwards was really waiting in ambush to pose: If the "agreeableness" of a motive is what determines the will, what distinguishes one man's perception of "agreeableness" in motives from another's? Edwards dealt with this in his earlier note with the reminder that *all* perceptions of agreeableness are, after all, ideas and are thus relative to "the inclination and disposition of the soul." Such an answer is, of course, a tautology, since it immediately swallows up the earlier categorizations he had so painstakingly made to conclude at the end, "It is ridiculous to say that the soul does not incline to that most, which is most agreeable to the inclination of the soul."[98] But it was a useful and Calvinistic tautology, and Edwards picked it up again in *Freedom of the Will* and rested the whole question of "agreeableness" on "the particular temper which the mind had by nature."[99] The greatest good will not necessarily be the greatest apparent good unless the mind is of such a constitution as to perceive it. This explained why persons were always moved by different "goods," as they saw them.[100]

Edwards had already said that truth is nothing more than the consistency of our ideas with the ideas of God, and that the truth of God's beauty and excellency can only appear to those who have "a sense" to perceive them. Therefore, one could say that not all men choose *the* good, but only the greatest apparent good, because their "education, example, custom, or some means" has conditioned them to view *the* good only speculatively, whereas the "new spiritual sense" would prepare the Christian to be moved by the excellency of God. "Right fear, sorrow, Joy, Hope, dependence &c. all These things arise from a sense of the d[ivine] B[eing]." Either way, men's choices are contingent on a "greatest apparent good," the perception of which is dependent itself on the whole "previous disposition" of the mind.[101] It is "utterly impossible," Edwards wrote earlier, "but . . . that the inclination and choice of the mind should always be determined by good as mentally or ideally existing," since "we mean nothing else by 'greatest good' but that which agrees most with the inclination and disposition of that mind."[102] Or, to put it another way, it depends on the disposition of the understanding and will as they are united to the affections by a new sense. "The will, in all its determinations whatsoever, is governed by its thoughts and apprehensions of things with regard to those properties of the objects of its thoughts wherein the degree of the sense of the heart has a main influence."[103]

This was, on the whole, a very simple skein of reasoning. Acts of the will are effects; effects must have causes; the cause is the appearance

of the greatest apparent good in the view of the mind, and since understanding, perceiving, and willing are inseparable, what the mind is
pleased to perceive and understand, the will is pleased to act on for it.
This effectively dismissed one of the principal tenets of libertarian "Arminians"—that the will could ever be self-determining—and it did so
simply by defining the will as an effect, the *by which* the mind chooses
the good it is pleased with.

This dismissal was not going to be let pass easily, and for three
reasons, the first of which was (as Edwards expected) a blunt refusal
to accept his say-so in defining the will as the determined rather than
the determiner. Undeterred, Edwards happily offered to compare his
definition of the will to that of the Arminians. "Their notion of liberty,"
Edwards stated in one of his notebooks, "is, that there is a sovereignty
in the will, and that the will determines itself, so that its determination
to choose or refuse this or that, is primarily within itself."[104] Nevertheless, as Edwards pointed out, choosing and determining to choose
are both volitions. Hence, a choice is produced by the will's choosing
to choose, which is itself a choice. But if the will must determine its
own choices, then all of these acts of determination to choose (which
are only choices themselves) must themselves be determined by a determination to choose; and they too are choices, so that there must be
yet a determination in back of them, and so on to infinite regress, "or
else we must come at last to an act of the will, determining the consequent acts, wherein the will is not self-determined, and so it is not a
free act, in this notion of freedom." Allow that, and "none of them all
can be free."[105] Of course, one can simply assert that the chain of
willings began spontaneously, but Edwards would not permit such an
escape. Something that began without a cause must, by definition,
begin by chance, and if "the determination of the will be from blind,
undesigning chance, it is no more from the agent himself, or from the
will itself, than if we suppose, in the case, a wise, divine disposal by
permission." Thus, "this Arminian notion of liberty of the will"
evinced itself to be so repugnant to good sense that it elicited from
Edwards one of his rare bursts of humor:

If some learned philosopher, who had been abroad, in giving an account of the
curious observations he had made in his travels, should say, he "had been in
Tierra del Fuego and there had seen an animal, which he calls by a certain
name, that begat and brought forth itself, and yet had a sire and a dam distinct
from itself; that it had an appetite, and was hungry before it had being; that

his master, who led him, and governed him at his pleasure, was always governed by him, and driven by him as he pleased; that when he moved, he always took a step before the first step; that he went with his head first, and yet always went tail foremost; and this though he had neither head nor tail": it would be no impudence at all, to tell such a traveler, though a learned man, that he himself had no notion or idea of such an animal as he gave an account of, and never had, nor ever would have.[106]

And that was essentially Edwards's explanation for the existence of Arminians in New England: such people had no idea, no "ideal apprehension," of what the will was in the context of divine truth, but only the pale, shallow "speculative knowledge" of those who lacked a "new spiritual sense." The will is not to be internalized so that external performance waits on the will to decide whether to do or not to do. As Edwards described and defined it, the will remains in unity with the mind as an expression of the overall disposition of the affections, and cannot roam free at its own impulse.

There was another way of objecting to Edwards's definition of volition, one more serious because it struck at a sensitive point in Edwards's argument. If the will is only that by which the mind chooses, then what separates this from the necessity of Hobbes, who said something very similar when he wrote that the will was only the last in a succession of appetites caused by some outside agent? In truth, Edwards did not necessarily disagree with the one-stage psychological model proposed by Hobbes and (initially) by Locke, but only with the materialistic and hard-determinist conclusions drawn from that model. Nevertheless, from the libertarian point of view, reconciliationists and hard determinists are wrong for the same reasons, notwithstanding the differences that otherwise separate them, and almost any reconciliationist psychology proposed by Edwards would to the Arminians have seemed as if it might as well be Hobbesian necessity.

As with his discussion of *will*, Edwards chose to disarm the opposition not with apologies for Hobbes, but by a call for a proper definition of what is meant by *necessity*. "To say, that a thing is necessary, is the same thing as to say, that it is impossible [it] should not be": that, Edwards observed, is what people generally mean by necessity. But to use the term in this fashion is to use it only as a "relative term." In other words, this usage implies a relation existing between self-conscious persons and some extrinsic circumstance that interferes with the exercise of the will. "The common notion of necessity," Edwards observed, generally puts this relationship in negative terms, as "something that frustrates endeavour or desire." So, in the relative sense, necessity describes a situation in which the full activity of will is engaged only to have something happen which makes the willing of no avail. "Things are said to be necessary *to us* which are or will be notwithstanding all oppositions supposable in the case *from us*."[107] Necessity, in this "relational" sense, describes a situation in which the will must struggle with something extrinsic to it.

Edwards, however, discerned a problem, and that was his perception that people have a propensity to use *necessity* as a "term of art"—to elide the "relative" sense of *necessity* into situations where *necessity* actually means something quite different. To start with, Edwards insisted that *necessity* when used by "philosophers and metaphysicians" had always commanded "a sense quite diverse" from the "common use." This "philosophical necessity" describes the relationship of *terms*, "really nothing else than the full and fixed connection between the things signified by the subject and predicate of a proposition, which affirms something to be true." There is no struggle between a will and an interfering "relative" circumstance, because terms imply one another and have no wills to exert. In the "relative" sense, the circumstance imposes a kind of connection that ruthlessly necessitates a result, volition notwithstanding; in the "philosophical" sense, the terms, as terms, already possess a "full and fixed connection" with each other, likewise necessitating a result but without the painful implications of resistance.[108]

Edwards went on to list the kinds of "full and fixed connection" that exist between the terms. There is, to begin with, simple logic: "*in and of themselves*," Edwards said, two and two necessarily equal four, and all the radii of a circle are necessarily of equal length. Also, there is *past time*: "the connection of the subject and predicate of a proposition . . . may be fixed and made certain, because the existence of that thing is already come to pass."[109] To supply an illustration, in the proposition "George Washington was the first president of the United States" we know that it is necessary that the subject be linked to the predicate because history has already established a full and fixed connection between them. And then there is also *consequence*: this involves two or more propositions, one acting as a given and the other expressing a "thorough" or "perfect" connection that makes it necessary. Hence, if we grant that turning the light switch will make the light go on, then we may say, "If John turns the switch, the light will go on."

And we may say that this latter proposition is philosophically necessary because "things which are perfectly connected with other things that are necessary, are necessary themselves, by a necessity of consequence." Happily, this allowed Edwards to reduce all likelihood-of-future-action propositions to necessities of consequence. "All things which are future, or which will hereafter begin to be, which can be said to be necessary, are necessary only in this last way." Because future actions can be, in this present moment, only so potentially existent as terms, then future occurrents ought only to be described as terminological possibilities, and not in "relative" fashion.[110] It becomes possible, then, to speak of the causation of future events (such as an act of will) purely as the occurrence of an antecedent condition upon which the event or act simply and certainly follows. Had Edwards wished, he might have rested a case for Calvinism simply on the necessity of future consequents.

But Edwards was interested not only in the kinds of *connection* which philosophical necessity involves, but also in establishing the kinds of *terms* which can thus be connected. He isolated two basic sorts of terms which operate under the rubric of philosophical necessity, *natural* and *moral*. There is, said Edwards, what we may call a *natural necessity* that something will happen, when the subject and predicate which are philosophically connected involve "natural causes." Examples of this occur when men

feel pain when their bodies are wounded; they see objects presented to them in a clear light, when their eyes are opened: so they assent to the truth of certain propositions, as soon as the terms are understood; as that two and two make four, that black is not white, that two parallel lines can never cross one another: so by a natural necessity men's bodies move downwards, when there is nothing to support them.[111]

This natural necessity is, in one respect, similar to the relational necessity Edwards had just left behind, and that is that natural necessity is "extrinsic to the will" and concerns itself with items of the natural world. The crucial difference lay in this distinction: in relational necessity, there is always resistance by, or putting forth of, volition. In a word, there is struggle. But some natural phenomena are *by definition* so involved with other natural phenomena that one never thinks to associate them with struggle. We cannot think that the soldier's body, so Edwards observed, puts forth resistance to the pain of a wound; the mathematician does not struggle to prevent two and two from equaling four; the aeronaut may regret that he is falling earthward, but there is no sense other than metaphor in which we may say that he is resisting his fall. All these terms are natural, but their arrangement in these series makes them necessary by virtue of their obvious intrinsic connection with each other, and there is no sense in which the will struggles against the mind or the other faculties.

Edwards saw a similar kind of "full and Fixed connection" existing within another category of terms, which he called *moral* and which guaranteed *moral necessity*. There is, in this case, a moral necessity that something will happen when the subject and predicate involve certain "moral causes," such as the "strength of inclination, or motives, and the connections which there are in many cases between these, and such certain volitions and actions."[112] Here we are not talking about external phenomena, like wounds and bodies, but about internal, mental phenomena. Nevertheless, Edwards insisted that, though the terms were different, the same kind of necessary relationship can be seen to exist between "moral causes" like these, and natural ones. "Moral necessity may be as absolute, as natural necessity," Edwards insisted. "That is, the effect may be as perfectly connected with its moral cause, as a naturally necessary effect is with its natural one."[113] Given Edwards's definition of the will, it is easy to see how this could be so. Suppose for a moment the existence of a greatest apparent good—here we are plainly talking about a "moral cause." By definition, the will is as the greatest apparent good is at the moment of perception. Simply by this definition of the will, a "full and fixed" terminological connection exists between the good and the will; so, let this good be perceived, and it is necessary that the will should be as that good is. *Morally* necessary, because the terms are moral rather than natural; *philosophically* necessary, because the necessity occurs, not by compulsion, but as an expression of a linkage inherent in the terms themselves. Once again, no sense of struggle is involved, for how can the will struggle against what it is by definition?

All of this definition-mongering had a practical result for Edwards, because anything one says about necessity invariably issues in some view of moral ability, and, with that, praiseworthiness and blameworthiness. A natural necessity cancels the possibility of connected natural causes functioning in any way otherwise: it creates a *natural inability* for bodies moving downward by gravity to float off sideways. "We are said to be *naturally* unable to do a thing, when we can't do it if we will [N.B.: as opposed to 'relational' necessity, which says we can't do it when we will] because what is most commonly called nature don't allow of it."[114] Likewise, a moral necessity cancels the possibility that moral causes can function in any other way: it also creates a *moral inability* for a will to behave otherwise than as the greatest apparent good is perceived. Moral inability consists "either in the want of inclination; or the strength of a contrary inclination; or want of sufficient motives to the contrary."[115] The sequence of psychological events in the case of moral inability will then run like this: A man, otherwise possessing full natural ability to repent (in that there is no defect in his "understanding, constitution of body, or external objects"), also is possessed of a wicked "temper." He perceives that which he understands to be an opportunity for wickedness; his "temper" is such that he perceives it as the greatest apparent good; his will at once embraces the opportunity, and all issues in a wicked action. He is morally unable to do otherwise because, having perceived wickedness as the greatest apparent good, his will by definition becomes "as" that good is. Thus "a great degree of habitual wickedness may lay a man under an inability to love and choose holiness; and render him utterly unable to love an infinitely holy being."[116]

And it is all done freely. This was the conclusion Edwards was all along maneuvering toward: *An action can be necessary and yet still be free.* Free, because, for one thing, the man with the wicked temper has full *natural* ability to embrace wickedness or goodness. As far as natural causes go, nothing extrinsic compels or restrains him. "All that men do in religion is their own act," Edwards explained, in that "everything they do, they themselves do, which I suppose none will contradict. 'Tis the exertion of their own power." On those grounds, Edwards continued,

It can't be truly said, according to the ordinary use of language, that a malicious man, let him be never so malicious, can't hold his hand from striking, or that he is not able to shew his neighbor kindness; or that a drunkard, let his appetite be never so strong, can't keep the cup from his mouth.[117]

And he is free, too, because the causes that necessitate the wicked action are moral. These "causes" are causes only in the most attenuated sense, since the strength of moral necessity lies solely in the terms involved, not in the compulsive force of the connection. Moral causality is not the mechanistic push and pull of material substances; it is merely an observed relationship which the terms themselves require, "any antecedent with which a consequent event is so connected that it truly belongs to the reason why the proposition which affirms that event is true."[118] The perception of a wicked motive as the greatest apparent good produces a wicked action because it is the definition of the will to be as the greatest apparent good is. The perception does not smite and bind the will—that is outside the boundaries of the definition of perception. It does not lay hands on the will—perceptions do not have hands. The will is not kicked along, biting and screaming—it can only be "as" the good "is," or else it is not a will. Hence, there is necessity, but "cause" is not the best word to associate with it. One can no more say that the will is "caused" by perception than one can say that a bird is "caused" to lay eggs—our definition of "bird" implies egg-laying. Moral "cause" is only connection, consequent following on its antecedent. And there is no struggle. The will freely follows perception just as the bird freely lays eggs.

The morally necessitated choice is neither bound by natural causes, nor do the moral causes of necessity imply the application of force. And if "there is nothing in the way to hinder his pursuing and executing his will, the man is fully and perfectly free."[119] Of course, the most obvious objection to this would be to notice that the wicked man's temper warped the procedure at the beginning. If a wicked temper guarantees that only wicked motives can be perceived as the greatest apparent good, then it is purely academic that the will chose evil. But Edwards was not to be distracted by this objection. We are, he reminded potential objectors, only trying to establish *if the will is free*; establishing where someone's wicked temper came from, or what it was, remains an entirely different subject from establishing *if the will is free*. "Let the person come by his volition or choice how he will," said Edwards, loftily dismissing the objection; so long as the will itself can function, it is free. "Liberty," then, is "that power or opportunity for one to do and conduct as he will, or according to his choice."

Thus a man may have it in his power to sell his estate and give the money to his poor neighbor, and yet the case may be so at the same time [that] he may have so little love to his neighbor and so great love to his possessions and the like that he certainly will not do it. There may be as much of a connection between these things in the qualities and circumstances of the man and his refusing to give his estate to his neighbor as between any two theorems in the mathematics. He has it in his power as much as he has other things, because there wants nothing but his having a mind to do it, or his being willing to do—and that is required in all other things, and in this no more than in everything else.[120]

By thus clearing his theory of volition from connection with impossibility and relative necessity, Edwards also absolved himself of the charge that he was little better than a sanctified Hobbes.

At the same time, this managed to satisfy a third matter in Edwards's mind, that of the validity of awarding praise and blame for actions that men had no "choice" in performing. It seemed to Edwards that there is nothing unreasonable in rewarding a man for actions done out of moral necessity, since, after all, the man has done them on his own power and under the influence of moral, rather than natural, causes. "If one should promise another a certain reward if he would appear . . . his faithful friend by a persevering adherence to his interest . . . the man certainly would not fulfill this condition unless he be a sincere friend, but yet the fulfilling is in his own power and at his own choice."[121] Edwards appealed repeatedly to the "common sense" of "the common people" to confirm "that liberty is only a person's having an opportunity of doing as he pleases," which meant in turn that "men don't think a good act to be the less praiseworthy, for the agent's being determined in it by a good inclination, or a good motive; but the more."

Thus, for instance, if a man appears to be of a very haughty or malicious disposition, and is supposed to be so by his natural temper, 'tis no vulgar notion, no dictate of the common sense and apprehension of men, that such dispositions are no vices or moral evils, or that such persons are not worthy of disesteem, odium and dishonor; or that the proud or malicious acts which flow from such natural dispositions, are worthy of no resentment. Yea, such vile natural dispositions, and the strength of 'em, will commonly be mentioned rather as an aggravation of the wicked acts that come from such a fountain, than an extenuation of 'em.[122]

This was an extremely adroit maneuver, since, as Edwards was prepared to point out, the Arminian who denied the validity of attributing blame or praise to the acts of those who were simply bad or good by nature was demanding that the actions of the will be entirely severed from the character of the agent. But since not even an Arminian was prepared to make such a separation, it followed that the Arminian really regarded the "nature" of the agent as a moral cypher, since "the least degree of antecedent bias must be inconsistent with their notion of liberty."[123] Edwards's word for this sort of empty and neutral temper was *indifference*, a state or disposition that, although connected to the will, exerts no influence on it one way or another.

But this introduced the absurd notion that, to preserve free choice for the will, one had to erase any and all motives from one's nature. "So long as prior inclination possesses the will," Edwards theorized, "it binds the will, so that it is utterly impossible that the will should act otherwise to it"; ergo, for the will to be free from necessity to do anything, the "nature," or disposition, or mind, must be in a perfect state of indifference.[124] One tip of the balances either way will produce a stronger preference, and the will will be bound to execute it. The corollary of this is that a good man's horror of sin and love of good are no longer laudable things: the horror of sin enslaves the will to choose against sin; the love of good enslaves the will to choose good. For the will to be truly free, the good man ought instead to be perfectly indifferent in his heart and mind to both sin and good, "nay, 'tis absolutely necessary in order to any virtue in avoiding them, or vice in doing them."[125] There can be no true virtue, then, in having (for instance) good habits, for if they influence the will to do good, then the actor deserves no credit; nor can there be anything wrong in being seized with bad habits, because if they lead an actor to do bad things he isn't really to blame. His will has been enslaved by his bad habits, and therefore he has not been able to choose freely and cannot be held responsible. Nor, for that matter, should ministers (Edwards and Chauncy alike) try to preach morality to men, or set good motives before them, because by doing that they put men out of a state of indifference and jeopardize their freedom of will: " 'tis vain to set before them the wisdom and amiableness of ways of virtue, or the odiousness and folly of ways of vice . . . for though these things may induce men to what is *materially* virtuous, yet at the same time they take away the form of virtue because they destroy liberty."[126] The result is that the Arminian cannot praise any action that is born of good habit, and excuses from blame any evil act that is committed from bad habit, "and in all cases, the stronger the inclinations of any are to virtue, and the more they love it, the less virtuous they are; and the more they love wickedness, the less vicious. Whether these things are agreeable to Scripture, let every Christian, and every man who has read the Bible, judge."[127]

In fact, as Edwards was delighted to remind "every Christian and every man who has read the Bible," there is no better example of a

being whose nature is immutably fixed but whose actions are "supremely praiseworthy" than the God whom the Arminians professed
to worship. "Because he is under necessity," Edwards reasoned, and
because "he can't avoid being holy and good as he is," then on the
Arminians' premises "he is deserving of no commendation or praise"
and "therefore no thanks to him." No Arminian who wished to retain
a semblance of orthodox Christianity could deny the a priori necessity
of God's goodness without denying the Bible and orthodoxy, so that
Edwards had no need to prove this contention in the "secular" fashion
he had heretofore employed. "There needs no other confutation of this
notion of God's not being virtuous or praiseworthy, to Christians acquainted with the Bible, but only stating and particularly representing
it," and hence Edwards could move from a position of unchallenged
strength.[128]

He moved, in fact, to extend that reasoning to Jesus Christ as well.
Was not "the holy and excellent temper and behavior of Jesus Christ"
praiseworthy precisely because "his will was not indifferent, and free
. . . but under such a strong inclination or bias to the things that were
excellent, as made it *impossible* that he should choose the contrary"?
Judged by Arminian standards, he "is less worthy of reward or praise,
than the very least of saints; yea, no more worthy than a clock or mere
machine, that is purely passive, and moved by natural necessity." Under
those circumstances, Edwards suggested that no Arminian would ever
want to offer Jesus Christ to others as an example of morality, for "if
there was nothing of any virtue or merit, or worthiness of any reward,
glory, praise, or commendation at all, in all that he did, because it was
all necessary, and could not help it; then how is there anything so
proper to animate and incite us, free creatures, by patient continuance
in well doing, to seek for honor, glory, and virtue?"[129] Presumably,
instead of wasting sympathy on the trials of Jesus, the Arminian would
be more consistent in sympathizing with the crime of Judas. After all,
Judas before his betrayal had already had Jesus declare "his certain
damnation, and that he should *verily* betray him."[130] Judas's will could
not have been free, on those terms, and therefore it must be said by
the Arminian that he could not have helped betraying his Master, and
could thus be guilty of no sin.

All of which is absurd, and Edwards knew it. "Freedom of will, to
speak very improperly, don't infer an absolute contingency, nor is it
inconsistent with an absolute necessity of the event to be brought about

by his free will."[131] To will is not to choose in a vacuum, or, as he had demonstrated earlier, to choose choosing. To will is to perform an act of volition, caused by motives which move the understanding and will together to an intelligent choice. When the understanding and will together function only by "signs" or "notions," they respond only to nonspiritual motives, and so their resulting actions will only ever be nonspiritual, even though they have the physical apparatus to perform spiritual duties. But the godly man, who has been given a "supernatural sense" by the Spirit of God, perceives spiritual motives in all things, including nature, and so is inclined to the performance of spiritual duties which please God. The will is not free to choose *what* to will; freedom consists only in willing *as* a man is "pleased." To conceive of freedom of will as an internal, uncaused, autonomous function can only land the Arminian in the position of excluding any good or bad motives from choice lest the will's freedom be endangered; or, if good or bad motives do happen to creep in, to withhold praise from any resulting good acts, and excuse any resulting bad ones—which is contrary not only to common sense but to the nature of God as well. Who, then, is the generous protector of the validity of human choice and human ethics from the Hobbesian abyss? Not the Arminian. " 'Tis the Arminian scheme, and not the scheme of the Calvinist, that is utterly inconsistent with moral government, and with all use of laws, precepts, prohibitions, promises or threatenings."[132]

CHAPTER 2

Jonathan Edwards

Critics and Criticism

I

Commentators on the text of *Freedom of the Will* have often been so forcibly struck with the deadly neatness of Edwards's general arguments against those "modern prevailing notions of that freedom of will" that they have overlooked the fact that Edwards spent a considerable amount of time (including several whole chapters of *Freedom of the Will*) taking apart in a painfully specific manner three individual proponents of those "modern prevailing notions." This oversight is unfortunate because Edwards's comments on these three champions of free will substantially extend the scope of his critique. But it is also baffling, since Edwards introduces all three in the Preface to *Freedom of the Will* and carefully marks off the boundaries of the damage he intends to do to each of them.[1] The three are Thomas Chubb, an artisan-turned-philosopher; Daniel Whitby, an Anglican priest; and Isaac Watts, a prominent Calvinist dissenter.

Edwards gives no one of these three any particular priority. The one furthest removed from Edwards, theologically as well as temperamentally, was Thomas Chubb. Born in 1679, Chubb was in that long tradition of radical Whig artisans exemplified by Benjamin Franklin in America. First a glover, and then a tallow chandler, Chubb had plenty of opportunity to read and think. He first put his thoughts and his Whiggery on paper in 1714 in an anti-Trinitarian religious tract, *The Supremacy of the Father Asserted,* and at once found himself the center of marveling curiosity from prominent proto-Unitarian dissenters in London. Brought to London, he was shuttled from salon to salon as the Midlands version of the noble savage, "a kind of rational and highly-civilized backwoodsman."[2] But, too shrewd to be taken in by

the condescending applause of heretical high society, Chubb returned
to his native Salisbury after two years, and spent the rest of his remarkably quiet life writing one controversial religious tract after another. A comfortable annuity provided by an admiring member of
Parliament secured him from the political consequences of his opinions.

Although Chubb is often described as a deist, that judgment is not
entirely appropriate. He needs to be read, not as a deist but as a
unitarian who believed that Christianity was "corrupted," not wrong.
Take away the corruptions and "christian salvation, or the way which
Christ propos'd to save men in, is *strickly just* and *rational,* suitable
to the *nature of God,* and the *nature of man*; and therefore, it is highly
worthy of *all* acceptation."[3] He was particularly eager to smooth down
corruptions that might afford hand-holds for an assault by atheism,
and he served notice to the partisans of unbelief that he did not intend
to concern himself if they overran the more perilous outposts of orthodoxy:

If its [Christianity's] professors make any blunders, lay down false principles,
or draw unjust conclusions; these ... are charged only upon their several
parents. . . . And therefore, the *Skepticks* and *Unbelievers,* if they, at any time
oppose christianity, by way of argument, ought not to blend it with the *doctrines,* and *principles,* and *fancies* of men, and argue against these, as against
Christianity.[4]

One corruption he found especially fraught with mischief was the
Calvinist view of man, and it became his burden to prove that uncor-
rupted Christianity did not attribute to men the natural moral evil that
Calvinism did. He did not deny that moral evil existed, but he did deny
that God was in any sense responsible for it. "God is always capable
of doing what is most *worthy* and *valuable* in itself," he claimed, "and
which, in the nature of things, is *right, good, best* and fittest to be
done ... so he *always will act thus.*"[5] But, if God is not responsible
for the existence of moral evil, who is? The answer was contemptibly
obvious: "This is occasioned by that *liberty* and *freedom* of actions,
which God, by constituting us *moral agents,* has rendered us capable
of."[6] If there was such a thing as moral evil, men had to look no farther
than their own free choice to find its source.

Yet that, as Chubb realized, only provoked a further question: What
is "liberty"? His reply to this question was not nearly so forthright and
it contained within it elements Edwards would point to later as utter
contradictions. Chubb wrote:

By liberty, in this case, I mean, that every man has *power* to act, or to refrain from acting, *agreeably* with, or *contrary* to any motive that presents, without being *constrained* to it by any foreign power or agent whatever.[7]

This definition has in some respects a curiously Edwardsean ring. Motives are "*necessary* to action, seeing the active faculty will not be exerted without some *previous reason* to induce to it"; and whatever motive finally prevails in the mind of a willing agent "is as effectual to *produce* or *prevent* the action as physical necessity."[8] Taken on these terms, Chubb could have been Edwards's ally rather than his antagonist.

But three words in his definition completely reverse this initial similarity: "or contrary to." Although motives are "*necessary* to action," Chubb tried to sharply curtail the force of that necessity and denude motives of any causal power. Motives, he began, "are only the *ground* and *reason*" of action—that eliminated any notion of instrumentality and reduced motives to being merely an opportunity for action:

... as motives are not the cause of action, so all, that is necessary to the exertion of a self-moving principle is not a cause, but an *occasion* of such exertion; and this is the case of *motives*; they do not cause, but only give occasion for the *exertion* of the self-moving power; they are only reasons.[9]

Since motives merely represent opportunities, they can be set aside as easily as they can be seized upon. In this way "every man has power to *comply* with, or to reject these excitements, that is every man is at liberty to act, or to refrain from acting, agreeably with, or contrary to what each of those motives . . . would excite him to."[10]

This power to set aside motives also rendered illusory any impression that Chubb was saying the same thing as Edwards about the "strongest motive." When Chubb allowed that the motive "which will finally prevail" could really produce results as "effectual" as "physical necessity," what he meant was that the motive, *once it has been chosen*, has consequences on subsequent actions which amount to predictability. He did not mean, as Edwards did, that the strongest motive has the power to command the choice itself. In fact, Chubb declared, "in many other cases, our appetites and passions lead us to act, not only *without*, but *against* our judgement" of what is the strongest motive.[11]

Implicit in this was Chubb's conception of the self as a tri-compartment of "understanding," the "self-determining power," and the "passions." Suppose that a strongest motive appears to the understanding— in the first place, it can easily be overpowered by the "appetites and passions" which would lead the understanding astray, before it even has a chance to apprehend the truly strongest motive (the strongest motive, being "passive," could offer no protest). But even if the understanding beats off the passions and apprehends the strongest motive, the understanding has no guarantee it can persuade the self-determining power to do anything about it. Hence, the will is radically free to take its own counsel about action.[12] For Chubb, this, and only this, notion of voluntarist libertarianism allowed for shifting the responsibility for moral evil from God to human beings. It also did several other things dear to Chubb's heart: It permitted him to dispense with divine predestination as the usual means of accounting for human action, and it eliminated a need to blame human nature as the root of evil, since the self-determining power was a more likely candidate. Further, and linked to that, it no longer required supernatural grace as a cure for natural depravity, that disease having now been banished from mankind. "Upon the whole," Chubb said, "there is just ground to presume . . . that mankind (bad as they are, or as their case may be represented by an artful complainer) have much more *virtue* than *vice* amongst them."[13] He added, as if to fire a parting shot at Calvinism, "As to supernatural ability, I fear these are terms with which men *amuse themselves* and *others*."[14] These soothing sentiments were a black flag to Calvinism, and no one could have seen that more plainly than Jonathan Edwards.

Edwards struck Chubb at the weakest point in the whole scheme, his concept of cause. "If every act of the will is excited by a motive," Edwards noted—and Chubb had plainly said that motives are in some sense "necessary" to action—"then that motive is the cause of the act of the will." And if, in *any* sense, "volitions are properly the effects of their motives," then they are necessarily connected with their motives, and it becomes "manifest, that volition is necessary, and is not from any self-determining power in the will." In a sense, this was not quite fair to Chubb: he had allowed motives to be *distant* causes, initially influencing the understanding, and only then being presented to the will as a "passive" opportunity. But, in the first place, by making at least the presentation of the motive "*necessary* to action," Chubb had granted causal status—if not instrumental cause, then at least material cause—to motives, and that was all the opening Edwards needed.[15] Edwards simply could not allow Chubb to enjoy the luxury of his trichotomized self. Edwards's notion of a united self, in which perception flows directly into volition, automatically excluded the possibility that the "self-determining power" could hold debates with the understanding.

From that basic criticism, Edwards spun off five subsidiary ones. First, it was evident that Chubb wanted the will to have power to choose or refuse whatever the mind presented to it; but, at the same time, the mind would have had to choose *what* it is going to present to the will, thus making what was supposed to be "a ground of volition" actually "*consequent* on the volition or choice of the mind." Now, Edwards asked, reveling in the contradiction, "how can these things hang together? How can the mind first act, and by its act of volition and choice determine what motives shall be the ground and reason of its volition and choice?"[16] Secondly, Edwards pressed for an explanation of how Chubb's motives could act as a "passive ground" for volition, and yet at the same time exercise any real influence on the will. If Chubb meant by "passive" that motives are strictly nonactive, then Edwards wanted to know how volitions could ever take place at all, since volition, no matter how it takes place, has to be motivated by a motive which "finally prevails." Of course, it was possible to say that the volition reaches out to the "passive" motive and apprehends it to use as a motive to volition. But Edwards pointed out that this only multiplied contradictions: the volition which reaches out to apprehend the motive cannot be the same as that which is motivated by it, since a volition cannot be the actor and the acted-upon at the same time. But if they are not one and the same volition, but two separate ones, then the first volition has to have a motive itself (i.e., to apprehend the motive, which, in turn, motivates volition number two), and that would lead to the infinite-regress argument Edwards had already deployed against Arminianism in general:

So that at last it comes to just the same absurdity: for if *every* volition must have a previous motive, then the very *first* in the whole series must be excited by a previous motive; and yet the motive to that first volition is passive, but can't be passive with regard to another volition, because, by the supposition, it is the very first: therefore if it be passive with respect to any volition, it must be so with regard to that volition that it is the ground of, and that is excited by it.[17]

Edwards next turned to Chubb's denial that the "strongest motive" necessarily is the one that would "finally prevail." Since Chubb had agreed that volition always follows on whatever motive *does* win out among the welter of motives, Edwards professed bafflement that this motive was not to be deemed the "strongest." Indeed, Edwards wondered how it was still possible to talk about motives in these terms. If the will is caused by a motive to prefer one thing over another, then the natural implication is that the one thing offers more of what the will prefers than the other—not less of it. To have the will reach over a motive it prefers to another it does not renders meaningless the whole business of employing motives in choice at all. "If the mind in its volition can go beyond motive, then it can go without motive," Edwards said, and it really meant that "with regard to the mind's preference of one motive before another, it is not the motive that disposes the will, but the will disposes itself to follow the motive."[18] Thus, Chubb's "motives" are frauds, mere cloaks for a will that wills itself—a conclusion that led directly into the trap of Edwards's infinite Arminian regress.

Edwards's fourth and fifth arguments also grew out of questions about cause and infinite regress. Did Chubb claim that volitions were self-determined, "the product of free choice"? This "is to suppose the first free act of choice belonging to the case, yea, the first free act of choice that ever man exerted, to be 'the produce' of an antecedent act of choice."[19] In other words, infinite regress again, an argument Edwards had employed so often he now needed only to allude to it to consider the case clinched. In his last comment on Chubb, Edwards returned to the simple question of cause itself that underlay the infinite-regress argument, and hammered again on Chubb's attempt to divorce a motive's "excitement" of volition from out-and-out cause of it:

Now if motives dispose the mind to action, then they *cause* the mind to be disposed; and to cause the mind to be disposed, is to cause it to be willing; and to cause it to be willing is to cause it to will; and that is the same thing as to be the cause of an act of the will.[20]

If Thomas Chubb had been determined to protect the nobility of man from Calvinism, Daniel Whitby—Edwards's second opponent—was equally determined to protect the sincerity of God from Calvinism, and he spent much of his career indignantly protesting that God was not what the Calvinists were leading people to think he was:

A God of absolute Sovereignty, who by virtue of his Prerogative over his Creatures, can pass an Act of Reprobation on the Generality of Mankind, when he had equal Reason to make them as well as any others, Vessels of Election . . . is a Predestinarian Idol, God being incapable of exercising any such Sovereignty over his Creatures, which is repugnant to his rich Grace, Goodness, Love, Mercy and Compassion.[21]

An Anglican priest whose *Paraphrase and Commentary on the New Testament* (1702) gave him a reputation for biblical and linguistic learning, Whitby seems to have spent most of his life in search of a God palatable to enlightened eighteenth-century opinion. His tracts against both Roman Catholics and Calvinists were inspired not so much by a sense of their particular errors as by the fear that both were an embarrassment to polite religion. When he died in 1726, a posthumously published fragment of his revealed that he had strayed over to unitarianism at the end.[22]

Whitby seems to have been more sure of what God was *not* than of what he was. "It is necessary," Whitby conceded, "that we should believe that God ordereth all things both in Heaven and earth, that we may own his Providence in all Events; but then it is not requisite that we should know how he doth order all things."[23] Or possible, he would have added, which at once jaundiced his view of Calvinism. Jaundiced, however, is perhaps too mild a word. "There is a plain agreement," Whitby declared, "betwixt the doctrine of Mr. Hobbes, and of these men, concerning this matter, as to the great concernments of religion."[24] Whitby found relief from both Hobbes and Calvin in his own private list of what God could *not* be. God could *not* decree to damn men, "for if God had so blinded their eyes that they could not see the light, or so hardened their hearts that they could not embrace it, Christ would not, or rather could not, have exhorted them to believe."[25] God could *not* simply decree salvation either, because that "disparages the power of God to suggest that it is power, not appeal to reason which operates in conversion."[26] God could *not* be so insincere as to demand compliance with terms of salvation that sinners were spiritually unable to meet, because this conflicted with God's "compassionate inquiries" about sinners and made God into a "deluder."[27] God could *not* have limited the benefits of Christ's atonement only to the elect, because Christ's death now "hath put all men in a capacity of being pardoned and justified" and "rendered it consistent with the justice and wisdom of God, with the honour of his majesty, and with the ends of his government, to pardon the penitent believer."[28] And, most important, God could *not* be the manipulator of human wills, because this would render morality pointless. Or, perhaps even worse from Whitby's point of view, it would make conversion a purely divine act and eliminate the need for an established clergy or the preparatory use of the means of grace:

> If such a divine, unfrustrable operation is necessary to the conversion of a sinner, then the word read or preached can be no instrument of their conversion without this divine and unfrustrable impulse, because that only acts by moral suasion. . . . If man be purely passive in the whole work of his conversion, and it can only be wrought in him by an irresistible act of God upon him, then can nothing be required as a preparation or as a prerequisite to conversion.[29]

Still, even after Whitby had enumerated what God was not, he was still forced to admit that God was, after all, the powerful Creator whose "Providence" we must own "in all events."[30] The task for Whitby was, then, to reconcile this fact with all his other deductions of the divine character, and to that end he labored to redefine terms and develop an accommodating psychology in his *A Discourse Concerning the True Import of the Words Election and Reprobation* (1710).

The psychology Whitby fashioned wears two aspects: the first, which appraises the human will in the overall context of the self, is stolidly conventional. "What makes the will chuse," said Whitby, "is something approved by the understanding and consequently appearing to the soul as good." What seems to have delighted Whitby about this was that, as with Chubb, it gave him grounds to dispense with the need for supernatural grace in conversion, and thus reduced preaching to the level of genteel discourse:

> . . . to say that "evidence proposed, apprehended, and considered, is not sufficient to make the understanding to approve" . . . is in effect to say "that which alone doth move the will to chuse or to refuse, is not sufficient to engage it so to do". . . . It therefore can only be requisite, in order to these ends, that the Good Spirit should so illuminate our understandings, that we, attending and considering what lies before us, should apprehend, and be convicted of our duty.[31]

However, when he came to consider the will in itself, Whitby showed himself, if not more wise, then certainly more shrewd. He began by insisting that the human will, whatever it was, had to be considered in the context of being in a state "of trial or probation."[32] The significance of this emerged only later, for Whitby was planning to head off the very criticism that Edwards later used to such good effect, that a necessitated human will was no obstacle to morality since God's will was necessarily holy but still free. Whitby preempted this with his location of the human will specifically in a context of trial and temptation. He could thus concede that God was indeed necessarily holy; but on the other hand, Whitby added, God "is in no state of trial, nor can be tempted to do evil." Only men are the objects of moral temptation; and as such, men need freedom of will "to render us capable of trial or probation, and to render our actions worthy of praise or dispraise." In a state of "trial and temptation," freedom of will "cannot consist with a determination to one . . . seeing this determining operation puts him out of a state of trial."[33]

Whitby also seems to have been anticipating his critics in his attempt to formulate what this freedom was. He eliminated at once any distinction between theoretical kinds of necessities. A man cannot "be said to be free to do what is spiritually good because his faculty of willing still remains, provided he be equally lame and impotent as to spiritual things, and therefore equally disabled from walking in the ways of God."[34] No separation would be allowed between the will and its freedom. As for defining the will, Whitby once more proved himself more adept at eliminating possibilities than in creating them, and in fact the closest he would be nudged toward defining the will was his declaration, "that only is voluntary which we lie under no necessity to do or forebear; and what we do, being unwilling, we do out of necessity, liberty being a power of acting from ourselves, or doing what we will."[35]

That does not seem to have discouraged Edwards. Although Sereno Dwight believed that his great-grandfather Edwards regarded Whitby as his most important antagonist, that judgment could only have been true in the sense that Whitby enjoyed a reputation as a scholar and some degree of renown among English Congregationalists as an advocate of increased toleration for dissenters.[36] As a speculative divine, Whitby was much less impressive than Chubb, and Edwards expended less effort on Whitby than on any other of his chosen opponents. Edwards seized first on Whitby's definition of the will. "If liberty consists, as Dr. Whitby himself says, in a man's 'doing what he will,'" Edwards wrote, "one of these two things must be meant." (1) *Doing what you will is the same as doing as you will*: in other words, according to Edwards, the essence of freedom lies in having the liberty to do according to the dictates of the will, without saying where the will came by its dictates. Doing what you will could be construed as saying the same thing, provided that we mean merely "that a man has power to will, as he does will; because what he wills, he wills; and therefore has power to will what he has power to will." Obviously, if this little affirmation of I-can-do-what-I-can-do is all Whitby meant, "then all this mighty controversy about freedom of the will and self-determining power, comes wholly to nothing," and he winds up saying the same things as the Calvinists whom he accuses of being Hobbesians. On the other hand, it might mean (2) *that Whitby is able by an act of will to choose what subsequent acts of will he shall choose.* This, however, as Edwards never wearied of demonstrating, merely shows that every act of will requires an antecedent act of will to will it, at which point the trapdoor of infinite regress opens again and another victim falls through:

And so the question returns *in infinitum,* and the like answer must be made *in infinitum*: in order to support their opinion, there must be no beginning, but free acts of will must have been chosen by foregoing free acts of will, in the soul of every man, without beginning; and so before he had a being, from all eternity.[37]

Beyond this, Edwards was content mainly to point out inconsistencies, such as Whitby's momentary allowance that the will chooses whatever is "appearing to the soul as good" and "approved by the understanding."[38] This, Edwards hoisted up as proof that even Whitby had to acknowledge that Arminianism had misdiagnosed the structure of the will, and that the will really is "as the greatest apparent good is":

I am sensible, the Doctor's aim in these assertions is against the Calvinists. . . . But whatever his design was, nothing can more directly and fully prove, that every determination of the will, in choosing and refusing, is necessary; directly contrary to his own notion of the liberty of the will. For if the determination of the will, evermore, in this manner, follows the light, conviction and view of the understanding, concerning the greatest good and evil, and this be that alone which moves the will, and it be a contradiction to suppose otherwise; then it is *necessarily* so, the will necessarily follows this light or view of the understanding, not only in some of its acts, but in every act of choosing and refusing.[39]

Edwards disagreed with Whitby on several further theological issues, such as whether God's foreknowledge (which Whitby allowed, though only as a species of generally reliable forecasting and nothing more) entailed foreordination as well. Curiously, he left almost entirely untouched Whitby's most unusual point, on the specific context of the human will in trial and probation, thus showing at least that, however well Whitby could bar his front door with ingenious arguments, the

Arminian house was full of other unguarded and perhaps unguardable holes through which the Calvinist could slip to despoil the house.

By contrast, when Edwards turned to Isaac Watts, he left no stone unturned. The very fact that Isaac Watts appears at all as an object of Edwards's criticisms must have been one of the most striking features of *Freedom of the Will* to its contemporaries, since Watts was one of the most prominent figures in dissenting Calvinism in eighteenth-century England. Whereas with Chubb and Whitby the disagreements with Edwards's Calvinism lie open on the page, with Watts the first things likely to be noticed are the similarities between Edwards and Watts. In their schools—Yale for Edwards, Rowe's Academy in London for Watts,—they read the same authors: Heereboord, Burgersdyck, Rohault, Downame, and Henry More; both taught out of Newton and both dipped into Locke's *Essay* like misers into a chest of gold; both were ordained as pastors of important Congregational churches; and, to make the comparisons converge, it was Watts who edited and arranged for publication in England Edwards's first important work on New England revivals, the *Faithful Narrative of Surprising Conversions* (1737).[40]

But there are Calvinists, and then there are other Calvinists, and Watts belonged, temperamentally and intellectually, to the Calvinism Edwards most feared was about to give way before the blandishments of Arminianism. For all Watts's well-known piety, his Calvinism was a reed shaking in the wind. Like Edwards, he clashed with the deists over the doctrine of original sin, but, unlike Edwards's arguments, his were timid, and he signed away huge tracts of Calvinism. He was an eclectic philosopher, and not always in the best sense of the word, and toward the end of his life he inclined toward unitarianism, influenced, it is said, by reading Samuel Clarke on the Trinity. Although Watts maintained lively and influential contacts with New England, the aging Cotton Mather was suspicious of his orthodoxy; and while Watts knew at first hand most of the great Calvinistic revivalists of the early eighteenth century, he candidly admitted that he thought Whitefield was "deluded," and his edition of Edwards's *Faithful Narrative* carefully pruned out (to Edwards's immense irritation) anything in which Watts scented "enthusiasm."[41] In short, if Chubb had wanted to show that man was not what the Calvinists said, and Whitby had wanted to show that God was not what the Calvinists said, Watts was eager to show that Calvinism itself was not what the Calvinists had said. His career, along with those of Richard Baxter and Dr. John Taylor (later, a target of Edwards's wrath in *The Great Christian Doctrine of Original Sin*), became a demonstration of how closely a Calvinist could conform to the spirit of the Age of Toleration, for the Baxterians of one generation routinely became the Arians and libertarians of the next.[42] And that, of course, was exactly the problem for Edwards: while Chubb and Whitby were formidable, at least they were easily recognizable as the Enemy, both for what they were as well as for what they said, but Watts, who enjoyed a credibility that disarmed the unwary, could easily lead the faithful down to the naturalism and rationalism of the Enlightenment by a soft and gentle slope. If the others were formidable, Watts was dangerous.

Watts was eager to find any philosophical grounds he could to repulse the threat of materialism. Just as quickly as he nervously denounced anyone he thought bore the slightest resemblance to Hobbes, he embraced anyone who looked as though he disagreed with Hobbes. He attacked Locke for, as he thought, teaching that the soul was material, as well as for Locke's disbelief in innate ideas. But at the same time he professed to admire much in Locke, and called him "that great genius" and "the ingenious director of modern philosophy."[43] He also declined to find refuge from materialism in immaterialism. He admitted that Malebranche "has many excellent chapters in his Treatise of The search after Truth, yet has vented a strange opinion, that we see all our ideas in God."[44] On the other hand, Watts vented opinions of his own ironically similar to Malebranche, especially when he explained how color, coldness, and sweetness cannot arise from sensation alone:

It is only God the author of our nature who really forms or creates these sensations and all these ideas of sensible qualities in a soul united to a body, and he has appointed these ideas to arise when such particular impressions shall be made on the brain by sensible objects.[45]

He rejected Bishop Berkeley's doctrine of continuous creation as an implication that God was the author of evil, while at the same time he admitted that there might be something to be said for that point of view, after all:

Now if God every moment create wicked men and devils, and cause them to exist such as they are by a continuous act of creation, must he not at the same time create, or give being, to all their sinful thoughts and inclinations, and

even their most criminal and abominable actions? . . . I own there are difficulties on the other side of the question, but the fear of making God the author
of sin has bent my opinion this way.[46]

Moreover, much as he admitted "the Cartesian doctrine" on the origin
of ideas as "the most evident and most defensible of all," he declared
his favor for the Newtonian physics, declaring "whether there be a
vacuum or void space is now no longer doubted among philosophers,
it having been proved by Sir Isaac Newton and others, beyond all
contradiction."[47] But even there Watts hesitated, and, before endorsing
Newton's theory of attraction at a distance, added that it would be
just as well not to call entirely into doubt the reality of mechanical
cause and effect in the universe. It was with this patchwork of piety
and philosophy that Watts proposed to defend Christian theism.

Watts's theory of freedom of will, as articulated in "An Essay on
the Freedom of Will in God and in Creatures," reflects this penchant
for balling together popular philosophy and Calvinist rhetoric. Like
both Whitby and Chubb, he was a voluntarist libertarian who asked
only for a "comparative liberty" where "the mind has some inward
reluctance or aversion to those actions which yet it wills to perform
for other more prevailing causes"; he arrived at this libertarianism not
by speculating freely on the nature of God or the creatures, but by a
strict Ramist dichotomization of the term *liberty*.[48]

Watts's voluntarism, like Chubb's, was predicated on a faculty of
psychology that sharply separated understanding and will to the benefit
of the latter, and in his "Philosophical Essays" he particularly chided
Locke for appearing to blend intellection and volition.[49] Although
Watts (again like Chubb) admitted that the will could sometimes be
run away with by the appetites and passions, nevertheless "the will has
the power to withhold the assent in many cases, and to delay the
judgement where things do not appear to the mind with full and bright
evidence . . . and even where things appear with a pretty good degree
of evidence, the will is able to delay our assent." Or, even more than
delay judgment, "the will has a great deal to do in our judgements
concerning objects proposed to the mind."[50] Watts's evidence for this
seemed perfectly commonsensical, since the pious often choose sensual
objects despite their full knowledge of the sensuality of what is chosen.
And further, there was the classic example of Buridan's ass: "sometimes two things are proposed to the will, wherein the understanding
can give no dictate, because it sees no manner of difference."[51] Left

without such a dictate from the understanding, the will must take over and "it must make its own choice only by its own determination."[52] In such cases, the understanding "has no pretense of power to direct and determine the will, because it sees no superior fitness, and the will would be forever undetermined, if it did not determine itself." In fact, to push matters even further, Watts suggested, in the case of "an unwise being" the will "may possibly determine itself without regard to the understanding, and even contrary to what the mind judges to be fit and good."[53] The will had not only triumphed over the understanding—it had effaced it.

Watts then moved to offer an unexpected demonstration of this: the will of God. God has established by reason the great moral truths and laws by which he runs the universe, thus making Christian morality eminently "reasonable" by Enlightenment standards. But not everything God has created has moral properties. When it comes to specifying "what should be the precise shape, and what the precise place of every corporeal being in the world"—such as "whether this single atom of mould or clay should be part of the glebe at Taunton or York"—there was no call for an act of moral legislation.[54] Thus, the disposition of these inconsequential items is left wholly to God's will in an arbitrary, unguided, undictated-to fashion:

Thus whether we consider man as a natural or a moral agent, and whether we consider God either as a Creator or as a governor, there seems to be several instances wherein there is no superior fitness or unfitness of things, that appears to the understanding to give any direction to the will in its choice or self-determination, so in these instances it eminently appears that it must be left to determine and choose for itself without any direction of the understanding.[55]

Stood beside Whitby's list of activities in which God was not permitted to engage, Watts's liberation of God's will to do what it pleased in the world seemed to be a thoroughgoing Calvinistic response. Watts certainly seemed to have seen it that way, and he congratulated himself for having devised a system that "allows the blessed God a full freedom of choice in distributing his favours to which of his creatures he pleases, and in what degree."[56] He made no allusion to the fact that this ultimate proof of the reality of free will was virtually identical to the argument used by Samuel Clarke against Leibniz's doctrine of "sufficient reason." No matter: the fact that he could wield Clarke's weapons could only have given him pleasure to think that he, the Calvinist, was worthy of the company of rational Anglicans. And anyway, did not the alternative to this "introduce Mr. Hobbes's doctrine of fatality and necessity into all things that God hath to do with?"[57]

Edwards was not nearly so enthused, but he was considerably more circumspect in how he handled Watts than in how he handled Chubb or Whitby. He never actually used Watts's name in *Freedom of the Will,* preferring to refer to him only as "the author of *An Essay on the Freedom of Will in God and the Creature.*" Although it is possible that Edwards did so because he was working from a copy of Watts's text in which the author's name did not appear (Watts arranged for one printing of his "Essay" to omit his name as the author), there is also the slim possibility that Edwards was hoping to divorce his attack on Watts's ideas from the matter of Watts's reputation. Although it does not seem likely that anyone willing to take up Edwards on freedom of the will would be so ignorant of Watts's treatise that he would fail to recognize the references to "An Essay on the Freedom of Will in God and the Creature" as meaning Watts's book, surely Edwards realized that too much in *Freedom of the Will* sounded like Hobbes for Edwards to hazard any further pejorative identifications by announcing that he was about to disagree with the psalm-singer of English Calvinism about free will.[58]

Still, if Edwards ever did experience any qualms about laying hands on Watts, the thoroughness of his critique does not betray them. Edwards's assault, in which it can be said that he found himself playing Leibniz to Watts's Clarke, deployed along two lines of argument. First, Edwards ridiculed the notion that the will could ever act in lieu of an undecided mind. Since the will moves by motives, and motives are perceived through the mind, Watts's idea of a self-actuated will moving without any impulse from the mind is the same as to say that no motive at all existed, and that the will moves solely by chance:

To suppose the will to act at all in a state of perfect indifference, whether to determine itself, or to do anything else, is to assert that the mind chooses without choosing. To say that when it is indifferent, it can do as it pleases, is to say that it can follow its pleasure, when it has no pleasure to follow.[59]

But on a deeper level, Edwards is really criticizing Watts's whole notion of what happens when volition takes place. Watts's stance for observing volition is from a distance, and his analysis of volition may therefore be called a macroanalysis. When he is told to touch any one of the sixty-four squares of a chessboard, Watts is aware that he has no more reason for touching one square than another, and he sees that his judgment can issue no particular order to the will. Assuming that this situation will induce a permanent paralysis, there is nothing left to consider when the moment for choice comes but to attribute autonomous action to the will and choose whichever square one chooses. But Edwards's analysis of volition was always a microanalysis; he consistently limited his discussion to what was happening at the precise moment of choice. In that sense, then, although "objects may appear equal, and the mind may never properly make any choice between them," that is never the real cause of action at the split second of volition itself:

... the next act of the will being about the external actions to be performed, talking, touching, etc., these may not appear equal, and one action may properly be chosen before another. In each step of the mind's progress, the determination is not about the objects ... but about the actions, which it chooses for other reasons than any preferences of the objects, and for reasons not taken at all from the objects.[60]

So it was possible to say with Watts that at the moment of viewing a chessboard, the mind might see nothing that would urge a choice. But if choice actually did take place, the reason was not that the will took over from a stymied mind, but that the object of choice itself changed by the time the touching of the chessboard took place:

... in this case, my mind determines to give itself up to what is vulgarly called accident, by determining to touch that square which happens to be most in view, which my eye is especially upon at that moment, or which happens to be then most in my mind, or which I shall be directed to by some or suchlike accident.[61]

There could never be a time when some motive does not preponderate; if not a view of the chessboard, then the view of acting of the chessboard or some such other: "The question they dispute about, is, whether the mind be indifferent about the *objects* presented ... whereas the question to be considered, is, whether the person be indifferent with respect to his own *actions*."[62] Watts thus stood guilty not only of giving the wrong answer, but of asking the wrong question about volition.

The second major axis along which Edwards advanced against Watts led to Watts's voluntarist conception of the will of God. Wild a notion as it appeared to Edwards, it was particularly threatening because he had repeatedly used his own notion of God's necessary will to beat down Arminian objections that necessity was inconsistent with moral choice. His response had a strikingly Leibnizian ring, perhaps because, even if it is impossible to say for sure that Edwards had read Leibniz (the *Theodicy,* after all, had not been translated into English in Edwards's lifetime), it is still difficult not to suspect that he had at least some familiarity with the celebrated Leibniz-Clarke correspondence on necessity. Edwards actually sets quotes from Clarke's *Demonstration of the Being and Attributes of God* into footnotes where they will appear to contradict Watts.[63]

Like Leibniz, Edwards began by objecting to Watts's glorification of the voluntarist God as mere show. Edwards complained that Watts's argument would make sense, and glorify God, only if it could be thought that there was something glorious in having no reason for doing whatever one does, or something shameful in having one. "All the seeming force of such objections and exclamations," Edwards wryly remarked, "must arise from an imagination, that there is some sort of privilege in being without such a moral necessity, as will make it impossible to do any other, than always choose what is wisest and best."[64] Far from its being glorious, the lack of a "sufficient reason" for the will of God was a recipe for calamity, since "to suppose the divine will liable to be carried hither and thither at random, by the uncertain wind of blind contingence," with "no wisdom, no motive, no intelligent dictate" to steer it, would "argue of a great degree of imperfection and meanness, infinitely unworthy of the deity."[65] To think, as Watts did, that this divine will was a demonstration of how the human will functioned would force Watts to define freedom as

a full and perfect freedom and liableness to act altogether at random, without the least connection with, or restraint or government by, any dictate of reason, or anything whatsoever apprehended, considered or viewed by the understanding as being inconsistent with the full and perfect sovereignty of the will over its own determinations.[66]

If a sufficient reason must come into play for every volition, then it is nonsense to talk of splitting the objects of volitions into categories of moral and nonmoral, significant and insignificant, since their moral status and significance are merely relative descriptions, and all atoms, whether in Taunton or York, are products of the determinate counsel and foreknowledge of God. For Watts to say otherwise was to roll God's purposes back up and out of view, behind his will or behind man's unwillingness; and once these purposes have been successfully obscured, they may as well never have existed—which are exactly the conclusions Edwards accused the Arminians of reaching in their effort to appease the demon of materialism. Characteristically, Edwards sought to defeat materialism not by safeguarding God from absolute contact with the world but by ensuring the absoluteness of that contact:

But I think it would be unreasonable to suppose, that God made one atom in vain, or without any end or motive. He made not one atom but what was a work of his almighty power, as much as the whole globe of the earth, and requires as much of a constant exertion of almighty power to uphold it; and was made and is upheld understandingly, and on design, as much as if no other had been made but that. And it would be as unreasonable to suppose, that he made it without anything really aimed at in doing so, as much as to suppose that he made the planet Jupiter without aim or design.[67]

Looking back over the wreckage of these three antagonists, Chubb, Whitby, and Watts, one begins to suspect that Edwards has gotten away with his refutations a little too easily. Although Edwards gave some glancing attention to the opinions of Samuel Clarke and to the writings of some secondary figures like Dr. John Taylor of Norwich and the Scottish moralist George Turnbull (both of whom would appear again as targets in Edwards's later book on original sin), he made no attempt to construct a serious case against Clarke or to deal straightforwardly with Hobbes. Instead, he chose to cross swords with antagonists who were anything but the last word on the subject of free will. Although Chubb, Whitby, and Watts were not exactly unknowns, they were simply not thinkers of the first rank, and that raises a very good question as to why Edwards chose to respond to these three.

It is not likely that he selected them merely because they presented easy targets, for in fact they plainly put Edwards off his stride in some important places. To correct Whitby, Edwards employed a notion of causality he himself did not really share; to find loopholes in Chubb, Edwards may have subtly manipulated the intent of Chubb's statements; in his scorn for Watts's idea of an undirected will, he never confronted the factor which pushed Watts to that idea, that if God was absolutely conscious of everything he had created, and continuously created it all, then he must be consciously involved in the production of evil.

What seems to have attracted Edwards most to these three was the symbolic value he could derive from standing them in the pillory of criticism. All three were voluntaristic libertarians, and they essentially differed only in the degree of libertarianism they required for the will, ranging from Chubb's virtually complete libertarianism, through Whitby's "imperfect" liberty, down to Watts's "comparative" freedom. By holding up an entire spectrum of libertarianism to scorn, Edwards was serving notice that no form of libertarianism—Arminian or dissenting Calvinist—was as good a defense against atheistic materialism as an aggressive, reconciliationist Calvinism. Even more to the point, in holding up a churchman like Whitby as a spokesman for Arminianism, Edwards was tacitly reminding his readers of the close associations of Arminianism with the dreaded minions of the Established Church. No matter what attractions Arminianism might have for New Englanders, Edwards knew that even Charles Chauncy hated episcopacy, and Edwards himself (who had been witness to the Great Apostasy of 1722) seems to have tarred Arminianism with an episcopal brush in his own mind. Performing that tarring for the benefit of his readers would have come instinctively. Likewise, by offering a unitarian like Chubb up with the Arminians, Edwards was once again indicating yet another bird of the feather he saw all Arminians flocking together with. It is noteworthy, too, that Edwards particularly chose an artisan Whig for this role, even perhaps seeing in the pesky independence of the Chubbs and the Franklins the same contemptuous shopkeepers who "wouldn't worship a wig" and who had helped drive him from Northampton. As for Watts, whom Edwards served up the hardest, his quashing was a warning that a half-hearted Calvinism which yielded every time the Arminians warned of the wolf of materialism at the door was worse than useless. In the long run, Edwards selected for his book the people who would best serve the polemical purposes of dogmatic Calvinism, not those who would help him toward a calm analysis of selected theories of volition.

II

Edwards's method of handling this opposition reminds us that *Freedom of the Will* was written not as an exercise in philosophical investigation but "that ye may believe." As such, it is a strategic, even manipulative, book fully as much as it is a search after truth. This is apparent not only from his handling of Chubb, Whitby, and Watts, but even from his very first definition of the will, where Edwards, far from exploring possible definitions of the will, simply assumes one. Indeed, he assumes a definition that can lead in the Calvinist direction only,

thereby rendering his subsequent reasoning an exercise more in definition than demonstration. Nothing in the balance of the book would
make sense unless the first definition is granted: if it *is* granted, then
the hook is in the mouth and one is led inexorably to a Calvinistic
conclusion. Edwards's definition of Arminianism was equally tailored
to usefulness. Just as he chose for opponents three men whose arguments were conventional rather than critical, so he preferred to view
Arminian libertarianism only at the most fierce and dogged extreme
of radical contingency. The "Arminians" he sought to stone for the sin
of random chanciness argued only for indeterminism, not raw Epicu-
reanism, and for some kind of sphere (however small) for the will. But
Edwards did not want to understand Arminianism: he wanted to leave
it for dead, and so he herded the entire spectrum of Arminian libertarianism far enough out on the Epicurean limb that he could saw
them all off at once. And that, of course, only subverted his intentions,
since the mild indeterminist, not recognizing himself on Edwards's
pages, would simply walk away wondering what all the fuss was about.

Certainly his most unusual manipulation was his appeal to "common
sense" to establish that liberty of acting, and moral necessity of motives, are not incompatible. Edwards himself was no democrat, and it
does not need much explaining to realize that the appeal to the "common people" was an intellectual fig leaf used to conceal the impression
that Calvinism was becoming naked of supporters. It had been one of
his goals, back in 1752, to refute the contention "that the Calvinistic
notions of God's moral government are contrary to the common sense
of mankind." But he was not doing it solely for the benefit of the
common people. By enlisting the "common people," Edwards satisfied
himself that he was turning the impression that Calvinism was immoral
and sterile into an accusation that Arminianism was the religion of an
aloof and aristocratic elite. As politics, this was a sensible tactic, and
if the successes of Edwards's followers, the New Divinity men, mean
anything, the tactic seems to have worked. As philosophy, it was prob-
lematic. "Common sense" is a shifting, changeable thing and always a
dubious authority. What was more, he was contradicting some of his
own principal tenets in making appeals to common sense: if it is
granted that only the elect can have an "ideal apprehension" of things,
then the sense of the "common people" about the will ought to be
even more risky. Indeed, he had seen for himself that only the regen-

erated souls of the Awakening had given proper credit to Calvinistic ideas—the "common people" were precisely the ones resisting such ideas.[68]

More serious than Edwards's explicit predilection for arbitrary definitions (and authorities) are the definitions he never offered at all for a series of will-related problems. The biggest definitional vacuum Edwards left in *Freedom of the Will* concerned what he meant by *nature*. The crucial element in distinguishing one motive from another, and ultimately determining the will, depended on "the particular temper which the mind has by nature." Edwards's Calvinist contemporaries would probably have assumed that by *nature* Edwards was referring to the same thing Calvin spoke of when he declared that, beneath the conscious intelligence, there existed "an immortal essence."[69] But Edwards was not in fact thinking along those lines. Since an "idea is only a perception wherein the mind is passive," there was no way to discover a substance or essence which might underlie that idea.[70] "We have no evidence of immaterial substance," Edwards conceded; "what we call body is nothing but a particular mode of perception; and what we call spirit is nothing but a composition and series of perceptions."[71]

Yet, Edwards recognized that there had to be some way to establish continuity between ideas—*something* had to confirm the self-evident fact that we are not merely random moments of consciousness. On that point of urgency he was in agreement with Locke, but this led Locke simply to eschew terms like "Being" and "substance" and to locate the foundation of consciousness in our personal memory of a continuous personal identity. Edwards, on the other hand, embraced "Being" and "substance" by redefining both as God, and branding as erroneous the supposition that this continuity rested on "a sameness or identity of consciousness."[72] Edwards thought it better to understand consciousness as an immediate and continuous creation of God. Hence, our ideas are connected to each other not because of something in them or in their surroundings but by God, who joins them by the word of power:

That which truly is the substance of all bodies is the infinitely exact and precise and perfectly stable idea in God's mind together with his stable will that the same shall gradually be communicated to us, and to other minds, according to certain fixed and exact established methods and laws.[73]

There was, then, no fixed "essence" or spiritual substance in which particular human qualities inhere, or whose moral temper governs human behavior. Just as the essence which "upholds the properties of bodies" is really "he by whom all things consist," so all our ideas proceed in a relationship issuing not from ourselves but from God.[74] The *nature* which the mind has, and which governs its temper and its liking or not liking of motives, resolves ultimately into the act of God himself.

Edwards later used this to good effect in 1758 in *The Great Christian Doctrine of Original Sin Defended*. Westminster Calvinism had explained human sinfulness in terms of a depraved nature, transmitted by nature from one generation to another. Faced with the need to justify yet another Calvinist doctrine in an age prone to cry "unfair" when the sins of the fathers were visited on the children, Edwards resorted to his notion of continuity (in this case, continuity in sin) by divine constitution rather than inherited nature. Mankind, Edwards suggested, is guilty not because we inherit Adam's sin but because we committed it with him. This is the case, said Edwards, because "all dependent existence whatsoever is in constant flux, ever passing and returning; renewed every moment."[75] In this flux, God decrees a *constituted* sharing of moral identity, so that "Adam's posterity are from him, and as it were in him, and belonging to him . . . as much as the branches of a tree are, according to a course of nature, from the tree, in the tree, and belonging to the tree."[76] When he grasped that forbidden fruit, "guilt . . . and also depravity of heart, came upon Adam's posterity just as they came upon him, as much as if he and they had all co-existed, like a tree with many branches."[77] In Adam's fall, we sinned all, because God simply constituted a shared moral identity between us and Adam:

Thus it appears, if we consider matters strictly, there is no such thing as any identity or oneness in created objects, existing at different times, but what depends on *God's sovereign constitution* . . . for it appears, that a *divine constitution* is the thing which *makes truth*, in affairs of this nature.[78]

Edwards made no allusion to this divine constituting of ideas in *Freedom of the Will*, and yet this concept of substance (or lack thereof) is vital to the most important distinction he makes in the book, that between natural and moral necessity. Remember that the key to how natural and moral necessity could guarantee reliably necessitated results without infringing on liberty lay in the fact that their connection was in the nature of the terms themselves, not in the nature of the connection. It is not physical force or compulsion that causes the malicious person to strike his neighbor, but rather the inherent connection between the perceptions of a malicious person and malicious volitions. There is no tactile causality at work. Malicious perception does not "push" a will that might otherwise choose not to be malicious, for wills (by definition) do not choose otherwise than as the greatest apparent good is.

This description of necessity is only the divine constitution writ small. Edwards's inability to define the substance that causes things to be what they are led him to replace substance with divine energy. That which kept bodies "indiscerpible" was only "some arbitrary, active and voluntary being that determines it"[79]; our ideas of bodies were not the product of impact on the senses but only "the determination that such and such ideas shall be raised in created minds upon such conditions."[80] Even the organs of sense are "no other than God's constitution that some of our ideas shall be connected with others according to such a settled law and order so that some ideas shall follow from others as their cause."[81] Therefore, what we perceive as *cause*—one thing hitting another and moving it—is merely a sequence of ideas whose connection lies wholly in the creative power of God to make us see that way. This is so similar in theory to Malebranche's occasionalism that it is tempting to see this as a direct borrowing from the French Oratorian. In both Edwards and Malebranche tactile causality is an error of imaginations duped by appearances, of those who mistake signs for reality, of those who do not enjoy the divine and supernatural light that would allow them to see God's hand at work. Thus, there is, really, no such thing as a "relational necessity" (and it is worth noting how quickly that half-defined concept disappears from Edwards's discussion once he has moved to philosophical necessity). Simply because the only relationships that exist *are* those induced by the divine connection of ideas, the only necessity *is* philosophical necessity—natural necessity when natural terms are involved, moral necessity when moral terms are used.

If the notion of divine constitution served to legitimize Edwards's reduction of volition to nominal connection, it also served to show how the ambiguous certainty of moral necessity could really rise to the level of absolute predictability. Edwards had acknowledged at the beginning of his discussion of moral necessity that, in common parlance, to talk of moral causality was only to talk of likelihood. "So we say," he wrote, "a man is under necessity, when he is under bonds of duty and conscience, which he can't be discharged from." The "bonds" of duty and conscience are only metaphorical speech; there are no physical bonds at all, no absolute guarantees of dutiful behavior, so that, "in this sense, 'moral necessity' signifies much the same as that high degree of probability, which is ordinarily sufficient to satisfy, and be relied upon by mankind." But Edwards then turned and insisted that "moral necessity may be as absolute as natural necessity." Why? Because, on one level, likelihoods can sometimes be piled so high as to be functionally absolute. But, on another level, moral necessity acquires absolute force because moral necessity is, after all, a "full and fixed connection between the things signified by the subject and predicate of a proposition," and such connections are ipso facto absolute.[82] "Truth," Edwards had written in his notebooks in the 1720s, "is the perception of the relations there are between ideas."[83] That duty and conscience do not attach physical shackles to the dutiful and conscientious is accurate, but irrelevant; shackles, duty, and conscience are all *ideas,* and where there is a relationship by divine constitution between *ideas,* that relationship *is* the truth. "Necessary being" exists "as it is a necessary idea." The great mistake, as Edwards saw it, was to assume that, in the realm of ideas, duty and moral action belong together but that in the "real" world, duty alone could only sustain likelihood of moral action. There was no such "real" world—"all existence is mental," Edwards insisted, "the existence of all exterior things is ideal."[84] There was no dichotomy between our knowledge of a "real" world where nominal connection supported merely the probable, and knowledge of an ideal world where nominal connection produced certainty. The "real" world of common language dropped away, leaving only the ideal world where such connections were absolute. Hence, while it is true that in common speech we think of moral necessity only as likelihood, common speech itself is in error. "Corporeal things exist no otherwise than mentally," and in such an ideal world, absolute nominal connections, which in the "real" world were thought only probable, turn out to be the truth.[85]

The divine constitution of ideas also served to defend Edwards from what was to be the most persistent criticism he would sustain, and that was that his idea of necessity from moral causes was simply a spiritual abstraction. Admittedly, the whole conception of moral necessity is an a priori one. It deals with terms rather than human experience. Like the Cartesian rationalists of his own day, Edwards was confident that truth could be found in the mind. But, as with many other rationalists, Edwards was left prey to the charge that he is manipulating terms that can be rendered conveniently air-tight by definition, rather than describing human beings. We recall, for sake of illustration, Schopenhauer's critique of an earlier Christian rationalist, St. Anselm. St. Anselm's contention that necessary existence is contained in the concept of a supremely perfect being (and so God *must* exist) was mocked by Schopenhauer as "the sleight-of-hand trick" in which "where the law of causality demands a *cause,* he substitutes a *reason.*" The apparent force of the ontological argument is thus dismissed as "a charming joke" whose force rests chiefly on its ability to switch terms without the restraint of experience:

After all, the simplest answer to such ontological demonstrations is: "All depends upon the source whence you have derived your conception: if it be taken from experience, all well and good, for in this case its object exists and needs no further proof; if, on the contrary, it has been hatched in your own *sincipit,* all its predicates are of no avail, for it is a mere phantasm.[86]

Similarly, for Edwards, it may be all well and good that one can have an idea of a malicious human temper so purely malicious that it always defines what a man will find agreeable. But people, as they are met on a day-in, day-out basis, seem to be considerably more complex than that, and therefore behave more erratically. Experience would also seem to dictate that the line Edwards drew between natural and moral necessity was not nearly so hard-and-fast as he made it. Edwards would have granted, for instance, that a man bound with cords is under a natural necessity of staying put; but suppose a soldier has a musket pointed at his head while being given an order to surrender. If the soldier surrenders, it is certainly not because natural causes have conspired to make him surrender (he had not been wrestled to the ground), but on the other hand, it would be a little stiff-necked to say that the soldier is only operating under moral causes and is still perfectly free when he surrenders. As John Hospers has observed, it can be hard to determine exactly when an act is "compelled" by natural causes and when not:

Our actions are compelled in a literal sense if someone has us in chains or is compelling our bodily movements. When we say that the storm compelled us to jettison the cargo of the ship . . . we have a less literal sense of compulsion, for it is at least open to us to go down with the ship. When psychoanalysts say that a man was compelled by unconscious conflicts to wash his hands constantly, this is also not a literal use of "compel," for nobody forced his hands under the tap. Still, it is a typical example of what psychoanalysts call *compulsive* behavior: it has unconscious causes inaccessible to introspection, and moreover nothing can change it—it is as inevitable for him to do it as it would be if someone were forcing his hands under the tap.[87]

By contrast, Edwards's characters appear as stick figures—not as people in the throes of moral dilemmas, but as terms, not as a person but a wooden construct called "malicious man," who is granted fixed moral attributes in the same way we grant fixed moves to a chess piece. In a word, was not Edwards's conception of human nature naive?

By his own experience, Edwards could only respond, *no.* For if Edwards had learned nothing else from the Great Awakening, he had learned that human psychology was not complex at all, but simple and unitary. The fathers of New England, subscribing as they did to intellectualist and voluntarist paradigms, were inclined to speak of the self as a hierarchy of faculties, through which assurance of salvation could be grasped only gradually, as psychological conflict was resolved and doubts erased. "Morphologies of conversion" appeared as checklists to soothe those well on the path to salvation, and to indicate to those not yet there how they could "prepare" themselves for grace. But the Awakening disrupted the preparationist pattern, for nothing was more remarkable in the behavior of the awakened than the dramatic shift of personality that occurred. Edwards recorded, in his observations of his parishioners in Northampton, not a gradual persuasion of truth emerging out of slow change, but the abrupt substitution of a completely new way of seeing things. Phoebe Bartlett was only four years old when grace came to her, but when it came, it took only the last Thursday of July 1735 for her to conclude, "Mother, the kingdom of heaven is come to me!" Abigail Hutchinson "saw the same things that she had seen before, yet more clearly, and in another, and far more excellent and delightful manner."[88]

From this evidence, it was plain to Edwards that there was a metaphysical mandate for his notion that human ideas were simply "the infinitely exact and precise and perfectly stable idea in God's mind." Bartlett and Hutchinson and thousands of others had given testimony that their conversion was God's, simply and graciously, changing his way of ordering their ideas. Now, God was granting them truth, and since Edwards had, a decade before, established for himself that truth was "the consistency and agreement of our ideas with the ideas of

God," then it followed that there was no evidence of conflict and complexity. Salvation came with the awarding of a new sense—not part of a new sense, but an entire one. "I think the Scripture knows of but one sort of sincerity," Edwards concluded, "and that is a truly pious or holy sincerity."[89] Conversion was a complete and thorough experience. This conviction led him to drop whatever "preparationist" rhetoric he had employed in his early sermons and to demand conversion from his hearers as "an immediate and instantaneous work, like to the change made in Lazarus when Christ called him from the grave."[90] And ultimately, years later, it would lead him to attribute the attraction of the will to just a single, new, simple idea: the greatest apparent good.

Given this all-or-nothing notion of spiritual life (and it is striking in Edwards just how little there is on the subject of *growth* in grace), it is easier to see how the conduct of a saint, by moral necessity, could be as inevitable as physical mechanics. Virtuous women sometimes do not behave virtuously, and hopeless drunkards sometimes do dry out, in some human experience. But in Edwards's experience, human nature had less potential. Because true supernatural virtue admitted of no degree, virtuous women were, all the time, predictably and necessarily virtuous; and drunkards, who plainly did not have such virtue, were always drunkards without the slightest hope of sobriety—unless, of course, the grace of God interposed. So, if Edwards's examples of moral necessity seem often nothing more than hypostatizations of terms, that is because, in a very real sense, that was precisely how he thought of people. It gained no ground with Edwards to complain that he spoke in abstractions. "For a man to go about to confute the arguments of his opponent, by telling him, his arguments are 'metaphysical' would be as weak as to tell him, his arguments could not be substantial, because they are written in French or Latin."[91] Life itself was abstract, consisting only "in the determinations of God that such and such ideas shall be raised in created minds upon such conditions."[92] The idea of moral necessity only described experience as Edwards knew it.

The other problem mentioned here—that of the exact boundary between natural and moral necessity—might have been easier to draw had Edwards given us a better definition of motives. Since "motives" are responsible for morally necessitated acts of will, knowing exactly what constituted a motive would go a long way toward fixing the bounds between moral and natural necessity. It is easy to say that

motives are mental causes, in contrast to natural necessity, which involves terms of physical cause, but when it is remembered that Edwards
saw both kinds of cause as ideal, that statement tends to fall flat.
Edwards himself seems to have deliberately fuzzed over the ontological
status of motives precisely so that he would not have to become en-
tangled in such distinctions, and he spoke of motives as being "some
way or other in the mind's view." The result, however, is that Edwards
never really divulges his notion of the exact nature of motives: "It is
sufficient to my present purpose to say, it is that motive, which, as it
stands in the view of the mind, is the strongest, that determines the
will."[93]

Nor do we get an altogether clear view of how motives operate.
Motives determine the will; but so does the greatest apparent good;
yet the will is as the greatest apparent good is; is the will *as* the motive?
Grant in "the view of the mind" something that constitutes the
"strongest motive," and it would then seem that the act of volition is
what Arthur Murphy called "a piece of superfluous mental machinery
that registers this result and somehow passes it on to ensuing bodily
movements."[94] Moreover, if the will is *as* the motive, and God creates
and presents the motive, then does God create the will? And are we
not back to what Edwards strenuously tried to avoid, that "there is no
positive act in God, as though he put forth any power to harden the
heart"?[95] So long as the matter of motives remains unclear, so will the
distinction between natural and moral necessity.[96]

The redefinition of causality as divinely constituted connection serves
to throw some light on that problem, even if it did not solve it entirely,
for once volition has in fact become thus superfluous in psychological
terms, then the critical factor in understanding human action becomes,
not the will, but *temper* or *nature*. The notion of "constituted connection" aided Edwards in dealing with the objection that *any* divine
involvement in human affairs renders God responsible for the evil in
human life. It stands to reason that if God makes some people with
"natures" such that they can do nothing but sin, then it might appear
that God and not men still deserves to be blamed as the perpetrator.
Superficially, Edwards's scheme of "motives" averted this blow. Edwards could "utterly deny God to be the author of sin . . . if by the
'author of sin,' be meant the sinner, the agent, or actor of sin, or the
doer of a wicked deed," and that because, in strict terms, God (1)
merely withholds the new spiritual sense from some men who do not

deserve it anyway, and (2) presents them only with motives to ungodliness.[97] God never *performs* sin, and therefore is not a sinner. Still,
Edwards realized, God could be accused of being an accomplice, if not
by performing, then by decreeing someone else's performance of evil,
or at least motivating it. But, insisted Edwards, the two are not really
the same:

> We do not mean by decreeing an action as sinful, the same as decreeing an
> action so that it shall be sinful. In decreeing an action as sinful, I mean de-
> creeing it for the sake of the sinfulness of the action. God decrees that they
> shall be sinful, for the sake of the good that he causes to arise from the
> sinfulness of the acts, whereas man decrees them for the sake of the evil that
> it intends.[98]

The examples Edwards offered are persuasive: for instance, "no Christians will deny it was the design of God, that Christ should be *cruci-
fied*." Nevertheless, no self-respecting Arminian would deny that this
was "for excellent, holy, gracious and glorious ends . . . and thus considered, the crucifixion was not evil, but good."[99] Of course, the force
of Edwards's theodicy would depend, as Edwards would have expected,
on the readiness of the reader's trust in God, and Edwards was counting
on an audience of Arminians who trusted God. So, he concluded, "I
don't deny that God's being thus the author of sin, follows from what
I have laid down; and I assert that it equally follows from the doctrine
which is maintained by most of the Arminian divines."[100]

Yet, even if we find it safe, under certain circumstances, to transfer
the responsibility for causation of evil to God, it is questionable
whether that makes any difference for the larger context of the problem.
If motives *cause* the will to act, how is that essentially different from
the causation compelled by natural necessity? They differed, Edwards
would answer, because we ought to think of cause not as the push that
impacts on another substance, but as a perceived relationship. Cause
exists only as the perception, according to "God's constitution that
some of our ideas shall be connected with others as their cause." The
divine and supernatural light God shines upon men does not actually
"consist in any impression made upon the imagination"; instead, Edwards said, he "unites" himself "with the mind of a saint, takes him
for his temple, actuates and influences him as a new supernatural principle of life and action."[101] In that context, then, motives did *cause* the
will: one observed the presence of a motive and the presence of a
corresponding act of will and sequence. After that observation, there

was no point to inquiring whether one had pushed the other. Hence, God could "cause" evil or good without having to sully his character by "pushing" it on men. One observed that a relationship had been observed between God and evil and called it what you had no good reason not to call it: a cause.[102]

III

One certain judgment that can be made about *Freedom of the Will* is that many judgments of it have been wrong. Perry Miller greatly exaggerated Edwards's debt to Locke, and thus dismissed *Freedom of the Will* as a mere elaboration of a psychology he supposed Edwards to have borrowed from Locke.[103] This is not to deny similarities. As in Locke, Edwards interpreted the mind as a single, conscious mental state with but two "faculties," the "understanding" and the "will," and he remained skeptical of the notion that unconscious states were real entities; he agreed with Locke's original contention in the first edition of the *Essay* that liberty is an attribute of the willing self, not the will; and he is certainly echoing Locke (although again only the Locke of the first edition of the *Essay,*) with his suggestion that the will is as the greatest apparent good is. Above all, Edwards agreed with Locke's general thesis, that minds have immediate knowledge only of ideas.[104] But Edwards also departed from Locke in ways that were to have far greater significance than the ways in which he followed him, beginning with the fact that, whereas Locke was confident that most of those ideas were derived from the impact of objects on the senses, and then reliably mediated knowledge concerning those external objects to the mind, Edwards believed that any communication between those external objects and ideas of them within the human mind was purely an activity of God. Likewise, Edwards would not rest the personal identity of the willing self in a continuous conscious memory, for that would jeopardize any moral connection with Adam and so undermine the doctrine of original sin. He also would not allow what Locke later resorted to in subsequent editions of the *Essay,* the power to suspend choice in order to establish free will, and it seems evident that Edwards thought Locke had not gone far enough in examining the actual process of volition. Repenting of his one-stage analysis of volition, Locke fell back to a two-stage theory and introduced distinctions between desire and actual preference. Locke accomplished this simply by shifting his analytical point of view from microanalysis to macroanalysis, and his image of "desire" thus became something that could be made remote in time or place from the actual preferring. Edwards thought that this, whatever it might say about the strength of memory, shifted the focus off what actually happened at the moment of willing itself. At that moment, desiring was indistinguishable from preferring. "When I say, the will is as the greatest apparent good is," Edwards cautioned, "it must be carefully observed, to avoid confusion and needless objection, that I speak of the direct and immediate object of the act of volition; and not some object that the act of will has not an immediate, but only an indirect and remote aspect to."[105] Of course, many acts of will may include factors which are "remote," but to Edwards the heart of the willing process was the moment of willing itself, and it was all he cared to analyze. "We commonly call that the will," Edwards had insisted long before, "that is the mind's inclination with respect to its own immediate actions."[106] It goes almost without saying that an attempt to open a crack between the willing and a motive to will would have left a vacuum that would have been filled eagerly by hosts of hostile Arminians.

Edwards seemed to have been less worried about being judged by a Lockean and more fearful of being accused of Hobbesianism—not just for defending determinism, but for some of the ways in which he did it. Although Edwards claimed, "I never read Mr. Hobbes," that is true only insofar as he probably had never read one of Hobbes's books by 1754; but he had evidently read Hobbes's arguments somewhere, since Hobbes is cited very early in Edwards's *Miscellanies*. [107] And, one is tempted to say, he appears in *Freedom of the Will* too, whether Edwards really wanted him there or not. It is going to be very hard to frame any secular argument for determinism, hard or soft, or any kind of one-stage microanalysis of volition, without employing a psychological explanation very similar to Hobbes's. And, sure enough, Edwards's description of the will as the greatest apparent good, or motive, or being the executor of the mind's preferences, sounded from a distance very much like speaking of the will as the last item in a series of mental exercises just before acting—which was, of course, just the way Hobbes described it. To be sure, Edwards was thinking of the will also as an aspect of the affections, motivated by spiritual apprehensions rather than appetites. But those who had not had the benefit of reading Edwards's preparatory psychological observations in *The Religious Affec-*

tions, or of peeking into his *Miscellanies,* were not likely to see that, especially with Hobbes's ideas conjured up by the very mention of freedom of the will. It did not help that Hobbes's definition of freedom *was* the same as Edwards's: freedom of acts from external coercion. It probably eased few anxieties to be reminded that Edwards shared this definition with Luther and Calvin fully as much as with Hobbes.

Edwards died in 1758, before he could improve or rework any of his arguments, but sketches for future work on "A Rational Account of the Main Doctrines of the Christian Religion" show that he was far from finished with the subject. His plan for "The Natural History of the Mental World" contained at least five new directions he wanted to explore concerning volition, such as "How fare there may be acts of the will without our adverting to it" or whether "truth be not also the object of the will."[108] Gordon Wood has taken Edwards as a paradigm of American thinking in the decades before the Revolution, not because Edwardsean thinking led in some peculiar way to Whig politics, but because *Freedom of the Will*'s relentless insistence on "sufficient reason" for volition characterized America's practical suspicions that the machinations of the British government were not just aimless blunderings. If no man acted from indifference, there must be discoverable causes for men's outward behavior. In the case of British imperial politics, it appeared that since there must be a morally necessary connection between evil mercantilist legislation and evil mercenary motives, then mercantilist Englishmen must be of corrupt and designing hearts. "Indeed," comments Wood, "never before or since in Western history has man been held so directly and morally responsible for the events of his world."[109]

Edwards could have supplied Wood with a concrete example of that, though it was drawn not from imperial politics but from New England ecclesiology. For if all men had not only "sufficient reason" for doing what they wanted to do but also natural ability to do it, there was every reason to suspect the sincerity of the Half-Way Covenant, preparationism, and, above all, Stoddardeanism. In his termination of Stoddard's open-door policy in Northampton in 1744, and his skillful defense of that termination against Solomon Williams in the *Humble Inquiry,* Edwards had in fact put into practice beforehand that direct demand for moral responsibility Wood saw so vividly enshrined in *Freedom of the Will.* Even though *Freedom of the Will* was intended to address an intellectual problem in New England—how to salvage

Calvinism from Hobbesianism and still have predestination—it is not surprising, coming from Edwards, that it also managed to speak to a spiritual and ecclesiastical problem as well.

For Edwards gave no evidence that he was interested in political applications of *Freedom of the Will*. When he preached the utter passivity of men before an angry God in Enfield in 1741, and destroyed all sense of mechanistic causality by informing the congregation that nothing had enabled them to rise, to come to church, or even to avoid dropping at that moment into hell fire but the unobliged forbearance of an incensed God, he wanted to create humility, not rebellion. He sought, in Northampton, to loosen the natural bonds of family loyalties, and reerect a community founded on conscious, ideal apprehensions of God, and on wills submissively drawn out in love, rather than town oligarchy. "When the spirit that is at work amongst a people tends . . . to high and exalting thoughts of the Divine Being . . . winning and drawing the heart with those motives and incitements to love which the Apostle speaks of," then that Spirit "also quells contentions among men, and gives a spirit of peace and good will."[110] As Richard Bushman observed, "the Spirit of God appeared to be creating an entire society of saintly men, submissive to God and exquisitely sensitive to religion," and for Edwards that meant that, whereas Arminians could produce only a congeries of self-determined wills that guaranteed factionalism and disorder, Calvinism would guarantee a harmonious Northampton, a harmony that could even be heard as the revived turned to singing hymns in four parts.[111] It seemed as though he had nearly succeeded in the Awakening, when those who submitted to a sovereign God suddenly found a new sense of community with each other. Alas, the jealousies of self-determination struck back, and struck at Edwards. However, he never was persuaded that he had been wrong, and *Freedom of the Will* embodied his conviction that only an America moved to submit its self-determination to God could become a community of will, as John Winthrop had said so long before, "knit together in this whole as one man."[112]

CHAPTER 3

Bellamy and Hopkins

The Wisdom of God in the Permission of Sin

I

On January 18, 1758, Jonathan Edwards paid a last visit to Samuel Hopkins, his prize pupil and now pastor of a strife-ridden congregation in Great Barrington, Massachusetts. The trustees of the College of New Jersey at Princeton had beckoned to Edwards to come and succeed his dead son-in-law, Aaron Burr, as president of the college, and, despite severe misgivings, Edwards was going. To Hopkins, Edwards delivered a pile of manuscripts for safe-keeping, and the next day Edwards departed, promising to return in the spring to retrieve them. Hopkins felt a chill of foreboding about this parting, and before the day was over he wrote to Joseph Bellamy, Edwards's other great pupil and now also a pastor in Bethlehem, Connecticut. Mr. Edwards, he explained, "expects not to return till next May"—and then he added grimly, "Alas, his mantle has gone with him."[1] Hopkins's foreboding was all too well justified. The spring came, but Edwards never returned, dying of a mishandled smallpox inoculation at Princeton in March. The American Elijah (as Gilbert Tennent eulogized him) was no more.[2] He was fifty-four years old.

But what of this Elijah's mantle? Later historians of New England theology like George Nye Boardman or Frank Hugh Foster have proved all too happy to accept at face value Hopkins's comment that Edwards had taken away his mantle with him, implying thereby that he had not bestowed it, or a double portion of his spirit, on either Hopkins or Bellamy. It has made no difference that Hopkins and Bellamy spent the next forty-odd years constructing an enormous web of Edwardsean dogmatics, spun almost entirely from the explicit and implicit agendas of *Freedom of the Will*. To the contrary, their "New Divinity" has been dismissed as a ruse by which Edwards's defense of Calvinism was watered down in order to perform the kind of accommodationism Edwards had spurned. Moses Hemmenway accused the New Divinity of having "inlisted under the banner of the Remonstrants [Arminians]," and the Arminian antagonist of Ezra Stiles Ely's *A Contrast Between Hopkinsianism and Calvinism* (1811) claimed that the New Divinity was "actually one of my fraternity."[3] So, almost as a punishment for having bit the hand that often literally fed them, Hopkins and Bellamy and their New Divinity have been virtually read out of the history of American thought.

What is suspicious about the truncation of Edwards from the New Divinity is that, united as many commentators in the past have been that Hopkins and Bellamy betrayed Edwards, they are far from agreed on the particular form this betrayal took. In the eyes of their contemporaries, Hopkins and Bellamy erred in taking Edwards too far. Israel Holly declared in 1795 that

Mr. Edwards was a tall man, and when they presum'd to clamber up upon his shoulders, it carried them much out of their proper sphere, and higher than their capacities were able to bear, that it caused their heads to swim, and their brains to turn, till they were struck with a fit of delerium, and never have come out of it since.[4]

When Hopkins transferred to the pulpit of Newport's First Church in 1769, Ezra Stiles, then pastor of the Second Church, accused Hopkins of erecting "a new Div[init]y Connexion & Sect as distinct from all the N. Engld. Ch[urc]hs" whose theology was composed of a few "favorite *eurekas* which they hold the Xian World never knew anything of till since President Edw[ar]ds' Death."[5] Andrew Fuller, a Calvinistic English Baptist with whom Hopkins corresponded in the 1790s, likewise warned Hopkins and his fellows about taking Edwards too seriously:

I have observed that whenever an extraordinary man has been raised up, like Pres't Edwards, and who has excelled in maintaining some particular doctrine . . . it is usual for his followers and admirers too much to confine their attention to that doctrine, science, or manner of reasoning, as tho' all excellence was there concentrated. . . . I must say it appears to me that some of your younger men profess a rage of imitating his metaphysical manner, till some of them become metaphysic-mad.[6]

Charles Chauncy, who had found Edwards so distasteful in the 1740s, found this "Hopkinsianism" even more unpalatable in the 1760s. It was "the very essence of pagan fatality" and, he warned Ezra Stiles, would ruin Connecticut. "I had much rather be an episcopalian, or that others should than [that] I or they sh[ould] be Hopkintonians," Chauncy raged and, straining to think of something even more horrific than episcopacy, could only splutter, " 'Tis as bad, if not worse than paganism."[7]

In the eyes of later historians, however, the New Divinity's treason lay in their failure to take Edwards far enough. Frequently, this charge was based on the complaint that Hopkinsian theology was so deadening that it quenched the spirit of revival Edwards had cultivated so assiduously. Joseph Haroutunian's classic *Piety Versus Moralism: The Passing of the New England Theology* (1932) complained that the New Divinity took the living, glowing piety of Edwards and fossilized it into an overdogmatized, overorganized, moralistic religion. In the hands of Bellamy and Hopkins, "the logic of Calvinistic piety was being transformed into a vast, complicated, and colorless theological structure, bewildering to its friends and ridiculous to its enemies."[8] Edmund S. Morgan concluded that the New Divinity men were provincial bores, mute inglorious Edwardses who would have sent New England into terminal narcolepsy had not Timothy Dwight and Lyman Beecher arrived to liven things up. Modern chroniclers, even when moderately sympathetic, feel constrained to apologize for the New Divinity in similar ways. Stephen Berk, for instance, allows that the New Divinity did contain a few lively revivalists; however, their impact was softened by the dead weight of a "metaphysical" faction which "often completely lost touch with their congregations as they constructed their elaborate systems and descended into the labyrinth of polemical controversy."[9]

The irony of these conflicting judgments about the New Divinity's relationship to Edwards (foolish heirs or deliberate traitors) is that they really do not differ in substance. Neither denies that the New Divinity was "metaphysical." The first view implies that the New Divinity went in the direction of the *wrong* metaphysics; the second assumes that it was wrong to be metaphysical at all. Both hinge their interpretation not on what the New Divinity actually was but on what they assume it should have been. It was not simply the New Divinity's proneness to excessive metaphysics that aggrieved the critics, but metaphysics itself, for the very notion of metaphysics had become stigmatized as intellectually illegitimate. We get a whiff of this as early as 1820, when the anti-Hopkinsian New Englander Thomas Andros complained that "a New England divine, in Europe, had well become a term of reproach" for "discussing the plainest evangelical subjects, in a deep, abstruse, metaphysical way."[10] Here, the complaint is lodged against the New Divinity, not for what their metaphysics said, but rather for being metaphysical. That perception had darkened by the time Haroutunian wrote *Piety Versus Moralism*, for Haroutunian's neo-orthodox Calvinism disposed him to set a high value on the passionate and the irrational. Construing Edwards as a sort of New England Kierkegaard, a knight of faith in Northampton, Haroutunian rounded on the New Divinity as slaves of paltriness. Similarly, Edmund Morgan, speaking as a secularist, could not see theological systemization like that of the New Divinity as a pursuit of any great worth. Metaphysics was ipso facto boring. The real problem the New Divinity posed for the critics was not that it created vast systems, but that the critics, like Haroutunian and Morgan, were not prepared to regard systemization as a legitimate intellectual enterprise.

And what made the New Divinity even worse in their eyes was, more than the form, the situation—bad enough to waste time' on systematic divinity, but worse still to waste it on the pulpit. Had the New Divinity men occupied chairs of divinity instead of pulpit couches, and addressed university audiences instead of rural parishes, the critics could have been more forgiving. But the New Divinity sought no such credentials, and proceeded to serve up to rustic congregations an intellectual diet supposedly unpalatable to popular taste.

Boxed on both ears for having extended metaphysics beyond a legitimately Edwardsean line (and that line kept receding as time went by) and for having fallen short of the religious passion of Edwards because they tried to be metaphysical at all, the New Divinity has without too much difficulty been disinherited from the family of American Calvinism, and from the history of American thought. But it is certain that, as far as their own broad conception of their place in New England's theological community goes, neither Hopkins nor Bellamy ever revealed any inkling that they were in the business of betraying Edwards. Bellamy's anxiety, expressed to Thomas Foxcroft as early as 1749, was that people were not paying enough attention to Edwards. In 1756 Bellamy urged Hopkins to collaborate in producing a sort of Edwardsean primer that would keep Edwards's ideas before the ordinary theological reader. "I have it in my mind," Bellamy wrote, "to propose to correspond with you in a regular manner. Thus—let 2 or 300 questions be stated. You write on one, I on another, to assist young students in the study of divinity.—Mr. Edwards Books will be the better understood."[11]

Not only did the New Divinity men *think* of themselves as Edwardsean, they frequently *looked* Edwardsean too. Stiff-necked and stiff-mannered, Hopkins and Bellamy and their students often replicated the thorniest aspects of Edwards's pastoral character, and they acquired a long-lived reputation for giving neither themselves nor their congregations any refuge from the rigors of Edwards's moral absolutism. Nathanael Emmons, preaching his son's funeral sermon in 1820, declared that he had seen nothing in his son's life that suggested he was not in hell. What quarter they did not give to others, they did not seek for themselves. Like Edwards, they were painfully hardworking students. Emmons studied "for seventy-eight years . . . from ten to sixteen hours a day" and wore four holes in the floor where the legs of his desk chair rubbed.[12] And, like Edwards, they were stoically indifferent to the consequences of preaching hard things. Hopkins so exasperated his congregation at Great Barrington that he was forced to obtain a dismissal from it, whereupon he went to the First Church in Newport and there emptied it with his preaching against the slave trade. Jonathan Edwards the Younger, in a striking case of ministerial déjà vu, pressed his father's demands for visible sainthood so far that he too was compelled to seek a humiliating dismissal from his White Haven, Connecticut, church lest his congregation simply dwindle out from under him.[13]

It should be said in their defense that, if they often developed a resemblance to Edwards at his worst, the New Divinity men also successfully reproduced many of his virtues. Just as Edwards had prepared Hopkins and Bellamy for the ministry in his own home, so they in turn created their own parlor seminaries (like Emmons) and log colleges (like Bellamy). Although private theological tutoring had been a common feature of preparation for the New England ministry, it rapidly became the peculiar trademark of the New Divinity, as in their hands it became a way of shortcutting around the educational monopoly that lay in the unfriendly control of Yale and Harvard. Over the span of half a century, Bellamy trained some sixty ministers in the New Divinity theology, including some of the principal standard-bearers of Edwardseanism in the succeeding generation, such as John Smalley, Samuel Spring, Levi Hart, and Jonathan Edwards the Younger. They in turn engendered their own intellectual offspring: Edwards the Younger trained Samuel Austin; Levi Hart trained Charles Backus (and Backus himself trained some fifty other ministers, including Leonard Woods) and Asa Burton (who trained another sixty ministers between 1786 and 1816); and John Smalley trained (in conjunction with Nathan Strong) Nathanael Emmons, who set the record by training eighty-seven students in his fifty-five year tenure as minister of Franklin, Massachusetts.[14]

Their training was only an induction into an even more characteristically Edwardsean task, for if it is true that some of the New Divinity men were bounced out of their pulpits for too much systematized hell and organized brimstone, many others used their pulpits to restoke the fires of the Great Awakening in the parishes and humble the godless. Jonathan Strong enjoyed three revivals in his church in Randolph, Massachusetts; Asa Burton preached revivals in Thetford, Vermont, in 1781, 1784, and again near the end of his life in 1821 (he was described by an admiring student as greatly successful in "winning souls"); Emmons superintended revivals in Franklin in 1784, 1794–95, and 1809; Nathan Strong lit revival fires in Hartford in 1794, 1798–99, 1808, and 1815; and Edwards the Younger, soon after his dismissal from White Haven, settled into a new charge at Colebrook, Connecticut, and promptly saw a revival there bring twenty-seven new members into the church. By 1799 Samuel Hopkins was able to show the English Baptist John Ryland that revivals were sweeping "more than 100 towns" in New England, and that they were occurring "mostly if not wholly under the preachers of Edwardean divinity."[15]

In their revivals, the New Divinity men achieved the one thing which had eluded Edwards in the 1740s, and that was a measure of pastoral popularity. In a very short time, the New Divinity was all over Connecticut and Massachusetts; from numbering only four or five in the 1750s, Hopkins estimated in the 1790s that more than one hundred New Divinity men occupied pulpits in New England.[16] They dominated the parishes of Litchfield County, where (according to the disgruntled Ezra Stiles) Bellamy ruled as the "Pope of Litchfield County," making and breaking ministers at will.[17] Anything else west of the Connecticut River Valley, including Hartford (where Nathan Strong occupied a citadel) was by and large New Divinity territory. New London County,

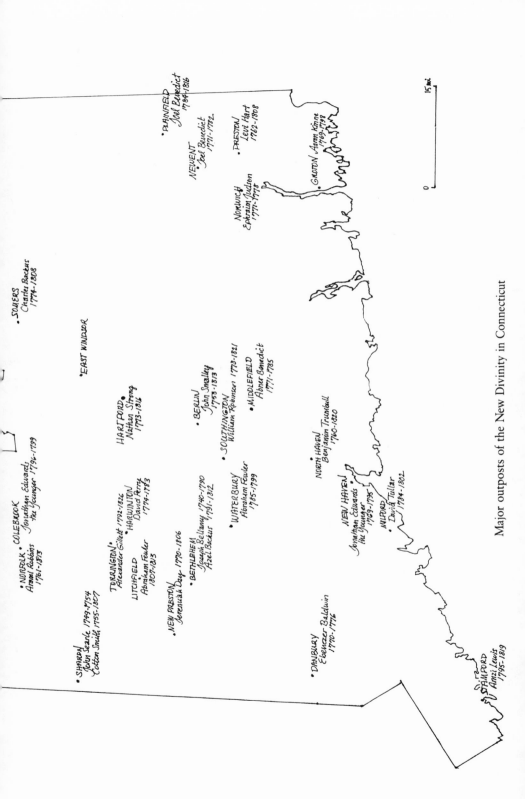

Major outposts of the New Divinity in Connecticut

WILLIAMSTOWN
Seth Swift 1779-1807

RICHMOND   Job Swift 1767-1774
           David Perry 1784-1817

STOCKBRIDGE
     Stephen West 1759-1818

GREAT BARRINGTON
     Samuel Hopkins

SHEFFIELD
     Ephraim Judson 1791-1813

WORCES
Samuel Au
1790-

Major outposts of the New Divinity in Massachusetts

NEWBURY-
PORT Samuel Spring 1777-1819
• BYFIELD
Elijah Parish 1787-1825
RAWLEY
Ebenezer Bradford
1782-1801
David Tullar 1805-1810

STONEHAM SALEM Daniel Hopkins 1778-1804
John Searle
1759-1776

BOSTON

BRAINTREE
Ezra Weld 1762-1816
RANDOLPH
MEDWAY Jonathan Strong 1789-1804
David Sanford
1772-1807 • ABINGDON
FRANKLIN Samuel Niles
• Nathanael Emmons 1775-1835 1771-1811
• WRENTHAM
David Avery
1786-1794

PLYMOUTH Chandler Robbins 1760-1799
• MIDDLEBORO
Joseph Barker 1781-1815

WAREHAM Noble Everett
1782-1819
ROCHESTER Gideon Hawley
Lemuel Lebaron 1758-1807
1772-1836 MASHPEA

0   20 miles

in southeastern Connecticut, was also rife with New Divinity men, whose principal there was Levi Hart of Preston. In Massachusetts, the Berkshires indisputably belonged to the New Divinity, but so did territory closer to Boston, which was hemmed in by New Divinity camps in Essex County (where Samuel Spring, Elijah Parish, and Hopkins's brother Daniel occupied pulpits), Norfolk County (Emmons reigned here along with David Sanford, Ezra Weld, and Jonathan Strong), and Plymouth County. To his father's Scottish correspondent, John Erskine, Edwards the Younger wrote in 1787, "I believe a majority of the ministers mean to embrace the system of my father and Dr. Bellamy," and he could not have been far wrong.[18] Five years later, more than one-third of the Connecticut clergy were New Divinity and Stiles was complaining that the New Divinity had as much as "half the ministers" in Connecticut and "all the Candidates" for the ministry as well.[19] In 1813 William Bentley, even less friendly to the New Divinity than Stiles, conceded that Hopkins's famous systematics text, *The System of Doctrines,* had become "the basis of the popular theology of New England."[20]

If, as the critics have had long innings saying, the New Divinity men were moral rigorists, it was because Edwards gave them a mandate for rigorism which they took with uncompromising seriousness. And if, as the critics have spent less time showing, they preached revivals, it was because their unspeakable "metaphysics" was built around the ideas Edwards had laid out in *Freedom of the Will,* for *Freedom of the Will* was Edwards's blank check to them upon which they would be able to write the sum of ultimate revival. His early death left Hopkins and Bellamy to function as the signatories as well, and all the evidence is that they did, for their *uses* and *applications* were precisely those that testify to the invisible hand of *Freedom of the Will.* Let us now delineate that hand.

II

There cannot be much question that the New Divinity shared with Edwards the one basic presupposition underlying *Freedom of the Will* (and indeed all Calvinism), the sovereignty of God. If their personal lives were tightly boxed in by the walls of their studies and the boundaries of their parishes, their theology was not, and they routinely ascribed all events, great and small, to the decree of God. "No material object can move, and no living creature can act," Nathanael Emmons wrote, "without the constant and controlling agency of him who made and preserves the world."[21] To David Porter, it was virtually impossible to think of God at all without at the same time thinking of him as sovereign in the full sense of the word. "To conceive of an infinite intelligent spirit, infinitely wise, powerful, and good, without choice and plan of operation" was a contradiction that, though perhaps embraced by Arminians, was incomprehensible to Porter.[22] And not only Porter's logic, but every glance Porter bestowed on the natural world seemed to agree in according to God all power in heaven and earth:

The system of natural philosophy proved true by actual experiment perfectly agrees with the idea of God having a fixed plan of operation according to which every thing is subordinated and managed. . . . Could all this order have sprung from unmeaning and blind chance? certainly not. The face of this earth wears marks of choice and plan in the mind of him who fashioned it.[23]

The world of the New Divinity was thus, as Bellamy put it, "created for a stage"—not for men to strut their little hour, but upon which God "designed to exhibit a most exact image of himself."[24] The proper human response was to be abasement, to be filled with "earnest longings that God would glorify himself" and "a free and genuine disposition to consecrate and give up ourselves entirely to the Lord forever."[25] And, according to one awed witness, Bellamy's preaching indeed "made God so great—SO GREAT." So much was this sense of abasement, this trembling before the Almighty, at the core of New Divinity Calvinism that Hopkins seized on it as the chief distinction from Arminianism. Like the youthful Edwards, Hopkins saw that the root problem with the Arminian understanding of volition was not just that it was theologically incorrect, but that it produced the wrong "sense"—it was "a scheme of doctrines exactly suited to gratify the selfishness and pride of man—to exalt man at the expense of the honor of God, and happiness and glory of his kingdom."[26]

When the New Divinity turned from the stage of the world to the inner world of the human will, their reflection of Edwards narrowed to a thorough replication of *Freedom of the Will.* "That we have a power of will or of determining is granted on all hands," Edwards the Younger wrote; however, it was not, as his father had warned, an independent psychological entity in men which reached out for what it pleased.[27] As Edwards the Younger averred, willing is merely "the mind willing," or "the mind in a different mode," and that volition is only "a modification of the mind" (as his father had said, will is that by which the mind chooses).[28] Otherwise, the will could well be pleased with something the mind loathed, and apprehend what the mind had no desire for, and that was the notion of willing and freedom Edwards had saddled the Arminians with. "Let this notion of freedom, as essential to moral agency, be true," warned John Smalley, and one would be presented with the farcical idea of a will not only "willing" its own willing, but doing it in blithe defiance of what the mind desires. This two-stage notion, so beloved of the Arminians, "must imply a power to will and do this way or the other, contrary to one's own mind, as well as according to it," a sort of schizophrenia (to supply a term) which Smalley could not comprehend. Such a notion would mean "an end, not only of all possible confirmation of creatures, but of all immutability in the Supreme Being"; and furthermore, the notion of psychological activity apart from the mind's consciousness of its activities—of struggle, competition, and conflict within the self—was utterly foreign to the unitary self Edwards had taken for granted in *Freedom of the Will*.[29]

The idea of a self-determining will involved a psychological model Edwards had rejected, one the New Divinity followed him in rejecting. "It is not necessary," Josiah Sherman thereupon concluded, that an "agent be independent . . . or that there be a self-determining power or sovereignty in the *will*" itself.[30] To ask "whether the *Will* is free," jeered Stephen West, echoing both Locke and Edwards, "is utterly unmeaning and impertinent."[31] The will is free *to choose*; not to choose *what* to choose. "LIBERTY," as defined by Levi Hart, could only mean the simple "power of action" itself, "a certain suitableness or preparedness for exertion"; or, once the will is actually engaged in willing, merely "a freedom from force, or hindrance from any external cause."[32] Thus, according to Edwards the Younger, "A man possesses liberty when he possesses a natural or physical power to do an action and is under no natural inability with respect to that action."[33]

The only sense in which it was meaningful to talk about the will being free was whether it had liberty sufficient to execute the commands of the willing self. "Men are free," said Smalley, "whenever they act their own choice"—whenever the will does what it is naturally formed to do, that is, to reach out to what pleases the mind as a whole.[34] Freedom of the will can only "denote a power of *doing as we please*," Levi Hart contended[35]; "*Liberty* . . . undoubtedly meaneth a *power of doing as we please,"* echoed Stephen West.[36] The will does not make choices for itself to will; the self, or mind, or soul desires, and willing is only the apprehending of the objects of those desires. Accordingly, the will could not be independent; just as, in *Freedom of the Will,* the will's subservience to another power was made a matter of a priori definition and psychological fact before the Arminian had half buckled-on his arguments, and before anyone had even so much as mentioned the bondage of the human will to God.

Edwards the Younger was well aware, however, that the stupefied Arminian, feeling tricked by such an a-prioristic sleight-of-hand, would at once seek to shift the question of freedom to more empirical grounds, and appeal to sensible evidences. "Self-determination," he coolly predicted, will then be "argued from our consciousness and experience." But, as he was also well aware, an appeal to facts was only as good as the interpretation attached to the facts:

When gentlemen speak of experience and consciousness, they ought to confine their observations to themselves; as no man is conscious of more than passes in his own mind, and in such things a man can with certainty tell his own experience only. . . . I am conscious of volitions of various kinds; but I never yet caught myself in the act of *making a volition,* if this means anything more than *having* a volition or being the subject of it.[37]

In fact, John Smalley neatly turned the question of freedom around by asking whether, even if we were to grant self-determination, it would really produce any more freedom than the Edwardsean plan entailed. "Because a man *must* act according to his own heart, or *as he pleases*; does this destroy freedom?" Nonsense, replied Smalley: "it is the very thing in which all free agency consists."[38] How could one ask for more freedom than to do as one pleases? "It is true that persons cannot act contrary to their pleasure," since the Edwardsean proclivity for absolute connections forbade such untidy contradictions as the choosing of something truly repulsive. But, Asa Burton demanded, are men "any the less worthy of blame for this? This is the very reason why they are blameable when they do wrong, because they *have* acted as they pleased."[39]

"Now it is easy," David Porter declared, "to see that the decree of God does nothing towards destroying the free moral agency of creatures."[40] As long as volition was strictly defined as a nondeliberative psychological function, naturally structured merely to execute the desire of the mind as a whole, then, ultimately, it was of little interest to God.

The divine decree, when it operated, was really directed to the heart and could confine its activities there in the sure confidence Edwards had inculcated; that loving, desiring, knowing, and willing were so closely intertwined as functions of the mind that what the heart loved, the mind would desire, and the will apprehend. No need, then, to imagine God twisting unpliable volitions. "The operations of the will are under the government of the heart," wrote Asa Burton; and since "liberty consists simply in the choice of the will," then Porter felt fully justified in his claim that "no act of God, whether in decreeing or causing choice can have the least effect on liberty."[41] One could thus have Calvinism *and* what was, in words at least, a free will; indeed, since Arminianism was predicated on the contradictory notion of a self-determining will, only Calvinism could guarantee a legitimate and correctly defined free will.

Still, if volition was, as Stephen West claimed, "nothing more than the mind's preferring the one to the other, by a free, *voluntary* determination," then it behooved inquirers to wonder where the mind acquired its preferences.[42] And again the answer came directly from *Freedom of the Will*: the influence of motives. "By a motive," Asa Burton explained, "I mean any thing which moves, excites, or induces an agent to act."[43] And since that accounted, in one sweep, for just about any human activity, Bellamy laid down as a psychological law that "all rational creatures, acting as such, are always influenced by motives."[44] This influence stems more from the nature of the perceiver of the motive than any power in the motive. Bellamy spoke of motives as that "which appear to us most worthy of our choice"; David Porter described the will as being "determined in view of the greatest apparent good"[45]; and Asa Burton further declared that "when several objects are in the mind's view, the object which is most agreeable, and from which the most pleasure is expected, is the *strongest* motive."[46] So the actual process of volition began not with an act of divine force but a perception of good. Josiah Sherman analyzed this process: "the Spirit causes truth to be placed before the mind, in the view of the understanding, and by his almighty efficacious power inclines the mind of the sinner to receive the truth in the love of it."[47] Here the outlines of Edwards's paradigm become clear again. The will obeys the mind; the mind perceives motive; the will apprehends the motive, and acts upon it freely and spontaneously (provided no obstacles are in the way), although not, of course, because it independently wished to; and yet,

God is still the "efficacious" cause of the entire process, not because he lays hands on the person to make him willing, but because he creates an occasion of willing which ensures that willing infallibly takes place.

To this, the New Divinity anticipated an objection, for if the mind merely acted to process desirable motives from the heart and the understanding to the will, and the will's sole purpose was to actuate the mind's desires, then there was little difference between saying this, and saying, as bluntly as Hobbes did, that motives always *caused* the will to do what it did. For this, they were ready with two replies. First, if choice was not contingent on a motive, then what was it contingent upon? Nothing? Then it was meaningless. This was Jonathan Edwards's favorite ambush for the self-determiners, and Edwards the Younger continued to spring it as though it were a family tradition. "If we have power to act without motive," Edwards the Younger pointed out, that must mean that "we have a power to act without end or design." But even any average-witted Arminian would admit that "such an action is as totally without morality, as the blowing of the wind, or the motion of a cannonball." Thus, "to choose anything without motive, is really a contradiction; it is to choose it and not to choose it, at the same time."[48] And it was not Calvinism which made people think like that, as though they were machines, but rather the Arminians, with their unmotivated volitions. "If man therefore could have an act of choice," said Samuel Whitman, "without an object chosen, or could act without design, he would be as destitute of accountableness as a mere machine."[49]

But secondly, and even more to the Edwardsean point, the New Divinity denied any resemblance to Hobbesian causality because, strictly speaking, no one had ever actually said that motives *caused* anything. Motives moved, excited, influenced, and inclined, but *caused* was a word the New Divinity carefully tacked away from. "Though motives have an influence," Asa Burton explained, "yet they are not the causes or agents which produce volition."[50] All that Edwards the Younger meant by *cause* was that "there is a stated Connection between volition and motive."[51] And that, he insisted, was all his father had meant, too: "All that President Edwards means by cause in this case is *stated occasion* or *antecedent*."[52]

Thus armed with Edwards's occasionalist notion of causality, the New Divinity could insist on the absolute certainty of outcomes and results of situations without ever having to identify the *thing* that caused those outcomes and results. They simply happened, and kept happening, and happening so often that one could take them for granted, if not for explained. And so long as this relationship between motive and the will was defined in these nearly Humean terms as merely a "stated connection," then the charges of mechanism bounced harmlessly away. One merely said, as Burton did, that "between the strongest desire of the heart and choosing the object of that desire, God has established an infallible connection," all the while denying that it is empirically possible to discover in just what the connection consisted.[53] A term—connection, tendency, influence—sat there to signify that something *happens* without offering a means for understanding more than just the happening. As Stephen West said, with what may have been deliberate opaqueness, "This foundation which there is in motives for engaging the choice and election of the mind, or in the mind itself for having its choice and election *engaged* by such objects, is what we mean to express by the term TENDENCY."[54] And even when some New Divinity men let their guard down and spoke of *causes*, West was quick to insist that even the significance of *cause* was only nominal: "the word cause, it must be carefully remembered, implieth nothing more than an occasion of the event."[55] God had merely *constituted* a "law of constant divine operation, that such particular effects should invariably take place under such circumstances." Whatever God called such arrangements, the human word *cause* was only a dim analogy. It was easy, then, for the New Divinity to pry the notion of cause loose from mechanism, and in the style of Edwards harmonize freedom and causality, and affirm with West, "Whoever acteth voluntarily, acteth in the view of motives."[56]

Nevertheless, just because motives were not causes, in the mechanistic sense, this did not mean that they could be thought of as powerless. Edwards the Younger, the earnest opponent of slavery, had seen enough motives presented in the slave trade to know better:

> . . . if it be pleaded, that the mind is still free, because motives are not the efficient causes of volition; I answer, that the same plea would prove that a West-India slave is free, because his actions are not efficiently caused by his master or driver, and they only exhibit such motives as influence the slave himself to perform those actions. . . . The slave, who always acts by motives exhibited by his master, is as absolutely controlled by his master, as the whip in the master's hand.[57]

Far from occasionalism's loosening the bands of necessity, it only bound them tighter. "It is," wrote Samuel Spring, "as impossible to commit murder from good motives, as it is to love God and prepare for heaven from bad motives."[58] But that only raised the further question from the Arminian as to how a man operating under the necessity of a "stated connection" was any better off than operating under any other kind of necessity. It was not immediately apparent how demonstrating that one's actions could be necessary without being mechanical made anyone more liable to praise or blame, or really granted other than puppetry to man. However, the New Divinity again resorted to *Freedom of the Will* for their rationale: in this case, they distinguished between a natural and a moral necessity. A natural necessity was, of course, the result of deploying natural terms, but a moral necessity, said Edwards the Younger, "is nothing but a previous certainty of the existence of any moral act."[59] And it arises from the connection of the moral terms involved. A drunkard (if he is a terminologically pure drunkard—again, realities are collapsed into nominalities) necessarily takes the drink because taking the drink is necessarily implied, even if it is not compelled, by the fact of drunkardliness. The same thing, according to David Porter, can be said of vice and virtue in general:

By moral necessity I mean a certainty of pursuing a course of action which certainly arises out of the disposition of the agent or actor. All moral beings, up to the infinite God, most certainly act from such necessity. It is certain God will pursue a course of holy action, which certainly arises from his holy nature. . . . Sinners are under the same moral necessity to do wrong and hate everything which is morally excellent and lovely. This arises out of the temper and disposition of the heart, and remaining sinners, it is morally impossible they should do otherwise than sin without cessation . . . . If then God can be under moral necessity without forfeiting his free agency, certainly creatures may be under the same necessity, and yet have perfect liberty.[60]

Hence, as Emmons put it, "if men always act under a divine operation, then they always act of *necessity*, though not of *compulsion*."[61] And so they were at liberty after all.

By the same token, the existence of a natural necessity implied a natural *inability* to do otherwise, consisting in a "want of understanding, bodily strength, opportunity, or, *whatever may prevent*, our doing a thing, when we are willing." Likewise, a moral necessity implied a moral *inability* to do otherwise, consisting "only in the want of a heart or disposition, or will, to do a thing." This last deduction of Emmons's served the practical purpose of explaining how unregenerate sinners could be commanded to repent without diminishing the sovereignty of

God in salvation. Samuel Spring explained, "As natural ability consists in having intellectual and bodily strength to perform every action required of man, it is evident that moral ability must consist in a willing mind."[62] However, it was an established fact, according to John Smalley, that "it is not God's usual way, to require natural impossibilities of any of his creatures; and to condemn them for not doing what they could not, if they would." That would not be the act of a responsible moral governor, and it would give wicked men the refuge of "unfairness" and "unable" to run to. Therefore, for salvation, "God commands none of us to fly above the clouds, or to overturn the mountains by the roots; or to do any such kind of impossibilities"[63]; he asks only faith and holy living, of which no man is *naturally* incapable. "To see the hatefulness of sin, the desirableness of salvation, and the universal loveliness of the Lord Jesus Christ, would be the easiest thing in the world," Smalley insisted—except for the problem of "the blindness of men's hearts," a *moral* problem.[64] "We have sufficient power . . . to avoid every thing which is prohibited and do everything required of us; by our Lord and Master," said Asa Burton—"if the heart were rightly inclined."[65] So, to continue Samuel Spring's observation,

It is, therefore, evident that the inability of sinners to repent, is of the moral kind only. The inability of sinners to repent lies only in the aversion of the hearts and wills from repentance.[66]

On this basis, it was possible to say that though an individual suffered from a moral inability to repent (from his wicked heart), he nevertheless had full natural ability to repent, and could be held accountable for it. And far from the moral unwillingness of the sinner's "rendering the sinner in any degree blameable or excusable." Hopkins claimed, "the more there is of this the more blameworthy and criminal he is."[67]

Of course, this did not mean that moral inability was a straw, something minor that could be more easily brushed aside than a natural inability, or that New Divinity Calvinism had thereby become Arminianized. "Moral sickness," said Smalley, "may be as hard to cure, and require as powerful means, and as able a physician, as natural sickness." In fact, to avoid understatement of moral inability, Smalley reiterated that "if mankind have lost the moral image of God intirely, it is easy to see, that nothing short of a new creation can restore it to them."[68] Bellamy, too, never stopped preaching that the work of God in conversion must be "an all-conquering, irresistible grace, or not at all."

There must be a *supernatural, spiritual* and divine change wrought in the heart, by the *immediate* influences of the spirit of God, whereby it shall become *natural* to look upon God as infinitely glorious and amiable in being what he is.[69]

What the moral/natural inability dichotomy meant was that, with this sovereignty in place, human beings could still be held responsible, even if the ability to repent was only putative. That such ability was only putative did not bother the New Divinity; given Edwards's occasionalism, *all* abilities and causes were putative.

From a technical point of view, this carried the New Divinity significantly far away from Continental Calvinism. In their determination to make it clear that men had full *natural* ability to repent, they allowed that no natural faculty could be rendered useless by moral depravity. "It is very certain," declared Smalley, "that no faculties, members or senses of the body, necessary for the performance of good works, are the things totally wanting in all men by nature, or the things created anew in regeneration."[70] Smalley was especially annoyed at those who place depravity "in the understanding," since the understanding was a natural rather than a moral faculty and would give men excuse on the grounds "that ignorance and mis-apprehension is the primary cause of all our enmity and opposition to God." Mankind's "infirmities and imperfections are not such comfortable extenuations of guilt, as they are sometimes ready to make of them," Smalley warned.[71] This jarred a good many other Calvinists, of both New England and elsewhere, who had been accustomed by Calvin and the Westminster Confession to regard man as "wholly defiled in all the parts and faculties of soul and body." When in 1769 Smalley presented his protégé Nathanael Emmons to an ordination council, one member named Edward Eels immediately wanted to know whether Adam's fall into sin "affected his understanding." Emmons dutifully responded, "No," and Smalley chimed in that moral qualities, or the lack thereof, were "no more upon Adam's understanding then upon his fingers and toes."[72]

It should be added that, in making this distinction between natural and moral faculties, Emmons, like Edwards, meant to distinguish the faculties but not to hypostasize them. Granted that the "merely intellectual or animal" powers—"such as natural conscience, natural understanding, natural sympathy, and the mere sensations of bodily pain and pleasure"—are, as Samuel Spring stated, "indifferent."[73] At the same time, these intellectual and animal powers are "indifferent" only when considered in and of themselves. In practice, they are always part of a complex of psychological events that includes the will, which is the moral faculty; the depravity which invariably skews the actions of the will seeps through and taints the thoughts of the understanding. "Moral depravity is of a blinding nature," Emmons wrote; "it flows from a corrupt heart, which blinds reason and conscience. . . . As a mote in the natural eye blinds its sight, so depravity of heart blinds the eye of the understanding and conscience."[74] That is why Nathan Strong believed that the mind, packed though it might be with information about Christianity, could never bring the soul to Christ. "Knowledge will be of no avail to change the heart," Strong explained, because no matter what the state of the mind, the state of the will can override and manipulate it. "Sinful minds do not seek evidence," Strong warned, because the will supervenes: "they are prejudiced against it; they do not see the glory of truth; they try to pervert it, that they may gratify their own hearts, and live with a quiet conscience, at ease in sin."[75] Thus, like any other natural ability, "errors in judgement respecting duty and divine truths in general, originate from a criminal source, blindness or sinful depravity of heart. Were it not for the wickedness or deceit of heart, the understanding would be luminous, and the decisions of the judgement correct."[76] Edwards Eels need not have feared, in one respect: the New Divinity proposed to wash the intellect clean only *as* intellect. The first step it took with the will would be as dependably depraved, by virtue of its association with a depraved will, as Eels could desire. In another respect, they were (perhaps unintentionally) calling into question the entire Joseph Butler-William Paley-Thomas Reid line of empiricist Christian apologetics, which had found so great an audience among eighteenth-century Calvinists. By flooding the will's evil over into the mind when it chose, the New Divinity were doubting that the mere presentation of evidences to some moral sense would ever accomplish anything. Despite Eels's misgivings, the New Divinity had left to the understanding not independence but only another putative ability.

On the other hand, by confining inability only to the will, and leaving the understanding and other natural faculties "capable" of free action, the New Divinity had forged a nearly perfect weapon for an Edwardsean revivalism that told men, with perfect sincerity, that God's decree of their eternal destiny would never exculpate their guilt for not repenting. The sinner, said Bellamy, is what he is, "not by *compulsion,* or through a *natural necessity,* but altogether *voluntarily.*"[77] Therefore, Hopkins plunged on, "there is no difficulty in the sinner's complying with the offers of the gospel, but what lies in his want of inclination and true desire to accept the salvation offered, and a strong and obstinate inclination to the contrary."[78] Even though "the Word of God requires sinners to be always so friendly to him as to be disposed and ready to believe every truth which he reveals and proposes to them, and to have exercises answerable to that truth . . . they are under no natural impossibility of doing this."[79] If it had been the case that men were "destitute of understanding to know what is right; or destitute of power to choose according to their choice; they would so far not be proper subjects of commands, and no blame could lie upon them for not obeying," Smalley gracefully conceded. "But no such powers of moral agency are the things wanting in natural men."

They have hands and heads sufficiently good; and a sufficient power to will, whatever is agreeable to them. All they want is a good heart. Their inability is therefore their sin and not their excuse. . . . The want of a good disposition is in itself sinful. It is the essence, the root, the foundation of all sin.[80]

Instead, Hopkins wrote, the sinner "is under no kind or degree of impotency or difficulty which is in the way of his repentance, loving God, and embracing the gospel, that affords the least excuse for not doing it or takes off the least degree of blame for his neglect."[81] All the burden must fall on the sinner alone: "there is nothing," claimed Smalley, "on earth; there is nothing in all the decrees of heaven; there is nothing in all the malice and power of hell, that can hinder your salvation, if you don't hinder it yourselves."[82] By thus juxtaposing the awful sovereignty of God with the obligation imposed by having a full *natural* ability, the New Divinity could create in their preaching a mentality of crisis suited ideally to provoking a new Great Awakening. Faced with the Calvinist God on one hand, and the terrifying responsibility imposed by natural ability, what else could men do but cry, *What must I do to be saved?* From this paradox, the New Divinity offered no escape but in submission. "What do you mean by being under an absolute impossibility to believe and repent," Bellamy demanded of sinners; "it is plain that there is nothing but the want of a good temper, together with the obstinate perverseness of sinners, that hinders their return to God; and that, therefore, all their pretenses of being willing to do as well as they can are mere hypocrisy."[83]

This suspicion of hypocrisy led the New Divinity to up the ante of crisis still further, and stage their most extravagant assertion. If men had full natural ability to repent (regardless of the moral inability of their hearts) then there was no reason why they should not do so *at once*. Sinners "have no excuse for neglecting to do their first work till a more convenient season," Emmons declared; "God now commands every one who is in the state of nature to put away his native depravity and immediately comply with the terms of mercy which he has proposed in the gospel."[84] Bellamy, too, insisted that the sinner was able and obligated "immediately to repent of your sins and return to God through Jesus Christ, looking only to free grace through him for pardon and eternal life."[85] So long as sinners "are under no natural impossibility of doing this," Hopkins warned, to delay repentance could only be laid to insincerity.[86]

The call for immediacy struck with particular force at the old preparationist model of New England conversion. The ancestors of New England Calvinism recognized that predestination, because it put the decree of salvation entirely in God's hands, left human beings with no means of determining until it was manifestly too late whether they, as individuals, were going to benefit from that decree. Hence, William Perkins, William Ames, and other English Puritan worthies urged their followers to look within themselves for signs of experiential grace they could then interpret as evidences of election and grounds for assurance. In time, these evidences were codified and standardized into "morphologies of conversion" that acted as checklists on one's road to complete assurance of salvation, and Thomas Hooker in particular suggested that even those who feared they were unregenerate could at least work at developing these evidences and "prepare" themselves to receive salvation. By Edwards's time, this gradualism, or "preparationism," had become the accepted mode of entrance into salvation in the minds of most of the New England clergy, and the idea of church membership in New England had been extended so as to put into the church covenants even those who had only begun to use the "means of grace" (attendance of preaching, praying, the use of the sacraments, and other such external duties which could be taken as evidence that the doers must be on their way to regeneration) to prepare themselves for salvation.

To Edwards, however, the upheaval of the Great Awakening made this gradualist mode of conversion absurd. His effort to exclude from church membership those who did not measure up to his stiffer standards of unquestioned visible Christianity cost him his Northampton pulpit. To the New Divinity likewise, preparationism only made sense if one assumed that sinners labored under some natural inability and could not respond to the Gospel. Smalley recognized that "many are ready to argue that since repentance and faith are gifts of God, and not in the power of sinners so long as they are in a state of unregeneracy; the only duty at present incumbent upon them" is to "make use of those outward means whereby saving grace is ordinarily communicated to the souls of men."[87] But the New Divinity strenuously declared that sinners *do* have natural power. Sinners, as well as saints, have wills; the essence of the will's freedom and power lies merely in the fact that *it can will*, not (as Edwards had shown) in a power to will its own willings. That the sinner always wills wicked things only establishes that there is a moral necessity between his heart and his will; that he wills at all shows that he really does have a natural power and freedom after all. In terms of natural power, a sinner's will can as easily will good as bad. "He is under no kind of inability or difficulty that is in the way of turning to God immediately," Hopkins said. "All the difficulty lies in the corruption of his heart . . . for if they had a real desire to repent . . . they would repent; for nothing is in the way of this but opposition of heart."[88]

III

If it seems remarkable that the New Divinity should so painstakingly reproduce the salient points of Edwards's thinking in *Freedom of the Will*, it is no less remarkable how they argued among themselves in just the places where *Freedom of the Will* turned vague. To the great annoyance of his critics, Edwards never sharply defined what he meant by *motives*, even though he laid much of the weight of his arguments on their operation. Most of the New Divinity men did virtually the same thing, and among those who did essay to clarify the meaning of *motives*, more heat than light was forthcoming.

On one side, Bellamy and Asa Burton considered motives as *ab extra* phenomena exerting an "influence" extrinsic to the agent and not interfering directly in volition. "When external objects impress the heart, they excite it to action," Burton taught, "and it is in this way only, that motives have influence." In that sense, "though motives have influence, yet they are not the causes or agents, which produce volition," and as such, "we do not mean they are agents; or have any active principle; or do anything more, than merely as means influence us to act, or give opportunity for the active principle in man to operate."[89] Once a motive is presented, the will appropriates it and, in sequence, volition results.

However, Stephen West and Samuel Spring replied that this was a naive oversimplification of the process of volition. "It cannot, I believe, properly be said, the mind of man is *governed by motives*," West complained, if by motives one meant to speak of entities that floated off outside the self. On the contrary, "the word Motive, as it is very frequently used in common conversation, importeth no more than some certain perception of the mind, and nothing different from the *real choice* and *exercise* of it." Perception of motives does not occur *prior* to volition; the act of perceiving a motive, far from initiating volition, is itself bound up with the action of the will. "When the mind feels, or perceives, the influence of a motive; it is then too late for the motive to *produce* effects on the mind," since the mind in reaching out to apprehend the motive is "already being moved." Nor are motives external to the self—rather, they are internal and immanent. Motives do not (so to speak) *transcend* the human psyche; things *become* motives only as one wills to be motivated by them. Hence, no motive can ever appear to the mind as the greatest apparent good unless the will has first been drawn out to it, to bring it to the understanding's attention. "No object, with qualities suited to the state, temper and disposition of the mind, ever cometh into *its* view without being actually chosen."[90] Or, as Spring aphorized the matter, "the term motive denotes not only an object of choice but it denotes the choice of an object."[91]

Naturally, this put West in the awkward position of explaining how the will "saw" a motive before the mind had perceived it as the greatest apparent good. But West merely replied that the will did not "see"— rather, it was acted upon directly by God, who moved it to bring a motive to the understanding's attention. "As in the moral world, we are compelled to resolve all into the divine disposal and . . . constant divine agency and operation."[92] Hence, the understanding does not need to perceive a motive before the will can act; like a divine matchmaker, God brings will and motive immanently together, sight unseen. "The will feels the tendency of a motive to engage its choice, *in actual choosing*."[93]

A more serious division, related to the question about motives, occurred over the nature of spiritual substance, and again the division occurred because the New Divinity were no more successful at arriving at a final definition than Edwards had been in *Original Sin*. The more conservative wing of the New Divinity continued to hold that there was an underlying spiritual substance of some sort in men, in which individual personal qualities inhere and which remains constant despite change in personal self-consciousness and self-identity, and they were resistant to any suggestion that spiritual substance, because it cannot be sensed, cannot therefore exist. Hopkins was distressed that people should embrace "the *new* notion of no spiritual substance," since Hopkins based his analysis of regeneration on the assumption that a sovereign God could regenerate a sinner's "nature" without relying on the active conscious awareness or permission of the sinner.[94] Regeneration is "wrought by the Spirit of God, immediately and instantaneously," but "altogether imperceptibly to the person who is the subject of it."

The subjects of this change know nothing of what is done, or that anything is done, with respect to their hearts, and are not sensible of any operation and change in any other way but by the effect and consequence of it. . . . All the notice we can have of this operation and change, and all the evidence there can be that our minds are the subjects of it, is by perceiving that which is the fruit and consequence of it by our own views and exercises, which are new. . . . We have no way to determine what is the cause of the ideas and sensations of our hearts, whether we are influenced by the Spirit of God or by a wicked spirit but by considering their nature and tendency.

It became useful for Hopkins to disentangle the silent renewal of the spirit from men's own response to it. The former he termed "regeneration," and the latter "conversion," thus distinguishing between that "which is the work of God in giving a new heart, and in which men are perfectly passive, and active conversion in which men, being regenerated, turn to God."[95]

No matter how nebulous the concept of spiritual substance, Hopkins was not alone in holding to it, nor even its most vocal proponent. Asa Burton was even more absolutely insistent that there existed "properties, or faculties, antecedent to the operations of thinking, feeling, and willing, and distinct from them."[96] Sinfulness was Burton's primary example of this arrangement, since it was obvious to him that, in fallen mankind, sin consists "in the entire want of a principle of benevolence, or holiness . . . and this privation of holiness must take place previous to the existence of any positive acts of sin . . . and in the existence or operation of those appetites with which we are born."[97] In short, "vice and virtue must exist antecedent to the need, or use, of liberty."[98] Both Burton and John Smalley acknowledged that this spiritual "nature is something beyond the direct view of men," and cannot be discovered by the mind's investigation or an impact on the senses; but, they replied, "we answer, just as well might it be thus concluded, that all invisible beings and things are unrealities, or that there is no evidence of their having existence."[99] More than that, neither Smalley nor Burton had any other way of accounting for why certain motives, and not others, pleased the mind, than by asserting the underlying influence of a spiritual substance. Unless it was said that "depravity of nature must be antecedent to all sinful actions, and the cause of them," then the only other cause for human pleasure over evil would be a direct divine influence, a conclusion in whose company even Edwards did want to be seen.[100] Josiah Sherman feared that "should God by his immediate efficiency determine the will to chuse without or against," then all of Edwards's reconciliationist labors (not to mention Sherman's too) would be for naught, and Hobbes and Arminius would conquer: "it would amount to the same as a self-determining power in the will, and would destroy the liberty of the agent and the morality of the exercise."[101] In the end, whether they called it "nature," or "heart," or "taste," or "disposition," most of the New Divinity men agreed with Burton that a spiritual substance underlay consciousness, and that "there is a plain distinction made [in the Bible] between the *heart*, and the *good or evil* which proceeds from it."[102] There seemed no other way open to explain how men could love sin and yet be held accountable for it by a sovereign Creator than to insist that the fault lay in themselves; and no way to maintain a credible Calvinism than to insist that the location of this fault was in one's nature, not in a self-determining will.

Vehemently arrayed against this "Taste Scheme" was a minority party, headed by Nathanael Emmons and Samuel Spring, which insisted that "all sin and holiness consist in positive exercises of the mind."[103] This "Exercise Scheme" read Edwards's speculation on spiritual substance in the most starkly phenomenological fashion, and concluded that the notion of a "taste" underlying and manipulating human personality was unprovable and detrimental to a "Consistent Calvinism." Stephen West announced that "there is nothing which can, with any propriety, be termed either a good or bad state of mind ... beside volition, or voluntary exertion."[104] What the Tasters, and the rest of

Calvinism, were content to call "the *tempers* and *dispositions,* or *moral habits* of mankind" were actually nothing more than God immanently stringing personal qualities together on the threads of his decrees.[105] In West's terms, the "nature" was "no more than certain laws, or methods of constant divine operation . . . no more than a certain fixt connexion between our *present* exercises of will and *future* voluntary exertions *of the same general nature and denomination.*"[106] Beyond the assertion that the human personality is simply God's constitution of affairs, West professed to have no idea, nor could he obtain any, of a spiritual substance. Even if it might exist, "Minds are conversant only with their own ideas," said West, and therefore cannot get behind their ideas to discover some substance prior to their consciousness of those ideas:

> If mankind have any consciousness of immediate perception of any power of will distinct from what they feel in the actual exercises of volition—if they are conscious of any power of action, distinct from the consciousness they have in actual voluntary exertion, and previous to it; they must nevertheless be conscious of this power as being in exercise.[107]

It is not surprising to see the same people who proposed this solution to the problem of spiritual substance campaigning the loudest for confining depravity and morality to the will alone. They pinpointed moral agency there because, ostensibly, they had no evidence in their consciousnesses that it could be anywhere else. But the driving force behind this confinement was the fear that they could not legitimately locate sin in natural faculty or taste or disposition without creating the same kind of natural handicap of natural power which the sinner could then plead as a moral excuse. The Exercisers were not attempting to be psychologists (Emmons denied knowing of any underlying substance, but then likewise denied knowing, or even caring about knowing, "how God upholds us every moment"). They simply wanted to define moral agency so as to leave the sinner neither room for inability ("my nature is depraved, *ergo* I am helpless") or Arminianism ("my will is the source of all my volitions")—to define it, as Stephen West did, so that "it will not carry away the mind into a dark apprehension of some secret and mysterious power, which exerteth influence upon itself, to rouse up and first awaken itself into action."[108]

Even sin, then, does not originate in a depraved "taste." Sin is "a wrong choice," said Samuel Spring[109]; "moral evil consists in a voluntary act, or, in an act of choice," echoed Samuel Whitman[110]; and Emmons added, "There is no morally corrupt nature distinct from free, voluntary, sinful exercises." But if sin consists only, as Emmons once replied, "in sinning," then where does sinning originate? Not, certainly, in a human nature, for that would create a natural inability to repent; nor in the will's own choice, for that would be Arminianism. "It seems necessary," concluded Emmons, grasping the nettle, "to have recourse to the divine agency, and to suppose that God wrought in Adam both to will and to do in his first transgression." Or to put it more bluntly, "a divine energy took hold of his heart and led him to sin."[111] And not only Adam: in all subsequent human generations too, even in infants, God "works in them . . . both to will and to do of his good pleasure; or, produces those moral exercises in their hearts, in which moral depravity properly and essentially consists."[112] In the most frighteningly direct terms, Emmons taught—and from his pulpit, no less—that "moral agents can never act but only as they are acted upon by a divine operation. . . . They cannot originate a single thought, affection, or volition, independently of a divine influence upon their minds."[113]

Not surprisingly, this answer won Emmons and the Exercisers few admirers. When Emmons published his first sermon on these themes in 1783, Hopkins was genuinely aghast at Emmons's proclivity for picturing God as the author of "every act of will, whether right or wrong," and especially "that the latter are as much the immediate production of God as the former."[114] Isaac Backus, visiting Franklin, Massachusetts, a few months later, recoiled in horror that "Nathl. Emmons, minister of the town . . . has carried the doctrine of predestination so far as to assert that God positively produces or creates sin; a shocking error!"[115] But Emmons was not dissuaded. Emerging from a meeting with the Taster Asa Burton, Emmons was accosted by a pupil anxious to learn the result. "No result," Emmons replied; "Neither of us broached the subject." Why? "We were both too much afraid of each other."[116] Even Hopkins dallied with Exerciser notions later on (as Edwards Amasa Park was at pains to show in his "Memoir" of Hopkins), and, in an effort to keep the New Divinity from getting "into divisions among themselves," Hopkins offered to define "taste" in occasionalistic fashion as a "divine [ie., immediate] rather than substantiall constitution."[117] It mattered little to Emmons, who campaigned for neither admirers nor concessions. He was looking only for Consistent Calvinism. The enemies of Calvinism were only too happy to concede that he had found it.

CHAPTER 4

The New Divinity

The True State and Character of the Unregenerate

I

The New Divinity followed the doctrinal blueprint Edwards had laid down in *Freedom of the Will*, and found to its satisfaction that Edwards's definitions more than adequately served the uses he had contemplated. The moral government of God had been vindicated, Arminian self-determination shown to be a blind alley out of the dilemma of materialism, and a prescription for fresh revival written. Had the New Divinity merely been content to hawk these *uses* as their wares, they might have attracted little more notice than one deserves for filial loyalty to a mentor. But it was not their formal loyalty to *Freedom of the Will*, profound though it was, which made William Bentley fume in 1790 that "the Congregational churches are infested with a sett of men called Hopkintonians, & who create contentions wherever they come."[1] What made them so notorious as to arouse Bentley's indignation, and so popular that students could flock to them, and so ferocious that Bellamy could be described as "slaying & turning out Ministers in Litchf[ield] C[ounty],"[2] was the peculiar brace of applications they developed from *Freedom of the Will*, aimed at revolutionizing and not just reviving the church life of New England. From Edwards they deduced four basic principles which they used to rack New England's theology and polity down to its roots—principles which were good Edwardseanisms. Good enough, in fact, that had not Princeton taken him out of New England in 1758, and death out of this world, Edwards would probably have applied them himself. In some cases he already had.

PERFECTIONISM

The first of these principles is a direct echo of Edwards's moral absolutism. The New Divinity had already established that, so long as men had wills, there was no natural reason for their not repenting, and likewise no excuse for not doing so at once. At best, then, the whole preparationist system (which Emmons sneered at as "unregenerate duties"[3]) now appeared "to be without the least foundation in scripture or reason"; at worst, claimed Nathan Strong, it is a dangerous error to suppose the inquiring, convinced sinner is gradually becoming holy, and in a slow manner acquiring a moral conformity to God."[4] But the denial of gradualism also meant the denial of the continuum between grace and reprobation along which the gradualist was wont to move people. If it was true, in practical terms, that "sin cannot by any melioration of its nature grow into holiness," then there was no reason why, in theoretical terms, it shouldn't also be true in general that "holiness and sin are essentially opposite in their nature."[5]

Hopkins, who also saw no reason why not, abruptly divided mankind into two, and only two, camps. "All men are in Scripture comprehended in two opposite characters between which there is no medium, viz., the good and the evil, the righteous and the ungodly, the children of God and the children of the Devil."[6] To those who protested that this flew in the face of reality—that in this world some of the holy and some of the unholy were less so than others—Emmons responded with another Edwardsean a priori declaration, based on the simple fiat of Scripture:

If there was only a gradual difference in the goodness of saints and sinners, we should naturally suppose that God would make only a gradual difference in his promises and threatenings to them. But when we find that he has promised sure, perfect, eternal happiness to saints in a future state, and threatened complete and eternal misery to sinners in the world to come, we must believe that they essentially differ in the moral exercises of their hearts;—or, in other words, that saints love God supremely, but sinners hate him supremely. We cannot conceive that any other than this essential distinction between them, should be a just ground for God's treating them so infinitely different in a future and eternal state.[7]

Nathan Strong, who agreed with Emmons that "the word of God describes sinners as being destitute of all holiness," nevertheless preferred an even more Edwardsean a priori, arising out of the terms employed:

There cannot be any thing that is pleasing to God, in the desires of an unholy heart, in whatever manner they are presented before God; and the solemn form of offering, which we call prayer, cannot sanctify them, for they do not thus lose their unholy nature.[8]

Thus Strong concluded that "the character and actions of sinners are wholly unholy," since "nothing, either in sentiment or practice, can be harmless, which arises from a wicked heart."[9]

All of this insistence on the sinner's utter perversion of heart went far beyond the customary Calvinist rhetoric of total depravity, since Westminster Calvinism still allowed, under the rubric of common grace, that the depraved were not as depraved as they might be and could still do acts of common decency or refrain from those of common indecency, and at least make the number of their sins one less. But if this absolutism exceeded Westminster's demands, it was perfectly in harmony with Edwards. And this stood to reason, for if a person had full natural power to repent (and not just to refrain from occasional outrages), and still did not do so, then there was no other way to explain so heartless and culpable a refusal other than to suppose an utter perversion of heart.

What aggravates this perversity, and makes the utterness of it appear still more bleak, is the fact of God. If God's nature was such that it required only ten degrees of love to be rightly loved, and our natural ability to love was thirty degrees of power, then we would be blamable for not loving God, but only to the measure of our ability—the thirty degrees—and not utterly so. But, as Hopkins delighted to demonstrate, God was the Being of Beings, the infinite God who loved his own glory to an infinite degree, and whose law was the "eternal rule of righteousness," and "infinitely binding." Not to love and obey was an offense against an infinite Being and an infinite law, and therefore an offense running up to our last degree of ability. And considering that, in this case, we have full natural power and liberty to obey God, and what Bellamy called our obligation "to love God in a measure exactly proportionable to the largeness of our natural powers," then there are (according to Hopkins) "no exercises or conduct of the moral agent which are indifferent . . . there being no medium in the case between right and wrong, virtue and sin."[10] In fact, said Bellamy, "the least disposition to love ourselves more than God, and be more concerned about our interest and honor than about his, and to be delighted in the things of the world, more than in him, *must,* consequently, be *infinitely* sinful."[11]

This same reasoning, which explained how sinners could only be completely sinful, also explained why the saint must live an exhaustively holy life. Just to have "a spiritual sight and sense in the ineffable beauty of the divine nature" was, for Bellamy, a motive sufficient to make clear the infinite obligation of saints to obey God's law completely:

When any person is lovely and honorable, reason teaches us that it is wrong to dislike and despise him: And the more lovely and honorable, the greater is our obligation to love and honor him; and the more aggravatedly vile is it to treat him with contempt. Since, therefore, God is a Being of infinite dignity, greatness, glory, and excellency, hence we are under an infinite obligation to love him with all our hearts.[12]

And when not only full natural power, but (as in the case of the saint) moral ability, is available, then it becomes a necessity to obey God "supremely with moral sincerity."[13] On those terms, "nothing is more plain and evident than that the true believer must needs feel himself to be under the strongest obligation to an entire devotedness to God, and a life of universal holiness."[14]

For the New Divinity, no halfheartedness, no reliance on mere good intention, would satisfy. At its gentlest, the New Divinity demanded a life of incessant asceticism, whether by spending fourteen hours a day in the study, or liberating one's slave on demand (as Bellamy did when Hopkins made emancipation an obvious obligation of disinterested benevolence). "Giving the heart is giving the whole man," Nathan Strong wrote; "where this is done, there is no reserve of self, or of any object that can be commanded."[15] At its naked ultimate, however, what they were preaching was perfection. If "the commands of God are all holy, and can require nothing but holiness," then Samuel Spring could not see that Christianity required anything "less of man in any respect than perfection."[16] Hopkins saw things the same way. The law of God requires "love exercised in a perfect manner and degree and expressed in all possible proper ways."[17] So did Smalley—"the gospel enjoins sinless perfection as much as the law."[18] So did Strong—"The command of God expressly revealed, creates a perfect obligation on creatures to obey."[19]

Given the Edwardsean logic, plus the Edwardsean history, there was really no avoiding this. Since it has been customary to look on the New Divinity men as extremists of some indeterminate sort, it is not often appreciated how much they thought of themselves as the enemies of extremism—at least the extremism of the antinomiam enthusiasts, whom they blamed for the ignominious collapse of the Awakening in

the 1740s. Hopkins had been a student in Edwards's home in Northampton in 1742 when he was witness to "Strange things," which he
was at first inclined to receive warmly. "Some Christians have been
filled with the Spirit of God to a surprising Degree," Hopkins wrote
in the short journal he kept in Northampton that winter. "They speak
ye Language of Canaan; yea, they manifestly Show that they have been
with Christ, that they are Children of the Day."[20] Hopkins changed
his mind, however, after the people of Northampton began lying in all-
day trances and then "running wild" with joy, and years later he denounced as frauds "many, it is to be feared, whose religion . . . consists
wholly in some extraordinary impulses and agitations of the mind, or
a set of religious exercises and experiences, as they call them; in great
discoveries and high flights of affection, joy, etc."[21] Bellamy, likewise,
had been a fiery itinerant preacher at the onset of the Great Awakening,
but the excesses of James Davenport had deeply shocked him, and he
withdrew from itinerancy, convinced that its evil reputation was stran-
gling true religion. It was just this spirit, Bellamy claimed in 1769, that
had sabotaged the Awakening: "Numbers of our converts in New England twenty years ago were to all appearances converted thus," he
recalled bitterly.[22] A forewarned Charles Backus, presiding over a New
Divinity revival in Somers, Connecticut, in 1797, "had been fully acquainted with the wild and fanatical spirit which had prevailed in some
parts of Connecticut in the previous years, to the great injury of the
churches; and he set himself with watchfulness and manly resolution
to exclude that spirit from his parish."[23]

But Hopkins and Bellamy remained deeply suspicious of those who
were "ravished with joy" for reasons that went beyond the simple
inexpediency of enthusiasm. At the root of enthusiasm they detected a
spirit that shrank from the true demands of Christianity and substituted a religion that permitted its devotees to be saved without any
effort. Behind the seemingly Calvinistic claim of the enthusiasts to have
received grace on the basis that "the elect are justified from eternity,
or from the resurrection of Christ, and that in due time their justification is manifested to them by the spirit, on which they commence
believers," Bellamy discerned a sinful longing to construe Christianity
as a religion of emotional play and no work, as though the only response true religion demanded was an ecstatic reception of salvation.
Of course, Bellamy protested that it is true that "we are justified by
faith alone" and not by works, but he added, "we are assured of our

justification, by a consciousness of our faith and other Christian graces, and by knowing they are of the right kind." In words that could have as easily been directed at Anne Hutchinson, Bellamy insisted that "sanctification, taking the word in a large and comprehensive sense is the evidence, the only Scripture-evidence, of a good estate."[24] As an antidote to enthusiasts and other potential revival-wreckers, the New Divinity required "a life of strict morality, and regular observance of all the laws and ordinances of Christ."[25]

To raise this requirement to the level of perfection was a conclusion possible only on Edwardsean terms as laid out in *Freedom of the Will*. The reality of full natural ability eliminated any need to limit oneself to one-by-one steps toward sanctification, and involved the saint in the obligation to obey down to the last degree of that ability. In so doing, the New Divinity's perfectionism only made explicit what was all along logically implicit in the words of *Freedom of the Will*.

THE USE OF MEANS

Though sinners had the natural power to will freely, it also remained true that they freely willed according to the desire of their minds and hearts. There were in Edwards's scheme no volitions apart from the heart and the mind. Consequently, the moral content of volition was also entirely dependent on the moral state of the heart or mind from which it sprang. Hopkins wrote, "Nothing is either duty or sin, if considered without respect to the heart, and as not implying any exercises of that; therefore there is not really any external duty or sin which is not considered in connection with exercises of the heart, and as the fruit and expression of these."[26] Volitions originating from an unregenerate heart were, thus, as a moral necessity, tainted by evil. "If sinners love to do things which they know are displeasing to God," Emmons hypothesized (knowing that this was the simple definition of "sinning"), "then they never do any thing merely to please him. Though they do a great many things which he has required them to do, yet they never do any thing merely for the sake of obeying or pleasing him."[27] This, for Hopkins, was a perfectly simple a priori deduction. Nothing "is more absurd than to suppose that a person under the dominion of a hard, impenitent heart, does, with such a heart, even with all his heart, desire a humble, broken heart, and truly and sincerely seek it."[28] Thus:

The unregenerate sinner is an enemy to God. The whole bent and all the exercises of his heart are in opposition to God's true character, and no influence on his mind, whether by the Spirit of God or anything else, antecedent to regeneration, or any change whatsoever, do in the least degree remove this opposition and enmity. . . . Therefore, all the exertions and exercises of the heart, under the greatest degree of this influence, by which the conscience is enlightened and awakened, are no more friendly to God, but as corrupt and as opposite to him as ever. . . . What natural principles are there but corrupt principles?[29]

Nothing, Nathan Strong repeated, "either in sentiment or practice, can be harmless, which arises from a wicked heart. Such a heart, with all its issues, is guilty in the sight of God."[30] Like the Midas touch in reverse, everything wicked men did turned to wickedness. "If he plows, his plowing is sin; if he prays, his praying is sin; or if he fasts, his fasting is sin," said Emmons. "God expressly condemns the best services of sinners."[31]

All of this might have been easier for the contemporaries of the New Divinity men to pass by had not the New Divinity chosen to apply it with special glee to the preparationist notion of the "use of the means." In this context, "chosen" is perhaps an unfortunate term, since the logic of *Freedom of the Will* drew them to this subject as inexorably as files to a magnet. For if the wicked heart could only ever produce thoroughly wicked volitions the unregenerate who attempted to use "the means of grace" could use them only sinfully. Even if a sinner became conscientiously troubled over his sins—became an "awakened, convinced sinner"—he was still a sinner and (Hopkins insisted) "has as much hardness of heart, and is really in a hardened state, as the secure sinner."[32] So, "even if they read [God's] word, they read it to please themselves," warned Emmons; "if they attend public worship, they attend to please themselves, and not [God]."[33] It will do no good to encourage sinners, who protest that they have not yet received the gift of divine preparation, to use "the means" so that they can at least "prepare" themselves to receive that divine gift. "The unregenerate," Smalley declared, "cannot warrantably be encouraged to strive to enter in, at the strait gate, by a serious attention to religion, with an assurance that if after all, they should not be saved, their sin will thence be less, and their condemnation lighter."[34]

It was not just the futility but the immorality of preaching up "the use of the means" to which the New Divinity objected. The "use of the means," instead of indicating good intentions, indicated that a pious fraud was being perpetrated. Not to repent at once, when full natural ability was available—to mill around in pretended helplessness amongst the "means"—immediately aroused the suspicion that those who claimed they *could not* repent at once were only disguising a *would not,* and a secret animosity to the Gospel. To nurse this sinful wickedness while at the same time handling the sacraments and hearing the word of God was a doubly blackened abomination. "The awakened, convinced sinner sins more directly and immediately against God and the Savior, and in the face of the clear dictates of his own conscience," Hopkins cried;

he thinks now a thousand times more about God and Christ than he did, and his exercises of heart are proportionately constant and numerous. But these exercises are all against God and the gospel; therefore, the more constant and numerous they are, the more guilty and vile the sinner is.[35]

"The use of the means" actually made the sinner *worse.* "The more means are used with the sinner, the greater advantages he enjoys, the more instruction is given him, and the more light and convictions he has in his own conscience . . . the more miserable he will be," Hopkins wrote; "yea, his heart is harder than it was in a state of security as much greater degrees of light and convictions are now let into his mind."[36] By the ostensibly pious use of the "means" to extenuate his wickedness, the sinner "becomes not less, but more vicious and guilty in God's sight, the more instruction and knowledge he gets in attendance on the means of grace."[37]

As might be expected, when Hopkins first unveiled this argument in the public press in 1767, it provoked howls of outrage from critics who complained that Hopkins was tacitly encouraging sinners to continue in their sins rather than risk making themselves worse by trying to do good. Hopkins stubbornly replied that his objection was not to the sinner's doing good, but to stopping with *only* doing good, a hesitation he thought preparationism was particularly guilty of sanctioning. "I place his greater guilt," he wrote, "not in his awakenings and internal light, nor in his amendment of life, but in his continuing obstinate and impenitent under all this light and conviction, and in his opposing and rejecting with his whole heart the free offers of pardon and salvation by Jesus Christ."[38] And the kind of sinner who did profess to be discouraged as the critics feared had to be a pretty suspicious character anyway. To such sinners, Bellamy put one question: Why should you think that the knowledge that your religious duties are worthless gives you a motive to wallow in sin? Simply because you see how these duties will do you no good? Then, Bellamy announced, that only proves what has been said: that a sinner really is a sinner, means or no. By this, "it is plain" that any sinner who gives up religious duties because he will derive no benefit from them was operating from depraved motives all along. Such "a sinner cares not a jot for God, and will not go one step in religion, only for what he can get."[39] Hopkins, too, had a question for the sinner who listened to his sermons and then abandoned the "use of the means" because he was afraid of sinning:

> If a sinner objects against attempting to pray and says he is afraid to do it, because the prayer of the wicked is an abomination to the Lord, he may be asked what he is afraid of. If he is indeed afraid of sin, and so avoids prayer that he may avoid sin, why is he not equally concerned to avoid all sin, or sin in any other way? If he is willing to do this, he may pray without sinning, and so the objection ceases.[40]

What the New Divinity wanted to do was not to make men more resigned to their sins, as if it were better to be hung for a sheep than a lamb, but to flush them out of their hiding places and tear from them the excuse of inability. "There is nothing," Hopkins warned, "which the unregenerate may be supposed to do, in order to obtain a new heart, which is not itself an act of opposition or consistent with the most perfect opposition to what which he is supposed to be seeking."[41] Repent, then, and be wise.

To their critics, the New Divinity men turned with even sharper questions and answers. What precisely was the assumption behind the use of means? Nathan Strong answered: "The supposition that means, by the most diligent use of them, will remove the corruption of human nature, implies that the heart is previously right; and that all sins are no more than pitiable mistakes, arising from doctrinal ignorance—Let this idea be followed in its genuine consequences, and it really denies the sin of human nature."[42] Hopkins bleakly suspected "that the doctrine that they who are the least sinners and have done the most duty are, on this account most likely to be saved . . . contains the substance and soul of the Arminian scheme, and, if followed in all its just consequences, will subvert every important doctrine of Calvinism." And even if the defender of "means" is not exactly an Arminian himself, he "has represented his awakened, reformed sinner in a light very agreeable to their notion of such." Thus:

> He is a humble sinner who, with tenderness of conscience and trembling at God's word, reformed all known sin, and complies with all known duty. . . . And what reason has such a person for any distress and terror of conscience?

He is prepared to be comforted, and told that all things are well and he has nothing to do but to hold on in this way of duty. This is exactly agreeable to their notion, and sets human nature in its fallen state in the light in which they [the Arminians] represent it. . . . And it follows from this that man is not in such a lost, helpless, depraved state as Calvinists have generally represented him to be.[43]

In Hopkins's eye, the "use of the means" had become the Trojan horse of the Arminians, or worse still, the golden calf of New England Congregationalism. "The Children of God," Hopkins resentfully complained, "make an Idol of their Preparations for Duties."[44] Nathan Strong saw blasphemy here, for "those who depend on the use of means to change their hearts are denying the power of God and resisting the Holy Ghost."[45]

Ironically, the New Divinity frequently performed an apparent volteface on this very issue of "means," and proclaimed—as Hopkins did—that "means are necessary to be used in order to prepare persons for regeneration."[46] Josiah Sherman recognized, as did other New Divinity men, that to bar sinners entirely from preaching, praying, and Bible-reading would be to cut them off from the very knowledge that they were sinners and needed to repent, thus turning them into theological solipsists. After all,

a man can have no idea of the love of food, though in the most starving condition, till he has the knowledge of food—the sense and the object must meet in order to produce the idea. . . . And it is impossible to exercise love in an object of which we have no knowledge; so that it is of great importance that sinners attend the means of instruction and conviction—and ministers should plant the seeds of knowledge in the understanding by instruction and water them by motives.[47]

Samuel Spring was "cordially ready to grant . . . that it is much more probable that sinners will be saved who read the Bible, and steadily hear the gospel, than though they were wholly inattentive, and stupid."[48] The New Divinity saved themselves from outright contradiction only by the not very helpful, or not very convincing, distinction that "means," while necessary to conversion, has neither "power or virtue adequate to the end proposed."[49] Although "the unregenerate are commanded to love God, and strive in this matter, and exert all their powers," Hopkins would concede only that "it does not follow from this that unregenerate men do thus love God," or (as Josiah Sherman explained matters) that we should any less "depend on God to give the hearing ear and the understanding heart."[50] Regeneration is only *con-*

nected to means; "that it is effected by the *power* of means, is what the scriptures are far from leading us to conceive."[51]

This shifting around is revealing, for even if we grant that the New Divinity's attack on the "use of the means" had painted them into a practical pastoral corner, it was still uncharacteristic of them to let practical concerns mitigate the force of a logical argument. At least they might have swept the nasty business under the rug instead of so often exposing a flank. But this only underlies what the assault on "means" really meant. The New Divinity, in their relentless pursuit of revival, could not allow anything to stand which might offer the sinner refuge; even if that *thing* was by itself indispensable to revival in practical terms, rhetorically at least, it had to go to the block. To this purpose, they appropriated the logic Edwards had supplied in *Freedom of the Will,* and hoped by this not to eliminate the actual use of "means" so much as to heighten the anxieties of personal religious crisis. That it was only an appropriation, a strategy, was evident from how blithely they fell back to the use of the means on other, less threatening occasions. But it was not an insincere strategy, if only because it served a larger Edwardsean goal. They did not want, as their critics charged, to discourage men from religion; to the contrary, they hoped to speed up the process of choice by eliminating every motive for hesitancy. "If sinners are but effectively awakened to see how dreadful damnation is," Bellamy believed, that "will make them also resolve to run for eternal salvation, till their very last breath."[52] To the sinner trying to use the "means" to prepare himself for salvation, Hopkins was delivering an exhortation not to loiter in preparation, but to repent completely and at once—not to halt halfway. To the sinner still in his sins, Hopkins was trying to close off all other avenues of escape and confront him with the immediate need of salvation. "Let him be convinced that this is the most likely course he can take to be saved," predicted Hopkins, "and that there is no other course likely . . . and it will be a strong and prevalent motive with him to take it, in proportion to his dread of eternal destruction and desires of future happiness."[53] Therefore, John Smalley demanded of New England's saints that no answer should be given to the all-important inquiry of sinners, *What shall I do to be saved?* except *Believe on the Lord Jesus Christ,* because "nothing short of thus entering at the strait gate, will ensure their salvation."[54] To New England's sinners, Bellamy would continue to thunder his command "immediately to repent of your sins and return to God through Jesus Christ, looking only to free grace through him for pardon and eternal life."[55] For the New Divinity, the proper model of conversion was not the gradualism of preparationism but the immediacy of Edwardsean revival; *Freedom of the Will* offered a logic, a means of its own, which they could appropriate in order to eliminate the one major rival to that model in New England Calvinism.

That *Freedom of the Will* was very much the hidden hand in New Divinity immediatism appears evident not only from the internal logic of the New Divinity but from the conclusions other Calvinists drew from *Freedom of the Will*. The English Particular Baptist John Ryland, pastor of the College Lane Church in the English Northampton, read *Freedom of the Will* and Smalley's sermons, and passed them on excitedly to Robert Hall, pastor of the Arnesby Particular Baptist Church in Leistershire, with the comment that Edwards's "distinction between natural and moral ability . . . would lead us to see that the affirmative side of the Modern Question [of revivalism] was fully consistent with the strictest Calvinism." Hall was similarly impressed—and shocked the hidebound Northamptonshire Association of Particular Baptists in 1779 with a sermon, "Help to Zion's Travellers," in which he announced that the Edwardsean logic had at last made it possible for strict Calvinists to preach conversion in the most uninhibited style: "The way to Jesus is graciously open for everyone who chooses to come to him." Hall then introduced yet another Particular Baptist worthy, Andrew Fuller, to *Freedom of the Will*, and Fuller was likewise convinced that at last an intelligible way had been found to reconcile evangelism and Calvinism. In 1785 Fuller (who struck up a correspondence with Samuel Hopkins) published *The Gospel Worthy of All Acceptation*, in which he insisted that there was no longer a contradiction between the "peculiarity of design in the death of Christ, and a universal obligation on those who hear the gospel to believe in him."[56] In England as well as New England, New Divinities sprang fully formed from the head of *Freedom of the Will*, and gave English-speaking Calvinism an impetus for mission that would propel them beyond their own boundaries to India and the Pacific Islands.

SEPARATION

Because Puritanism was devoted to inculcating and discerning purity, it had always had strong urges to create churches only for the pure; but the pure are always few in this world, and New England feared to be too pure lest its churches be occupied only by the few. So, although New England called its polity a Congregational Way (implying churches based on pure, separated congregations), it was split throughout the seventeenth century between those like Solomon Stoddard and Richard Mather, who organized their congregations on the simple basis of town membership and a good life, and those who wanted the church to be sharply separated from the town and reserved only for the pure. The Great Awakening made the pure unmistakably visible, and, no longer few, they emerged in unprecedented numbers. Edwards had fresh incentive to try to restore separatism to Congregationalism. Northampton foiled him by dismissing him from its pulpit. But the New Divinity caught the separatistic urge, and the agenda implicit in *Freedom of the Will* spurred them toward furthering Edwards's goal.

The New Divinity desired nothing so much as to repudiate the notion of a church-in-society—the comprehensive, Solomon Stoddard–style or Richard Mather–style church which embraced all members of a community as a covenantal entity, and which acted as the moral sheet anchor for the community at large. They sought instead to limit the church "to real Christians." whom Nathan Strong characterized as those "who have made a profession of evangelical obedience, by repentance towards God and faith in our Lord Jesus Christ."[57] John Smalley repudiated the traditional undergirding of a church-in-society: the need to distinguish between a visible church on earth, which is compelled to tolerate both the wheat and the tares, and the invisible church of the pure alone, known only to the sight of God. The kingdom of God, said Smalley, most emphatically is "the invisible church of Christ here below; comprehending all true Christians, and no others."[58] Bellamy warned that when "any man who is unconscious that he is united to Christ by faith is bold to put in claim to the heavenly Canaan, he is guilty of the grossest presumption."[59] The Church was only for those in whom visible and invisible Christianity coincided.

The chief roadblock in the path of implementing this policy lay in the fact that the concept of the church-in-society was sanctioned by law and by practice in both Massachusetts and Connecticut. Any outright repudiation of the established polity or any organization of separatist congregations would be unhappily redolent of the enthusiasm of the fanatical Separatists in the Awakening. Few New Divinity men ever went so far as to attempt the erection of illegal conventicles, but in many cases they did not need to: the rural parishes that welcomed so many of the New Divinity already shared the same urges after purity; they offered the New Divinity unhampered opportunity to experiment, legally, with functional separatism—a kind of congregationalism within established Congregationalism. In their own churches in Great Barrington and Bethlehem, Hopkins and Bellamy followed Edwards's effort in Northampton and ended the practice of admitting to provisional membership those who had made no profession of faith but who claimed church membership on the strength of their baptism as infants (Bellamy coined the phrase that still describes this practice: "the half-way covenant").[60] "Your baptism," Bellamy declared, bestowed no convenantal identity; it "gives you not the least right to any one of the peculiar blessings of the covenant of grace . . . but you are now, this moment, in fact, as liable to be struck dead and sent to hell, by the divine justice, as any unbaptised sinner in the land."[61]

Wherever else they could pursue it without penalty, the New Divinity would push still further the demands of purity, and separation of the pure from the impure in the churches. Bellamy did not hesitate to take sides in 1742 with James Davenport's Separatists against Joseph Noyes's First Church in New Haven.[62] Isaac Backus, the celebrated antiestablishment Baptist, was pleasantly surprised, first, to find New Divinity men like Ephraim Judson and Lemuel LeBaron "very friendly," and then to receive an invitation to preach in the pulpit of Joel Benedict (one of Bellamy's students), and then to see Baptists regularly preach in the church pastored by Joseph Barber (an admirer and possibly pupil of Hopkins).[63] Ezra Stiles observed other symptoms of aggressive separatism in the New Divinity in 1787, when Edwards the Younger "lately refused to receive a Communicant from the Rev. Mr. Streets Chh. in East Haven altho' recommended to him & his Chh. as a member in full Communion & regular stan[din]g in the Chh." In fact, Edwards proceeded to treat the hapless transferee "as a Heathen & Publican, and required a new profession of Religion as he would of a newly converted Heathen." Hopkins, also, "refused to admit a Member from another Chh. without a profession de novo," and Stephen West caused a sensation during a visit to his home town when he "refused to perform Baptisms there (tho' asked) because it was an impure Chh., or as he called it Stoddardean Chh. & baptized on owning the Covenant the Infants of those who did not come to the Lord's Supper." Far from fitting comfortably into the Standing Order, Stiles found that "they are determined to coalesce with none that are not in heart

New."[64] In the end, the New Divinity never went as far as Stiles feared they would—setting up an entirely new denomination of Congregationalists—but it was plain that they were very much a world to themselves, and, to Stiles, a singularly threatening one.

Hopkins declared that "the church is not a worldly society"; it "wants no support from the civil authority" and exists "distinct from civil, or worldly communities and independent of them."[65] Just how seriously they intended to make that distinction appears in the demands of Aaron Kinne, the New Divinity minister of Groton, Connecticut, who proposed in a spirit of pure come-outerism that a "Chh Committee settle all lawsuits—no coming to Law for Chh. members before civil Courts."[66] And that sectlike sense of hostility to a tainted world largely accounts for why, despite Alan Heimert's extravagant claims for the Revolutionary activism of the Edwardseans, they remained fundamentally aloof from secular political and social issues. Although Bellamy was generally sympathetic to the American cause in the Revolution, his deepest energies were engaged by revival, not revolution. Typical of his political indifference was his comment to his son in 1775: "My desire and prayer to God is, that my son Jonathan may be saved. And then, whatever happens to America or to you, this year or next, you will be happy forever."[67] Hopkins, in a letter to John Erskine in 1774, applauded the Boston Tea Party, but only because it would help to mortify unholy tea-drinkers. It "will save much needless expense; And there is a hopeful prospect of its putting an end to many other extravagances." Far from being thankful for the Revolution, Hopkins regretted that "political affairs" had put theological discussion "to sleep" and had dampened revival everywhere in New England except under Stephen West at Stockbridge.[68] Both Levi Hart and Hopkins thought the American rhetoric about liberty nothing but cant so long as those same Americans persisted in fastening a natural necessity of slavery upon blacks.[69] John Smalley also doubted whether "that ardent love of political liberty, which is common among men" was really "a virtue, acceptable to God," especially since "in Pagans and infidels, this flaming love of liberty is ever most conspicuous" and "may be nothing else, at bottom, than narrow selflove."[70] On later reflection, he was even more sure that the Revolution had lowered the moral tone of America and brought the ministry into disrepute:

In this country, the ministry was once accounted honorable. Religious pastors and teachers were some of the greatest men. But it is far otherwise now. The dignity of the clergy has been long declining; and it is likely, I apprehend, to sink still lower.[71]

The New Divinity cared too little for the grimy world of politics to stain their hands in it collectively, and it was as perilous to try to identify them with a single political philosophy in the new nation as it is to make them into a black-coat auxiliary of the Continental army. Where they manifested political interest at all, they expressed personal inclination and not that of a movement. It is true that Azel Backus was so vehement an anti-Jeffersonian that it nearly cost him a spell in jail for libel, while Emmons preached "excessive severe against Jefferson" and spoke of the Federalists as the "only real friends to the present government."[72] On the other hand, David Sanford, Emmons's brother-in-law, was a Jeffersonian, and Joseph Barker was actually elected to Congress as a Republican in 1805 (the only New Divinity minister to hold political office).[73] Even Emmons, despite his distaste for Jefferson, appeared to Archibald Alexander in 1801 to cherish "no malignity against anyone on religious or political grounds."[74] More in the spirit of Charles Backus, who advised his New Divinity brethren that they had no business in politics, the Edwardseans desired to claim a higher moral ground above politics (the one thoroughly New-Divinity-owned-and-operated periodical, the *Massachusetts Missionary Magazine,* was remarkable for confining itself purely to metaphysical and doctrinal subjects and eschewing social controversy).[75] They preferred the role of antagonist standing outside of society to that of protagonist within it.

Of course, again, the critics grew hoarse with complaints that closing off the churches to all but the pure would shut out nine-tenths of the population and give up the good influence the churches could exercise in society. Bellamy, however, cared only for purity, not good influence. He wrote, "were it not for the honour of Christ and Christianity in the sight of the Pagans, Jews, and Mahometans . . . and more for the good of their own souls that nine-tenths should be shut out of the church, if need so require, than to come in by wilful lying?"[76] He plunged in even further when he added, "God never did propose any covenant to mankind but which required real holiness on man's part; and any covenant short of this is a mere human device."[77]

And it is hard to see how, in the overall light of his own thought, Edwards could have come to any other conclusion. Bellamy not only had before him the concrete and sacrificial example of Edwards himself in Northampton, and Edwards's explicit teaching, in the *Humble Inquiry into the Terms of Communion,* that the church was a holy community for saints alone, but he also had the philosophical agenda of *Freedom of the Will.* After all, a comprehensive, parish-type church made sense only if it was assumed that purity could never be absolute, but could be cultivated in varying degrees by all who were not openly abandoned to profligacy. However, *Freedom of the Will*'s imputation of ability eliminated gradualism and, with it, the need to nurture a town or a church full of gradualists. The covenantal community was replaced by individual decision, and profession of faith replaced baptism as the sacrament of initiation.

Hence, the New Divinity viewed the notion of a church-in-society with what amounted to contempt. Those who yearned with Nathan Strong to love God "with the whole heart" had no time for "religious civilities," and Strong warned against expecting "civilization" to "alter the moral qualities of men's hearts and actions."[78] Given the sovereignty of God, said Smalley, place and title in society are meaningless, and since the giving of place and title are the only discernable functions of "society," society itself was rendered meaningless for all moral purposes, for all men are brought equally low by the divine decree. "The parentage or education of persons, is nothing whereby it can be determined, whether they will be truly virtuous or not. . . . The outward condition of persons, whether high or low, affluent or indigent, is not anything whence it can be known."[79] To the contrary, Strong believed that it was precisely the "influential and useful in the society of this world" who will be *"weighed in the balance,"* and *"they will be found wanting."*[80] The truth, as Nathaniel Niles discovered, is that formal society is a fraud. "Instead of improving their power and interests for the good of the community," the great ones "make use of the common interests as means of aggrandizing themselves and their families." Among the ordinary people, "ambition, pride, or avarice" makes them "diligent in their business, fair in their dealings, humane to their neighbors, or intrepid defenders of the public weal."[81] To Nathan Strong, the veneer of public morality given to these people by identification with, and acceptance into, a church never served to influence them to improvement. It merely gives "a more specious appearance to crimes, and better accommodate the principles of depravity to the taste of those who call themselves refined."[82] It may be true that

they may often come where God hath appointed social prayer to be offered, and may sit before him as his people; but their service is more fitly called the civility of a christian land where providence hath placed them, than a worship of the Father in spirit and in truth. . . . Is this religion? . . . No, it is not.[83]

ATONEMENT

The most startling departure from received Calvinist doctrine which the New Divinity undertook concerned the central doctrine of Christian theology, the atonement. European Reformed dogmaticians, in an intellectual tradition extending back to St. Anselm, interpreted the death of Christ as a substitutionary sacrifice. Christ died for the ungodly, but not only "for our convenience and good, but also in our room, by substitution strictly so called." In this substitution, God the Father legally accounted, or imputed, to Christ on the cross all the guilt of his elect people, and when Christ died, their real guilt legally died with him. At the same time, God then also imputed Christ's real righteousness to his elect, making them legally justified and righteous in his eyes.[84] Boston's Samuel Willard described this double imputation as an "exchange" in which "all the guilt which was before ours, now became his, and was translated on him."[85] Hence, as the Saybrook Platform of Connecticut put the matter, the elect are justified by God "imputing Christ's active obedience to the whole Law, and passive obedience in his death, for their whole and sole righteousness."[86]

This meant, first, that justification was plainly a legal transaction made by God, objective to the sinner and not dependent on the sinner's own labors to make himself righteous. Second, it meant that the atonement could be intended only for those whom God had predestined to salvation: obviously, if the atonement involved a receipt of imputed righteousness that would entitle the bearer to a place in heaven, this imputation of righteousness had to be confined intentionally only to those whom God willed to have there. Redemption was particular in nature, and necessarily implied a definite, or *limited atonement*.

The New Divinity's rejection of this model of the atonement began as early as 1750 with the publication of Bellamy's *True Religion Delineated,* which remained the principal exposition of New Divinity theology for as long as it was a theology to be reckoned with. Divided as the New Divinity might be on what linked Adam and his posterity in sin, they were united in proclaiming that it was decretive and occasionalistic—a "connexion" or "constitution"—rather than imputed. "It has been thought," Smalley acknowledged, "that Adam's act in eating the forbidden fruit, is so imputed to all his children, that they are condemned for it, just as if it had been their own personal transgression."[87] Emmons replied that this impugned the strictly moral nature of God's government of the universe, since it amounted to saying that one man's sin compelled another man to be a sinner without any real action of the other's will. However, Emmons added, God did have a right "as a sovereign" to create Adam as a kind of moral test-model for the entire human race, and to use the results of that test as the basis for forming judgments about how to treat all other human beings. In that way, God merely established between Adam and his human posterity "a connection between his first sin and their future sin and misery," which, rather than inflicting a burden of inherited sinfulness on men, instead influenced God to create them sinful and sinning all on their own.[88] Adam, if not actually the cause of human depravity, was without question its occasion:

> God placed Adam as the public head of his posterity, and determined to treat them according to his conduct. If he persevered in holiness and obedience, God determined to bring his posterity into existence holy and upright. But if he sinned and fell, God determined to bring his posterity into existence morally corrupt and depraved. Adam disobeyed the Law of his Maker; and according to the constitution under which he was placed, his first and single act of disobedience made all his posterity sinners; that is, it proved the occasion of their coming into the world unholy and sinful.[89]

Of course, both imputation and Emmonsism came out with the same result: that men are sinners because of Adam. The crucial difference was in the method, for by Emmons's method, human guilt and sinfulness were not treated as forensic hypotheses or poses which God strikes over against sin, but spiritual realities. Sin exists in men, not by *fiat* imputation but, as Hopkins said, "by virtue of a holy and wise constitution, which connects the sin and ruin of all Adam's children with the rebellion of their first father."[90] And the efficiency of "connexions" was not to be underestimated merely because the word "cause" was absent. "Though there is an established connexion between the sin of Adam and the sin of his posterity," Samuel Spring reminded David Tappan in 1789, "yet sin is a personal quality."[91]

If guilt could not be imputed without emptying it of personal reality, neither could righteousness. "In the case of our blessed Saviour and the sinner," Nathan Strong wrote, "Jesus Christ was never guilty, either by his personal actions or an imputed transferral."[92] Nor was his righteousness ever transferred by imputation in order to justify sinners.

"Merit is ever personal," John Smalley protested. "Another's having been righteous, doth not make me righteous, if I have not been so myself." Just so, Christ's death for sinners "did not design to deliver them from obligations to perfect obedience."[93] To dismiss our just condemnation as sinners under God's law with a legal fiction was as subversive of God's moral government as the infliction of imputed guilt without actual transgression. "This is the very thing Antinomians formerly held," Bellamy asserted.[94] Spring added, "Christ is not a minister of sin. He did not come into the world to abate the demands of the law but to magnify the law and make it honorable."[95] Under the terms of imputed righteousness, the New Divinity imagined that sinners would throw off all restraint. "Had we the righteousness of Christ as a perfect cloak for all our sins, so as to have no occasion for forgiveness," Smalley declared, "it might more reasonably be expected that we should be unforgiving"—or even worse. "They would have no sins to confess; they would deserve no punishment and need no pardon."[96]

Restraint, if it were applied anywhere, would now be applied to God. If the righteousness of Christ was to be "so imputed to them as to become to all intents and purposes their righteousness," then "the justification of such a one would be of debt."[97] Smalley could imagine those receiving such an imputation leaping for joy at the prospect, for, with this imputed righteousness in hand, they held a promise of grace God was obligated to honor regardless of their real condition or behavior. "According to it, all obligation is now on God's part; all the grace is ours! . . . All the debts of mankind, both of duty and suffering, are forever cancelled! . . . If they now love or serve God, it is of mere gratuity."[98] Such an apparently impersonal, artificial relationship reminded the New Divinity of exactly the sort of aggressively commercial society New England had become, and which they spent so much time denouncing. Smalley warned,

all notions of supererogation, and of a fund of merit to be sold and bought, or any way communicated from one to another, proceed upon the maxims of commercial, not of rectoral justice. Everything of this kind is going off entirely from the ideas of sin and duty, to those of debt and credit, damages and reparations.[99]

Smalley was woefully confident that, having conjured up such notions of unholy competition, "many may not be able to enter into the kingdom of heaven, because they expect it on account of the righteousness of Christ, without any righteousness of their own."[100]

In the place of an atonement involving the imputation of guilt and righteousness, the New Divinity substituted a governmental model. Images of law and order came naturally and frequently to the New Divinity, since they had taken up the Edwardsean burden of proving that God was a moral, and not an arbitrary, governor of creation. And, in a universe where God was primarily conceived of as a *governor*, it became just as natural to think of sin, not so much as wickedness, but as lèse-majesté. "The great evil of all the unrighteousness, as well as the ungodliness of men," Smalley concluded, "consists in the disrespect shown to the supreme Governor of the world, and the reproach cast upon his great and holy name."[101] That meant, as Bellamy saw it, that when God was "injured and offended by our sins," his principal concern was "to maintain the honor of his majesty . . . of his law and government, and sacred authority."[102] After all, Smalley hypothesized, "Better never to give a law, than to let the violation of it pass with impunity."[103] Therefore, to reassert moral order in the universe and show that his laws can and will be enforced, God would have been perfectly within his rights to have exterminated the entire boastful, heaven-daring human race. "The truth and justice of God required, that this threatening of his law should be executed upon every child of Adam," Smalley declared—"unless in some other way an equal manifestation could be made of the governing righteousness of the Most High."[104]

That was an important *unless,* since God, who desired to "show the infinite hatefulness and ill desert of sin," was still benevolent and preferred not to destroy mankind.[105] "And now Christ stepped in," Bellamy wrote, and "offered to undertake to frustrate Satan's scheme . . . opening a way in which glory might come to God, and salvation to fallen man."[106] Christ died for the ungodly—not to take their sins upon himself, but to show, in his mortal sufferings on the cross, how very real God's anger and power against sin were. The principal purpose served by this atonement was not to make propitiation for human sin, but to demonstrate that God was no weakling, hated sin, and had all the necessary power to punish it.

> The pangs of our expiring Lord
> The honours of thy law restor'd:
> His sorrows made thy justice known,
> And paid for follies not his own.[107]

The atonement did not provide redemption for sinners: it provided "an opportunity" for God to show that God meant business about sin.[108]

On those grounds, God could now proceed to forgive sinners and regenerate them without being accused of inconsistency with the rules of his own moral government. "And now," rejoiced Bellamy, "this door being opened, mankind may, through Christ, be considered as subjects to whom God may show favor consistently with his honor."[109] In Christ's death (Smalley proclaimed), "a foundation was laid for God, to the eternal honor of his remunerative justice, to give grace and glory, to all who believed in Christ and belong to him."[110] So Christ did not actually die in the place of any individuals. His atonement was intended to justify God, not humans, and when God forgave anyone, it was not because Christ had merited it for them personally. Christ had only "opened a way for the sinner's salvation" by making it possible for God to forgive in general. Smalley warned that God had sent his Son, "not to be laid under obligation in justice, to justify anyone," but only to make his justifying of sinners "honorable."[111]

Indeed, far from God being placed under obligation, God's forgiveness was restored as a matter of pure grace and sovereignty. The atonement arranged matters so that God *could* forgive; there was no guarantee that God actually *would* for any individual. Salvation remained an act of sovereignty. Smalley continued, "He is at full liberty to choose the subjects of his renewing mercy, as he thinks proper. Even the obedience and sufferings of Christ, do not lay God the Father under any obligation which is inconsistent with his most sovereign grace. . . . God hath left himself at liberty in his word, to regenerate or to leave in unregeneracy any impenitent sinner whom he pleases."[112]

In the end, this meant that our faith—not Christ's righteousness—is really what is imputed to us for righteousness. "As perfect obedience was a compliance with the covenant of works," wrote Bellamy, "so faith is a compliance with the covenant of grace."[113] And salvation comes, added Smalley, as Christ "produces in them personal righteousness."[114] It also put a stop on the doctrine of a limited atonement among the Edwardseans. Christ's death did not provide redemption for a tiny band of the elect. Rather, it served to allow God to save any and all. Thereby, "a way is opened," said Bellamy, for "all and every one of the human race," who shall fall in with the gospel design":

The *obedience* of Christ has brought as much honor to God and his law, as the perfect obedience of Adam, and all his race, would have done: the rights of the Godhead are as much asserted and maintained. So that there is nothing in the way, but that mankind may through Christ, be received into full favor, and entitled to eternal life.[115]

This is so far from Westminster or Dordrecht Calvinism, and at first glance from Edwards as well, that numerous commentators have seized on the New Divinity doctrine of unlimited atonement as a prime example of the New Divinity's "betrayal" of Edwards, and they have hypothesized that Bellamy must have found his way to Hugo Grotius and dredged up his governmentalism from there.[116] But a little reflection will show that the New Divinity doctrine of the atonement represented hardly more than an elaboration of what Edwards had himself laid the foundations for. First, by abandoning the imputation of Adam's sin as the ground of natural depravity, Edwards had already undercut any similar imputed connection between Christ and the elect. Second, and far more important, the New Divinity balked at the idea of a limited atonement because it seemed to conflict with Edwards's notion of the natural ability of all sinners to repent. Limited atonement implied that, for some, repentance was doomed to be a natural inability. As Bellamy saw it, the chief virtue of an unlimited atonement was precisely that, in this way, "it is attributed to sinners themselves that they perish at last—even to their own voluntary conduct."[117]

It is true that nothing in Edwards's published works openly promotes a governmental or unlimited atonement; but he did employ vocabulary concerning the atonement in sermons predating 1733 which clearly points toward the New Divinity doctrine:

All the sins of those who truly come to God for mercy, let them be what they will, are satisfied for, if God be true who tells us so . . . so that Christ having fully satisfied for all sin, or having wrought out a satisfaction that is sufficient for all, it is now no way inconsistent with the glory of the divine attributes to pardon the greatest sins of those who in a right manner come unto him for it.—God may now pardon the greatest sinners without any prejudice to the honour of his holiness. The holiness of God will not suffer him to give the least countenance to sin, but inclines him to give proper testimonies of his hatred to it. But Christ having satisfied for sin, God can now love the sinner, and give no countenance at all to sin, however great a sinner he may have been. . . . God may, through Christ, pardon the *greatest sinner* without any prejudice to the honour of his majesty. The honour of the divine majesty indeed requires satisfaction; but the sufferings of Christ fully repair the injury.[118]

It is also true that Edwards's private notebooks and *Miscellanies* would have revealed an Edwards whose doctrine of justification had veered over into a denial of the imputation of guilt or righteousness, and it is difficult to believe that Edwards was not teaching his pupils what he was confiding to his theological notebooks.

Of course, at the close of *Freedom of the Will*, Edwards was careful to lay out the particular ways in which his construction of the freedom of the will undergirded the "quinquarticular points" of Calvinism, including the limitation of the extent of the atonement to the elect, and if we were to confine our attention solely to that passage, we would indeed be wondering how Bellamy ever came up with the formulas that so distinguish *True Religion Delineated*.[119] But it has to be remembered that Bellamy's construction of the atonement in *True Religion Delineated* also turns out, for all of its un-limitedness, to be as particular and definite as the more classical constructions of the doctrine, since God in the end always has the final say in who shall be forgiven—in fact, Bellamy thought his notion of the atonement superior to the "quinquarticular points" precisely because it gave God more, not less, control over whomever would benefit from the death of Christ. It would not have been difficult at all for Edwards or anyone else to have embraced such an idea of the atonement—indefinite in theoretical scope, limited in actual application—and still insist that he was within the ambit of Westminster Calvinism.

The really odd fact that must be stacked against the last chapter of *Freedom of the Will* and its apparent "limited atonement" is that it was Edwards who contributed the preface to Bellamy's *True Religion Delineated* in 1750, describing it as "a discourse wherein the proper essence and distinguishing nature of saving religion is deduced from the first principles of the oracles of God."[120] Even if we disregard all the other evidence pointing to Edwards's governmentalism, and the direct implications of un-limitedness which governmentalism always carried into discussions of the extent of the atonement, it is plain that Edwards had no hesitation about putting his imprimatur upon the New Divinity doctrine of the atonement; to the contrary, he pledged his own reputation on its appearance.[121]

II

The New Divinity men were not original speculative thinkers—that much we may as well concede to their manifold critics, now as well as then. Speculative they were, and their enemies never tired of harping on the speculative quality of their theology as though that, ipso facto, rendered it anathema. But, interesting though their forays into psychology and theodicy occasionally were, their preaching and teaching were, looked at in the long run, still the stuff of Calvinism given yet another working over. As such, the New Divinity was hardly more than a set of variations on certain Edwardsean themes.

In their defense, it must be said that originality, no matter how much it may be prized for its aesthetic appeal, was not their intention. They set themselves to a more useful task, and that was the drawing out of the practical consequences of *Freedom of the Will,* for they believed that Edwards's doctrine of the will was the key to reviving what appeared to them as the moribund state of New England's religion. Since most, if not all, of the first generation of the New Divinity (like Bellamy and Hopkins) had experienced the gracious excitement of the Great Awakening, everything that followed the 1740s had to seem like a careless cooling of that terrible spiritual crucible in which their spiritual lives were reborn. *Freedom of the Will* represented the soul of the Awakening, the justification of unalloyed New England Calvinism, and Hopkins and Bellamy thought they need only labor to inundate the flat spiritual plain of New England with a new flood of Awakening.

Of course, they paid a price for this. For in using *Freedom of the Will* to drive New Englanders toward grace, they blurred the international focus of Edwards's work, for at least one important aspect of *Freedom of the Will* was to speak to a transatlantic as well as a provincial audience. To Edwards, the Great Awakening was substantial proof that the only workable theism was a Calvinistic theism. Let the Clarkes and Bentleys wring their hands in anguish over Hobbes and flee to Arminianism as their port in the deterministic storm—Edwards had experiential proof that deterministic atheism could be effectively stopped and routed only by an equally deterministic theism. *Freedom of the Will* was his endeavor to turn the reality he had seen in Northampton in the 1740s into theory and fix it on paper for the entire English-speaking world to read. The New Divinity substantially shortened the range Edwards had in mind, and their applications of *Freedom of the Will* were centered less on the reading public of the British Empire and more on the stubborn unregeneracy of New England. The conventional criticism that the New Divinity men were provincial in outlook is, on this score, entirely right—provided that the term is used geographically and not as a pejorative metaphor.

Part of that can be explained by the Revolution: the New Divinity wrote for New England because they had lost their political identity with Great Britain and, with it, the urgent search after recognition that led earlier colonial intellectuals to write their books for English readers, search out English publishers, and cultivate membership in English societies. But that does not explain why even in Bellamy and Hopkins, in the 1760s, the intellectual landscape is so foreshortened, unless one sees that the casting off of America's cultural dependence on Britain had really been ongoing as early as Hopkins's first blast of the trumpet against the use of means in 1767, and that Americans were becoming provincial in the most exact sense of the word because their American geography now held for them such interest that they no longer required a transatlantic perspective to keep their minds busy. Especially for Hopkins and Bellamy, who had weathered the storms of the Awakening, the American landscape had acquired its own significance as the land which their mentor, Edwards, had thought a likely place for the Millennium to begin. In that respect, the New Divinity was the first indigenous American theology.

Indigenous, and yet not utterly divorced from a transatlantic past. The problems the New Divinity claimed as its own had long lain at the bottom of New England's Calvinism, and stretched back beyond the 1630s to the anxieties of the last Elizabethan Puritans. The first generation of New Englanders had already built for themselves in old England an elaborate rationalization of divine determinism and human responsibility that historians have since called the Federal Theology, and this was at the root of many of the enmities of the New Divinity. Whatever its other achievements, the Federal Theology managed principally to grant to men a putative power to act; and, having imputed that power, the Federal Theology and the men who preached it supplied to their followers the precious possibility of meaningful human action in a divinely determined world. It was predicated, however, on the notion of preparationism, and, as it turned out, not everyone who came to New England was sure of preparationism's validity. John Cotton was one doubter, first in England and then in New England; the numerous congregations who resisted the introduction of the Half-Way Covenant were among the others who never lost that original Puritan urge for purity whose logical resting place was strict separatism and come-outerism. The social consequences of separatism, however, were more than even the doubters could bear—not even Cotton could stomach the raw spiritism Anne Hutchinson advertised as Cotton's "real" message.

The alternatives during the century that stretched between John Cotton and Jonathan Edwards thus stood at only two: gradualism or immediacy, preparationism or separatism. Up until 1741, most chose gradualism. What happened after 1741 convinced Edwards that gradualism was not a legitimate alternative, even though to abandon gradualism also meant the loss of that putative power of action. What Edwards did for New England in *Freedom of the Will* was to rid Calvinism of the need for gradualism by replacing the Federal Theology with an entirely new model of putative power, this time based on psychological analysis rather than metaphysics. Edwards thus supplied to New England Calvinism what the separatists within it had all along been searching for: a workable theory of possible human action that would, at the same time, lift up the gates into the creation of a pure, separated church polity. In this way, we may say that Bellamy and Hopkins were decoyed off into provincialism because so much in *Freedom of the Will* offered answers to New England's most fundamental provincial problems, and also because New England provincialism offered such a rich intellectual vein to follow.

Rather than quibbling about provincialism, the critics of the New Divinity might have made more progress if they had struck at a more serious weakness in the New Divinity, the overall validity of the enterprise itself. Joseph Bellamy believed in the sovereignty of God, and that God did indeed determine all things. What is unusual, then, is that he felt compelled to resort to numbers to prove it. As much as Bellamy preached his Calvinism with a whole and untroubled heart, his entire life's work moves against the backdrop of a New England in which Calvinism was on the defensive, and Bellamy was compelled to perform the intellectual version of miracles in order to have an audience. As such, the New Divinity was often an exercise in appeasement, for, while they aggressively promoted the wisdom of God in the permission of sin, they did it in such a way as to show that no Arminian could have any ground to complain against them (in fact, that the Arminian did not do *enough* to ensure real freedom of will). It does not seem to have occurred to them simply to state the terrible facts and leave them at that. Instead, they dressed up their Calvinism to look both offensive and inoffensive at the same time and then offered this to their hearers or readers just as if they had offered to an auction a sheep carefully disguised in wolves' clothing. Of course, if is easy to say from a distance that they really ought to have dispensed Calvinism pure and unmixed; in their minds, they were merely making it more explicable. But the line between explanation and rationalization is often a thin one, and they broke over it many times.

It should be quickly added that this is not the same thing as "watering Calvinism down," which they certainly did not do. However much Hopkins and Bellamy attempted to provide explanations/justifications of the wisdom of God in the permission of sin after the fact, they did so only after asserting the fact in the most unvarnished of terms. And they asserted them out of no sterile urge to follow the logical implications of divine determinism down to the last repulsive detail. If they professed confidence in the wisdom of God in the permission of sin, it was because hard and tragic experience had left them no other way to make sense of a world in which infant mortality carried off to tiny graves a hideous percentage of New England children, and in which many a man or woman in the prime of life had only the time to look up to see sudden death coming at them in an Indian hatchet. Emmons recorded that, after the death of his first wife, the two children born of that marriage sickened and died of "the dysentery" within twenty-four hours of each other. Frantically watching the hopes of his posterity wilting in maddening and helpless succession, feeling himself spinning into the abyss of lunacy, Emmons saved himself from falling into that black gulf only by clutching desperately to the doctrine of God's absolute sovereignty. Only by the conviction that absolute Purpose had directed his catastrophes could he gradually recover himself and go on to rebuild his shattered life.[122]

If Emmons later seemed hard and unflinching in his notion of divine sovereignty, it was because men saw only the hard shell. Hopkins, too, in the death of one of his children, could find consolation for his stony grief only by composing a sermon "on the subject of sin, the occasion of much good," for otherwise such a death made no sense.[123] If they retailed outrageous opinions at times, it was because New Divinity came by them, not only by Edwardsean logic, but out of personal crisis. And Edwards would have expected nothing less—*Freedom of the Will*, after all, was the ultimate statement of the proposition that "with a cold and unaffected heart . . . there can be no true spiritual knowledge of divine things."[124] The New Divinity were only the uses and applications of that single idea.

CHAPTER 5

Old Calvinism

The Obligation and Encouragement
of the Unregenerate

I

Thus time, Stephen West seemed to have gone too far.

The Reverend Mr. West, who succeeded Jonathan Edwards at the mission church at Stockbridge, Massachusetts, had been converted to New Divinity opinions by the aggressive overtures of Samuel Hopkins, and the publication in 1772 of his *An Essay on Moral Agency* located him squarely on the most radical flank of the Edwardseans. As true to the New Divinity mold in church practice as he was in theology, West refused baptism to the children of nonprofessors of grace no matter how upright the parents' lives, and refused communion and fellowship to any other churches he suspected of Arminian laxity. And then in 1779 the hard hand of New Divinity purism swung against West and created the most sensational ecclesiastical case in the history of Berkshire County.

The trouble began with Mrs. John Fisk, or rather with her husband, Captain John Fisk. Shortly after leaving the Revolutionary Army, John Fisk had taken up the job of schoolmaster in Stockbridge. Then a bachelor, he boarded at the Widow Deane's. Soon Captain Fisk and Mrs. Deane announced their intention to marry, but to this, Stephen West entered a vehement objection. Mrs. Deane was a member of the Stockbridge church; Captain Fisk not only was *not*, but showed no signs of grace, not to mention many disturbing holdovers from the habits of army life. Believers were not to be unequally yoked to unbelievers; ergo, Mrs. Deane was not to marry the rough-tongued captain. Mrs. Deane, unawed by West and the rest of the Stockbridge congregation, married Captain Fisk anyway, whereupon West excommunicated her. So dreadful did West regard this penalty that it does not seem to have occurred to him that Mrs. Fisk would do other than slide into cowed silence, if not outright submission. Instead, Mrs. Fisk demanded that an ecclesiastical council be called to review her case and authorize her reinstatement.[1]

It is doubtful whether Mrs. Fisk seriously entertained either hope or desire of reentering the Stockbridge congregation. More likely, she intended to bring the almighty Mr. West down several pegs, which, as West soon realized, was an imminent possibility. The excommunication of Mrs. Fisk had proceeded on scraps of evidence about the captain that looked ominous in Stockbridge but would look meager in New Haven or Boston. West was careful to see that the council was composed overwhelmingly of New Divinity men, including Bellamy, Hopkins, and Levi Hart. Mrs. Fisk, permitted to choose a spokesman for herself, chose the Reverend Mr. Joseph Huntington of Norwich, Connecticut.

Under the circumstances, she could not have chosen better. Brother of the governor of Connecticut (Samuel) and of a signer of the Declaration of Independence (Benjamin), Joseph Huntington was a member of the most powerful political family in Connecticut. Although in his parish "the state of religion . . . was scarcely ever otherwise than depressed," the temporal fortunes of his church were not, and his congregation, grateful for tranquility, had rewarded him by building him the most expensive new meeting house in the region. In his first published sermon in 1774 he had gone on record as opposing the New Divinity, although his opposition consisted mostly of a lofty disdain for the intricacies of New Divinity "metaphysics," not a painstaking rebuttal of matters point by point. He was respectably, if not impeccably, orthodox (only after his death in 1794 would his horrified family discover a lengthy manuscript in which he embraced Universalism), and when he arrived in Stockbridge in October 1779 to stand as Mrs. Fisk's champion, he stood as the representative of everything in New England Congregationalism that the New Divinity loathed.[2]

Huntington knew it, too, and since he also knew that his pleas for Mrs. Fisk were going to fall on predeterminedly deaf ears, he aimed directly at the assembled moguls of the New Divinity. He began by asserting that the real issue before the council was symbolic rather than legal or ecclesiastical. The promoters of Mrs. Fisk's humiliation had no real interest in Mrs. Fisk, or in Captain Fisk, Huntington argued; in fact, they had proven "no certain degree of immorality, and profaneness, in the man they think it is so criminal for a sister of the church to marry."[3] Captain Fisk was only a token for the real object of Stephen West's attack, which was the peculiar combination of secular and sacred in the nature of marriage itself. For, while marriage was a holy estate, "the original design of marriage was, that the social inclination of mankind might innocently enjoy its proper object, the human race propagated under good regulations, children well-educated and provided for and the like; and all in proper subservience to the glory of God and the everlasting good of mankind."[4] New Divinity men like West expected that men and women with full natural ability for spirituality ought to be looking for other things in marriage than satisfying their social inclinations, and they expected that marriage, like church membership itself, would be an exercise in visible sainthood.

What the New Divinity men could not abide, Huntington said, was the implication posed by Mrs. Fisk's wedding: that marriage was a social as well as a religious institution that could be entered into by the unregenerate even if they lacked spiritual virtue, without in any way jeopardizing their ability to be decent husbands and wives. Like the "use of means," grace of course made a marriage gracious, but the proper use of marriage by the unregenerate would certainly make the unregenerate better. "I readily allow, that grace makes the best husbands and wives, parents and children, rulers and subjects," Huntington pleaded, but this was no reason to forget that "marriage is purely a transaction of the civil kind, as any transaction in all the world: This is the great point that has been strangely unobserved and passed over by the Gentlemen that oppose me." Always, in this world, the civil and the sacred are intertwined: they can either oppose each other or help each other but they cannot be disentangled, and men cannot by mere will escape their culture into a utopia of spiritual purity. Grace can complement and even perfect the relations of state, marriage, and family, "but to say that saving grace is essential to these relations, is wild talk indeed."[5]

And this case, Huntington insisted, was the prime example of how wild the New Divinity's talk was. If it is true that believers must not, on God's authority, marry unbelievers, then, on the same authority, Mrs. Fisk's marriage to Captain Fisk was null and void, no matter what civil recognition they enjoyed. Hence, Mr. West ought to be ex-communicating her for fornication, since "Mr. Fisk and she ought by no means to be deemed husband and wife." This was come-outerism at its furtherest stretch, but to Huntington it proved that, cry as West might for pure sainthood, not even he was willing to refuse recognition that a lawful marriage had taken place, though it was one he disliked. If West were true to his own logic, Huntington insisted, "it is only for a man that wants a new wife to call himself a believer, and his wife an immoral profane person, and then put her away, and justify himself by the authority of this church." Not even West could deny civil law that far, although (and here Huntington cast an eye back to the shadowy figure of Edwards that he held to ultimate blame for this foolishness) almost anything could be logically rationalized in Stockbridge, "*so re-markable for important new discoveries.*"[6]

Huntington lost, not unexpectedly, and the unrepentant and excom-municated Mrs. Fisk emigrated to Vermont. But he had made his point: let Edwardseanism have its way and it would unchurch all of New England society. Nor was he the only one to fear that, in *Freedom of the Will*, Edwards had let loose a demon that would induce a fatal divorce between the church and its society.

II

For more than a century after the publication of Joseph Tracy's land-mark study, *The Great Awakening* (1842), the conventional wisdom on that subject had seen it as an event that destroyed the superficial unity of the New England churches and split them into two warring camps: the New Lights, led by Edwards and stimulated by the booming denunciations of George Whitefield, who preached a reinvigorated Cal-vinism; and the Old Lights, led by Charles Chauncy of Boston, horrified at the fanaticism of the revivalists, who were eventually to reject Cal-vinism in favor of Arminianism, Unitarianism, or a genteel deism.

This simple division has encouraged historians of post-Awakening New England religion to assume that all subsequent religious conflicts up to the Revolution merely play out this dichotomy. Just as Tracy offered only a choice of New Light or Old Light *during* the Awakening, so Alan Heimert and a host of others offer us only New Divinity or Arminiamism-Unitarianism-deism *after* the Awakening. The image of the veil of Congregationalism being rent in two, and only two, parts has been too appealing to resist. But the conflict of ideas rarely falls so evenly into such convenient sorting bins. It is much more realistic to think of New England Congregationalism as a spectrum including one large center party, with the noisy jumble of Edwardseans, Old Lights, Baptists, Separates, Anglicans, and others clustering in narrow bands on either side. The center party was composed (and perhaps even that word is too strong, since composition implies intelligent arrangement) of an amorphous and almost undefinable assortment of New England Calvinists who represented solid Trinitarian orthodoxy and who became known, for want of a more decisive term, as the "Old Calvinists."[7]

Historical neglect is only the last injury Old Calvinism has had to endure, for in their day the Old Calvinists suffered all the indignities regularly heaped on those who attempt to walk in ideological paths that occupy the unhappy juxtaposition of moderation and tradition. Hopkins scornfully described the Old Calvinists as those "who would be thought to be Calvinists" even though "they appear to dislike, and never preach, some of the important doctrines of Calvinism; such as the total depravity of man."[8] Samuel Spring called Old Calvinism "a jumble of arminianism and antinomianism both"—Arminian because it teaches men that they can use the means of grace and at least make the number of their sins one less, and antinomian because it teaches them that the inherited and imputed taint of original sin makes it pointless to go all the way to repentance and faith. "He pleads with the former," Spring complained, "that sinners are morally capable of some conformity to the moral law; and he pleads with the latter . . . that they cannot repent because they are destitute of a principle of repentance or because they are dependent."[9] John Smalley accused them of the same duplicity:

> they would have it maintained, indeed, that sinners are unable to do much . . . but then they apprehend, it may, and must be admitted, that sinners are able, by the help of *common* grace to do those things which are connected with, and may be considered as a sort or preliminary conditions of salvation . . . that is, they suppose, if sinners will seek and pray, use the means of grace, and do the best that persons under the circumstances, and having such hearts as they have *may* do: God will not be wanting on his part, or leave them to perish.[10]

On those terms, Hopkins professed surprise that "they choose to call themselves *moderate Calvinists*" when they "might as well, and perhaps more properly, be called *moderate Arminians*."[11]

Not all of this abuse was unjustified, and for two reasons. One is that, in all truth, Old Calvinism sheltered under its wings a number of ministers who stretched the meaning of *Calvinist* to just the breaking point that Hopkins, Spring, and Smalley had indicated. Samuel Langdon, president of Harvard during the Revolution, vehemently declared himself "a Trinitarian and also a Calvinist, in those points which were discussed at the Synod of Dort," and even adopted a governmental conception of the atonement which might as well have been pure New Divinity.[12] But Ezra Stiles pegged him aright when he compared Langdon to Isaac Watts: the Arminianism which "he renounces, I think, has got the ascendency & greatest hold of his Reasoning Powers."[13] Langdon certainly gave to Hopkins, no less than to Stiles, all the evidence needed to support that judgment, and more, when in 1794 he tried to correct Hopkins on what could not be readily corrected. Predestination had nothing to do with divine election, Langdon blurted out, because God only predestinated the activities of large groups, not individuals.

Upon careful enquiry it will appear that the Apostle did not mean to exhibit the doctrine in this latter view . . . but to decide the great question then in dispute whether the Jews, as a nation, were so peculiarly the chosen people of God, or his elect people, that none of the Gentiles could be admitted into his church . . . but they are quite silent as to the election of individuals to eternal salvation by the absolute decrees of God.[14]

If the presence of such waverers accounts for some of Hopkins's contempt for Old Calvinism, it must be conceded that the rest of that contempt was manufactured out of embarrassment. Despite the Langdons, by far the largest number of Old Calvinists drew their dogma from the old standards, from the Westminster Confession and the Saybrook Platform, and not from Edwards. Call it Arminianism or call it antinomianism, it was still the old doctrine, and only by fervidly denouncing the Old Calvinists as half-hearts could the New Divinity obscure the fact that it was they, and not the Old Calvinist regulars, who had departed from the New England Way. Consequently, what one most often hears from Old Calvinism is not sterile liberalism, but the standard orthodoxy of sixteenth- and seventeenth-century Reformed scholasticism. Elijah Sill, delivering an ordination charge in 1770 to a young minister suspected of New Divinity propensities, exhorted him to preach a traditional orthodoxy that was as much at odds with Arminianism as it was with Hopkinsianism.

Insist much, in your preaching, on the great essential truths of the gospel; such as the fall of man, with all its inconceivably awful consequences, and his recovery thro' the unsearchable riches of free grace in Christ;—the nature and necessity of the new birth, with its blessed and happy effects:—that great, fundamental and precious doctrine of justification by the imputed righteousness of Christ, thro' faith alone. And as to that important doctrine of a thorough conviction of sin, or the work of the law on the conscience, as antecedent and preparatory to a saving faith and conversion, be careful to give it due place and weight in your preaching.[15]

Ezra Stiles, convinced that the New Divinity was as much a threat to Congregationalism as deism, labored as president of Yale to keep New Divinity men off the Yale Corporation; he repudiated them precisely because he thought they had strayed from "the Evangelical Doctrines, the Doctrines of Grace as held by the good old Puritans and our Ancestors."[16] Moses Hemmenway declared that his favorite authors were John Owen and Francis Turretin, the standards of the seventeenth-century Reformed confessional literature.[17]

Far from running off wholesale into Arminianism, the Old Calvinists were often as vocal in their resistance to Arminianism, and in their friendliness to revival, as the New Divinity itself. Although Thomas Clap, as president of Yale College, earned the everlasting enmity of the New Divinity for his treatment of David Brainerd and the Cleaveland brothers during the Awakening, and for slandering Edwards afterward, he was also the "main architect" of the campaign against the Arminian Robert Breck in 1734; and the same Clap who organized a virtually "separatist" college church at Yale to protect students from the Arminian influences of the minister of New Haven's First Church, Joseph Noyes; and again the same Clap who was once more inviting Whitefield to Yale by 1755.[18] Jedidiah Mills, who had been the first to make a public attack on Hopkins for promoting "new divinity," also had a long record of published hostility to Arminianism (especially in controversy with his Anglican neighbor Samuel Johnson); he had preached on an itinerating circuit with Bellamy during the Awakening, had fitted David Brainerd for the ministry after his expulsion from Yale, and had endorsed the *Testimony and Advice* of 1743, in which 111 ministers in Massachusetts, Connecticut, and New York joined in support of the Awakening.[19] Solomon Williams, who clashed so bitterly with Edwards over the terms of communion, nevertheless invited Whitefield into his pulpit in Lebanon, Connecticut, and remained his "decided friend."[20]

The very presence of ministers like Huntington and Langdon and

Mayhew among the Old Calvinists, however, acts as a reminder that Old Calvinism, taken as a whole, was an exercise in ambivalence. Unlike the tight codifications of the New Divinity, it was a spectrum of opinion, held together by loyalties of place and time, and for just that reason it could embrace the New Lightism of Jedidiah Mills, the traditionalism of Moses Mather, and the quasi-Arminianism of Experience Mayhew. These variations are so great that it is worth wondering just what kind of loyalties of place and time could hold such diverse types of men together, or, better still, it is worth wondering what induced the New Divinity to address them as though they all did partake of a common identity.

Two things stand out as banners around which Old Calvinism gathered. One was a strange kind of loyalty to the "doctrines of grace"—depravity, election, limited atonement, and so forth. Ministers might quality, redefine, or even ignore these doctrines in their preaching, but they never openly repudiated them either, even when they were in places where, as in Joseph Huntington's Norwich, they could probably have gotten away with it. This may have been because in the mind of Old Calvinism the dogmas of predestination and the like had assumed the status of a historical icon—an ideological version of what later became Plymouth Rock. Long after some New Englanders had stopped loving election as a theological truth, it remained for them an ideological symbol that preserved a needed sense of intellectual continuity with the past. Thomas Clap made the doctrines of grace sound more like an element of genealogy than dogmatics, and even Charles Chauncy, though he eventually wound up beyond the pale of Old Calvinist tolerance, predicated his massive attack on Edwards in 1743 upon the history of New England Calvinism, not upon Calvinism itself.

And not only did this tactic protect ideological supply lines to the past, it also engendered stability in the present, for, once the New Lights had disappeared from the scene of their contentions, the chief threat felt by the established clergy of New England was from the Church of England—whose agents, like Samuel Johnson, wore their Arminianism as brazenly as a campaign badge. Predestination remained vitally important to these New Englanders as a badge of their own. Which point, incidentally, goes some way toward explaining why few Old Calvinists felt any compulsion to perform elaborate metaphysical reconciliations of election and free will. People do not explicate icons; they parade them; they use them as points of resistance; and every now and again, the icons are trotted out to show that they still work, even in defiance of modern rules. And with that, Old Calvinism was content. It did not like being pushed into a more radical version of Calvinism, or being flayed as Arminians when it pushed back.

The other rallying point was a fundamental image of New England society, an image that linked these heterogeneous theologians precisely because it was an image and so ran deeper than the specific tenets of theology. It was the image of a *church-in-society,* the old-as-Winthrop New England idea of a moral community in which the church covenant was the central, unifying political document, identifying who belonged to the town by identifying who belonged to the church. For, however much the notion of covenant may have originally suggested the creation of God's mere *nomina* of a relationship with a specific individual, it eventually came to describe an organic relationship between the generations and among individuals in a certain place (like New England). Under these terms, "covenantal" came to describe an intrinsic linkage of all the parts of a society, not by will, but by birth and deference. The church acted as the outward expression of that organic relationship, and its purpose was not to pluck out the elect from the reprobate and withdraw them into a kind of holy hibernation, but rather to unify potentially disparate elements of society into a declaration of "covenantal," visible holiness—what Philip Henry called "a face of godliness."[21] The baptism of the community's infants, conferring on them at least a "half-way" membership, would underscore the unity of the generations, past and future; participation by all in the public sacraments and in public discipline would unite the community across the present in moral order. As Moses Hemmenway explained, the church exists

for the purpose of observing the ordinances of worship and discipline which Christ has instituted for the edification of the whole body and the several members, and that the light of the Gospel might be held up to the world by . . . the reading and preaching of the word; and that its proper influence and effects might be manifested and exemplified in the christian and orderly conversation of the members in their several places.[22]

Idyllic though the image was, reality had warred against it time and again. The first definition of *covenant*—that of the relationship between God and the individual—described a relationship of *willing,* while the second—that of a relationship between entire generations and places—described a relationship of *being.* Given the Puritan urge toward spiritual purity, the first was constantly threatening to overturn the second. Furthermore, even while John Winthrop preached political community to the first generation of New Englanders, the fact was that their emigration from England had evaporated whatever sense of community they had been born into. The emigration was itself an act of will that disrupted community, and part of the urgency of Winthrop's *Arabella* sermon, "A Model of Christian Charity," was his realization that he faced the difficult task of creating a new sense of community. The Congregational polity, too, was similarly disrupting at the outset, being after all a localized association of covenanting wills, existing in voluntary, not organic, harmony, but only at the outset, for New England's emigrants were by no means of all one mind about the structure of their churches. What was semiofficially known as the Congregational Way soon came to look like parish presbyterianism under Peter Hobart, and mere Anglicanism in a black gown under Richard Mather and Solomon Stoddard. Only after a sleep of one hundred years did the Great Awakening reawaken Congregationalism's voluntaristic and separatistic urges from their slumbers.

What is surprising in all this was not that the Great Awakening challenged the organic notion of covenant, but that it took New England so long to erupt over it. The Great Awakening brought the terrible significance of individual religious experience back to explode this, and the New Divinity swarmed after the Old Calvinists, setting the gracious against the not so gracious, the people against the ministers, and, worst of all, the lone saint against his community. The Old Calvinists never did manage to develop a single strategy to fight back, but, ironically, whatever their confusion over how to respond to Hopkins and Bellamy, the assault of the New Divinity probably gave the Old Calvinists a more startled sense of self-identity than they had ever enjoyed. It also brought them to a common realization of what they could plainly blame their troubles upon: "the very abstruse reasonings of President Edwards on the freedom of the Will."[23]

III

The intellectual ambiguity of Old Calvinism also touched its relations to the person of Jonathan Edwards. Joseph Huntington freely lauded Edwards as "that great luminary of the church" and "our Great Countryman."[24] Both William Hart and Moses Hemmenway tried to invoke

Edwards against the New Divinity at points, and in 1762 Thomas Clap, despite a vicious quarrel with Edwards in the 1740s, introduced *Freedom of the Will* as a textbook in moral philosophy at Yale.[25] For Ezra Stiles, Edwards was one of the "ementissimi" of Yale College, "a great Divine—a good Linguist especially in Hebrew—a good scholar."[26] And it should not come as a surprise to hear these conventionalities trip off Old Calvinist tongues. Edwards was a son of the Connecticut establishment and a member (professionally at least) of the Massachusetts establishment, and if William Hart recognized the danger inherent in calling Hopkins names, that danger was no less concerning Edwards. Moreover, there was a substantial amount in the body of Edwardsean writings that Old Calvinists could appropriate with ease, and the reputation Edwards enjoyed at home and abroad as a reviver of true religion made such an appropriation eminently worth their while.

But it had to be a selective appropriation, because, however much they could admire Edwards as a person, and even as a scholar, they could not swallow his immaterialist metaphysics. Although the Scottish philosophy is so often associated with John Witherspoon and Princeton that it is almost assumed that Witherspoon was the first to bring it to America, it had already begun to acquire a considerable readership in America almost two decades prior to Witherspoon's arrival. Edwards had read Francis Hutcheson, the forerunner of Scottish "common sense" thinking, by 1746, and in 1765, when Edwards's *True Virtue* and Thomas Clap's *An Essay on the Nature and Foundations of Moral Virtue* were published, both Edwards and Clap condemned Hutcheson in terms detailed enough to reveal an intimate reading of him, not to mention betraying an anxiety that many others in New England had done likewise.[27] Hutcheson was also being used by students under Francis Alison's tutelage at the College of Philadelphia in the 1750s, and subsequent Scottish books were evidently in use at Harvard and the College of William and Mary.[28] That the Old Calvinists (with exceptions like Clap) read and approved the Scottish philosophy appears, first, from the fact that so much of the Old Calvinist leadership was Harvard-generated (James Dana, Moses Hemmenway, Jedidiah Morse, and David Tappan were all Harvard graduates); and second, from the fact that Tappan then used Scottish writers like Hutcheson and Thomas Reid as textbooks during his tenure as Hollis Professor of Divinity at Harvard. Almost a century later, Edwards Amasa Park could claim with demonstrable justice, that his Old Calvinist forerunners "were adepts in the philosophy of Reid, Oswald, Campbell, Beattie, Stewart; and this has been termed the *philosophy of common sense.*"[29]

On those terms, however much else they may have respected Edwards, the Old Calvinists could hardly have helped rejecting most of the central premises of his immaterialist metaphysics, and, with them, the theory of will enshrined in *Freedom of the Will.* Beginning with the problem of *substance,* they simply refused to be budged from what the common sense of mankind attested was the only possible foundation for identity and self-consciousness, that of qualities inhering in an underlying essence. "Is not this the most familiar idea we can form of man," asked Samuel Langdon, "that he consists of a body inhabited or animated by an intelligent spirit, with which it is mysteriously united, and continues united until death dissolves the union?"[30] It was Huntington's chief (and probably only) philosophical complaint, years after Edwards's death, that Edwards had fostered a movement which, like "CORNICULA" the spinster, "believes that her soul is not in her body, but her body in her soul; and that she has neither body nor soul, except what consists of a certain assemblage of ideas, maintained by the constant exertion of deity."[31] And Ezra Stiles thought he saw the same legacy at work as he objected to Stephen West turning "the Berclean Ideal Philosophy into Divinity."[32]

In practical terms, this meant that the quality called grace, or the lack of it, might not be part of the immediate consciousness of the individual and hence cannot be judged reliably by the church. "It may be asked," said Moses Hemmenway, posing a rhetorical Edwardsean question, "Are not exercises of grace matter of sensible experience? Are not the acts of our will subject to our own consciousness, as well as to the acts of our judgment? Why then should not one, who has any grace in exercise, be conscious of it, and be able to profess it?" Hemmenway's answer was that grace exists first as a quality in the soul before it ever ascends to the level of consciousness. It is possible to have it without knowing it. Hence it is folly to expect that grace automatically registers itself in its hosts for the direct inspection by the consciousness. "In doing this men are exceedingly liable to deceive themselves; to take those things for signs of grace, or evidences of a gracious state, which are not so"—or, Hemmenway might have added, to create churches full of none but saints rapturously conscious of their sainthood.[33]

In theological terms, this means a rejection of the arbitrary constitutionalism of Edwards in *Original Sin* (and, although the Old Calvinists could not have known it then, the final entries in Edwards's "Notes on the Mind"). Experience Mayhew affirmed that, in the Fall of Man, mankind was present substantially in Adam: "the Persons of their offspring did not then, indeed, personally subsist, but the whole human Nature, and all that was essential to it, did."[34] As a consequence, spiritual death passed on to all men, not because their exercises or lack of them were constitutionally linked to Adam, but because they had been deprived of the "Principle" from which virtuous exercises spring. "This death," Mayhew explained, "does not, properly speaking, consist either in Men's doing that which they should so; but in their Want of such a Principle as is necessary to their doing that which is . . . holy and good."[35]

Similarly, the Old Calvinist stalwarts dismissed Edwards's Augustinian voluntarism in preference for an intellectualism more in accord with the intellectualist psychology of the Scottish philosophers. Samuel Langdon seated depravity in the mind rather than the will, because in his schema the mind continued to be the same leading and directing faculty it had been for John Calvin. Sin results, not from an evil heart or will, but because

the mind is filled with ideas arising from flesh and sense, which have the most powerful effect upon us, too powerful for meer reasonings upon right and wrong. Reason is dethroned, and the flesh has assumed the government of the soul; which must remain enslaved until it is furnished with those heavenly truths which the gospel reveals.[36]

For that reason, it was possible for James Dana to believe that sin was primarily a problem of knowledge rather than affections. "The mind of a moral agent is the true cause of his own election and volitions," Dana wrote; hence, in order to find salvation, " 'tis previously requisite that there be"—not a changed will—but "some competent doctrinal acquaintance with the main articles of the Christian religion." As Dana explained, "Faith has its foundation in reason. . . . Consequently our obligations to believe can extend no farther than our knowledge, or means and opportunities of being inform'd."[37] From there it was but a short space to preaching up the "use of means," since, as Hemmenway never tired of warning, "the saving truth will not be received into the mind and heart of those who never attend to those means."[38]

The popularity of the Scottish philosophy among the Old Calvinists also helps to account for their most visible bone of contention with

Edwardseanism, the *moral sense*. "There is in man a natural faculty whereby he is rendered capable of discerning and distinguishing between moral good and evil, as well as natural," insisted William Hart, a sense which naturally "perceives the one to be right, amiable, and worthy of esteem and honor, the other wrong, hateful and blameworthy, immediately, as soon as these objects are seen by the mind in their true light."[39] Of course, Edwards had been happy to grant that all men have common intuitions about the good—all *natural* men, that is. True virtue, however, was beyond the grasp of mere human intuition and could only be perceived as a result of divine regeneration. But that distinction mattered little enough to Moses Hemmenway: "mankind however depraved in all their faculties, are capable of feeling the force of moral obligation." Men may not love God, but their common moral sense can still dictate that it is proper to serve him. "They who have no holy love to God and his laws, are yet sensible, from the dictates of conscience, that it is their duty to be obedient to the great creator and lawgiver."[40] Nothing could have put more philosophical enmity between Edwards and Old Calvinism than this referring of the deepest moral questions, over the head of the ugliness of human depravity, to a natural internal monitor which could intuitively perceive goodness without the help of grace.

All of these antagonisms with the real Edwards posed a serious problem for those Old Calvinists who wanted to promote an image of Edwards as their own; it was going to be necessary to pick and choose what in Edwards remained congenial to the spirit of Old Calvinism and somehow truncate what from the speculations was not. So they applauded the Edwards of the five great sermons on justification, the "History of Redemption," and the Northampton revivals, and treated the "metaphysics" of Edwards as though it were an eccentricity that needed to be detached from the true Edwards, who was after all very much a staunch Calvinist like themselves. Edwards "had too much sense, and too much grace ever to introduce any of his metaphysics into his divinity," Joseph Huntington disingenuously assured his readers:

Look into his sermons, all his writings in divinity, his History of Redemption, which in my humble opinion, is the most instructive body of divinity that ever was written, by any man uninspired, and you will find him attending to the gospel, and the plain dictates of conscience, and quite as intelligible to persons of good hearts and plain common sense, as any other writer in all the world.[41]

It is hard to believe that Huntington meant a single word of that, and yet Ezra Stiles, too, thought that Edwards's metaphysics could be detached from his theology as an ephemeral embarrassment and the Old Calvinist Edwards salvaged. "In another Generation" Edward's speculations will "pass into as transient Notice perhaps scarce above Oblivion, as Willard or Twiss, or Norton," to be "looked upon as singular & whimsical."[42] This denatured Edwards could then be used to bless the doings of Old Calvinism, and simultaneously serve to expose the New Divinity men as pseudo-Edwardseans, who had manipulated the true Edwards either by overmagnifying his metaphysics or by attaching their metaphysics to his reputation.

There were other Old Calvinists, however, who were from the beginning suspicious of the plausibility of trying to dress Edwards up as one of their own. Chauncey Whittlesey and James Dana believed that Edwards's metaphysics was frankly dangerous and could not be disguised; nevertheless, they were wise enough to see that this danger would never be safely disposed of until someone came up with a Calvinistic theory of will which would justify the sovereignty of God with the same sophistication as Edwards in *Freedom of the Will,* but without involving as a result the drastic separatism of the New Divinity. Whittlesey, who twenty-six years before had been the butt of David Brainerd's scorn and had evidently never forgiven Edwards for taking Brainerd's side, complained to Ezra Stiles in June 1768 about the then-current use of *Freedom of the Will* as a text at Yale. He was convinced that Edwards had, in his efforts to fend off Hobbes, only infected Calvinism with Hobbes's own ideas and definitions. "Hence he from time to time speaks of the Arminian Notion of Liberty which he asserts to be absurd and inconsistent, and of the Liberty which Calvinists maintain, which he asserts to be the only Liberty in the Universe." In particular, Whittlesey could not accept the ultraism inherent in *Freedom of the Will*: not only did it define Calvinist orthodoxy too narrowly, but it did it in ways indistinguishable from Locke or Hobbes. By Edwards's logic, Whittlesey said, "Dr. Watts is the Arminian, and Mr. Locke the Calvinist," and if that were the received truth at Yale, then "some, I fear, will become Deists from their dislike of what is said to be orthodox Christianity; others will become practical, if not speculative Atheists by substituting in their Minds, Fate instead of Deity, or necessity in the Room of an Intelligent Moral Governour."[43]

Whittlesey admitted to Stiles that he was a trifle late in sounding his alarm, but he pleaded, "while his book was regarded as a critical, metaphysical Treatise upon a dark, abstruse, unimportant Subject, I was little concerned about it." But the year before, Jedidiah Mills and Samuel Hopkins had opened the first round in what was branded by Mills as "new divinity," and suddenly the scales fell from Whittlesey's eyes and he beheld the real meaning of *Freedom of the Will*. Now, "the Errors of Arminianism," Whittlesey noted anxiously, "are not only called *Errors*, but damnable and fatal Errors." The New Divinity's demand that New England toe Edwards's line in *Freedom of the Will* was bound to split churches, driving out many who were content with a predestination which did not press them personally out of the churches and into the arms of something much more dangerous. "I fear the Consequences, lest Deism, if not Atheism, should ensue," Whittlesey bleakly confessed.

His scheme, in proportion as it is admitted by any mind, will, I think, unavoidably lessen the odiousness of Sin, in the view of that Mind; yea, if that Mind is not habitually virtuous before, will wholly destroy the Sinfulness of Sin.[44]

Whatever the depth of Whittlesey's apprehensions, the task of confronting *Freedom of the Will* head-on instead fell to James Dana, who would later succeed Whittlesey as the pastor of Old Calvinism's foremost pulpit, the First Church of New Haven. Dana was reputed to be somewhere out near the fringe of Old Calvinism with Experience Mayhew, and when in 1758 he had been called to the pulpit of the First Church in Wallingford, Connecticut, a minority of that congregation vigorously protested the call on the grounds that Dana was a closet Arminian. Thus ensued a year of bitter controversy over who had authority to call whom, with the Consociation of New Haven denying the legality of Dana's call (siding with the minority) and the majority of the congregation denying the Consociation's authority to tell it what to do. In the end, the church declared its own independence, and retained Dana.[45] Many issues, both political and ecclesiological, were sucked into the Wallingford business, but to James Dana the most obvious issue it resurrected was the old conflict of New Light and Old Light. When Jedidiah Mills's clash with Hopkins in 1767 made it apparent that the New Divinity proposed to reawaken this conflict all across New England, Dana needed no further encouragement to strike back at it, and he did so by striking at the New Divinity's basic text. Although, like Whittlesey, Dana initially skimmed *Freedom of the*

Will after its publication, he had hastily concluded "that few who might read it might bestow enough attention to understand it; and of those who should attentively read and understand it, few would admit its foundation principles." But, just as they had for Whittlesey, the New Divinity's applications of *Freedom of the Will*'s principles rapidly disabused him of this complacency, and "from the great reputation of Mr. *Edwards,* and the prevalence of his doctrine, he came to a resolution of giving the book another and attentive reading."[46] The result was Dana's two-part *Examination of the late Reverend President Edwards's 'Enquiry on Freedom of Will,'* published in 1770 and 1773.

Dana began his assault on *Freedom of the Will* by calling into question Edwards's most basic premise about volition, that willing was the mind's choosing. If "liberty consists not in a power of willing, but in an opportunity of doing what is already willed—of *executing* a choice already made, not in a power of chusing," then Dana could see no sense in describing such a mere execution of orders as worthy of the adjective *free.* "How is it possible that action and conduct should be free, and yet be the effects of a necessary cause?" Dana asked, "Or how can that be called a voluntary determination, which is the effect of necessity?"[47]

Nor was Dana in a mood to be put off by Edwards's answer that liberty referred to means and not origins, to being free to choose something, not in being free to use a power of choosing choices. "The *act of volition* or *choice* is a different thing from the *pursuit* or *execution* of what is willed or chosen," Dana acknowledged, but to restrict liberty to "the latter only" was to make nonsense of "moral agency and accountableness."[48] If "the only things wherein human liberty consists, is, a power of executing what is already willed—if volition springs not from man as the source, cause, or efficient of it—if he is only the *subject,* the *doer,* the *actor* of sin," then Dana wanted to know exactly who was the source of volition. "Who then is the positive cause and fountain of it? If not the creature, who but the creator?"[49]

And yet Dana was not so foolish as to then go ahead and ascribe a self-determining power to the will—Edwards had prepared too well the trap of infinite regress for those headstrong enough to rush in that direction. Dana instead declared that, while men were indeed free to determine themselves, freedom belonged to the mind, and the authority for this discovery lay in the power of the moral sense. "Let a man look into his own breast, and he cannot but perceive inward freedom—

Inward Freedom—For if freedom be not in the mind it is nowhere."[50] In contrast to Edwards, who made the will's actions an extension of the mind's perception of the greatest apparent good, Dana pried apart will and mind, giving to the mind freedom to perceive and then deliberate among perceptions and then choose, after which only then did the will proceed to the actualization of the choice. "And," Dana added, "liberty in the mind implies self-determination." He was, in short, a classic intellectualist. "The mind of a moral agent," Dana reiterated, "is the true cause of his own election and actions."[51]

With this fundamental objection in place, Dana now moved out against Edwards along two parallel lines, one theoretical and the other practical. Along the axis of theory, Dana had two objections in mind, the concept of *motive* and the natural/moral distinction. Dana at once sensed the elusiveness of Edwards's definition of motives and his desire to show "that the strongest motive is the *immediate* cause of every act of choice."[52] However,

We are very sensible he had no *fixed* meaning to this word in his writings. . . . In the sense he sometimes uses the word, it is not *extrinsic* to the mind, nor even *antecedent* to volition, nor *distinct* from it—consequently, hath not a tendency to excite volition, is not the cause [but rather] the occasion of it.[53]

Dana understood what Edwards was up to in his occasionalist explanation of cause, and flatly rejected it as a viable understanding of *cause*. Dana's more conventional notion of causality demanded that motives, if they were to cause anything, had to function as efficients. And if motives operated as efficient causes, then their operation must be of absolute necessity. In that case, the question of ultimate blame once more recurred. "If the highest motive were allowed to be the *next* and *immediate* cause of volition, this is no resolution of the question," Dana repeated, "as it doth not show the *original* and *true* cause thereof."

To what extrinsic cause then, or to whom, are the volitions of men to be ascribed, since they are not the cause of them themselves? . . . According to Mr. *Edwards,* it is the strongest motive from without. But motives to choice are exhibited to the mind by some agent: By whom are they exhibited? . . . Will it now be said, that GOD is the cause of those dispositions of heart, and acts of the will, which are so odious in their nature? On Mr. Edwards's scheme, this must be said.[54]

The real absurdity in this (to Dana) was not only what it implied about God, but what it tried to make motives into. In fact, said Dana, motives have no necessary causal power at all, occasional or efficient.

"It cannot be that motives are themselves efficient causes," Dana wrote, because it is evident that people often choose what is neither compelling nor good.[55] "Moral agents many times sin immediately against present light and conviction, while they have *full in their view* the wiser choice. And what is this but to determine themselves contrary to the greatest apparent good?" Edwards had been in error to link perception and willing, mind and volition, so close together as to think that the first necessarily involved the second. "Perception and volition are as different as sight and taste," Dana declared; "we think nothing is more evidently false than the opinion, that the affections evermore follow the last practical judgment of the understanding."[56] On that basis, Old Calvinist logic dictated that motives had no real role to play in volition; and if not motives, nor still God, then men themselves were the real determiners of their own volitions. Dana reasoned that "if (as has been shown) volition is not always as the highest motive; then when these meet, it is not necessarily . . ."[57]; and "if motives are not efficient causes, nor the Deity through the intervention of them, then moral agents themselves are."[58]

Dana did not go so far as to deny that motives have *some* influence. But beside Edwards's "motives," Dana's were piddling. For Dana, since volition and understanding were entirely different functions of the mind, then motives always remained extrinsic, purely *ab extra* phenomena which never could be so far taken into the knowing process as to have an immediate impact on the will. So long as motives remained exterior to the knower, without exercising determining power over him, it was pretty much up to the knower to decide which motives he would be influenced by. Hence, Dana concluded:

a moral agent either hath power to originate an act of suspension, and so bring himself into the view of new motives; or the suspending act proceeds from a motive extant in his mind at the same instant with some motive to immediate election or action.[59]

Dana also rejected the other keystone of Edwards's theory of will, the natural necessity/moral necessity distinction. Dana was dubious from the beginning about describing necessity in any but relational terms, and he seems to have foreshortened his definition of *necessity* so that it stuck solely to mechanism. To assume that there was a necessity resulting from any other than efficient, mechanical causes seemed to Dana to be little more than airy talk. To base necessity on terminological connections alone (whether moral or natural) seemed

The Reverend Jonathan Edwards. Oil portrait, c. 1750–1755, by Joseph Badger
Yale University Art Gallery. Bequest of Eugene Phelps Edwards, 1938

A careful and ſtrict

ENQUIRY

INTO

The *modern* prevailing Notions

OF THAT

FREEDOM of WILL,

Which is ſuppoſed to be eſſential

TO

Moral Agency, Vertue and *Vice, Reward* and *Puniſhment, Praiſe* and *Blame.*

By JONATHAN EDWARDS, A.M.

Paſtor of the Church in *Stockbridge.*

Rom. ix. 16. *It is not of him that willeth——*

BOSTON, N. E.

Printed and Sold by S. KNEELAND, in Queen-ſtreet, MDCCLIV.

(Left) Title page of Jonathan Edwards's *Freedom of the Will*, published in 1754 by S. Kneeland. *Courtesy, Massachusetts Historical Society*

(Below) Congregational church, Northampton, where Jonathan Edwards succeeded his grandfather, Solomon Stoddard, as minister in 1729; he was dismissed in 1750 as the result of a disagreement with his parishioners over the qualifications for communion. *Courtesy, First Church, Northampton*

(Left) Samuel Hopkins, student of Jonathan Edwards and leading proponent of the New Divinity; his rendering of Edwards's ideas came to be known pejoratively as "Hopkinsianism." Oil portrait by Joseph Badger
Courtesy, Massachusetts Historical Society

(Below left) Jonathan Edwards the Younger, second son of Jonathan Edwards, trained for the ministry by Joseph Bellamy. He was New Divinity minister in White Haven, Connecticut, for twenty-six years until, like his father, he was dismissed for excessive emphasis on visible sainthood. Oil painting by Reuben Moulthrop
Courtesy, Schaffer Library, Union College

(Below) First issue of *The Connecticut Evangelical Magazine*, published in Hartford in 1800, popular source for accounts of revivals under New Divinity preaching.

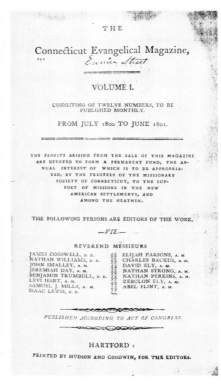

THE

Connecticut Evangelical Magazine,

VOLUME I.

CONSISTING OF TWELVE NUMBERS, TO BE
PUBLISHED MONTHLY.

FROM JULY 1800 TO JUNE 1801.

THE PROFITS ARISING FROM THE SALE OF THIS MAGAZINE ARE DEVOTED TO FORM A PERMANENT FUND, THE ANNUAL INTEREST OF WHICH IS TO BE APPROPRIATED, BY THE TRUSTEES OF THE MISSIONARY SOCIETY OF CONNECTICUT, TO THE SUPPORT OF MISSIONS IN THE NEW AMERICAN SETTLEMENTS, AND AMONG THE HEATHEN.

THE FOLLOWING PERSONS ARE EDITORS OF THE WORK,

—VIZ.—

REVEREND MESSIEURS

JAMES COGSWELL, d. d.
NATHAN WILLIAMS, d. d.
JOHN SMALLEY, a. m.
JEREMIAH DAY, a. m.
BENJAMIN TRUMBULL, d. d.
LEVI HART, a. m.
SAMUEL J. MILLS, a. m.
ISAAC LEWIS, d. d.

ELIJAH PARSONS, a. m.
CHARLES BACKUS, a. m.
DAVID ELY, a. m.
NATHAN STRONG, a. m.
NATHAN PERKINS, a. m.
ZEBULON ELY, a. m.
ABEL FLINT, a. m.

PUBLISHED ACCORDING TO ACT OF CONGRESS.

HARTFORD :

PRINTED BY HUDSON AND GOODWIN, FOR THE EDITORS.

(Above) Ezra Stiles, president of Yale during the late eighteenth century, earlier, Congregational minister in Newport, Rhode Island; an "Old Calvinist," who accused the New Divinity of "mediocrity."
Yale University Art Gallery. Bequest of Dr. Charles Jenkins Foote, B.A. 1883, M.D. 1890

(Right) Ezra Stiles Ely, chaplain of New York City Hospital and author of *A Contrast Between Calvinism and Hopkinsianism* (1811), which berated the New Divinity.
Courtesy, Bob Robinson, Old Pine Street Church, Philadelphia

(above) Edward Dorr Griffin, president of Williams College and popular revivalist during first half of the nineteenth century; a student of Jonathan Edwards the younger, he was a third-generation New Divinity preacher.

Courtesy, Franklin Trask Library, Andover Newton Theological School

(above right) Nathanael Emmons, third-generation New Divinity preacher who, in turn, trained eighty-seven students during fifty-five years as minister of Franklin, Massachusetts.

Courtesy, Massachusetts Historical Society

(right) Asahel Nettleton, third-generation New Divinity preacher and successful New England revivalist who, according to Bennet Tyler, awakened "no less than thirty thousand souls."

Gift of Adelbert Henry Stevens. The Connecticut Historical Society, Hartford

Andover Theological Seminary, the first Congregational seminary, founded in 1808; it provided an alternative to Harvard and Yale or the parlor seminaries and log colleges of the New Divinity preachers.
Courtesy, Massachusetts Historical Society

Princeton Seminary, founded in 1812, the center of Presbyterian teaching in the nineteenth century, standing in opposition to New Divinity Presbyterianism; to the far left is Archibald Alexander's house.
Courtesy, Speer Library, Princeton Theological Seminary

(Left) Leonard Woods, student of Nathanael Emmons and professor of theology at Andover Theological Seminary for thirty-eight years; he moved away from New Divinity Edwardseanism.
Courtesy, Franklin Trask Library, Andover Newton Theological School

(Below, left) Archibald Alexander, advocate of Old School Presbyterianism and first professor of Princeton Theological Seminary.
Courtesy of Office of History, Presbyterian Church (U.S.A.)

Nathaniel William Taylor, Yale's first professor of Didactic Theology when
the Divinity School was founded in 1822; an advocate of old Calvinism,
Taylor challenged Edwards's position on the will, seeking to counter both
the New Divinity and Unitarianism.
Yale University Art Gallery. Gift of Students of Divinity School in 1843

even more an exercise in useless distinctions. But even if Dana had been willing to grant that natural necessity could be the result merely of stated connections between certain natural terms, Dana could not see how it was possible to claim that a moral necessity, resulting from the connection of moral terms, was in principle or in reality any different from natural necessity. He was even more skeptical that Edwards could say that the one necessity was devoid of moral connotation, and the other full of it.

What Mr. *Edwards* intended by a *moral* cause, we cannot satisfy ourselves. Sometimes he appears to reason as if he supposed there was *really no distinction* between a moral and natural cause, or none to be perceived; while more generally he seems to suppose a distinction of great importance; which however, he hath not so clearly pointed out as were to be wished.[60]

In a more blunt mood, Dana simply declared the famous distinction a fraud. "After all that hath been said, *moral necessity* is, properly speaking, *natural necessity*; *moral* power is *natural* power," Dana wrote; "the latter is interwoven in our frame no otherwise than the former."[61]

Dana appealed to two sources to support this dismissal of Edwards's cherished logic. First, he asked simply whether it corresponded to anything anyone had ever observed in human moral affairs. Dana saw as clearly as Bellamy and Smalley that a person under moral necessity had to be constantly and completely of a certain moral character; i.e., the virtuous woman in Edwards's example had to be completely virtuous all the time before a terminological connection like moral necessity could be established between the woman and her necessary morality. "Necessity is *fixed* and *uniform,* admitting of no dissonance of character," Dana shrewdly observed; the problem for Edwards is that no one Dana knew had ever lived like that. "Upon the whole," Dana found that even where "powerful motives to holiness" are "joined with a prevailing propensity this way," even then "there are in many instances contrary volitions." Edwards might have been too holy himself to have noticed this, Dana hinted, but it was nevertheless true that even the best men "are called to watch and pray. . . . They are, therefore, under no moral necessity of being perfect nor indeed can be free from sin in this life."[62] Contrary to Edwards's habit of seeing the world in either-or terms, the *real* world, according to Dana, labored under "the *joint* influence of moral and natural necessity in moral events—their influence is closely linked together" and cannot be separated either for theoretical or ecclesiastical purposes."[63]

Dana's second objection to the natural/moral distinction grew out of another sharp insight into the implications of Edwards's logic, for Dana also saw that by wedging apart natural and moral necessity, it was possible to put all the explanation for moral behavior on the actions of the will alone. Human nature, the tainted substance that claimed so large a role in the classical Calvinist scheme, was relegated to unimportance, and maybe even put out of the way completely. Dana had seen that Edwards "blends together moral motives and inducements with moral habits, inclinations and dispositions, as though they were precisely the same"—as though habits and dispositions were as ephemeral and ideational as motives.[64] He now saw that "if moral necessity lies in the will, and is the will's propensity, it either follows that there is no good or evil in any dispositions implanted in the hearts of men by nature"—or that there is no nature.[65] The elimination of substance, dimly perceived as it was by Dana in *Freedom of the Will*, was still enough to give him further ground for dismissing Edwards. By that thinking, not even God could be holy, for "would Mr. *Edwards* deny, that the holiness of GOD, his moral rectitude in general is necessary *in its own nature?*"[66] Again, everything in Dana's theological and philosophical legacy rose up against this, and together convinced him that Edwards had wrought a net of words lacking in either theoretical worth or observable confirmation.

Having demolished to his satisfaction the two great towers of *Freedom of the Will*, Dana turned an ominous finger to what had propelled him and Whittlesey to a confrontation with Edwards: the practical danger of *Freedom of the Will*. The work was, to begin with, offensive and dangerous to the churches of New England. So long as Edwards posited "such a constant and unfailing connection or co-incidence between volition and the greatest apparent good," then Dana realized that "it seems hardly proper to speak of *tendency* and *influence* in motives to choice," since "so *sure* and *perfect* a connection of causes and effects, antecedents and consequents, as he hath endeavored to make appear, leaves no room to speak of a *meer tendency* in motives."[67] This abolition of moral gradualism rendered the Half-Way Covenant, the "use of means," and the whole notion of the church as a covenantal entity obsolete, and Dana rightly pointed to Edwards as the chief engineer of the catastrophe the Hopkinsians were bringing down on the steeples of New England.

The doctrine of necessary connection of means and ends as stated by Mr. *Edwards* implies one or other of the following things: Either that no means are employed with the unregenerate to their conversion—or none that have a tendency to that end—or that they have not a moral power of using them— or their use of them is certainly and infallibly successful.[68]

Obviously, Edwards was not guilty of the second or third of those options. That left to Edwards only the denial of the use of means. "By his own confession and argument," announced Dana, "commands, invitations Etc. are of no use where there is a moral necessity of being biassed, or going the contrary."[69] And in that case it was Edwards and *Freedom of the Will,* rather than just the New Divinity, that was the real menace.

Since Edwards was so dangerous to the churches, Dana felt no compunctions about appealing to the galleries of those churches in a series of *ad hominem* attacks. First, Dana said, Edwards was *no Calvinist.* True to Old Calvinist propensities, Dana denounced Edwards not just for being wrong but for being an iconoclast along with it. "Whatever moral inability belongs to unregenerate men by nature," Dana proclaimed for all to hear, at least "Calvinistic divines have ever considered the inability of mankind to holiness as the natural and judicial consequences of sin." Unlike Edwards, "they don't represent this inability in the race of Adam as merely moral, but as both natural and moral. They assert the impotency of the understanding, as of the will."[70] Furthermore, Dana insisted that "Calvinistic divines have ever maintained" that depravity and inability were not "*original, but consequent to the fall.*" And on he went: "Calvinistic divines" held to "*original, internal* freedom in man," to "moral imbecility" as "the *punishment* of the first offense," and to so many other tenets Edwards had plowed aside that it appeared as though Edwards were somehow un-New-Englandish—which was, of course, the whole point of the exercise.[71]

Dana's next popular indictment was that Edwards, no longer fully Calvinistic, was now *too metaphysical.* Metaphysics, as Dana expected his readers to know, was a poison best left alone, especially since the moral sense was already sufficient to detect right and wrong.

Principles manifest on first proposal, if men will open their eyes, neither need nor can receive any assistance from metaphysics; and those who would make them undergo the peril of a metaphysical scrutiny may find they have exposed them to be rejected. It is often said, that physic oftener kills than cures. Such is metaphysic to the mind. . . . The plainest and most important principles of revelation would not endure a metaphysical disquisition.[72]

Alas, poor Edwards! this was just the unhappy quagmire into which he had stumbled while speculating on the will. Although Dana made the ritual genuflection to Edwards as a great divine, and congratulated him on having "had a strong practical sense of religion, which over-balanced his theory," nevertheless, the truth was that in *Freedom of the Will* he had well-nigh "philosophized" himself into "skepticism."[73] Dana, with cruel generosity, called for pity on Edwards, rather than casting stones. On *Freedom of the Will* itself, however, Dana had no mercy: there, he cried, lurked outright *skepticism,* the great Edward-sean sin. To make the offense of *Freedom of the Will* all the plainer, Dana arranged in parallel columns quotes from *Freedom of the Will,* Spinoza, Trenchard and Gordon, Collins, Hume, Leibniz, and Hobbes, demonstrating not so much that Edwards was in error as that he was keeping bad company. Whether *Freedom of the Will* "was copied from Mr. *Hume, Hobbs, Spinoza,* or any of the old heathen Philosophers, we do not say," Dana concluded.[74] He might as well have insinuated that Edwards was taking dictation from the Devil.

What Edwards ought to have done, Dana decided, was to have heeded the moral sense (and Dana included copious allusions to Thomas Reid for the benefit of those who wanted specifics). "That we have internal liberty is apparent from our *moral discernment,*" Dana wrote, and if only Edwards had cultivated something that sounded very much like Scottish common-sense thinking, he would have seen that "if any truth be plain, this is, that man is free," because "next to the consciousness of our own existence is that of our moral freedom."[75] But Edwards had long before rejected the Gospel according to the moral sense, both in *Freedom of the Will* and in *True Virtue,* and on the counts of both consciousness and freedom. In the long run, it was as much for that as for the specific offenses contained in *Freedom of the Will* that Dana marched out against him.

It must be conceded that Dana's campaign was not an ill-conceived one. He challenged Edwards at several important points, and if his grasp of the entirety of *Freedom of the Will* had its weaknesses, he had unquestionably acquired a sound hold on its basic premises. But as loudly as Dana blew his trumpets, the walls Edwards had built would not come tumbling down. To have been successful in squelching *Freedom of the Will*'s usefulness in New England, Dana would have first had to attack Edwards's occasionalism head-on and refuted it. Instead, Dana contented himself with ignoring it and explaining how, on *his* terms, Edwards's "motives" made no sense. Second, Dana's rejection of the moral/natural distinction was predicated on his own personal observation that on one ever really lives according to the all-or-nothing categorizations this celebrated distinction implied. Dana overestimated the impact of simple observations of fact on the armor of ideology. It mattered little to Hopkins or Bellamy that James Dana was not himself of this absolutist temperament, or had no parishioners who were. To Hopkins and Bellamy, Dana was not describing a simple reality; he was confessing his own deadness and articulating—not solving—the problem Edwards had been trying to solve. What if Dana had never seen such a virtuous woman as Edwards described? That only meant, to Hopkins and Bellamy, that New England churches like Dana's had not demanded enough virtue.

Dana might have given serious embarrassment to the Edwardseans if he could have pressed harder on Edwards's departures from traditional Calvinism, and especially on the subject of *nature,* and shown that Old Calvinism could never comfortably embrace Edwards, and that the New Divinity was really a departure from New England orthodoxy. But Dana discerned the problem of substance too dimly to make a good case of it, and the doctrines he borrowed from "Calvinistic divines" were just the sort of wishy-washy Isaac Watts–type statements that engendered respect for Edwards's forthrightness. Ultimately, however, Dana failed to embarrass the Edwardseans by anything he had said chiefly because he said them too late. Had Dana taken Edwards more seriously at first reading, and written his *Examinations,* say, in 1758, at the beginning of his ministry, he might have done more in nipping Hopkinsianism in the bud. By 1770 the New Divinity was already too far down the road to be caught by Dana's arguments.

The comparative ineffectualness of Dana's critique rests simply on the fact that it was a critique, and not an alternative. The practical dangers posed by the Edwardseans to the equilibrium of New England Congregationalism were all predicated on the formidable analysis of volition Edwards had provided in *Freedom of the Will,* for both Whittlesey and Dana saw that *Freedom of the Will* was the bridge between Edwards's "metaphysics" and the violent agitations of the New Divinity. To halt the Edwardseans in their relentless tracks would require the offering of a rival theory of volition, stated in terms as formidable as Edwards's and fully able to satisfy the demands of theological Calvinism for doctrines of depravity and responsibility, but which would somehow avoid leading people to the conclusions that *Freedom of the Will* had led the Edwardseans to. Without such a positive alternative, Dana's negativism could do little more than annoy.

Dana thought to save Calvinism by blending, chameleonlike, as far into the background of self-determination as he could, and he resisted Edwards's attempts to flush New Englanders out of hiding to go fight the spirit of the times in open combat. Much as he wanted to embarrass Edwards by connecting him with Hobbes, he was embarrassed at being even formally connected with the kind of Calvinism espoused by Edwards. Only three years before the publication of the first of his *Examinations*, Dana had been telling a Harvard graduating class that "God's permitting sin is to us unsearchable" and that "humility and modesty teach us to acquiesce in the sovereign pleasure of the all-perfect governor of the world, rather than attempt a solution of this abstruse point."[76] This tactical agnosticism allowed Dana to ignore questions put to him by Hobbesian materialism while permitting him to retain intact his reputation as a Calvinist. *Freedom of the Will*, by tackling these abstruse points, made such humility and modesty now look like cowardice; only by attacking Edwards could Dana continue to enjoy his truce with the spirit of the eighteenth century undisturbed.

IV

If some Old Calvinists were suspicious of Edwards for not playing by their rules in *Freedom of the Will*, many others were furious when the New Divinity began applying the doctrines of *Freedom of the Will* to church affairs. Israel Holly denounced the New Divinity as "that vile and hateful novelty," and William Hart declared that "this new system, or rather chaos of divinity, is a hard-hearted, arbitrary, cruel tyrant, a tormentor of souls."[77] And not only was the New Divinity cruel, it was also haughty and presumptuous. "Am I a competent judge to pronounce a sentence of inability against God," Beach Newton asked Hopkins and Bellamy; and if not Beach Newton, why should Bellamy and Hopkins have authority to speculate on God's wisdom or lack thereof in the permission of sin? "How can I prove that the world would not have been more perfect if there had been no sin, no disorders, no devils. . . ?"[78] Others found outlet for their rage in scorn, holding up the New Divinity as the butt of ridicule. "I did think these Doctrines could not . . . be believed by a rational man," Israel Dewey told Samuel Hopkins, who was then his minister in Great Barrington.[79] The New Divinity, added William Hart, "offers as great affront to reason, common sense and experience as the doctrines of Rome." So, Samuel Moody asked Bellamy, "so dextrous in arithmetical Calculations," if so much sin produced so much happiness, weren't people just dreadful bored when virtuous? "How did the inhabitants of Heaven do for Happiness before this Apostacy and Misery? Why, upon Mr. *Bellamy's* Scheme they were very poorly off; and wanted some of the most essential and exalted Ingredients of Happiness."[80]

Worst of all, the Old Calvinists thundered against the New Divinity as disturbers of the peace and public morals. Of John Bacon, Stephen West's chief ally in the Fisk case at Stockbridge, Joseph Huntington said, "he is a great incendiary, and has been rejected from place to place, advanced monstrous doctrines, and is like to do mischief all his days, unless his bad influence is suppressed."[81] When Bacon protested this charge, Huntington merely asked that Bacon's New Divinity doctrines speak for themselves.

Would he have us send to Sturbridge and summon the whole congregation, to give us some account of his much famed sermons and prayers in that place on the Lord's Day, concerning the infinite excellency and utility of all sin in general, and every great sin in particular? Shall we now prove to his face, that when he was reproved in the evening, by a very wise, judicious, and godly gentleman, for the shocking work he had made, he broke out in great wrath, that he had said nothing more in favor of sin than he ought to, that he would give thanks to God for all sin, and every sin, as he had done that day, and that *if his wife should cuckold him that very night, he should give thanks to his God for it in his morning prayer.*[82]

By preaching morality like that to sinners, and then telling them that attempts to reform those sins could make them even more damnable, the New Divinity would be instrumental in "the introduction of paganism in this land—the expulsion of family prayer—the neglect of public worship—the profanation of the holy Sabbath—and the ruin of candidates for, and young gentlemen in, the sacred ministry."[83] Ebenezer Devotion declared that the attack on the use of means "mightily co-incides with the indolence, backwardness, and wickedness" of the "graceless" who now were provided with pious excuse for wallowing comfortably in their sins.[84] "When we turn our eyes and behold," Jedidiah Mills lamented, what do we see?

once famous towns, churches, and societies, lying in ruin, broken, as in the place of dragons, altar erected against altar, to the number of four or five in a single parish; universal benevolence, with every social and divine vertue, in a sad degree banished . . . the adversary triumphing over all attempts to restore peace, charity, good order, and unanimity in the worship of God.[85]

Beach Newton even offered personal testimony of the danger posed to morality by the New Divinity, for "I found by reading such as E———s, B———y, and I know not whom, my abhorrence of sin did much abate, and a more favourable idea of vice grew up insensibly in my mind."[86]

But worse than just encouraging New Englanders in their native, home-grown corruptions, the New Divinity's doctrines had opened the door to the foreign menace of deism, and worse. "These principles vacate all the obligation of natural and reveal'd religion," Ebenezer Devotion expostulated, thereby having (according to Joseph Hunting-ton) "a great tendency . . . to promote the cause of deism and even of atheism."[87] The deist "appears to be an intimate friend and special companion" of the Hopkinsians, Huntington remarked; "they seem both to have read the same new divinity, so called."[88] The kind of God proposed by the New Divinity was so arbitrary, so heedless of human merit, that Samuel Moody believed that Christianity offered in these colors will "tend to increase Deism and infidelity. For if the most zealous Advocates for the divine Authority of the Scriptures draw the Proof of such Doctrines from thence; will it not naturally lead men to disbelieve and reject them?"[89] This view of God as the ordainer of sin "may make a thousand deists and profane profligates under the gos-pel," Jedidiah Mills prophesied, "but sure has not the remotest ten-dency to make one true and real Christian."[90] Hence, Israel Holly concluded, "many fly to those sectaries for refuge, to shun this vile and abominable doctrine. And the advocates for this novelty are eventually driving the country fast into Deism and Universalism."[91] In other words, the New Divinity were guilty of precisely the same things for which Edwards and *Freedom of the Will* were being condemned by Newton and Dana.

However, once the Old Calvinists had exhausted their criticism, they settled down to shoring up three major breaches which *Freedom of the Will* had made in the walls of established Congregationalism, and through which the New Divinity had been irresistibly pouring. Their first, and admittedly most ineffectual, counterattack was launched against the Edwardsean psychology. Not surprisingly, it was in many ways a repetition of Dana's critique of Edwards. The two major critics of New Divinity psychology, Samuel Langdon and Moses Hemmenway, were, like Dana, intellectualists and owed a heavy debt to the Scottish philosophers. Langdon aired a particularly intellectualist complaint when he found that Hopkins did not properly subordinate will to understanding as distinct categories within the mind, "and represents it as chusing, or willing without any regard to light in the mind, or rather without any distinct views of one or another." That was something of an exaggeration, but that did not prevent Langdon from understanding that for the Edwardseans the will was sovereign: "it is not under the direction and government of the understanding."[92]

To Langdon, this was impossible, chiefly because he found it difficult to think of willing as a rational function of the mind unless it worked on the basis of perceptions already processed into rational options by the understanding. "Can the Dr. mean anything by the choice which such a kind of soul makes, when it has no objects of choice in view?" Even if we concede a little and say that the will responds to simple perceptions in the mind, the case is no better to Langdon's thinking. Perhaps the will could function, and even function freely according to these perceptions (which was the essential point demanded by Edwards's description of the will being *as* the greatest apparent good). But to Langdon, that kind of volition was neither rational nor genuinely free.

if its volitions are determined by the appearance of objects, then indeed it may have liberty in preference or rejecting; but this liberty must be exercised according to the light in which objects appear desirable, or undesirable; and if it has no choice in this respect, it is no longer a rational being or moral agent, but a mere machine under an impulsive power.[93]

In Langdon's psychology, "the first and simplest idea we form of ourselves is that we are thinking beings, or have an intellectual faculty." Depravity was a fact of the mind, not the will; sin occurred when "reason is dethroned, and the flesh has assumed the government of the soul"; redemption ensued when the understanding is "furnished with those heavenly truths which the gospel reveals."[94] In the face of an intellectualism so thoroughly dug in, the Edwardseans' glorification of the will was a simple and fundamental error. Langdon even saw clearly enough that the New Divinity had made the will so important that it had totally obscured not only understanding, but nature. In Langdon's estimate, Hopkins's "philosophy . . . seems to be this, That the Will is most properly the soul itself."[95]

Moses Hemmenway preferred to hammer away at this last point even though he was as thoroughly an intellectualist as Dana and Langdon, and shared their criticism of the Edwardsean will. But to prove the error of the New Divinity, and show that all sin did not lie in sinning or willing at all, Hemmenway himself proposed to revise the traditional psychology. Essentially, he objected to Edwards's proclivity for phasing "inclination" into "will"; in reality, will was, with the intellect, simply a "remote" power for knowing or willing. He dared to one-up the New Divinity by agreeing that, *contra* classical Calvinism, the understanding was morally indifferent. But in that case, so was the will, for both were merely instruments, "remote powers" of the soul, "indifferently capable" of either sin or holiness. These remote powers actually stood in contrast to the "inclination," for in the "inclination" were located the real underlying moral principles and direction of the soul, which provided the "next power" for action. While the faculties may *act,* the moral content and direction of their actings are dependent on some underlying "subjective meetness and disposition of the agent" which provides the moral objective of the soul's actings.[96]

Hemmenway's psychological formula was striking, though hardly entirely original, and its chief purpose appears to have been not to chart new theoretical waters but to push out into the open the New Divinity's tendency to do away entirely with substance and make man a chain of willings. And, as William Breitenbach contends, Hemmenway was more successful than any other Old Calvinist critic of Edwards or the Edwardseans, since he helped in large measure to throw an apple of discord into the New Divinity camp.[97] By forcing the Edwardseans to decide for themselves just what Edwards meant by will and by inclination, Hemmenway contributed to splitting the New Divinity into the Taste and Exercise schemes. But it cannot be said, all the same, that Hemmenway or Langdon grappled with all the problems they needed to solve. Ill-focused, and in Hemmenway's case as much a departure from orthodoxy as the New Divinity itself, Old Calvinism's psychological critique lacked the subtlety it needed to do more than just slow the New Divinity down. Their own distaste for metaphysics, and suspicion of what Jedidiah Mills sneered at as "too great a fondness for, and dependence upon the conclusions come into, as the result of subtle metaphysical reasoning," left Old Calvinism vulnerable at just that point to the most subtle metaphysicians in America.[98]

Old Calvinism had more trenchant and interesting things to say about the New Divinity's applications of Edwards to the churches. So long as depravity was rooted in nature, prior to exercise, Old Calvinists would deny that men had the kind of full natural ability to repent which the New Divinity ascribed to them. And in that case they likewise denied that a church could demand a conscious act of complete *consent,* or a profession of saving grace, before allowing people to church membership. As both depravity and grace were substantial qualities, men lacked ability to change their condition through an act of will; and, lacking the ability to will such a change, men could never hope to become gracious by an instantaneous decision.

There was no purpose, then, to extorting from people a confession of an experience or a sanctity they could not possibly attain, nor excluding those who could not confess either one. "I find no warrant in the Gospel to excommunicate a rightful church member, a serious and credible professor of an unblameable life," said Moses Hemmenway, simply "because he has not such an undoubting confidence in his own fitness."[99] Besides, Moses Mather objected, a requirement of consciously willed sanctity for church membership would wreak havoc with infant baptism. If gracious affections are "the Band of Union to the visible Church; it will follow, that no Person in an unrenewed State, can be a Member of it." Since infants are not born regenerate, by New Divinity logic they "ought not to receive the seals of the Covenant . . . for to administer the seals of the Covenant to one not included in the Covenant itself, is trifling; yea, trifling with Things sacred." All of which, as Moses Mather knew, "makes Infant-baptism a mere Nullity, or Thing of Nought."[100] If, Joseph Huntington warned, "a baptized person is not one of God's visible, covenant people, baptism is without any signification at all."[101]

True to their intellectualist framework and the "Half-Way Synod" of 1662, the Old Calvinists insisted that churches could only look to a formal *assent* to the Gospel as the basis of admission, or to the assent of one's parents to one's baptismal vows, instead of a profession of infused grace. "Certain evidences of inward sanctification are not necessary," Hemmenway reiterated; if people were turned away from his church, "it is not the want of grace, but the want of credible evidence of grace which renders one unfit for admission."[102] As far as he was concerned, more than that was not necessary.

All who credibly profess christianity are to be considered as belonging to the household of faith; as holy brethren, partakers of the heavenly calling. And some special acts of brotherly fellowship seem to be due to them. . . . There seems to be some brotherly relation between all who profess the common faith.[103]

In fact not only was it not necessary, it was humanly impossible. "No profession which can be delivered in words is a certain discovery of the true sentiments and dispositions of the heart," Hemmenway declared, and that was because, as Huntington patiently explained the obvious, "no mortal knows, or can know, who has grace or who has not."[104] Men may have grace substantially and not know it; or think they are conscious of it when their hearts lack it. Either way, "we can look no further than the profession, life and conversation."[105] Hemmenway thereby concluded that "if inward holiness be not visible to the eye of man; then it cannot be the visibility of this which gives any one the title of a visible saint, and a right of admission."[106] To the contrary, said Moses Mather, "according to this Rule, the Church may admit such as are not regenerated, when they make a credible Profession of free Grace."[107]

Not only *couldn't* the church bar the visibly credible, it *shouldn't* either. In the eyes of Old Calvinism, the source of the New Divinity's mistaken application of the strictures of ability to the church was a fundamental misconception of the purpose of the church in this world. The church existed "to direct christians how to regard and behave towards men in this world," said Hemmenway, teaching saintly men how to live and order their world, or, as Moses Mather added, helping sinners obtain "needed Assistance" and "to use means with them for their Recovery."[108] It did not exist, Hemmenway snapped, "to enable them to search and know what is in the hearts of each other."[109] The church was not a refuge for the pure: "The good and the wicked are as fully commanded to be one in everything of a civil and temporal nature, as the children of God are among themselves," Joseph Huntington told the New Divinity elders at Stockbridge, in 1779: "to run away from human nature is not the part of a Christian but a madman."[110] What Old Calvinism most begrudged the New Divinity was its thus running away, and then calling it holiness.

They also resented the implication that such a way of thinking had packed Old Calvinist churches full of hypocrites who owned the covenant of a particular church without at the same time giving proof that they were sincerely converted and had an interest in the covenant of grace. Ebenezer Devotion protested that this phased the objectivity and visibility of the church's covenant into the invisibility and subjectivity of God's covenant of grace in regeneration, as though objective relationships had no validity apart from spiritual sincerity. "You make the obligation of a covenant to depend, not upon the words of the covenant but upon the meaning of the covenanter," Devotion protested.[111] In that case, almost any kind of civil arrangement ought to be dissolved upon the discovery of impure motives. And that was a principle so corrosive of social unity that Devotion could not believe that even the New Divinity took it seriously. In an argument that Joseph Huntington would use a decade later to defend Mrs. Fisk, Devotion in 1770 had challenged Bellamy to

suppose you and your neighbor assented to the same covenant verbatim, when ye were married. You yourself assented to it with great sensibility, solemnity, and understanding; meaning to keep your vow. But your neighbor assented to it, only in a formal customary way with great inattention, and without so good a meaning as you had. Upon your principle, sir, ye have entered into different things, yours is binding, but his is not. According to you, sir, instead of entering into vows, he has only *lied*—has lived in fornication, his bedfellow in whoredom, and his children are bastards.[112]

There was a point at which even the most separatistic churches had to drop the pretense of purity and rejoin society. And if the New Divinity were willing to regard the formal covenant of marriage as binding whether or not a sincere personal covenant of love lay behind it, there seemed to be no other reason why they should not recognize the validity of other objective social arrangements.

There is, concluded Moses Mather, "a real external Covenant-Relation subsisting between God and his *visible* Church, as well as an *internal* or spiritual Covenant-Relation between God and the invisible Church," and the two are neither to be confused nor put into competition to see which is the more "real."[113] After all, as Hemmenway was quick to point out, even "the scripture terms those holy or saints, who cannot with rational probability be judged, to be all the subjects of internal sanctification."[114] Consider "this external Covenant with the visible Church, as it was made with Abraham," Moses Mather urged:

it will evidently appear, that God had not a Respect to a gracious State of Heart, as that which should be the distinguishing Qualification of such as should be taken into it . . . as there were some true Believers who were not taken in: So there were others expressly required to be included who were not themselves truly regenerate.[115]

Furthermore, said Hemmenway, on the same principle, "the whole congregation of Israel are called a holy people." And in the New Testament, "visible churches are called holy, and all the members of them, not excepting the infant children." Whatever the relationship of visible covenanting to invisible grace (and Mather was convinced it "is in close Communion with it"), there was no doubt in Hemmenway's mind that "there are therefore two sorts of persons, who in scripture have the title of saints, and are *really such in their kind.*"

All therefore, who are comprehended in that covenant by which the church is formed, are relatively or federally holy. . . . This external holiness is not merely a show and appearance of something whose existence is doubtful; but it is real in its kind; though it be a different kind from that which arises from an invisible and saving relation to God.[116]

This in turn put considerable amounts of logic at the service of the "use of means." The unregenerate were brought into a church covenant precisely because it was assumed that the unregenerate were naturally or morally unable to leap over to grace and needed the stepping stones of the means, and help in using them—which, of course, could only be had in the church. If God is truly a sovereign and lofty Deity, then the mere "manifestation of the glory of God in the face of Jesus Christ to the mind and heart of a sinner," reasoned William Hart, "is the most unsuitable means that can be used to convert and reconcile; it is like throwing oil into the fire in order to quench it."[117] Instead of driving men to despair in order to provoke immediate repentance, Old Calvinism preferred to quiet men's fears and guide them steadily to grace through the understanding and the means of grace—in practical terms, that meant to "read and hear the word of God . . . meditate on what we read and hear . . . examine our spiritual state by this rule . . . pray to God for that grace and mercy we need . . .[the] Lord's Day must be remembered and kept holy . . ." and so forth.[118] The doing of these things indicated that there was at least *some* grace at work, or else one would not be interested in doing them; and, moreover, using these means had the additional advantage of putting the user in the proper place to take further, more important steps to salvation.

While it was true, Hemmenway conceded, that "acts of religious obedience performed by the unregenerate" are "defective and unholy," nevertheless they benefit the unregenerate since they "tend to and often issue in their everlasting good."[119] The work of grace comes in "gradual advances," with the state of unregeneracy yielding so gradually to holiness "that is is impossible to determine, with any certainty, how far these illuminations and encouragements were preparatory to conversion, and at what point of time the principle of spiritual life was first infused."[120] The New Divinity, its heart being set on purity, was not interested in comforting the sinner; they treated the "use of means" as if it were a declension rather than an alternative.

The Old Calvinists, forced to defend that which they had merely assumed, struck back with emotion. "What!" asked Jedidiah Mills, "is there no possibility that the drunkard, the thief, and liar, the profane swearer, the adulterer, the murderer and blasphemer should become, on the whole, less vicious in God's sight while unregenerate, by reforming all this atrocious wickedness?"[121] To abstain from murder, theft, and so on, Ebenezer Devotion reasoned, may not render one gracious, but obedience to God's commands at least renders one steadily less sinful than if one *had* murdered or stolen. "To say that obedience to God may in a strict and proper sense be unlikely, is a contradiction in terms. Obedience to God, be it greater or less, and proceed it from what it will; so far forth as it is obedience, is always holy."[122] To impugn the validity of the "use of means" would remove all incentive to greater holiness among the prepared and convinced sinners. "This thought," William Hart remarked, "that let him do his best he only becomes more guilty, vicious and vile than he would be if he shut his eyes and sinned away in the dark, at all adventures, will not greatly encourage him."[123] Hart, in a satirical pamphlet aimed at the New Divinity, scornfully advised sinners that there was no longer any point, on New Divinity terms, in *seeking* for salvation: there was nothing of a religious nature one could do until it was actually given.

Shall I advise you, as the very last resource, to pray for the gift of a new heart, by which you may pray for all other gospel blessings? I would do so, if I was applying the doctrines of Jesus Christ. But these new doctrines have shut your mouths and mine. For according to them, you can't desire a new heart till you have it.[124]

Nor was there point any longer for the hapless parishioner who labored under the preaching of a New Divinity minister to pray for deliverance from sin—unless he prayed along such lines as Hart provided:

O Lord have mercy upon me, and give me a new Heart——But, O *dreadful*! I must retract this request: I do but lie in making it. I don't truly desire a new heart, but hate it, and *reject it with perfect abhorrence*. So my minister tells me. I could pray to be saved from misery . . . but this, I know, will not and ought not to be granted. So I find I can't pray at all, though I attempted it, any more than a devil. So dreadfully do these doctrines, which my minister teaches me to believe, shut up the way against me. O, how am I perplexed, distracted, and *rent sore,* like one possessed by an unclean devil! How can I live so, how can I die! Cursed be the day of my birth. Amen.[125]

It was plain to someone like Jedidiah Mills, who prized public morality as much as private spirituality, that, despite the temptation the "use of means" provided to foster self-righteousness, "profaneness" is "at least as fatal to the souls of men as self-righteousness."[126] And more, according to Ebenezer Devotion, who defined the "awful effects" of the New Divinity in social rather than theological terms: "Yea these principles vacate all the other obligations of natural and reveal'd religion, and thence burst the bands of social life, strike at the foundations of civil government, and even at all God's moral government of the world."[127] Old Calvinists like Mills never worried (in print, at least) that the theology of the New Divinity would send souls to hell, but, like Mills, they feared it would send churches into disarray and society into immorality, and *that* would send souls to hell. They did not always discern the evil lurking in their own good intentions, the selfishness in their benevolence. The notion that a covenanted, orderly community of decent godless persons might be destitute of worth stung Moses Hemmenway into a peculiarly revealing response: on New Divinity principles "it is then no privilege to be in the way of these means, and they who are brought up and live all their days among the savages of Africa, have as desirable a lot as we who are both in a christian land, educated in the profession of true religion . . . and the gospel faithfully preached to us."[128] But indeed it was not, according to Hopkins. Only a man who assumed that grace was a tribal inheritance, and religion merely a moralizing motive dangled before the eyes of a morally minded but self-determined community, would automatically assume that an unregenerate white man was immediately better than an unregenerate black man.

What the Old Calvinists preached was a community of being rather than doing or willing. It finally found its champion, and the deviser of the Great Alternative to Edwards, in the person of Nathaniel William Taylor, and in the context of the new academic theology of nineteenth-century New England.

CHAPTER 6

Presbyterianism

No Objection to the Sinners' Striving

I

On Wednesday the 22nd Inst. died at Nassau-Hall, an eminent Servant of God, the Rev. and pious Mr. Jonathan Edwards, President of the College of New Jersey; a Gentleman of distinguished Abilities, of an heavenly Temper of Mind; a most rational, generous, catholick, and exemplary Christian, admired by all that knew him, for his uncommon Candour and disinterested Benevolence: A Pattern of Temperance, Prudence, Meekness, Patience and Charity; always steady, calm and serene, a very judicious and instructive Preacher, and a most excellent Divine; And as he lived chearfully, resigned in all things to the will of heaven, so he died, or rather as the Scripture emphatically expresses it, with respect to good men, he fell asleep in Jesus, without the least appearance of pain. (*The Pennsylvania Journal and Weekly Advertiser*, March 30, 1758)

Edwards had only enough time as president at Princeton in 1758 to give out his first set of theological questions to the senior class before submitting to the smallpox inoculation that killed him. Years later, Ezra Stiles sighed that his brief tenure was probably for the best. Edwards would not have been happy at Princeton. "He was rather adapted to a recluse, contemplative, serious Life, than to the Labors & Activity of the Head of a College," Stiles explained, "the Volatility of 100 youth would have disturbed his calm Quiet & made him unhappy."[1] The fact that Edwards had labored without complaint and with a fair amount of success in the midst of a non-English-speaking tribe of Indians, plus the combined obstinacy of the Williams clan and a major Indian war, without disturbance to the writing of *Freedom of the Will* or *Original Sin* does not refute Stiles's claim, but it does make us wonder if Stiles thought privately that other things about Princeton besides the students would have posed severe problems for Edwards. The Presbyterians into whose bourne he was journeying were philosophically aligned with the

Old Calvinists he had repudiated, and many of them would have scant sympathy with the ideas he had been ready to publish in *Original Sin*. The anonymous eulogist in the *Pennsylvania Journal* who praised Edwards's "uncommon Candour and dissinterested benevolence" had unwittingly stumbled over two of the numerous things in his "Temper of Mind" that might have brought on a conflict anything but "heavenly."

Presbyterianism was the other major codification of Calvinism besides Congregationalism in colonial America, and thus also the other great proponent of theological reconciliationism, and as such it was bound to be sucked into the discourse surrounding *Freedom of the Will*. Edwards's entrance into Presbyterianism at Princeton only accelerated the need for that reckoning, for if there is one outstanding characteristic of Presbyterian literature in the pre-1740 period, it is its complete contentedness with the formulae of the Westminster Confession—a pre-Hobbesian document which Edwards had long since found unable to provide answers to his questions about volition, not to mention the related questions about original sin and depraved natures. Ministers like John Tennent of Freehold, New Jersey, routinely affirmed that, as the Confession dictated, "original depravity is conveyed to all the Sons of *Adam* by *Generation*." Tennent, who with his brothers Gilbert, Charles, and William constituted the first family of colonial Presbyterianism, preached a salvation predicated largely on doctrinal precision, and within the framework of a faculty psychology predicated largely on an intellectualist theory of will.

Our first parents were made after God's Image . . . the *Understanding* being the guide and governor of the Soul's Faculties, had clear perceptions of the mind and will and *God*; the *Will* was subject to the Understanding's directions, having an inherent inclination to will that which the Mind by it's native light, shew'd to be good. The whole train of *Passions* freely follow'd the guidance of these superiour Powers, without the least reluctance.[2]

And, predictably, the Presbyterians also preached that this salvation was to be had through the diligent use of the means of grace. Thus, when one hopeful convert appealed to Ashbel Green to know what he should do to be saved, Green told him to keep out of bad company, read the Bible statedly, and pray to God for a new heart. "Continue this . . . and press forward in duty; and the Spirit of God will convert you."[3]

The antique psychology implicit in the Confession was manifestly at odds with Edwards's theory of will, but surrounding that was a larger notion of society which grew out of that psychology, and with which *Freedom of the Will* had long been at war in New England. Colonial Presbyterianism was an overwhelmingly ethnic affair in both of its major centers, New Jersey and Pennsylvania, and especially in Pennsylvania both clergy and congregations were almost entirely Scots-Irish immigrants in the 1740s. Understandably, their notion of church and society was Old World, organic, and, like the Old Calvinists, tribal. In their minds, salvation was a continuum that began with baptism, developed through catechesis, and gradually culminated in full communion, requiring no mighty crisis of will. It was expected to fall along family lines, binding together the generations of a community in covenantal union—not shattering them with an unexpectedly gracious blow.[4]

Unhappily for the Scots-Irish, maintaining this covenantal society called for more exertion in Pennsylvania than among their obvious counterparts among the Old Calvinists of Connecticut or Massachusetts. Presbyterianism enjoyed no established tax support; in addition, before 1746 it had no institution of learning in which to train a clergy to mediate its ideas to the people; and it was frankly outnumbered, thanks to William Penn and his open-door policy toward all religious sects. Its only advantages were ethnic homogeneity and geography; Presbyterianism was Scots-Irish, and its numbers were concentrated in the frontier counties of western Pennsylvania and the hills of northern New Jersey. There, at least, they seem to have succeeded in re-creating the church-in-society they had once known in Europe, for John Williamson Nevin remembered a late-eighteenth-century boyhood in the Cumberland Valley as

based throughout on the idea of covenant family religion, of church membership by a holy act of God in baptism; and following this as a logical sequence, there was regular catechetical training of the young, with direct reference to their coming to the Lord's Table. In a word, it proceeded on the theory of a sacramental, educational religion, that belonged properly to all the national branches of the *Reformed* Church in Europe from the beginning.... The schoolmaster stood by the side of the pastor as the servant of the Church; the school was regarded as its necessary auxiliary; and the catechism stood in honor and use everywhere, as the great organ or ruling power, which was to promote a sound religious education for all classes in the congregation.... The children of church members were all baptized with few or no exceptions and received into the Christian covenant at an early day as a matter that allowed of the least possible delay.[5]

Loyalty to the Westminster Standards, and conversion through the gradual use of the Presbyterian means of grace, were ideas that sprang from both a deep-seated conception of human community and a tactical necessity of protecting that concept where they had managed to transplant it from Europe to America. Against this, Edwards would have made little more progress than he had against Stoddardeanism in Northampton.

Or would he? A note of skeptical objection to Stiles's prophecy of gloom has to enter here because the contented (or else somnolent) picture painted by Nevin contained one important logistical flaw. Communities that subordinate will to intellect need teachers, but, in America, Presbyterian teachers were hard to come by. Francis Makemie, the renowned father of American Presbyterianism, ran out of available Presbyterian clergymen almost at once, and was forced to an expedient that came within a hair of destroying Presbyterianism: he turned to New England. Beginning in the 1690s, when Makemie recruited (through Cotton Mather) the services of Jedidiah Andrews, then a young Harvard graduate, the presbyteries in Long Island and New Jersey frequently resorted to calling New Englanders to their empty pulpits. The resulting accumulation was formidable. During Edwards's lifetime, the entire Presbytery of Long Island was Connecticut-born and Yale-educated; thirty-one New Englanders ministered to New Jersey Presbyterians, two more labored in Pennsylvania, and another in Delaware; and of the New Jersey contingent, twenty-four were Yale College graduates, and another six were Harvard men.[6]

In a strictly dogmatic sense, there was nothing unusual about this, for in the not-very-distant English past, Congregationalism had been very much a branch out of the Presbyterian trunk. The 1653 Savoy Declaration, the first organizing document of English Congregationalism, was little more than a retouched Westminster Confession; in the 1690s Cotton Mather rejoiced to see English Congregationalists and Presbyterians join hands as the United Brethren; and Connecticut's 1706 Saybrook Platform enshrined in its principle of "consociationism" a polity distinguishable only by its name from Presbyterianism. Samuel Willard's great opus, *A Compleat Body of Divinity,* was, in fact, a series of 250 lectures on the Westminster Shorter Catechism. Even the names Congregational and Presbyterian were used interchangeably, most notably in Franklin's *Autobiography.* Edwards himself had begun his ministerial career in a Presbyterian church in New

York City, and thirty years later he had found the boundary between
the two polities still so porous that he could agree to assume leadership
of America's only Presbyterian college. As late as 1801 the two polities
could still find enough common ground to stand on that they would
arrange for a joint church-planting effort in upstate New York known
as the "Presbygational" Plan of Union. That others, over the same span
of time, should find the boundary similarly thin is not surprising.

Whatever the surface similarities in polity, New England's Congregationalism contained within it the seeds of purism and separatism,
and it had been traveling a different path from Scots-Irish Presbyterianism for a long time, and as the numbers of New Englanders in the
presbyteries increased so did conflicts with the "old side" Scots-Irish
clergy. In 1722 the Scots-Irish party, anxious to ensure the integrity of
Presbyterianism, began agitating for strict subscription to the Westminster Confession. Objectively, the New Englanders had no objection
to this; subjectively, they interpreted the demand as a declaration of
no confidence in their theology, and Jonathan Dickinson of Elizabethtown, New Jersey, emerged in the forefront of the New Englanders as
he argued that men ought to be received for the ministry for the quality
of their religious experience, not for their allegiance to the Confession.
A compromise was reached in 1729, but in the 1730s more trouble
occurred when William Tennent, Sr., and his four sons organized an
ad hoc college—the famous "Log College"—at Neshaminy, Pennsylvania.

Although the Tennents were pure Scots-Irish, they were fervently
evangelical and pietist, and their manner split the Scots-Irish into two
bitterly quarrelsome factions. Fumbling for allies, the Tennents found
men of like spirit in the New Englanders, and a fateful détente took
place. When schism split the Synod of Philadelphia into Old Side and
New Side synods, the New Englanders threw their weight behind the
Tennents and the New Siders. With their assistance, and Gilbert Tennent's borrowing of the shock tactics of the New England revivals,
Presbyterianism in New Jersey and Pennsylvania went through its own
Awakening in 1742. The unrepentant Old Siders, led by Jedidiah Andrews and Robert Cross, declined to be thus awakened, and fought
back with their own condemnations of the revivals as bringing on
"Anarchy and Confusion, and Overthrow of all Order and Government."[7] In the end, neither side completely triumphed, and although
the sundered synods were reunited in 1758, the Old Siders were far

from reconciled. But their control over Presbyterianism's future had been badly shaken, and it was quite plain to them that it had been the sympathies of the New Englanders that had sustained the New Siders in staging their rebellion.

The influx of New Englanders into the Presbyterian churches did more than merely lend a pious and friendly arm to the Tennents. By the 1750s it was becoming clear that the ties of many of these New Englanders led to one specific place in New England: Stockbridge, Massachusetts. The kingpin of New Jersey Presbyterianism, Aaron Burr, married an Edwards daughter; New Jersey Presbyterianism's most famous martyr, David Brainerd, was Edwards's short-lived protégé; his brother, John Brainerd, who continued Brainerd's mission to the Indians, was a student of Bellamy's, a trustee of the College of New Jersey, and one of the two (the other being Caleb Smith, still another New Englander) deputized to bear to Edwards the news of his election to the college's presidency; Samuel Buell, who had been Edwards's pulpit supply in Northampton back in the wild days of 1741–1742, and tagged Samuel Hopkins around the Berkshires on an itinerant preaching tour, now presided over the Presbytery of Long Island. Jonathan Dickinson, the greatest mind among the colonial Presbyterians and first president of the College of New Jersey, enjoyed substantial contact with Edwards and, with Aaron Burr, had vainly interceded with Thomas Clap to have David Brainerd restored to Yale.[8] Even Samuel Davies, in faraway Virginia, fell under the Edwardsean spell after reading *True Religion Delineated*. After Edwards's dismissal from Northampton, Davies begged Bellamy to cooperate in a plan to lure Edwards to Virginia; failing in that, he tried to lure Bellamy himself, assuring Bellamy that *True Religion Delineated* had been such a blessing to the cause of revival that Bellamy himself was needed to keep the revival fires burning.[9] And not just Davies: in 1753 New York Presbyterians also tried to draw Bellamy from Connecticut, dangling as bait a £250 salary that would have made him the highest-paid clergyman in America.[10] The College of New Jersey itself at Princeton had in its founding a whiff of the Edwardsean to it, for "if it had not been for the treatment received by Mr. Brainerd at Yale," Aaron Burr declared, "New Jersey college would never have been erected."[11]

No matter, then, rowdy students or Old Presbyterians—when Edwards arrived at Princeton, he had allies and even disciples. Only, he had not counted on Dr. Shippen's inoculation.

II

Death, not the Old Side, did the most to prevent New Englander Presbyterians from grabbing the reins of control within Presbyterianism. The first five presidents of Princeton were all either New Englanders or admirers of Edwards, but all of them died after disappointingly brief tenures of office, the shortest being Edwards's own. But even without firm leadership, Edwardsean influence in the Presbyterian churches proceeded to grow along ideological lines similar to those laid out in *Freedom of the Will*, just as had Hopkinsianism in New England. During the half-century after Edwards's death, Presbyterianism developed its own New Divinity faction, and, with it, its own Edwardsean brand of voluntarism and reconciliationism.

If the Presbyterians could in any way claim to have a direct counterpart to Edwards himself in their ranks, it was Jonathan Dickinson. Born in western Massachusetts and a graduate of Yale the same year Edwards matriculated there, Dickinson was settled as pastor over a congregation of Connecticut immigrants in Elizabethtown in 1719, and spent the rest of his life there, including the last brief year before his death in 1747, when he acted as the first president of the College of New Jersey. He has proven a maddeningly elusive figure: he left behind no important set of manuscripts, and the active role he played in Presbyterian affairs has been eclipsed by the colorful stridency of the Tennents. And yet those closest to his time consistently bracketed Edwards and Dickinson as the leading lights of American Calvinism. Edwards himself eulogized Dickinson as the "learned and very excellent Mr. Jonathan Dickinson"; John Erskine averred that "the British Isles have produced no such writers on divinity in the eighteenth century, as Dickinson and Edwards"; and the nineteenth-century antiquarian-cum-clergyman W. B. Sprague (who was himself highly sympathetic to Edwardsean divinity) doubted "whether with the single exception of the elder Edwards, Calvinism has ever found an abler or more efficient champion in this country than Jonathan Dickinson."[12] The real proof of these connections, however, lies in Dickinson's published writings, for just as Dickinson was reckoned as Presbyterianism's Edwards, his most substantial work, *The True Scripture-Doctrine concerning some important points of Christian Faith* of 1741, contains some striking anticipations of *Freedom of the Will*.

The *True Scripture-Doctrine* devotes most of its attention to a rather

conventional apologetic for the main points of Calvinism, and, unlike
Edwards, Dickinson dealt with questions concerning the will and its
freedom as difficulties to be pushed out of the road that led to explaining more interesting dogmatic tenets, and not an end in itself. All the
same, something about volition must have intrigued Dickinson, for
when he did have to offer a reconciliation of the ways of men to God,
the conventional vocabulary dropped away and Dickinson began speaking in a very un-Presbyterian tongue.

One root of Dickinson's theory of will certainly lay, as it had with
Edwards, in his observations of the psychology of conversion, for in
June 1740 Dickinson watched in Elizabethtown the same outburst of
surprising conversions take place that Edwards had seen for the first
time six years before in Northampton. Round about him in northern
New Jersey he saw people awakened in ways he could not doubt for
sincerity, and yet which violated the intellectualist model of salvation
through knowledge. Although Dickinson was careful to see that "new
converts were all for a considerable time under a law work before they
were brought to any satisfying views of their interest in Christ and the
favour of God," he was later of the opinion that this "law work" had
been divinely inspired only to act as a restraint to prevent "those ecstatic, rapturous joys that were so frequent in some other places."[13]
This knowledge of the Law was not itself a cause of spiritual awakening, since, as he observed, many "had a doctrinal knowledge before,
that they were sinful, guilty, helpless and hopeless in themselves" and
yet "this had no special influence upon their affections or their conduct."[14] What decisively distinguished "those who are brought up under Gospel-Light" from those converted in the revival was not a
difference in the content of what they knew about salvation, but the
way in which it was known, for while the former had knowledge, the
latter had "a feeling sense" of that knowledge. Those who not only
knew of God but were "brought low" by it possessed what Dickinson
had earlier called a "feeling sensible Impression" that set them off from
the others.[15]

Old Side Presbyterians might have accounted for this difference simply by writing off the awakened converts as excitable enthusiasts who
had let their passions run away with them. But to Dickinson it merely
proved that intellection of the Old Calvinistic variety could never be
wholly sufficient.[16] "A True and saving Faith is a realizing and sensible
impression of the Truth of the Gospel," Dickinson later wrote, and

therefore true religion must lie beyond the intellect, in what Edwards was at that moment defining as the affections. And as that "feeling sense" was imparted to the affections, "the ways of piety and holiness" would for the awakened "necessarily become their objects of choice."[17] By that token, the will was not a faculty subservient to the understanding nor could it be reduced to a rational appetite—it was what Dickinson could only call the "result" of a compounded movement "of our own understanding, affections and appetites." Accounting for the indifference of the ungodly, or the semigodly, now took on a different dimension.[18] Individuals wallowed in sin, not because they were ignorant of truth, but because their hearts were evil and in love with darkness. "Our grand impotency," Dickinson declared, lies not in a depraved intellect "but in our wills."[19] And that, for Dickinson, was also what showed that the impotency of the will was nevertheless compatible with its freedom.

It cannot be said of any man, that he is truly willing to comply with the terms of salvation, to accept of Christ as offered in the gospel, to depend upon him only as the fountain of grace and life, and to live conformably to his will. . . . The inability of a natural man to repent of his sins, consists especially in this, that he cannot be sincerely willing to forsake all his sins, and to live a life of holy obedience to God.[20]

Dickinson might have taken this in the same direction Edwards followed in *Original Sin* and denied even the existence of a depraved nature exerting a compulsion on the will to sin. And to a certain extent he did, for of the two means by which mankind inherited Adamic sin— natural generation and forensic imputation—Dickinson simply removed the former from consideration. "It will not follow that [Adam's] sin and guilt descends to us by natural generation," Dickinson wrote; it was enough that Adam "sustained a public character, and was considered as our representative in that covenant-transaction."[21] But denying a corrupt *inherited* substance was not the same thing as eliminating substance entirely. Dickinson was profoundly uneasy in talking about a depravity which was not in some sense natural. "There must be some cause of these corrupt affections, appetites, and passions, of this universal depravity of our natures, and corruption of all our powers and faculties," he insisted, and he was not prepared (as Emmons would be) to put it into "the hands of God" or explain depravity as a divine constitution of conscious, sinful ideas.[22] To do that, Dickinson wrote, carefully picking prudence over valor, it "would be proper for us to know something more about the time and manner of the union of our souls and bodies, before we decree too positively in this matter."[23] Therefore, Dickinson was content to conclude that man was controlled by a sinful nature, a substance somehow polluted when "we were all in the loins of our father Adam, when he broke the first covenant." It was not a significant problem for Dickinson that he could not quite explain in just what way we were in Adam or how this depravity was imparted: "in how lax a sense soever this be allowed to be true, it serves to clear up the justice and equity of God."[24]

The other visible root of Dickinson's thinking on the will was certainly Locke—not only does Dickinson mention him by name, but he employs some telltale Lockean definitions. His most obvious appropriation of Locke was the declaration that it was erroneous to speak of the will as *free*. "I cannot but think (with Mr. Locke) that it is a very inaccurate and obscure way of speaking, to attribute freedom, or want of freedom, to the will," Dickinson explained. "Free agency implies personality, which I think no man applies to the will." Freedom applies instead to the person doing as he wills, without "coaction or constraint."[25] But, more like Edwards than like Locke, Dickinson then turned this innocuous psychological conclusion into a stick to beat sinners with, for "if freedom consists in acting agreeably to our inclinations, then unconverted sinners are in a state of freedom, for they always act in their moral conduct as they incline to act." They have, he is almost ready to say, a natural ability to repent. Indeed, "God has decreed to give even to the reprobate more power and ability, than they will ever improve."[26]

Dickinson also used Locke in a more peculiar way, as he foreshadowed Edwards's use of the first edition of Locke's *Essay* by borrowing from Locke the idea that appears in that edition only, that "the choice of the Will is every-where determined by the greater apparent Good." Although Dickinson was aware that in later editions Locke had changed this to identify the direction of the will with a sense of "uneasiness," Dickinson chose to follow Locke's earlier version by asserting that "every free agent must necessarily will what his understanding, appetites and affections represent to him as the most fit object of choice; he can't do otherwise."[27] And in vocabulary that looks back not only to Locke but to the Clarke-Leibniz debate, Dickinson went on to add that "every rational agent must, in all he does, be always actuated and influenced by the highest motive and inducement before him."[28] Hence, in the context of Calvinistic psychology, God presents "motives" to the subject; given the subject's temper or nature (let us assume a good one), the motive presented "makes such a powerful impression" that the understanding, appetites, and affections cannot but perceive it as the greatest apparent good; and since willing is only the "result" of this perception, and follows it naturally, then the subject's appropriation of that good is neither a self-determination by the will nor an unfree compulsion. All of which serves to demonstrate that divine predestination in no way strips men of moral responsibility or reduces them to machines; as Edwards would be at pains to prove, it was the notion of a self-determining will, not Calvinism, which made a chaos of the human psyche:

> a power to will or not to will, any particular object of choice, or a power to choose indifferently either one or the other of two contrary objects, is so far from freedom, that it is utterly inconsistent with it; and is what cannot be predicated of any being that is perfectly free. We could not be free agents, if we had not a power to will what appears to us from our present view of things most fit to be chosen; or if we had a power to will what appears to us from our present view of things unfit to be chosen. For either of these supposes the will itself to be the effect of some constraint from something without us; and not to be the result of our own understandings, affections, and appetites, as it always is in every free agent.[29]

It is no wonder, on those terms, that William B. Sprague later was struck by how Dickinson wrote "in a tone not unlike that which characterizes the works of Edwards, written about the same time, and on the same subject," and we would like to know just how much contact Dickinson enjoyed with Edwards, or how closely Edwards may have read Dickinson—questions Dickinson's scanty manuscripts and Edwards's *Catalogue* of reading have not answered, and maybe will never answer.[30] What is at least certain is that Presbyterianism had in Dickinson a close reader of Locke and probably of other British moral philosophy; his reading and revival experiences led him to many conclusions marvelously coincidental to Edwards.

Dickinson died in 1747 without leaving a noticeable corps of converts to his proto-Edwardseanism. But following after him all the same, whether due to Dickinson's ideas or Edwards's or even someone else's, came John Blair, preaching what looked very much like New Divinity. A graduate of William Tennent's Log College in the early 1740s, brother and successor to another Log College New Sider, Samuel Blair, and very briefly professor of theology and acting president at the College of New Jersey, John Blair was as much and more of an Edwardsean in style and tone than Dickinson. He enthusiastically endorsed the same glorification of willing and affections Edwards had espoused in *Religious Affections*. "The power of the soul to any activity lies formally in the will," Blair wrote, and conversion especially offers proof that the understanding and the will—the material and formal causes of the soul's activity—are bound much more closely than the traditional psychology allowed.[31] "Thus when the regenerate are called *light*, the matter is not confined to the understanding only, but includes the approbation of the will, and to be willing, certainly includes the view of the understanding," Blair said; "to see the glory of God must include both the view of the understanding, and the approbation of the will."[32] From this, Blair, like Edwards, concluded that spiritual knowledge is "not gained by way of conclusion from premises, or by argumentation," but is "an immediate intuitive sense or knowledge of the moral perfections and character of God . . . arising from the approach of God to the soul by way of gracious presence." This kind of illumination of the soul by love—by a divine and supernatural light—consciously separates the believing soul from the unbelieving, and also, as Blair was fully aware, from routine intellectualism. "This is a way of knowing," he admitted, "very different from that received merely by description and report of the word, and, therefore, a different kind of knowledge, viz: by way of spiritual sense and experience."[33] But, at the same time, Blair was also persuaded that this unified way of knowing was, as it had been for Edwards, a better way of developing a reconciliationist psychology. For when a man, whose will is that by which the mind chooses, "sees this glorious object represented as in a glass; from thence the reflection is so strong and lively as irresistable, though in a moral way, to determine the will."[34]

With these fragments in hand, we would like to have seen what a treatise by John Blair on freedom of the will would have looked like. He did not, however, favor his readers with one, perhaps because after 1754 he did not have to. Instead, he vaulted over that step into two of the most radical corollaries the New Divinity had drawn from *Freedom of the Will*. The first of these was strictly psychological, for Blair dared to wonder aloud whether, since the will was so vital to all of the soul's activities, the soul might be simply a chain of exercises and ideas rather than a passive underlying substance. "For any one . . . to pretend to tell what the principle of divine life is, Antecedent to all exercises of the heart, and undertake from thence to demonstrate and explain those exercises," Blair declared, "is a vain attempt."

When he distinguishes this life from all its exercises, and goes about to tell us what is antecedent to them all, he must talk in the dark about a certain something, of which he has no idea. To give it a name, to call it, for instance, a new temper or taste, is not to tell us what it is. Let any man explain what he means by a new or holy temper, without including some exercise of life in heart, if he can.[35]

Hence, in regeneration, what occurred was not the infusion of a new taste or disposition but simply a "principle" of acting or thinking, a "new view of the mind" or "determination of the mind, to right activity towards spiritual objects" and a "determination or approbation of the will."[36] Of course, strictly speaking, the soul was not constantly popping up and down with violent activity: "the graces of the Holy Spirit are not always in exercise," but they are on the other hand never latent either. At the least, "there is always such a sense of things as makes the soul restless and uneasy in such a case."[37] In terms that would have done justice to Nathanael Emmons (ordained but two years before Blair's death), Blair insisted that we must "conceive of it as a moral determination of the soul towards God . . . including some apprehension of God in the understanding, and an act of the will embracing him."[38] If we try to consider spiritual substance as an "effect which includes no acts of the understanding and will, but is absolutely antecedent to them," then we must define it as "a mere physical and not a moral effect."[39] Implicit in all of this was the immanent sovereignty of God: if, as Edwards had discovered, there was no way to prove the existence of a substance in which personal qualities and consciousness inhered and were rooted together, then the only other alternative was to consider that it was God, by direct action, who preserved the self's sense of personal identity. And that served perfectly the purposes of the Log College's revivalism, for on those terms it was good philosophy and not just piety to insist, as Blair did, that "regeneration is the communication of a principle of spiritual life to the soul of a sinner . . . by the agency of the Holy Spirit."[40]

If on the other hand one persisted in speaking of regeneration as an unwilled transformation of the soul's substance, then one at once removed any moral responsibility or power to repent. Blair was no more willing than Hopkins to grant such a revival-discouraging concession. On his terms, there was no such physical obstacle to repentance—and that brought Blair, as it had brought Hopkins, to a second corollary, to the demand for immediate repentance and the denial of the "use of means."

Plainly, Blair did not enjoy endorsing Hopkins. After Hopkins's collision with Jedidiah Mills over "unregenerate doings," Blair commented, "As to the newly invented plea, that God commands no unregenerate Duties (a very odd phrase) or does not command unregenerate Men, as such to do Duties . . . it really does not deserve a serious answer." And Blair continued to open the sacraments to his unregenerate parishoners, if they chose to use them, maintaining "that ministers and church officers have no more authority to debar from the Lord's Table those who desire to attend than from any other duty of God's worship." But if he would not agree with Hopkins that the unregenerate were actually making themselves worse by wallowing in the means, he could not avoid agreeing that they were certainly not doing anything to make themselves better. "To have Matter of Encouragement, and to have a Ground of Confidence and Claim," Blair warned, "are not the same Thing, as some seem strangely to imagine."[41] Let men come to the "means"—but let them not suppose that they are by that doing enough, or all that they could do. "It will by no means follow, that awakened sinners, are in a degree, accepted of God on account of their being less sinful than they were in the days of their security; for the divine law still condemns them as falling short, infinitely short of its demands."[42] If this militated against the Old Side ecclesiology, and left Blair to try to hold together the threads of a "means"-oriented majority and a revivalistic minority, it was a conflict he was not forced to resolve. That would remain for those who followed him.

And there were many in Presbyterianism who followed him through the strait gate of New Divinity. Blair and Dickinson were only the best and most prominent of the proto-Edwardseans (assuming that they had not actually borrowed ideas directly). Neither the immigration of New Englanders nor the importation of New England ideas in any way slowed after Blair's early death in 1770; Presbyterianism continued to nurture in its bosom the corrosive absolutism of Hopkins and Bellamy. Some, like Samuel Davies, who helped bring Presbyterianism to the Shenandoah Valley, or like James Patriot Wilson, pastor of the First Presbyterian Church in Philadelphia, were converts to the New Divinity, but sometimes not to all of it. Others, like Jacob Green, pastor of

North Hanover, New Jersey, and Gardiner Spring, pastor of New York City's Brick Presbyterian Church and both son of Samuel Spring and nephew of Nathanael Emmons, were almost literally born into it. Either way, from the time of Green and Davies (roughly the 1740s until the 1790s), through the tenure of Wilson in Philadelphia (1801–1830) and up through the long life of Gardiner Spring (pastor of the Brick Presbyterian Church from 1810 until 1873), the Presbyterian Hopkinsians sang the same infuriating song for the Scots-Irish Old Siders and Old Schoolers that earlier had been sung for Old Calvinism.

Like their New England counterparts, they flaunted their Calvinism, even up to the wisdom of God in the permission of sin. "The whole work of divine Providence is one perfect plot and design—laid in the eternal counsel of divine wisdom—which cannot be altered for the better, nor adjusted more wisely than it is," Samuel Buell announced. "In it there is nothing amiss—it is perfectly wise and good: so that if there was the least alteration . . . it would not be so well."[43] By contrast with such aggressive assertiveness, Old Side Presbyterianism paled into a wishy-washy Arminianism, a condition James Patriot Wilson laid to the Old Side's intellectualist psychology. "If the will is *reached through the understanding,*" then God's action on the soul "is mediate, not immediate with respect to the will," Wilson complained. That, he went on, made the Presbyterian little better than the Arminian: "they agree . . . in this, that the sinner is left to yield to, or reject, the light communicated to his understanding, by a sovereign act of his own will."[44]

In the place of this self-determined will, picking and choosing from what the understanding offered to it, Wilson offered a radical brand of voluntarism that entirely reversed this order by putting the action of the will prior to the understanding. "The will uses the understanding for its own purposes, and sends it out a pioneer, to discover the path to happiness," Wilson claimed; the so-called " 'leading faculty,' the understanding, seems to be led and directed."[45] But in practical terms, Wilson did not significantly differ from Edwards. The will is by no means a self-determining entity: the will contains a moral quality which fixes its actions without any sense of debate within it. The will always moves first, but its movement is forever biased by its moral condition. In the case of the sinner, Wilson said, "the governing faculty, the *will,* being dead, or indisposed to good, renders the whole man dead, it misapplies or prejudices the intellectual powers, closes the eyes and ears, and shuts up every avenue by which truth might reach the man."

So it is "an aversion to holiness," not a lack of doctrinal precision in the sinner, "which determines the will to direct the understanding."[46]

On that basis, "impotency to believe proceeds from disaffection or unwillingness," not from some natural cause. "The natural liberty or free agency of man is no more destroyed by efficacious grace than by slavish corruption," Wilson declared, because "*both the saint and the sinner pursue the objects of their choice.*"[47] Sinners cannot take refuge in God's decrees and cry inability. When they say "they *cannot believe* and *cannot* come to *Christ*," Jacob Green wrote, "the *cannot* is not to be understood in the natural common Sense, or of natural Inability."[48] Given the will's primacy in choosing, *cannot*s are really *will not*s. "When a Person had no Desire, Inclination, will or endeavour to that which is reasonable, fit and proper to be done, which is attended with good consequences when done, and to the doing of which there is no insuperable difficulty, then he is to blame." In short, Green implied, he could do right if his will was right; but the will not being right is what "is infinitely to blame."[49] Gardiner Spring assured an objector, "Your rational and moral faculties capacitate and oblige you to choose life." Such natural ability "leaves you in full possession of all possible liberty to accept, or reject the Saviour." Hence, "there is nothing in the way of accepting the offer, but a perverse will."[50]

Having pressed so far in order to reconcile human ability and divine decree, the New Divinity Presbyterians came a-cropper on the same rock of "taste" and "exercise" that sundered the New England Hopkinsians. For someone like Jacob Green, orthodoxy demanded that the will's aversion to holiness be in some way "a Taste, an Inclination or Heart" which lay behind the actual conscious willing itself.

Fallen Sinners have a Wicked perverse Nature; they are bent to sin; they have no Heart, Will or Inclination, to that which is spiritually Good. They have such a corrupt Taste and vicious Heart that Light and Reason do not influence them to Holiness.[51]

Samuel Davies likewise was appalled at an ultraism that called spiritual substance into question. "Do they not know, that a principle, a disposition, a power of holy acting must precede, and be the source of all holy acts?" he asked indignantly.[52] But appalled indignation did little to discourage James Wilson or Gardiner Spring. To Wilson, clinging to the notion of a fixed underlying taste undercut all hope of appealing to the sinner's consciousness of sin.

The doctrine of an inability, by supposition natural and immoveable, except by supernatural power, and as culpable as if moral, impeaches Divine justice, exculpates the impenitent, hardens the wicked, and has a tendency to drive the hopeless saint to despair. . . . To induce men to believe that there is any other supernatural influence or aid necessary, than that which is to remedy *moral inability*, or help them "to will and to do" what they are already bound unto, and have natural talents for, is to furnish them with an excuse.[53]

Instead, Wilson argued, "the will is the source of moral actions, and therefore the principal seat of moral depravity" by itself; what Green and Davies called the heart is nothing more than the exercises of the will "metaphorically called the heart."[54] Hence, "original sin" was for Wilson simply our *"inclination & propensity to evil"* which only "arises from the first temptation offered to the soul."[55] Gardiner Spring, as Emmons's nephew, knew far more exactly what he was espousing when he denied that sin exists anywhere else but in conscious exercises. "Sin is an internal emotion of the mind," he wrote; those who claim not to be conscious of the location of their sinfulness, and hence are unable to do anything about it, say so "because they have a wrong state of heart."[56] Even though Spring later lost his enchantment with the exercise scheme, he nevertheless admitted that he could find no proof of a spiritual nature behind those exercises. "I am certain," he was still saying in 1866, "that we cannot prove we have a mind which is distinct from, and the foundation of, all the mental powers and faculties of which we are *conscious*."[57]

No matter which scheme best served to free persons from the trammels of inability, they all agreed that the preaching of ability demanded the elimination of at least two things: imputation and the "use of means." "Sinfulness is not transferrable," Wilson declared, either from Adam, or to Christ; nor is "Christ's righteousness . . . transferred to them, for it is of a personal nature."[58] Christ's atonement served a governmental purpose, demonstrating God's consistency as a moral governor, rather than a substitutionary one providing a righteousness that men had not willed. Gardiner Spring explained, "When God determined to save a part of mankind, he had it in prospect to provide such an expiation for the sins of the world, as to justify him"—not sinners—"in the unlimited offer of pardon, and in the full and complete justification of all who accept it."[59] Even Gilbert Tennent was willing to agree that, in the atonement, God "is to be considered as a Governor, who by an Act of Supremacy and pure Jurisdiction, may dispense with the Execution of the Law, upon such considerations as fully answer the Ends of Government."[60]

The use of means, however, drew from the New Divinity Presbyterians considerably more vehemence, as much for the theory itself as for the larger concept of the church that lay behind it. "Means are nothing to an awakened sinner," William Sprague remarked; "they are only fitted to abate a sense of guilt, and finally to bring back to the soul its accustomed spiritual torpor."[61] They worked this way, said Gardiner Spring, merely on their own inherent logic. "Are not the hearts of unregenerate men entirely sinful?" Spring asked, faultlessly deploying the absolutism so dear and so close to the heart of Edwardseanism. If so, "is not all their moral conduct therefore entirely sinful?" How, on Spring's terms, could it not be? "Therefore . . . all the use which unregenerated men make of them is unholy and sinful."[62] Better for the unregenerate not to pray as unregenerate, but better still, and the real purpose of this absolutism, was for the unregenerate to repent at once. "The only proper direction to be given them is, *REPENT AND BELIEVE THE GOSPEL*," Spring thundered, "No matter what they perform beside, until this is done, not a step is taken in the business of their salvation."[63] Of course, Spring was aware that many of his Presbyterian brethren feared turning up the fires under the sinner, lest the lids blow off the pots of many a church. But, for Spring, such eruptions were exactly what the Church was for—not nurturing the godless and godly alike, but separating them and flinging the unregenerate out over the fires of damnation to bring them to their senses.

Do you say, sinners will not be satisfied with these directions, and these directions will only discourage and distress them? Be it so. We do not wish to satisfy them, but to render their condition more and more distressing, as long as they stay away from Christ. . . . You feel it your duty to keep them from despair, and therefore you direct them to the use of means, and comfort them with the hope that if they wait God's time, all will be well! . . . It is just as though you said to them, *You need not repent; God does not require it*. . . . It is the business of a minister so to preach as to leave the impression on the minds of sinners, that he has a right to expect that they will at once cease to do evil, and learn to do well.[64]

In pursuit of that happiness, the next logical step would have been the call for practical, if not theoretical, separatism, and indeed some of the New Divinity Presbyterians heeded that call. Gardiner Spring, after his installation at the Brick Presbyterian Church in New York City, terminated the covenantal practice of baptizing infants "without regard to the Christian character and profession of either of the parents. . . . I could not understand how any conscientious parent could consistently consecrate his child to God in baptism, who could not consecrate himself."[65] Jacob Green simply erected his own Morris Presbytery in New Jersey in which he could separate the sheep from the goats as he pleased, and bade adieu to the Synod of Philadelphia. More of them might have tried to do likewise had they been in Connecticut or Massachusetts and enjoyed the autonomy of the Congregationalism Edwards had ironically blamed for his misfortunes. But they were, after all, Presbyterians. They had the intellectual inertia of confessionalism to restrain them and an obedience owed to higher presbyterial and synodical authorities. And those authorities had the incentive and the power to strike back.

III

It is one measure of the resiliency of Old Side Presbyterianism, and its stubborn loyalty to Nevin's fond memory of a church-in-society, that Gardiner Spring was still conducting a lively argument about the "use of means" in 1833, the same year that Samuel Howe's dramatic diatribe ardently supporting the "use of means" was published in Philadelphia. Even after the Revolution, Presbyterianism still sought the kind of organic hegemony that had been denied them by the sectarians before the war and which the secular pluralism of the new Constitution threatened to put entirely beyond their reach. Surprisingly, they came closer to that goal after the Revolution than before it, not only in Nevin's Cumberland Valley but also in Philadelphia, where the Presbyterians forged an alliance of class and church in which Calvinistic theology offered to provide the moral fiber and moral restraints of society in return for public recognition of the Sabbath, the authority of the Bible, and special governmental aid for church agencies. Whether it was Nevin's pastor catechizing the village schoolchildren, or Archibald Alexander's early Sunday-School reciting the catechism around the woodstove in Alexander's Pine Street Church in Philadelphia, they worked—in the words of Fred J. Hood—"to control the development of character by control of the mind," since the will (as they knew) could not be moved by mere information, but the mind *could*.[66] And by those means, America could prepare itself ultimately for the receipt of millennial grace. And where they failed to receive such de facto recognition, they were quick to warn, as Jonathan French did in 1804, that societies with invisible churches were doomed. "To preserve a republican government," French said, "it is of great importance, that the minds of the people be well informed and religiously impressed"— and to that end the Church must have a public place within the society to act as its moral adhesive.[67] And when, from within, Presbyterians of Hopkinsian propensities drove at this public moral hegemony by advocating the church's withdrawal from the godless world, they held trials and purges.

The New Divinity Presbyterians were never subjected to the boiling wrath that was visited on the infidelity of the deists, perhaps because they were too badly needed and because not all Presbyterians could quite make up their minds whether they were entirely beyond the pale of Westminster orthodoxy. Attacks on New Divinity Presbyterianism were more of a series of isolated engagements, provoked as much by the personalities involved as the ideas, and as much by practical eccle-siology as by philosophy.

The first of these incidents occurred even before Hopkins's clash with Mills in 1767 over the "use of means," for in 1765 William Tennent the Younger of Freehold, New Jersey, published a blistering attack on those who denied the virtue of unregenerate doings. Although a New Sider by persuasion and yet another Log College Tennent, his revivalism resembled that of Jedidiah Mills more than Samuel Hopkins, and in the Freehold revival of the 1740s Tennent's preaching actually did more to cement Scots-Irish tribalism than to disturb it.[68] Elias Boudinot described him as "a moderate Calvinist . . . of sound ortho-dox principles," and although Boudinot esteemed him as one who "carefully avoided the discussion of controversial subjects," the abso-lutism of denying the "use of means" was evidently more than Tennent could bear.[69] To him, grace was apprehended first by the understanding, not the will. So long as the will was depraved, one could do no more than gradually stock the understanding with enough truth to tip the balances against unbelief. To call for repentance, now, without waiting for the knowledge of the Lord, was absurd. "Our souls are rational," Tennent protested; "we must hear, attend and consider, or else we cannot have faith." But, as Hopkins would have objected, can the holy person ever do anything holy which he does not make unholy in his use of it? Tennent's defiant reply was a most unrevivalistic *yes*. "It is true, the sinner, who is thus active, is less guilty than he who lives in rebellious contempt."

Now the sinner can pray, he can hear, he can do alms, he can do things materially good, tho' not formally so. The performance of these duties, as a natural man can perform them, is the way in which GOD usually confers his grace . . . and such performance leaves him less guilty, than if he did not perform them at all.[70]

Tennent was not about to allow *his* sinners, or his community in Freehold, to be driven into the evangelical chaos so beloved of Samuel and Gardiner Spring.

A more significant eruption occurred three years later around the person of John Witherspoon, the new Scottish president of the College of New Jersey, who was no less inclined to allow the college to be surrendered to Edwardsean philosophy than William Tennent had been to surrender Freehold to Edwardsean ecclesiology. Following Edwards's death in office in 1758, the college had gone through two more short-lived presidents, Samuel Davies and Samuel Finley, both of whom had strong sympathies with Edwardsean thinking. After the death of Finley, the Edwardsean tone of the college increased still more, with John Blair being appointed professor of theology and two of Bellamy's pupils, Joseph Periam and Jonathan Edwards the Younger, filling the tutors' positions. James Caldwell, the successor of Jonathan Dickinson in Elizabethtown and a trustee of the college, schemed to press even further, and in March 1767 sent Edwards the Younger to Bellamy so that both of them together could press Samuel Hopkins to come "as a professor at the College."[71] Alarmed at the prospect of the college's falling under Hopkins's aegis, Old Side Presbyterians offered a compromise candidate for the vacant presidency, a Scottish Popular Party man named John Witherspoon, on the theory that even a Scottish moderate was better than a radical Edwardsean. The Edwardseans, unable to oppose Witherspoon without looking embarrassingly partisan and sectarian, gave in to Witherspoon's election, perhaps reasoning on their part that a stranger from Scotland would be easier to maneuver around than a hard-line Old Sider.

If the Edwardseans thought that way, they could not have been more wrong. Witherspoon was a talented and subtle academic politician, a vigorous popularizer of Reid and "common sense" moral philosophy, and a determined enemy of immaterialism. Witherspoon's earliest biographer tersely described the formidable Scot's inevitable confrontation with the Edwardseans:

The Berkeleyan system of metaphysics was in repute in the college when he entered. The tutors were zealous believers in it and waited on the President with some expectation of either confounding him or making him a proselyte. They had mistaken their man. He first reasoned against the system and then ridiculed it till he drove it out of the college.[72]

The students, too, learned the new Princeton line. Ebenezer Bradford, class of '73, wrote to Bellamy in alarm that Witherspoon had declared war on "what they call Edwardsean, or New Divinity."[73] Since he had been advised "not to let my sentiments be known," Bradford raised a subscription for two hundred copies of *True Religion Delineated* and circulated them among the students with the title page discreetly removed so that Bradford could later have the pleasure of identifying the author to impressionable fellow students.[74] It did not work. Within two years of his arrival, Witherspoon had gotten rid of Blair on the grounds that he could save the college money by teaching theology himself, and he had driven Periam and Edwards the Younger into resignation from their tutorships. Periam and Bradford both went to the Presbytery of New York for ordination, but Periam was kicked out in 1775 for teaching that God was the author of sin, while Bradford joined Jacob Green's schismatic Morris Presbytery in 1781. The college had been made safe from the New Divinity.[75]

Further ecclesiastical and philosophical skirmishes flared up over the next several decades. In 1795 Hezekiah Balch, a Presbyterian frontier missionary and founder of Greenville College in Tennessee, toured New England to raise funds for his college. He fell under Hopkins's spell and brought back to Tennessee as much New Divinity as new money. The Presbytery of Abingdon in Tennessee acted to censure him for heterodoxy; in response, he and five followers imitated the example of Jacob Green and formed an independent presbytery, which (to the disgust of the Abingdon Presbytery) a synodical commission recognized as a legitimate presbytery. Balch's censure remained a live issue and was eventually taken all the way up to the General Assembly of the Presbyterian Church which met in Philadelphia in 1798, where he was found guilty of teaching false doctrine on the most objectionable Hopkinsian heads:

in making disinterested benevolence the only definition of holiness or true religion. . . . In representing personal corruption as not derived from Adam . . . thus, in effect, setting aside the idea of Adam's being the federal head or representative of his descendants . . . in asserting that the formal cause of a believer's justification is the imputation of the *fruits and effects* of Christ's righteousness, and not that righteousness itself.[76]

Unabashed, Balch would confess only to imprudence; he was restored to good standing by the General Assembly and went happily back to Tennessee, where for the next twelve years he made Greenville College a New Divinity hothouse.[77]

A similar contest had broken out in New York City over the ordination in 1810 of Gardiner Spring. The Brick Presbyterian Church of New York, having tried several times to obtain a pastor, turned to New England and invited Spring, a graduate of Yale, as a last resort. Spring's connections were all too well known, and an apprehensive New York Presbytery had Spring preach a trial sermon to them to take his measure. Spring chose to preach on "Human Ability," and his undisguised New Divinity sent the presbytery into an uproar. Only when the influential Samuel Miller interceded for Spring on the grounds that he was a "very pliable man" did the presbytery relent and install him at the Brick Church.[78]

But not all of the members of the Presbytery of New York were pleased at this indulgence. Ezra Stiles Ely, chaplain of the New York City Hospital and a razor-tongued zealot, resumed the battle over Spring by publishing in 1811 *A Contrast Between Calvinism and Hopkinsianism,* unquestionably the most savage treatment of the New Divinity ever written; in it Ely attempted to make the terms "Calvinist" and "Hopkinsian" mutually exclusive:

> It will be evident, that some of the doctrines of Hopkinsianism . . . if they have not sprung from doctrinal objections, or from a desire to compromise with the enemies of our God, Christ; and from the pride of "philosophy, so-called"; may certainly be traced down in their consequences, through various erroneous systems, to deism, and in some instances from deism to atheistical fatality.[79]

Or, if the New Divinity did not lead men to unbelief, it would lead them to the wrong kind of belief. "The advocate for a general and indefinite atonement cannot fail to have recourse to Arminianism for answers," Ely warned. After all, he reasoned, how "does the *written display* of God's glory, in loving mercy, while he loves his law and hates sin, make an atonement? . . . The manifestation of his holy indignation constitutes no expiation of guilt." And if it is not such an expiation that secures salvation, what? Human free will? "NOAH WEBSTER, ESQ. in his dictionary defines an *Arminian* to be 'one who denies predestination and holds to free will, and universal redemption,'" Ely reminded his readers. "In its proper place he might have introduced the name *Hopkinsian* before the same definition."[80]

Ely's most substantive quarrel with Spring was over psychology. For Ely, the vocabulary of faculty psychology might as well have been engraved on tablets, for intellectualism reigned supreme for him as the only safe theory of will.

Faith, then, implies knowledge of . . . testimony, assent to its doctrines, approbation of the plan it reveals, and acceptance of the offer which it makes to the sinner. In this way, and no other, it gives reverence, love, and worship to God . . . there can be no just views of God, or of his law, without understanding and accrediting the testimony, in which those views are exhibited. . . . There may indeed be a *disposition,* which will certainly be affected by a suitable object, when perceived; but there cannot be love without some previous knowledge. . . . Calvinists believe that before there can be any affection of love for any spiritual object, that object must *first* be presented to the eyes of his understanding.[81]

What Ely objected to in the New Divinity was, first, that they put the volitional cart before the intellectual horse. "The poets have represented their LOVE to be blind," he sneered; "this fiction has become a part of the new divinity," for in that scheme, "love is the effect to be produced and then the understanding is to be enlightened."[82] Second, Ely rejected the unity of the Edwardsean psychology, with both its absence of internal conflict between the will and the understanding and its consequent moral absolutism.

[the New Divinity] says there are no contending principles, no opposing dispositions in the good man; but all his desires are perfectly holy, or perfectly sinful. . . . Man is a complex being, composed of body and spirit, which constitute him a compound agent; and all his actions are therefore of a complex nature.[83]

To Ely, there was no way in which the will could be said to be free, in either a moral or a natural sense. Detached from the understanding, it could do nothing in its depraved state but fight against truth, rendering true obedience to the Gospel an utter impossibility. Talk as Spring might, Ely believed there was nothing to distinguish a moral from a natural necessity—let a man suffer under a moral impossibility "in relation to moral or religious subjects" and he may as well be under a natural one as well. "The fallen man has no more power of any sort to live, than the dead man to move."[84]

But the most formidable opposition to Hopkinsian Presbyterianism did not come from vehement men like Ely. Ely, in fact, was too vehement even for most Presbyterians, and when he moved to the Pine Street Church in Philadelphia in 1813, he continued to argue against Hopkinsianism so incessantly that the congregation split, a Hopkinsian faction organizing an independent Presbyterian church and the remainder of the congregation eventually asking Ely to leave. Undaunted, he prevailed on the Synod of Philadelphia to authorize a "Pastoral Letter" of his in 1816, in which he encouraged resistance to "the introduction of Arian, Socinian, Arminian, and Hopkinsian heresies," only to have the General Assembly, led by Samuel Miller, suppress the "Letter" as "offensive."[85] The real bulwark of resistance would lie in the Theological Seminary of the Presbyterian Church in the United States at Princeton, organized in 1812, and especially with its first professor, Archibald Alexander.

Unlike Ely, Alexander was no shouter and published no work denouncing Hopkinsianism. But in one respect, he never had to: Princeton Seminary became the narrow neck of the Presbyterian bottle through which all of Presbyterianism's subsequent leaders would have to flow, and he had but to inculcate any philosophy *except* immaterialism, any theology *but* that of Bellamy and Hopkins, any ecclesiology *but* that of the New Divinity, and Hopkinsianism (not to mention deism and infidelities of a paler sort) would be screened out at the source.

Just by occupying that strategic position almost anyone might have succeeded in stoppering up the Hopkinsian virus. But Alexander had peculiar qualifications for this task which made him all the more effective. For one thing, he had had his own youthful fling with Edwardseanism and had come away the sadder but wiser theologian. Born in 1772 in the Shenandoah Valley so assiduously evangelized by Samuel Davies, Alexander first studied under William Graham, an eclectic amateur who ladled out a potent mixture of Cartesian rationalism, Scottish realism, and Jonathan Edwards. Alexander's education accordingly wandered from reading in Locke and Witherspoon to "Edwards on the Will, on Original Sin, and on the Affections."[86] To judge from Alexander's earliest extant sermons, it was Edwards who made the biggest impression, for his early preaching was full of revivalistic fire about moral inability, heart language, and exercises. In his second preached sermon in March 1791, Alexander warned "careless sinners" that their claim to be "unable to come unto Christ" was purely a moral inability and really did nothing to restrain them from obedience to the Gospel. "You cannot because you will not," and since you "labour under such an inability, you therefore are inexcusable."[87] To another audience, he explained that they need only look to their wills to find the source of their sin. "The character of every man is determined by the habitual bent and purpose of his will," Alexander said. "All human actions flow from the will; this is, therefore, the mainspring of all good conduct. Man's depravity consists mainly in the opposition of his will to the will of God."[88] From there it was not far to the conclusion, which he aired before the Presbytery of Lexington in April 1791, that the "heart" was mainly "a ruling principle of action."[89] Men, he hinted in another sermon, ought not think that regeneration quickened some substance of which they were unaware and which otherwise excused their wills from repenting. Men could know only that they had ideas, and the ideas were either holy or unholy. "Let no man deceive himself with the deceptive idea, that this change may have been experienced without his being conscious of its effects."[90] The heart was thus known by its exercises, and by exercises alone.

But Alexander's training was not exclusively Edwardsean. William Graham had also put him to reading Thomas Reid and other Scots, and Alexander's early preaching shows traces of this Scottish influence, too. In 1795 his sermons offered people straight Westminster theology on imputed righteousness and frequent appeals to the "moral sense."[91] He would not go so far down the road of intellectualism as to suppose that the moral sense and "reason" were coterminous, but at the same time he could not be sure that having an evil will totally obliterated some inkling of what true virtue was. Whatever it was, Alexander claimed, "the soul of man has an inward monitor which, according to its light, accuses him of the sin which he commits." No matter what the condition of the will, within man is a sense which intuitively perceives error, and

Although the mind of man has fallen into an awful state of blindness, and disorder, yet conscience is not obliterated: as far as it has light, it still remonstrates against the commission of sin, and utters its voice of condemnation, when sin has been committed. Happily, some actions are intuitively seen to be morally wrong, and by no sophistry can the soul be persuaded to approve them.[92]

And so elements of both Edwardseanism and the "common sense" philosophy floated unresolved and unreconciled in Alexander's mind for almost a decade.

What finally tipped Alexander away from his youthful Edwardseanism was his tour of New England in 1801. Having sat in on the final approval of the "Presbygational" Union at Litchfield, Connecticut, as a representative of the General Assembly, Alexander took the time to acquaint himself with the New Divinity firsthand, and paid personal visits to Edwards the Younger, Hopkins, and Nathan Strong, even preaching in Hopkins's pulpit. But what he saw and heard caused him to shrink back abruptly from this New England embrace. That God was the author of sin, that people should be so disinterestedly benevolent as to be willing to be damned if it would glorify God, that the "use of means" was illegitimate—all these ultraisms shocked Alexander, no matter how carefully qualified, if they were qualified at all. The shock was made worse when one of Hezekiah Balch's associates dragged Alexander off to Franklin, Massachusetts, for a spell with Nathanael Emmons. "I have no doubt that he had a design in taking me to this venerable theologian," Alexander recalled, "believing that by his conversation I should be brought over, for I was already quite a follower of Edwards." He preached for Emmons, too, and found Emmons quite genial company, but also found him catechizing one of his theological students in how "to prove man's dependence on God for every thing, including every thought and emotion."[93] It may also have been Emmons whom he later recalled having heard

once undertake to prove that moral men and formal professors must, in all cases, be far more wicked than the blaspheming infidel and gross debauchee. The argument was plausible, but laboured under one essential defect; and I was of the opinion, and still am, that such a doctrine is highly dangerous, and calculated to encourage men to go to all lengths in wickedness.[94]

All this was more than Alexander could swallow. He was, in the end, too much a Presbyterian and too much a lover of the old Presbyterian church idea to surrender to this unalloyed picture of New England, and he instead experienced a profound revulsion against the New Divinity. "On his return from New England," Alexander's son wrote, "his views, which had been somewhat modified by eastern suggestions, began to fix themselves more definitely in the direction of the common Westminster theology."[95]

James Waddel Alexander might as well have gone on to add that his father also became a more convinced partisan of the Scottish philosophy after that. His personal experiences convinced him that immaterialism was bad philosophy as well as inducing bad practice and bad divinity, and when Archibald Alexander arrived at Princeton Seminary in 1812 as its first professor, he was as determined to establish in the seminary the Presbyterianism of Westminster Calvinism and Scottish philosophy as John Witherspoon had been fifty years before at the college. He went to work at once on the idea of substance, conceding at the very beginning what the Exercisers had always taken as the end of the argument that we have no empirical knowledge of a soul substance. "We know nothing of the soul but by its acts," Alexander told his classes at Princeton, "we have no consciousness of any thing but acts of different kinds." That, however, did not eliminate ipso facto any possibility of such substance existing, for although "we are not conscious of the existence of what is called disposition, temper, principle," nevertheless "we as intuitively believe in the existence of these, as in the existence of the soul itself."[96] By appeal to the common moral sense of mankind, sufficient proof of "moral or spiritual nature" was intuitively available to all men, even to the Exercisers. Of course, Alexander was aware that they were just the people most likely to denounce the common moral sense of man as depraved, and demand more purely experimental evidence. But Alexander's reply was simply that of the Scots:

this is a question not requiring or admitting of much reasoning. It is a subject for the intuitive judgement of the moral faculty. If there are minds so constituted that they cannot conceive of permanent, latent dispositions in the soul, both good and evil, I can do no more than express my strong dissent from their opinion, and appeal to the common sense of mankind.[97]

It is possible, therefore, that both sin and regeneration occur apart from the conscious acts of the will. Alexander thought it an "interesting question whether now there are any persons sanctified from the womb" and he was certain that "sin may be committed in sleep."[98] He was also certain that, as a rule, people were often genuinely unconscious of their sinfulness, or, if awakened, were unable by an exercise of will to get behind the conscious self to remedy the situation. "No man knows how much iniquity still lies concealed in his own heart," Alexander wrote, and even "they who are redeemed from sin" only discover the utter inability of man to extirpate it from his nature." Similarly, we cannot be entirely conscious of regeneration either, since regeneration is a renewal first of human nature. "Many persons, when they hear of the greatness of this change, are led to infer, that its greatness must always be manifest to the consciousness of the person who is subject of it."[99] But, Alexander demurred, "the operation of the Spirit cannot be traced in the work of regeneration."

We can neither explain the manner in which the work commences, the process by which it is carried on, nor its termination; but as in the case of the wind, we can hear its sound, so here we may observe the fruits and effects of the Spirit's operation.[100]

In that case, more than just the will of man may be depraved without the subject knowing it. "The root of sin is deep in the nature of man, and its ramifications extend through his whole constitution of mind and body" and not only the will.[101] For instance, "our affections," Alexander said, "are properly the subject of moral qualities, good and evil," and "the understanding," too, is "just as much a moral faculty as the will." Hence, he condemned as erroneous "that doctrine . . . which confines depravity or holiness to the will, and which considers the understanding as a natural and the will as a moral faculty. The soul is not depraved or holy by departments; the disease affects it as a soul; and of course all faculties employed in moral exercises must partake of their moral qualities."[102]

Having exploded both the Exercisers on substance and the Tasters on volitional depravity, Alexander shifted his critique from unconscious to conscious psychology. Predictably, his Princeton lectures revealed a by now full-blown intellectualism. "This noble faculty was certainly given to man to be a guide in religion, as well as in other things," Alexander claimed, because "every man's feeling & volitions are in accordance with the prevailing practical views of the understanding." He dismissed Edwards's location of true religion in the affections: Edward's "*Treatise concerning Religious Affections* is too abstract and tedious for common readers."[103] Not only true religion, but untrue as well, hangs on the understanding, since even "all sin arises from some error or deception of the mind."[104]

But, in the end, what does this mean for the will? Intellectualism had always carried with it frank implications of hard determinism, with the will dancing attendance on the understanding. And that posed the same problem that every other intellectualism interested in moral responsibility had encountered, and that was how to speak of a will controlled by a nature or a mind that could also be understood as unmanipulated and could be held responsible. Alexander as much as acknowledged the problem aloud in one sermon where he said, "Talk not of the freedom of the will: the will, as much as any other faculty, is under the influence of depravity. If the will were capable of putting forth one right volition, one holy act, the new creation would be unnecessary; for life, in that case, would have an actual existence in the soul of man."[105] But to leave matters there would also leave men saddled with a depravity they could not wholly conceptualize and which they could not psychologically alter. For Alexander, born in the wake of Hobbes and Hume but too early for Kant (in America, at least), nothing was more imperative than to squeeze human responsibility out of depravity. Edwards had shown one way, but that way was closed to Alexander. He appealed instead to the *fact* that all human beings intuit moral freedom; and the perception of that testimony as *fact* made its existence necessarily real. "In judging of the moral quality of an act, we never attempt to go further back than the spontaneous inclination," Alexander wrote; to discover whether or not "we possess liberty," we instead appeal to "the intuitive perception of every mind." And this intuition very often revealed that "man is conscious of liberty and nothing can add to the certainty which he has as a free agent." The will, therefore, is free—a freedom, true, to "will and act in accordance with his own inclinations," but then again those inclinations were not susceptible of empirical analysis, thereby leaving one with the simple fact of freedom.[106] So long as substance existed, it could be invoked to show that the will was self-determining; so long as substance remained known only by intuition, that same intuition could also decide in favor of free will. As for the role divine sovereignty was to play in this freedom, Alexander advised his students not to worry overmuch about it.[107]

IV

The appeal to intuition saved Alexander from the problem posed by a depraved substance's power over the will.

Objections to self-evident principles, however plausible, should not be regarded; for, in the nature of things, no reasonings can overthrow plain intuitive truths, as no reasonings can be founded on principles more certain. Though we may not be able to understand or explain with precision wherein freedom consists, yet this ignorance of its nature should not disturb our minds.[108]

This was, for Alexander, better than attributing all efficiency, and therefore blame, to God. It also allowed for something which may have lent Alexander's arguments more force: that no church could ever hope to have a consciously regenerate membership. Because the absolute fact of regeneration was buried in the inaccessible reaches of the nature, and only gradually and only fallibly revealed itself in converted behavior, Alexander opposed "all attempts by man to draw a visible line between the regenerate and the unregenerate" and warned the General Assembly against any inclination "which savours of greater strictness and purity, which considers none as properly members of the visible church, but such as exhibit evidences of vital piety."[109] To that end, he maintained that

Churches and church-officers are not to be censured for receiving into the communion such as make a fair profession, and even if they suspect their sincerity, they have no right to exclude them, until by some overt act or speech they clearly discover that their hearts are not right in the sight of God. The power of searching the heart belongs not to men—no, not even to apostles.[110]

Alexander's theory of will may have hung together by only a very few hooks, but they were also the hooks that held Old Side Presbyterianism together, too.

Alexander did not save Presbyterianism from Edwards single-handedly, although he was singularly effective at discomfiting New England students who essayed to break rhetorical lances with him. He was not even alone in his fight against Edwardseanism at Princeton, for he was joined by Samuel Miller in 1813 (who could tolerate a run-of-the-mill Hopkinsian but not Emmons), and later still by his protégé Charles Hodge, whose animus against New England theology would generate numerous polemical articles and a major two-volume critique of Edwards and the Great Awakening, both in New England and in Presbyterianism. But Alexander remained the dominant intellectual figure in the founding, organizing, and administration of the seminary. Miller remains a vague and shadowy figure in Princeton Seminary's history, while Hodge in his early years as an instructor was very much an extension of Alexander's mind. And, as the preceptor responsible for educating over 1,100 students between 1815 and 1840, Alexander made Presbyterianism and the Scottish philosophy to be very nearly a natural mating.[111]

Ironically, he never rid himself completely of Edwards's influence. In all of his critiques of Edwardseanism, he aimed only at the satellite problems and never at the core, Edwards's occasionalist causality in the natural world. This was not for want of knowing, since on the subject of miracles Alexander displayed a minute reading of Hume and devoted some attention to other works on causality. Perhaps Alexander pulled his punches because, whatever else he found reprehensible about

Edwardseanism, he still admired the deep piety of New England even while he condemned its conclusions. The enemy of Edwardseanism could still write in 1844 that, besides Edwards, "few men ever attained, as we think, higher degrees of holiness, or made more accurate observations on the exercises of others."[112] And in his inaugural address as Professor of Didactic and Polemic Theology at Princeton in 1812, he felt free to describe regeneration simply as "a lively impression made by the Spirit of truth" which "banishes all doubt and hesitation."

This may appear to some to savour of enthusiasm. Be it so. It is, however, an enthusiasm essential to the very nature of our holy religion, without which it would be a mere dry system of speculation, of ethics and ceremonies. But this divine illumination is its *life*, its *soul*, its essence.[113]

John Williamson Nevin cast a cold eye on this retrogression. As a student at Princeton in the 1820s, he was gratified that "Dr. Alexander was always careful to recommend the divinity and piety of the seventeenth century, showing that they formed the elements in which mainly his own piety lived, moved, and had its being." Still, he tacitly blamed Alexander for fostering, or at least not doing enough to suppress, "the unchurchly scheme" of New England which "continued to exercise a strong practical force at Princeton."[114] Nevin would spend the best years of his career elaborating on that complaint, and blaming Hodge and Alexander for not having hated New England enough.

In this ambivalence we catch again an overtone of the same ambiguity that plagued Old Calvinism's response to Edwards. Certainly, Old Calvinism and Old Side Presbyterianism shared a great deal in common: their mutual fascination with Scottish philosophy and with the church-in-society arrayed them both as philosophical and practical enemies of Edwards's achievement in *Freedom of the Will*. But co-belligerence does not necessarily mean the same as alliance, as the events of the year 1837 were to prove.

CHAPTER 7

The Waning of Edwardseanism

From Asa Burton to Lyman Beecher

Almost every theological party, faction, or movement in New England from 1758 (the death of Edwards) until 1858 (the deaths of Nathaniel William Taylor and Bennet Tyler) defined itself in some way or other according to "Edwards on the will." One measure of the sheer impact of *Freedom of the Will* was the extent to which it made volition, and especially reconciliationist theories of volition, the principal topic of New England discourse. Of all the efforts to cope with the theory of will spawned by *Freedom of the Will*, the New Divinity was the most ingenious, and had the most intense following, so much so that it is safe to suggest that the New Divinity represents the most vital and fecund intellectual movement in the early republic. Indeed, if intellectual vitality were all that counted, the New Divinity would never have fallen into the oblivion to which it was so long consigned.

There are three basic reasons why the New Divinity passed into intellectual eclipse: one was a problem inherent in its popular strategy, another was a problem in its leadership, and another—the largest— was the successful resurgence of Old Calvinism at Yale in the 1820s, which displaced Edwards's peculiar brand of voluntarism in New England affections with an intellectualist libertarianism. The demise of Edwardseanism dragged down with it the credibility of a reconciliationism built on an Augustinian voluntarism.

In another sense, the demise of Edwardseanism was part of the overall triumph of Scottish "common sense" philosophy within the structure of American religion and American higher education. And in still one further sense, the resurgence of Old Calvinism, particularly in the form of Nathaniel William Taylor, affords a bridge by which the parochialism of Richard Mather and Solomon Stoddard is linked to Horace Bushnell. It must be remembered that Old Calvinism represented the mainstream of New England orthodoxy, while Edwardseanism spoke for one strand of thought, the strand of separatism, standing aloof and critical on the fringe. To give it its due, Edwardseanism proved to be, for almost a century, a position to be reckoned with, and that was because Edwards had endowed it with the philosophical fruits of his genius. Thus, the intellectual progression from Edwards to Hopkins to Emmons is perhaps the single most interesting phenomenon in the history of American thought. But it remained a fringe position all the same, and all that Old Calvinism required to reassert its hegemony was someone to devise a satisfactory alternative to *Freedom of the Will* and its concomitants.

This would not have been possible, however, had not the ingenuity of Edwardseanism reached its zenith in Nathanael Emmons and thereafter declined. The first sign of decay in the New Divinity was its increasing incapacity to sustain the level of anxiety it sought to promote, and which smoothed the way to the embrace of its other teachings. In short, when it pricked people, they no longer bled. Part of that developed as a simple result of the law of diminishing returns. The New Divinity depended for its *popular* impact on the shock value of its preachings: no "use of means," no unregenerate doings, absolute benevolence, willingness to be damned for the glory of God, willingness (as in Emmons) to preach one's own offspring into hell for the sake of that glory. None of these items, strictly speaking, was ever more than logically peripheral to the theological core of Edwardseanism, but they moved to the fore because of their usefulness in promoting the atmosphere of crisis in which the exercise of the will Edwards had described could be seen to be all-in-all. These ideas became battering rams, to jar complacent parishioners out of their pews and onto their knees, acknowledging their perfect natural ability to repent and wailing over the moral inability that showed how sinful they were.

These ideas were also high-explosive, and they often backfired, but they just as often worked. They would, however, work only for a while, until the noise of them became routine enough that crisis ceased to flow from their application. The Great Awakening was the prime example that an undiluted diet of spiritual shock will last only so long. That the New Divinity kept it going so long in revivals that kept on flaring up until the turn of the century is a tribute to their adeptness and to the depths of thought locked away in *Freedom of the Will*. But even that formula could go only so far, and so the crises ceased to come. And in losing their capacity for crisis, the New Divinity men lost their reason for being. Edwards had originally sought to revive Calvinism as the only true means of staving off mechanism, for in his mind only Calvinism was capable of restoring that sense of supernatural immediacy Malebranche, Berkeley, and even Newton had sought to reinject into the universal machine. Hence, as much as the New Divinity talked of *law*, they meant only God's laws for himself; they denied the other forms of law (like the "use of means," and even causality itself) to make way for God's gracious arbitrariness toward his creation, the sense of a God on whose string we are dangled like a spider over the pit.

Hence, too, the psychology of the Exercise scheme, making all of man's consciousness float timorously on the waves of God's power; hence, the governmental scheme of the atonement, which left God no more obligated to save one soul after Calvary than he had been before Calvary. The difficulty with maintaining this sense of immediacy was that it was so often in the minority.[1] The New Divinity had chosen the route of immediacy when most of the rest of Anglo-American culture went over to theories of natural law, general providence, and common-sense libertarianism, and they came to lack an essential item of any successful intellectual system, simple *respectability*. When the battering rams of New Divinity rhetoric ceased to make breaches in men's hearts, the atmosphere of immediacy and crisis evaporated, and, with it, the New Divinity's principal consolation for the lack of respectability. After that, one by one, the underpinnings of the New Divinity psychology began to collapse.

This process is, by its nature, elusive of description and datability, but one can certainly see some of it in Asa Burton, the king of the Tasters. Burton was what we may call a "second-generation" Hopkinsian: born in 1752, graduate of Dartmouth and student of Levi Hart, Burton found in Edwardseanism "a new field in divinity" and during his fifty-six-year pastorate of Thetford, Vermont, acquired a formidable reputation as a preacher and preceptor. When his theological lessons were finally published in 1824 as *Essays on Some of the First Principles of Metaphysics*, they were hailed not just as the most thorough statement of the Taste Scheme but as "one of the great influential philosophical books of the world." What made Burton remarkable, however, was not that he had managed to state with greater felicity a case which had earlier been made by other Tasters like Smalley.[2] Burton had seen as clearly as anyone the problem posed for divine justice by the likes of Emmons, suspending as Emmons did the sinful exercises of men on the immediate agency of God. In search of a solution, Burton turned not only to Edwards and Smalley but to "every author who had made the mind the subject of his investigation, who was then in print." It was, at length, in the Scottish philosophers that Burton found satisfaction. From them, and from his own "reasoning, writing, and close application of the mind," he formulated a Taste scheme with a strongly Scottish tinge.[3]

To begin with, Burton broke apart the unity of the faculties that Edwards had proposed a generation earlier in *The Religious Affections* and *Freedom of the Will.* "If we . . . say that the mind is nothing more than a composition of thoughts or ideas, feelings and volitions, or as some have said, a bundle or union of exercises, then . . . we must alter" the English language.[4] His authority for prying the faculties back apart was, fundamentally, intuition. "From our thoughts," Burton insisted, "we infer the faculty called the understanding . . . and from our volitions we infer the faculty termed the will, which chooses or rejects," and the two must not be confused.[5] But in addition to these two faculties, whose existence (if not their exact relationship) had been fully acknowledged by Edwards, Burton also proposed to add another faculty of the mind, that of Taste, which he defined as "another faculty of the mind distinct from the understanding and from the will."[6] Burton described Taste as the "*feeling* faculty," or, alternately, "the heart," the "spring of action," and the "moral faculty." None of these faculties was permitted to obtrude upon the other: "The understanding *perceives,* but never *feels;* the heart *feels,* but never perceives anything."[7]

What happened, then, in volition was not a complex act but a fall of dominoes. Motives do not act on the will, nor does the will become as the greatest apparent good is. Instead, motives "affect" the heart; the heart in turn prompts the will; the will then acts to determine external conduct. Burton frankly allowed that the real cause of the will is *in* man. "The real active cause, which determines the will, or gives rise to volition, is in man, and a property of his nature."[8] The will itself may not have been self-determined, but, in Burton's scheme, the man choosing was.

Burton seems to have been quite aware that he had altered the alignment of heart and will within the framework of Edwards's voluntarism. "Scarcely any writer that I now recollect has considered the heart and will to be distinct faculties," Burton conceded; "they have generally been treated as one and the same."[9] What Burton did not recollect, or perhaps never knew, was that his tripartite division of the mind resembled nothing so much as the same three-way division of the mental faculties made by the Scots Presbyterian John Witherspoon and the Unitarian Samuel West. And with them, such a division had been made for the purpose of showing that the feelings were so hopelessly divided over their objects that it was the task of the will to arbitrate.[10]

This collapse of intellectual confidence within the New Divinity was accompanied by what can only be called the overall failure of nerve and imagination on the part of its leadership. By 1787 Ezra Stiles (with perhaps no little satisfaction) noted that the real "Pillars" of Edwardseanism had been removed or were "shaken or falling," and that their places were not likely to be filled.

President Edwards has been dead 29 years, or a generation; Dr. Bellamy is broken down both body & mind with a Paralytic Shock, & can dictate & domineer no more; Mr. Hopkins still continues, but past his force, having been somewhat affected by a Fit & nervous Debilitation; Mr. West is declining in Health, & besides was never felt so strong Rods as the others. . . . The very New Divinity Gentlemen say they perceive a Disposition among several of their Brethren to struggle for Preheminence—partly Dr. Edwards, Mr. Trumbull, Mr. Judson, Mr. Smalley, Mr. Spring, Mr. Robinson, Mr. Strong of Hartford, Mr. Dwight, Mr. Emmons, &c. They all want to be Luthers. But they will none of them be equal to those strong Reasoners, President Edwards & Mr. Hopkins. . . . Geniuses never imitate. Imitation may rise to something above laudable & very useful Mediocrity but can never reach originality.[11]

Stiles was, of course, premature to predict the intellectual demise of the New Divinity men in so wholesale a fashion: although Bellamy died in 1790, Hopkins lived on until 1803 (publishing in the meanwhile his greatest work, *The System of Doctrines,* in 1793) and West survived to 1818. Stiles was also wrong to shortchange the second generation so severely: Emmons, Spring, Edwards the Younger, Smalley, and Strong all had yet to reach their prime. But all the same, Stiles was right in one respect: the second generation was talented but it lacked the speculative daring that had made Hopkins and Emmons so remarkable. And though they still had yet to flower at the time of Stiles's prediction, their flowering was comparatively brief. Between Bellamy's death in 1790 and Hopkins's in 1803 the younger Edwardseans published a number of lengthy and interesting works, like Spring's *Moral Disquisitions* of 1789 and Nathan Strong's *Doctrine of Eternal Misery* in 1796; but after that, the fountain dried up. Edwards the Younger, probably the sharpest mind of the second generation, died prematurely in 1801 and never came to fulfillment as a theologian. What appear afterward from Edwardsean pens are mostly sermon anthologies, those traditional *nunc dimittis* volumes of the New England clergy. The only major treatise to appear from a New Divinity author after the turn of the century was Burton's *Essays,* and even these had been circulating in manuscript for twenty years or more before their publication. The second generation were not quite the mediocrities Stiles made them out to be, but they were not up to the level of their preceptors either.

Where Stiles's accusation of mediocrity fits best is on the third generation of the New Divinity men. This is not to say that these students-of-the-students-of-the-students-of-Edwards were not without talent. From 1815 to 1845 Hopkinsian ideas were still being preached with much of the old ruthless consistency by Edward Dorr Griffin, a student of Edwards the Younger, an enormously talented revivalist and president of Williams College; by Bennet Tyler, who early on served as a lieutenant to Azel Backus, Bellamy's successor in Litchfield County and later a president of Dartmouth and founder of the Theological Institute of Connecticut; by Leonard Woods, pupil of Emmons and for thirty-eight years professor of theology at Andover Theological Seminary; and by Asahel Nettleton, probably the most successful revivalist in New England's history of revivals after Whitefield, responsible by Bennet Tyler's breathless estimate for the "AWAKENING" of *"no less than thirty thousand souls."* Still, it is difficult not to read their essays, papers, and memoirs and not to conclude that in their hands Edwardsean voluntarism had lost its wonted force, and that the preachers of reconciliationism had fallen back on platitudes.[12]

Outwardly, the old flame of Edwardsean immediacy still seemed to burn in Tyler and Woods, in particular. But, inwardly, it is plain that the fuel for that flame had been exhausted, and that the precedent glimpsed in Asa Burton at the turn of the century had, further on, become routine. Although Tyler insisted that "moral necessity implied something more than simple certainty,"[13] Leonard Woods doubted whether moral necessity could be construed as meaning *more* than certainty. "All that we can say of men's dispositions of characters implies" nothing more than "that we can with more or less certainty predict what will be our feelings and actions on future occasions." To speak, for instance, of the necessity of depraved behavior in fallen men means simply *"that we can predict with certainty that it will in due time act itself out."*[14] In the same way, motives to sinful behavior acted on depraved men not as a cause (efficient *or* occasional) but as an "influence" that "induces" rather than guarantees certain results.

God himself constantly makes use of motives or rational considerations to induce men to right actions. This constitutes the whole system of influence, employed by the inspired writers and by the ministers and of God himself. Man is so formed as to be influenced to act by motives, and in no other way.[15]

To be sure, the results of such motives were *certain*—they would happen as though they were really necessary anyway—but without the sense of immediacy that necessity implied. As with Burton, the cause of men's sins could be attributed to the routine likelihood of certain behavioral features in men themselves.

No surprise, then that both Tyler and Woods also adopted the tripartite psychology of Taste that figured so prominently in Burton's *Essays*. Woods bluntly said that "it is a source of no small confusion in Edwards's Treatise on the Will, that he considers all the *affections* and *desires* as acts of the *will*," and he found it strange that "it has been said by some that volition, or the act of the will, always controls the affections."[16] Woods instead appealed to "consciousness" to prove that "the will, instead of having any direct control of the affections, is itself controlled by them."[17] And the "Affection is excited, and from its very nature must be excited, by a suitable object present in the mind's view, not by an act of will soliciting or requiring."[18] Tyler emphatically agreed. "There are certain laws of mind by which all our mental operations are governed," Tyler explained: "the will is controlled by the affections," and every motion of the affections to control the will is in turn caused "when a material object is presented to one of our senses," producing a sensation "without any act of the will."[19] Thus, the faculties of understanding, affection, and will are acted upon by each other rather than acting together, and, as with Burton, they act in a set sequence that needs no divine intervention beyond the dangling of a motive in the path; and yet, the sequence follows through of its own inherent weight, and not because of a necessary connection between motive and willing.

But that, of course, was precisely the weak link that the Exercisers and the Old Calvinists had pressed on: Did God make Adam sin by his immediate agency? If so, are then men not puppets, suffering from a natural inability to do good? If not, is there really any meaning to the word *necessity* with reference to human action? It is one measure of the flaccidity of these later Edwardseans that, unable or unwilling to work out an answer, they sought refuge from the dilemma by a singularly un-Edwardsean appeal to *fact*. Tyler would only declare that divine agency is a "fact," and human responsibility is a "fact" too— "that we can not see *how* they are consistent, is no evidence against the truth of either."[20]

The appeal to the simple, a posteriori facts of sin and sovereignty was itself a signal of a sharp methodological departure from the confident assertiveness of Edwards's a priori reasoning. This insistence on *facts* as an invocation of philosophical cloture was indicative of the degree to which New England Edwardseans (outside of Emmons) had abandoned immaterialism as their intellectual foundation in favor of the more respectable "Baconian" empiricism of the "moral sense" philosophers. So it is again no surprise to discover the disturbing degree to which not only Burton but Tyler and Woods embraced intuition as the ultimate arbitrator. "Appeal directly," Woods encouraged his students, "to man's moral sense," for every man will find by consulting his moral sense that he is intuitively (if not logically) a free and responsible creature.

These remarks disclose an important principle, namely: that *the feeling* of obligation is founded in the very constitution of the *human mind*; that it is an ultimate fact in our moral nature. And this is only saying, that God has made us moral and accountable creatures; that he has so formed us, that we are the proper subjects of law, and have an inward consciousness that obedience is our duty, and that disobedience is totally wrong and worthy of punishment.[21]

From there, Woods had nowhere else to go but further into the same amorphous libertarianism conceded by Alexander and Witherspoon. On those terms, Woods was ready to recognize a will, competent not only to mark out its own directions, but even to rearrange the moral disposition of the soul. The power to change our dispositions, said Woods, "is doubtless much greater than is commonly supposed." True, this power "is indirect and limited"—how could it not be when the consciousness could discover little of the existence of such underlying dispositions?—but all the same, Woods considered it "a well known fact, that some men by patient efforts acquire an ability to regulate their views and trains of thought in a manner quite above what others would consider practicable."[22]

The principal dissenter from this movement into "common sense" moralism was Edward Dorr Griffin, who with Enoch Pond (one of Emmons's last pupils) formed the last guard of the Exercisers. Griffin did not share Woods's confidence that "consciousness" can "extend farther than to intellectual and moral exercise" and discover the existence of that which may "*precede* action."[23] Griffin, to be sure, was willing to speak of the existence of a "temper," and even of a "heart" which "must be regarded as the seat of the feelings."[24] But by that, Griffin only meant what Emmons had meant, another species of exercise. The sinner's depravity of *heart* is merely "that *proneness to gratify himself,* growing out of the absence of love to God and the presence of self-love turned to selfishness." That which "constitutes the corrupt nature or temper" is simply "that *combination of inward circumstances* out of which will infallibly arise the exercises of selfishness and enmity against God." Accordingly, "the new nature" is not a new or renewed substance or heart, but new exercises; "not a new *existence,* but a new *relation* between the feelings towards self and towards God."[25]

Naturally this invited the predictable question: If we are nothing essentially but exercises upheld by an immediate divine agency, then how exactly did Adam or anyone else after him fall into sin? "How then can a holy being apostasize?" Griffin's answer, like that of his preceptor Emmons, was unflinching:

Not until the heart ceases to be inclined to fall in with the motives which moved it before. That cessation cannot be produced by good motives, and before it takes place bad motives cannot operate. It cannot therefore be the effect of motives. It must result from some influence, or some withdrawment of influence, behind the scene. If it results from a positive influence, God must be the efficient cause of sin; if it results from the withdrawment of an influence, the influence withdrawn was that which before inclined the heart to holy action; and that is the very efficiency for which we plead. Without resorting to efficiency and its withdrawment, how can we account for the fall of holy beings?[26]

But if God is responsible for all human exercises, how then can there be freedom? At that, even Griffin hesitated, and, like Tyler and Woods, he shrugged his shoulders.

It has been asked on our side, How can our faculties be constantly dependent and their operations forever dependent? There is nothing gained by anything delusive or by concealing any part of the truth. I admit therefore that the argument for divine efficiency involved in this question is not logical.[27]

Not to be logical: that for an Edwardsean was a significant concession, since so much of the argument of *Freedom of the Will* hung upon nice logical distinctions and connections between terms. Even for as sturdy an Exerciser as Griffin, the Edwardsean world had grown cold.

This shying away from the immediacy of Edwardsean voluntarism is evident not just on the theoretical level but even in the practical terms of Asahel Nettleton's revival preaching. In 1812 Nettleton, a Yale graduate (1805) and intimate friend of Tyler, commenced a circuit of itinerant revival preaching that produced the most striking series of "harvests" since the 1740s. He was the principal figure of the Second Great Awakening, and until typhoid fever permanently disabled him in 1822, he was the greatest revivalist Edwardseanism had ever produced; indeed, he was the revivalist for which Edwardseanism had always looked as a justification of its New Divinity. It is apparent from Nettleton's own writings that he took that responsibility so self-consciously that descriptions of his revivals are rhetorically patterned after Edwards's *Faithful Narrative*, right down to the case studies offered. But despite his unquestioned success, Nettleton relied for effect not on the shock tactics of the older New Divinity revivalism but on his uncanny skills as a casuist. His methods required quiet, not crisis, and instead of promoting anxiety, he preferred to defuse it.

When prayer was ended and the people were standing, he made a very close application of the subject to their hearts, in a short address, which was very silently and solemnly heard. He requested them to retire without making a noise. "I love to talk to you, you are so still. It looks as though the Spirit of God were here. Go away as still as possible. Do not talk by the way, lest you forget your own hearts."[28]

This was a far cry from the awesome boisterousness of Bellamy or the arrogance of Stephen West. No wonder Heman Humphrey had to go out of his way to affirm that Nettleton was indeed "an Edwardean," and Gardiner Spring had to be careful, half a century later, to remind his readers that Nettleton was a genuinely Hopkinsian product.[29]

In sum, then, by the 1820s the third generation of Edwardseans had run out of uses and applications for *Freedom of the Will*. The enormous burst of creative development of the premises laid down in *Freedom of the Will* had spent itself by the 1820s, and the generation of Tyler, Woods, Nettleton, and Griffin had, by and large, settled for rearranging and restacking the ideas of their predecessors to fit a less hospitable time. And the fault lay not so much in the New Divinity, which (abstractly considered) still had sufficient energy to carry them along on its back, as in the inability of the New Divinity men to do more with it.

But beyond the diminished capacities of the New Divinity leadership, there was another reason why the New Divinity was beginning to falter, and that was the means by which it translated the Edwardsean legacy from one generation of divines to another. Beginning in the first decade of the nineteenth century, massive changes were taking place in the ways lawyers, physicians, and divines were being taught their functions. The teaching of those specialized kinds of marketable knowledge in law, in medicine, and in divinity which came to be known as the "professions" were slowly being transferred out of the law office, the doctor's parlor, or the pastor's study into the law school, the medical school, and the theological seminary. The number of medical schools in the United States, for instance, jumped from three in 1800 to thirty-five in 1840, while the number of medical school graduates leapt from fifty in 1810 to 2,923 in 1850.[30] Similarly, the Congregationalists, who had no formal "seminaries" at all in 1800, suddenly hurried to found Andover Theological Seminary (1808), Bangor Theological Seminary (1815), the Theological Department at Yale (1822), and the Harvard Divinity School (approximately 1819, since this is when the first full faculty of theology existed at Harvard; Divinity Hall was not dedicated until 1826). The Presbyterians also sponsored their own flurry of seminary building, and within twenty-five years they had founded Princeton Theological Seminary (1812), Auburn Theological Seminary (1818), Union Seminary in Richmond (1824), Western, or Allegheny, Theological Seminary (1827), Columbia Theological Seminary (1828), Lane Theological Seminary (1829) and Union Theological Seminary in New York City (1836).[31]

The advantages of this movement for the theologians were threefold: first, by creating a professional level of training in a specialized theological institution, the ministry preserved at least the semblance of being on the same professional plane as law and medicine. Second, enormous power was concentrated in the hands of a very few practitioners of the profession, allowing them to impose uniformity on theological studies and also to limit, through admission and graduation policies, the number of fellow practitioners—in a word, it limited the pool of available competition. Third, the seminaries helped generate demand for their own services by creating a marketplace. Or, to put it another way, concentrating the production of professional practitioners under one roof made it easier for consumers of professional theological services to do their shopping. A graduate from a certain law school immediately carried an easily identifiable code, so to speak, depending on the reputation of that school; and theological seminaries made it vastly easier for churches to recruit candidates from a supply of ideologically predictable clergy.

To this social reorganization of knowledge the New Divinity men remained strikingly indifferent, just as they had been indifferent to most other schemes of social reconstruction. But this indifference was, this time, to be their undoing, for the parlor seminaries of Emmons and Bellamy became, after 1808 and the founding of the first Congregational Seminary at Andover, their albatross. Unable to rival the new seminaries in output or respectability, the log colleges went the same way as cottage industries in New England, leaving the seminaries in monopolistic control of clerical education. It was the unhappy fate of the New Divinity, who had spurned every aspect of a church-in-society, to be undone by shifts in the socializing of education.

The Old Calvinists, by contrast, profited immensely from this shift. They might have been derivative, unoriginal, and manipulative, but by the 1820s so were the Edwardseans. On the other hand, the Old Calvinists were anything but indifferent to the wants and needs of an audience. Precisely because they preached a church-in-society, they had learned to adapt to the demands of change in society. Dedicated to dominating social situations rather than propagating doctrinal systematics, they had no difficulty in founding and then using institutions that would foster still further domination.

What happened in the founding of Andover Seminary is the best example of how the Old Calvinists regained much of what they had lost to Edwardseanism, and did it not by outthinking them but by outmaneuvering them.[32] The story of Andover Seminary, simply put, begins with the capture of the Hollis Professorship of Divinity at Harvard by the Unitarian Henry Ware in 1805, a capture that, in symbolic terms, meant the seizure by heterodoxy of a system of clergy education that had stood intact for almost two centuries in New England. Previously the Hollis chair had been routinely filled by Old Calvinists, and although that did not enchant the Edwardseans, an Old Calvinist was the best they could expect at Harvard, and at least a man like David Tappan, who occupied the Hollis chair until his death in 1803, was far from an outright heretic. Ware the Unitarian was, and his election to the chair sent a tremor of alarm through New England.

Samuel Spring proposed, as a counter-measure, to organize a theological academy at either Franklin or West Newbury, Massachusetts, with his brother-in-law Emmons as instructor of theology. The proposal met with characteristically small response from Spring's fellow Hopkinsians, and might have gone for nothing had not the Old Calvinist Jedidiah Morse offered a counterproposal. Suggesting that Unitarianism represented a threat sufficiently vast to entice the New Divinity men out of their shells and into an alliance with Old Calvinism, Morse urged Spring to join him in founding a school in which both orthodox factions could jointly repel an infidel threat they could not repulse separately. Spring was at first hesitant to unite with those "who will not give up the half-way covenant, and are forever pleading for the duty which pertains to the BEST actions of sinners," but by degrees he warmed to the plan. Even though Morse insisted that someone less notorious than Emmons would have to be chosen as the professor of theology and a site less notorious than Franklin found, Spring was soothed by assurances that another Hopkinsian would be selected for the post, and that subsequent faculty appointments would always be neatly balanced between Old Calvinists and New Divinity men. Presumably, New Divinity money and Hopkinsian students would never be diverted or decoyed into other channels. Hence, when the new school opened in Andover, Massachusetts, in 1808, the professorship of theology went to Leonard Woods, the pastor of West Newbury and pupil of Emmons, while the professorship of biblical literature went to Moses Stuart, the protégé and successor of James Dana at the Center Church in New Haven.

This relationship, as Emmons had predicted, did not work nearly as well as Spring had envisioned (one Old Calvinist chuckled over the Andover graduate whose "sermon was all confusion—sometimes directing to repent, and sometimes to read and pray, in order to prepare for repentance"). Woods proved to be a bruised reed, and seemed every year to move further away from Emmons into a fuzzy amalgam of Edwardseanism and Scottish philosophy. The one undoubted Exerciser to join the faculty, Edward Dorr Griffin, lasted only two years as professor of pulpit eloquence, from 1809 to 1811, before moving on to the Park Street Church in Boston. And then, as Emmons had also predicted, once Samuel Spring had been removed by death in 1819, the Old Calvinist trustees felt free to stack the faculty with men of their own stripe. Emmons "apprehended that Hopkinsians, thus amalgamated with those whom they looked upon as Moderate Calvinists, would lose their distinctive character, so that the Hopkinsian party would after a time be extinct," and, Cassandralike, he was only too right.

But even Emmons could not disenchant the Hopkinsians from the aura of legitimacy that a seminary, or a seminary education, displayed. By successfully inveigling the New Divinity men to cooperate in the foundation of Andover, and then smothering them once they were inside, the Old Calvinists captured for their own use what became the sole institution for educating and legitimizing future clergymen in Massachusetts. Nor did the process of cooptation end there. In 1808 Morse and Spring also arranged the merger of the only New Divinity magazine, the *Massachusetts Missionary Magazine*, with Morse's *Panoplist*—and with similar results.[33] To Emmons's horror, and over his vehement opposition, Morse also succeeded in engineering the creation of a General Association of Congregationalists in Massachusetts, and although between 1806 and 1811 Morse was able to persuade only half the local Congregational associations to participate, that was bad enough to Emmons, who looked upon his own local Mendon (Massachusetts) Association with suspicion as trampling on the separate autonomy of individual congregations. By 1822, when Old Calvinists in Connecticut imitated the Andover seminary by establishing a divinity school at Yale, the New Divinity influence had been so diminished that no similar offer to cooperate was ever made.[34]

This resurgence of Old Calvinism was built upon more than just the cooptation of theological education. Even more serious was the appropriation by Old Calvinism of the figure of Edwards himself, a process which in some sense had been going for some time, but which became a major strategy at Yale under the aegis of Timothy Dwight between 1795 and 1817. Although Old Calvinism had never exactly disinherited Edwards, it had also issued severe and sustained criticisms of him, and a major rehabilitation of Edwards's reputation would seem a fairly tall order. But, for one thing, Old Calvinism had only ever needed to appropriate Edwards's piety, practical devotion, and preaching, not his doctrines; and, for another, Old Calvinism had in Timothy Dwight precisely the agent best suited to bring such an appropriation to pass. Indeed, the passage of Timothy Dwight out of Edwardseanism and into Old Calvinism is indicative, first, that the problems Congregational orthodoxy had to confront after the Revolution were greater than those posed in Edwards's day by polite Arminianism, and second, that the Edwardsean formula for volition would not only fail to drive men back to God, but would in the new circumstances of republican America actually open Congregationalism to infidelity.

Dwight certainly started off with all the credentials a legitimate Edwardsean could want: the grandson of Edwards and student of his uncle, Edwards the Younger, Dwight had been marked by Ezra Stiles in 1787 as one of the would-be Luthers seeking to seize preeminence among the New Divinity. The young Dwight wore his Edwardsean connections proudly enough. His anti–Old Calvinist satire, *The Triumph of Infidelity,* lauded his grandfather as "That moral Newton/And that second Paul," and in the same year that Stiles figured him for an Edwardsean, Dwight had announced that he "had as lieve communicate with all the devils in Hell as with that corrupt Church" of Northampton, then presided over by the Old Calvinist Solomon Williams.[35] Dwight also had carved out such a brilliant reputation for himself as a tutor at Yale in the 1770s that there had been talk of installing him rather than Stiles as president of Yale—talk Stiles darkly attributed to the Connecticut New Divinity men. In any event, Stiles won the presidency and Dwight resigned his tutorship, and a very promising career seemed to have gone up in smoke.[36]

Over the next two decades, Dwight survived both an external and an internal revolution. Buffeted by personal and family reverses, disappointed that the American Revolution had only opened up "strong temptations, for the sacrifice of integrity at elections, for caballing, bribery, faction, private ambition, bold contentions for place and power, and that civil discord, which is naturally accompanied by the prostration of Morality and Religion," and softened by the twelve tranquil years he spent as pastor of the Connecticut village of Greenfield, Dwight lost his taste for separatism and theological acrimony.[37] The man who had once refused to commune with Old Calvinists, and who was now granting that even a Papist could be a true Christian, had found that there were other, more ominous, dangers to worry about than sinners using the means of grace.

When at last Dwight returned to Yale triumphant in 1795 as Stiles's successor, he was less afraid of unregenerate doings than of the incursions made by French deism, infidelity, and atheism, and Dwight's ideological delousing of Yale in the 1790s has since become a piece of American folklore. He was also less afraid of the utility of a church-in-society, and of the organic unity of a covenantal community. He had seen in Greenfield the very real benefits yielded by parish nurture, and the equally enjoyable rewards of a parish which, if it could not be pure, could at least be decent. In "Farmer Johnson's Political Catechism," Dwight framed a question that his Edwardsean preceptors would not have dreamed of asking:

Q. How does religion make a man useful to his fellow?

A. By rendering him just, sincere, faithful, kind and public-spirited, from principle. It induces him voluntarily, and always, to perform faithfully in the several duties of social life. . . . All the real good of society springs from the performance of these duties, and cannot exist without them.[38]

Moreover, Dwight had also had a good look at just who was most strenuously advocating the separation of church and community, and it was not always the New Divinity purists. The come-outerism of the New Divinity, however well-intentioned, was playing into the hands of the atheists, the Jacobins, and the Jeffersonians, who sought to divide church from society in the interests of conquering both. Old Calvinism might have sunk its roots into the base earth of social impurity, but at least those roots would hold the society together as a covenantal unit against the erosion of infidelity, and for Dwight that was no small achievement. "From the intimate and inseparable connection between morality and religion," Dwight advised Yale seniors, "arises a most manifest necessity of religion for a nation."[39]

Hence, Dwight threw himself into the struggle to preserve Connecticut's church establishment. He campaigned vigorously to continue public support of the ministry ("Where will you get your ministers if you do not support them by law?") and scorned as unworthy and even suspicious the Baptists' plea of conscientious objection to church taxes ("those who do not wish to avail themselves personally of the direct benefits of religion, might as well plead an exemption from the support of roads, bridges, . . . because they do not use them, as excuse themselves from the support of the public preaching of the Gospel").[40]

Ironically, by the time Dwight took up his cudgels on behalf of the establishment, not all that much remained of it. Connecticut had been forced since 1727 to grant equal support to the Anglicans, and the Act of Toleration had extended public support to all Protestant churches in proportion to their membership. In 1792 Stiles had been forced to allow laymen onto the Yale Corporation in order to get state aid for the college; in 1793 a proposal to divert money from the sale of Connecticut's land claims in Ohio to the support of the ministry went down to humiliating defeat; and in 1795 the control of Connecticut's schools was passed from the ministers to lay societies. But Dwight was arguing for a principle, and against the individualism not only of the Republicans in the state but of the New Divinity in the churches. No lasting union, he warned, had ever been founded on the voluntarism of the naturally able.

Government, since the days of *Mr. Locke,* has been extensively supposed *to be founded in the Social Compact.* No opinion is more groundless than this. . . . It supposes, that they entered into grave and philosophic deliberations; individually consented to be bound by the will of the majority; and cheerfully gave up the wild life of savage liberty, for restraints, which however necessary and useful, no savage could ever brook for a day.[41]

Having unshackled himself from one of the principal corollaries of the New Divinity, he began to work backward, piece by piece, to the theory of will at the New Divinity's core. As he went, Dwight's new persona as an ex-Edwardsean did not escape attention. In Hartford, one wit sarcastically contrasted the two Dwights, new and old:

A minister of the Gospel, who ought to be an example to all men, sets at his desk in 1788, hates Yale College, hates Doctors [James] Dana and [Charles] Chauncy—is in contest with most of his brethren—hates sin and Pinckney, and a thousand more conscious men, puts it all into rhyme—issues it without his name—attacks without mercy men, who had been gaining fair characters before he was born. In 1800 is a President of a College, ay the head of a corporation of which his *milky Preacher* [i.e., James Dana] in the above poem is a member—is in high favor with the Clergy, and begins to rebuild the waste of character made by his indignant pen—and first foremost hails his former *hackney coachman of whores* as a pious man and real christian.[42]

And Dwight, for his part, candidly admitted that he was no longer the would-be Luther of Hopkinsianism. James Patriot Wilson, the Philadelphia Hopkinsian, was told by Dwight "that there were no Hopkinsians among them at Yale."[43] To John Ryland, one of Hopkins's English Baptist correspondents, Dwight declared in 1805, "I am not a Hopkinsian. . . . Their Systems I know, but do not believe; I think some of them [are] in danger of injuring seriously, the faith once delivered to the Saints."[44]

At Yale the principal evidence behind these declarations—and one which Dwight was the first to offer—was his repudiation of the rhetorical tactics of New Divinity voluntarism (Archibald Alexander had it repeatedly drawn to his attention in 1802 that Dwight "drew back from the opinion that God is the author of sin, and also from making a willingness to be damned a sign of grace") and especially his advocacy of the "use of means."[45] "The kingdom of God, as established by his pleasure, is a kingdom of means, regularly connected with their ends," Dwight wrote.[46] In passages reminiscent of Moses Hemmenway and Moses Mather—and it is incidentally of significance that Dwight's four-volume *Travels in New England and New York* makes no mention of New Divinity preachers, but reserves high praise for Moses Mather and other Old Calvinists—Dwight argued that the Old Testament afforded plenteous examples of the covenantal necessity of unregenerate doings.

God required *Moses* to command all sinners, of that nation, to labour; to cultivate their own ground; to circumcise their children; to celebrate the passover; to offer sacrifices; to be present at the public worship of God; to hear and learn his word from the mouth of their priests; and to teach all these things to their children. It will not, I presume, be questioned that Moses, in enjoining these things upon sinful *Israelites,* as well upon the virtuous ones, acted lawfully; or, in other words, was guilty of no sin. But what was lawful for *Moses,* in this case, is in itself lawful. Accordingly, it was lawfully done by all the Ministers, who followed him in the *Jewish* Church. It cannot therefore fail to be lawful to Christian Ministers, unless it has been plainly forbidden.[47]

And when an objector tried to fasten a logical inference on him—"*Do not sinners grow worse under convictions of Conscience, and in the use of Means?*"—Dwight impatiently dismissed the question as being beyond the experience of mortals to answer. "I am ignorant; and shall remain so, until I can search the heart, and measure the degrees of depravity."[48] The Hopkinsian students at Yale—among whom were Nettleton and Tyler—shook their heads in disbelief to hear Dwight preach so. Nettleton, who had come to Yale with Edwards's writings as his Gospel, and with Exercisers like Spring, West, and Samuel Whitman as his authorities, usually sat and listened to Dwight "without hesitation," but "on this point he differed from him, as did also a large part of the pious in New England."[49]

But Dwight was prepared to shock the pious still further, for, long before Nettleton heard those utterances from the pulpit of the Yale chapel, Dwight had stabbed even deeper at the heart of Edwardseanism. His encounter with David Hume (albeit secondhand, in the pages of Bishop George Horne) had convinced him that Hume's notion of causality was a sure ticket to atheism.

Mr. Hume declares,
That there is no perceptible connection between cause and effect;
That the belief of such connection is merely a matter of custom;
That experience can show us no such connection;
That we cannot with any reason conclude, that, because an effect has taken place once, it will take place again.[50]

But how different was this from Emmons? or Hopkins? or even Edwards himself on consciousness? Like James Dana thirty years before, Dwight concluded that "the Theology of a part of this country appears to me to be verging, insensibly perhaps, to those who are chiefly concerned, but with no very gradual step, towards a *Pantheism,* differing materially, in one particular only, from that of *Spinosa.*" In reaction, Dwight insisted that, by *cause,* "it will be observed, that I am speaking of what is called *the efficient cause*" and he denied as "totally erroneous" the "assertion" of "Mr. Hume . . . that *the connection between cause and effect exists,* or rather *is perceived, only in the Names.*"[51] In rejecting that, Dwight had shaken not only the New Divinity but the whole premise upon which the argument from moral and natural necessity was built.

His equation of Hume with Emmons eliminated any possibility of further interest in the Exercise scheme. "*That God by an immediate agency of his own, creates the sinful volitions of mankind,* is a doctrine, not warranted, in my view, either by Reason, or Revelation."[52] But he found little solace in the Taste scheme, not only because "the existence of the substratum itself cannot be proved," but principally because of the recurring problem the Tasters always had of explaining how, granting the existence of a *fixed* nature, and granting that Adam's fixed nature had been fixed as a *holy* one, Adam could possibly have committed sin—apart from the direct agency of God so beloved of the Exercisers.[53] This forced a not-entirely-willing Dwight to two conclusions. Unable to embrace either of the Edwardsean alternatives, Dwight first sought refuge from explanation by claiming metaphysical ignorance. "The nature of the cause itself, and the nature and manner of its efficiency, are in most instances, too subtle, or too entirely hidden from our view, either to be perceived at all, or to be so perceived, as to become the materials of real and useful knowledge."[54] When he spoke of nature, he meant only

a state of mind, generally existing, out of which holy volitions may, in one case, be fairly expected to arise and sinful ones, in another. . . . From these, we learn that it is not so powerful, nor so unchangeable, as to incline the mind, in which it exists so strongly to holiness, as to prevent it absolutely from sinning, nor so strongly to sin, as to prevent it absolutely from acting in a holy manner.[55]

Once the Edwardsean causality went, the absolutism went with it, and after that one could speak only of certainties and fair expectations rather than moral necessities.

Secondly, and almost inevitably, Dwight began to alter his grand-father's fundamental doctrine of the will's freedom. This process can be glimpsed in the organization of Dwight's Yale sermons (published in 1818–1819 in five volumes as a systematic theology), for, as Leon Howard noted in 1943, the published volumes contain more sermons than Dwight actually preached, and probably include sermons from the Greenfield days that did not fit into the Yale school calendar and were not revised.[56] Hence one can find Dwight assuring an audience at one point that God "certainly *will,* and *man* certainly *will not, be the Efficient.*" But in other sermons Dwight adjusts this to read, "Such a change then, as Regeneration or Renovation, exists in man, and is produced by the power of the Holy Ghost; yet is as truly active and voluntary in this change, as in any other conduct."[57] And to fend off criticism, he, too, invoked mystery:

Many questions may indeed be started concerning the nature and extent of the agency of the Holy Ghost in our renovation, our own agency, and the consistency of these doctrines; which may perplex the authors of them and their readers, and which may never be answered to their satisfaction. Still it will be exactly true, and highly important to us, that we must be born again; and that by the power of the Holy Ghost, exerted in co-incidence with our own agency; whether we do, or do not know any more of the subject than Nicodemus himself knew.[58]

As time went by, Dwight professed even more uncertainty about what went on in volition: "Concerning the Will, we are still more in the dark" and "have not yet determined in what Moral Obligation consists; or how far it extends: nor are we agreed concerning the nature of sin, or its guilt; or concerning the merit of virtue." Indeed, Dwight added, "we understand imperfectly the very *Reason,* by which we make discoveries."[59]

Dwight's disavowals of reason's capacity to explain volition, however much they express his humility, were also his excuse for falling back upon intuition as the primary evidence of freedom. "Men are intuitively conscious of their own free agency, being irresistably sensible, that they act spontaneously, and without any co-ercion or constraint."[60] Motives disappear from discussion, as does connection; and a vocabulary, if not the substance, of self-determination takes their place.

The certainty, perceived by mere mental inspection, that the changes passing in my own mind are produced by my own active power, is a higher certainty, than that, with which I perceive any other changes to be accomplished by any other active power. . . . Besides, if *we* are not agents, or active causes, possessing active powers, by which we can originate certain changes in the state of things, but are mere chains of ideas and exercises, it will be difficult to assign a reason, why GOD is not, also, a mere chain of ideas and exercises.[61]

Where Dwight talked about motives, it was not in connection with volition, but divine Providence. God's rule of the universe is a moral government, and "a moral government is founded by motives."[62] But what Dwight meant by motives in this sense was not that which the "will was as," but an "influence"—and, since he had confined causality to efficiency, influence could only hope to induce certainty indirectly rather than by absolute connection.

It will not be pretended, that all extraneous influence on the mind destroys its freedom. *We* act upon the minds of each other, and often with complete efficacy; yet it will not be said, that we destroy each other's freedom of acting. God, for aught that appears, may act, also, on our minds, and with an influence, which shall be decisive; and yet not destroy, nor even lessen, our freedom.[63]

But Timothy Dwight's greatest gift to Old Calvinism was his ancestry. Old Calvinism had always, in a general way, wanted to make Edwards out to be one of them, both to embarrass the Hopkinsians and to drape themselves in his reputation. Dwight, the grandson of Edwards and student of Edwardseanism, now made that possible. He never explicitly repudiated his famous grandfather, and indeed was fond of insisting that he was entirely in harmony with the Edwardseans on such issues as the atonement and imputation. He showed, in fact, what James Dana had not been able to show, that one did not have to be an Edwardsean and subscribe to *Freedom of the Will* to claim

legitimate descent from Edwards. Dwight further legitimized this conclusion by aggressively promoting that ultimate imprimatur of Edwardseanism—the revival—three times during his tenure at Yale, in
1802, 1808, and 1813.[64]

Relying on the unquestionable authority of his lineage—no small
matter, that; Samuel Spring had risked his life under British fire at
Quebec to rescue another Edwards grandson, the scapegrace Aaron
Burr—and on his position at Yale, Dwight in effect retouched Edwards
as a respectable Old Calvinist. Old Calvinists would not hesitate thereafter to publicly denominate themselves as Edwards's heirs, even while
they privately muttered criticisms into their notebooks. The New Divinity men, having nothing in their leadership to match "Pope" Dwight,
were at the same time often drawn into the bargain, and the wavering
and hesitating we hear from pristine Edwardseanism, on the part of
Tyler and Woods, owes as much to Dwight's influence (in the cases of
Tyler and Nettleton, direct influence) as to their own defects as creative
thinkers.

If Dwight was responsible for the cooptation of the New Divinity's
theology, it was Lyman Beecher who was most responsible for similarly
coopting the New Divinity's revivalism. Beecher has emerged as the
most famous of Dwight's students at Yale, and it is in fact to Beecher
that we owe the famous account of Dwight's cleansing-of-the-temple
at Yale in 1797. Beecher adored Dwight as "second only to St. Paul"
(thereby bumping Edwards from the niche Dwight had accorded him)
and "loved him as my own soul"—which, considering Beecher's capacity for self-esteem, is saying a great deal.[65] Dwight apparently returned some of the sentiment, for (according to Beecher) Dwight "loved
me as a son," and seems to have been the moving force in getting
Beecher translated from his first church on Long Island (ironically, this
was the old church where David Brainerd had once candidated and
where Samuel Buell had spent a half century as incumbent) to the
strategic pulpit of Litchfield, Connecticut (which had been vacated by
the New Divinity man Abraham Fowler. Thus did Beecher become an
apostle of Yale to the fiefdom of Joseph Bellamy).[66] Dwight had picked
his man with the precision of moral necessity, for the substance of
Beecher's entire colorful career was a dedication to preserving the
power and place of the church-in-society. Like Dwight, Beecher was
less concerned about picking out the pure within the church than about
trying to keep the church from being displaced by infidel forces from

without. For Dwight in the 1790s it had been French atheism; for Beecher in the 1810s it was the Unitarians.[67] For Dwight and Beecher alike, the disestablishment of orthodoxy was a cultural and personal disaster. "We shall become slaves," Beecher warned, "and slaves to the worst of masters." And when, a year after Dwight's death, a coalition of dissenting sects and secular politicians (including Edwards's youngest son, the irreligious lawyer Pierpont Edwards) succeeded in terminating Connecticut's public support of the ministry, Beecher sat "on one of the old-fashioned, rush-bottomed kitchen chairs, his head drooping on his breast, and his arms hanging down," moaning, "THE CHURCH OF GOD."[68]

Like Dwight again, Beecher regarded the purism of the New Divinity men as a dangerous luxury in the face of such threatening enemies. As one of Dwight's postcollegiate theology students at Yale, Beecher "read Hopkins's Divinity, but did not take him implicitly," and forty years later Beecher was still assuring audiences that "the doctrine for which I contend is not new divinity, but old Calvinism."[69] Like so many others, Beecher stumbled at the problem of how Adam's sinless nature could have been changed into a sinful one without either God being immediately responsible or Adam being responsible through self-determination. He spurned Emmons, as he wrote to his daughter Catharine (who was then sitting under Emmons's preaching), because he could not accept Emmons's reduction of consciousness to a chain of ideas.[70] Rejecting Emmons and the Exercisers, he had hardly more time for the Tasters, and he judged them guilty of the very natural inability they sought to escape. If God

could command a change of moral tastes or instincts which are a part of the soul's created constitution, upon which the will cannot act but which do themselves govern the will, as absolutely as the helm governs the ship; then also the things required would be a natural impossibility, and could not be reconciled with free agency and accountability.[71]

More troubling for Beecher than the problem of how Adam could be condemned for a sinful nature he didn't create was how infants who died in infancy could also be thus damned. The problems are really not all that different—in essence, both ask how that which is innocent can be made out to be guilty when it is agreed that the innocent are not actually able to make themselves guilty. And Beecher was hardly the first to put the problem in those terms; Emmons had done it in one of his most horrific sermons, with the predictable conclusion that

God made infants, as he had made Adam, put forth sinful exercises. But by the 1820s it had become routine for the critics of Edwardseanism to replace the abstract person of Adam with the more painfully familiar image of dying infants, probably because a nineteenth-century imagination which might not have balked at consenting to the dispatch of Adam or Aaron Burr to perdition was sentimentally revolted at consigning what was now perceived as an inoffensive infant to the eternal flames.

Beecher's solution was to rewrite the meaning of "depraved nature" as it applied to infants—and, presumably, to Adam. As early as January 1822 Beecher confided, "For some time past, I have noticed a leaning of my mind to *heresy* on this long-disputed and very difficult topic."[72] In March 1825 he spelled out what he meant in a letter to Asahel Hooker (Bennet Tyler's old theological teacher) in which Beecher, with what would once again prove to be something less than originality, proposed that the concept of a *nature* in infants be retained, and even that this *nature* be regarded as the *certain* cause of sin, but without regarding that *nature* as itself sinful or sin as ever more than the *certain* result of it. Like Dwight, he did not try to pretend that the way out of the dilemma of the cause of sin was to redefine causality. Beecher could not but believe that causality was efficiency. But he could redefine what the agent of that efficiency was like, and so he did. As he explained to Hooker,

That nature in infants which is the ground of the certainty that they will be totally, actually depraved as soon as they are capable of accountable action— which renders actual sin certain, I call a depraved nature; and yet I do not mean by 'depraved nature' the same exactly which I mean by the term as applied to the accountable sinful exercises of the hearts of adult men. Nor does Edwards or Bellamy. Edwards calls it 'a prevailing effectual tendency in their nature' to that sin which brings wrath and eternal undoing; but he does not consider it as being sin in itself considered, in such a sense as to deserve punishment.[73]

Of course it was perfectly possible, as Emmons had done, to set the moment of accountable, and certainly sinful, action so close to birth as to make negligible the difference between becoming a sinner and being born that way. But it was the principle of the idea that Beecher enjoyed: no one was born sinful, nor was their subsequent sinning the exercise of God.

And what role did Beecher now propose to ascribe to the will, since action now took place apart from the control of either God or nature?

That would be easier to say if Beecher had been a systematic theologian; as it was, Beecher's intellect revolved around two poles only. "If I understand my own mode of philosophizing, it is the Baconian," he declared. "Facts and the Bible are the extent of my philosophy."[74] But even that is a revelation of Beecher's affection for the Scottish philosophy, and his comments in the 1830s indicate his predilection toward the Scots' intuitive libertarianism.

> Of nothing are men more thoroughly informed, or more competent to judge unerringly, than in respect to their mode of voluntary action, as coerced or free. . . . Our consciousness of the mode of mental action in choice, as uncoerced and free, equals our consciousness of existence itself; and the man who doubts either, gives indication of needing medical treatment instead of argument. . . . There is a deep and universal consciousness in all men as to their freedom of choice; and in denying this, you reverse God's constitution of man.[75]

Of course, Beecher did not propose to grant to the will "complete exemption from any kind or degree of influence from without." But for him, *influence* was as strong a word as he would use to describe the action of motives. When Beecher spoke of "God's government" as "a moral government, by motive and not by force," he had really come to think in terms of human, republican government, not moral necessity, to explain God's divine sovereignty over men.[76] God's will was manifested in terms of incentives, not decrees; of coaxings, not commands.

> What is family government, what is civil government, what is temptation, exhortation, or persuasion; what are the influences of the Holy Spirit, but the means, and the effectual means of influencing the exercises of the human heart, and the conduct of human life? . . . Natural government is direct, irresistable impulse. Moral government is persuasion; and the result of it is voluntary action in the view of motives. . . . The influence of motives cannot destroy free agency; for it is the influence of persuasion only, and results only in choice, which, in the presence of understanding and conscience, is free agency.[77]

At this point, with causality confined to efficiency, and efficiency reduced to producing certainty rather than necessity, Beecher had crossed the boundary separating Edwardsean reconciliationism from the foothills of libertarianism.

But in all this, Beecher was merely partaking of Dwight's new-fashioned Old Calvinism, and his invocation of Edwards and Bellamy in the letter on infant depravity is an indication of the degree to which the image of Edwards was being successfully coopted by Old Calvinism.

Like Dwight, Beecher embraced the Edwardsean doctrine of the atonement. Once more one finds the explanation of the atonement as a justification of moral government:

The gospel is not, as some have imagined, an expedient to set aside a holy, just, and good law, in order to sustain an inferior one, brought down more nearly to the depraved inclinations of men. God did not send his Son, to betray his government, and compromise with rebels, by repealing the law which offended them. He sent his Son, to vindicate and establish this law, to redeem mankind from the curse, and to bring them back to the obedience of the same law from which they had revolted.[78]

Extending that still further, Beecher consistently draped himself in a vocabulary which, on the surface, implied his solidarity with *Freedom of the Will.* "From Augustine to Edwards, and from Edwards to this day, the ability of man, as a free agent, has been taught as consisting in a biased and perverted will," Beecher told the students at Andover, thus neatly blocking himself in with Edwards; and to western Presbyterians, Beecher submitted a bewildering reading list when he wrote, "the authors which contributed to form and settle my faith, were Edwards, Bellamy, Witherspoon, Dwight and [Andrew] Fuller."[79]

But Beecher, more an organizer than a thinker, aimed less at coopting Edwardsean ideas than at coopting New Divinity activism—in this case, revivals. "It has already been made apparent," his son Edward explained, "that the one idea of Dr. Beecher was the promotion of revivals of religion, not merely in his own congregation, but as a prominent instrumentality for the conversion of the world, and the speedy introduction of the millenial reign of our Lord Jesus Christ."[80] As early as 1809 Beecher was stimulating revival on Long Island, and in 1822 in Litchfield, even as he was doubting infant depravity, Horace Mann (who had spent his youth writhing under Emmons's sermons in Franklin) heard Beecher preach a particularly *"hopkinsian"* revival, perhaps made all the more so by Beecher's use of Asahel Nettleton on the spot as his revivalistic coadjutor.[81]

The mention of Nettleton in conjunction with Beecher points to the fact that Beecher coopted not only New Divinity revivalism but also the revivalists themselves. It is significant that the recognition Nettleton enjoyed in New England as a revivalist did not begin until 1813, when Beecher invited Nettleton to come and preach in the Litchfield area, and thereafter much of Nettleton's career was centered in Litchfield County, probably under Beecher's management and perhaps for the

purpose of deflecting criticism from Beecher in the old Bellamy territory. When Nettleton came to New Haven and preached his greatest
revival at Yale College in 1820, he did so in the company of Lyman
Beecher. Nettleton would afterwards deeply resent the implication that
he was nothing but Beecher's man, but others believed it, and in 1827
Charles Grandison Finney would interpret Nettleton's actions at the
New Lebanon Conference as those of a stalking horse for Beecher.

Charles Grandison Finney affords yet another and more striking
example of Beecher's ability to manipulate the later Hopkinsians. Although Finney is unquestionably the best known of all nineteenth-century revivalists, he is more often interpreted as an expression of
Jacksonian America than of Edwardsean New England, and yet it is
only against the backdrop of the latter that his career has any real
meaning. We know little about his early religious training, and not
much more about him at all before 1818, except that he was born in
Warren, Connecticut, in 1792, moved with his parents to upstate New
York in 1794, and undertook a brief stint as a schoolteacher back in
Connecticut after 1810. He began to be noticed only after his return
to Adams, New York, in 1818, where he studied law and where, in
1821, he experienced a violent conversion that impelled him to leave
the law and become an itinerant evangelist.

Finney liked to think of himself as self-taught, but it soon became
obvious that, wherever his ideas had come from, they had a strong
Hopkinsian tinge:

Soon after I was converted I called on my pastor, and had a long conversation
with him on the atonement. He was a Princeton student, and of course held
the limited view of the atonement—that it was made for the elect and available
to none else. Our conversation lasted nearly half a day. He held that Jesus
suffered for the elect the literal penalty of the Divine law; that he suffered just
what was due to each of the elect on the score of retributive justice. I objected
that this was absurd . . . on the contrary it seemed to me that Jesus only
satisfied public justice, and that that was all that the government of God could
require. . . . I asked him if the Bible did not require all who hear the gospel to
repent, believe the Gospel, and be saved. He admitted that it did require all to
believe and be saved. But how could they believe and accept a salvation which
was not provided for them?[82]

And for the next six years he preached what sounded very much like
the New Divinity:

Instead of telling sinners to use the means of grace and pray for a new heart,
we called on them to make themselves a new heart and a new spirit, and pressed

the duty of instant surrender to God. . . . We taught them that while they were praying for the Holy Spirit, they were constantly resisting him; and that if they would once yield to their own convictions of duty, they would be Christians. We tried to show them that every thing they did or said before they had submitted, believed, given their hearts to God, was all sin, was not that which God required them to do, but was simply deferring repentance and resisting the Holy Ghost.[83]

Indeed, for one who claimed to be sui generis, Finney showed marked resemblances to the Exercisers. "I assumed that moral depravity is, and must be, a voluntary attitude of the mind," Finney remembered, and in his first published sermon he defined the "*spiritual heart*" as a "*deep-seated but voluntary preference of the mind,*" and regeneration as a change in "that abiding preference of our minds, which prefers sin to holiness."[84] A far from friendly observer, James Waddel Alexander, heard the same things from Finney in New York in 1837, and likewise concluded that Finney's sermon was "an odious caricature of old Hopkinsian divinity."

How did Finney come by these ideas? Perhaps they came from his Connecticut-born parents, perhaps from others in that flood of immigrants from New England into upstate New York in the 1790s that turned the area into a virtual Yankee colony; perhaps it was his own sojourn as a teacher in New England—whatever the source, the New Divinity element in his preaching struck a sympathetic note among the New England immigrants in New York, and that sympathy accounts for much of his fabulous success as a revivalist there. What must also go into the calculus of his success was the brazen impudence of his manner.

They used to complain that I let down the dignity of the pulpit; that I was a disgrace to the ministerial profession; that I talked to the people in a colloquial manner; that I said "you," instead of preaching about sin and sinners, and saying "they"; that I said "hell," and with such emphasis as often to shock the people; furthermore, that I urged the people with such vehemence, as if they might not have a moment to live; and sometimes they complained that I blamed the people too much. One doctor of divinity told me that he felt a great deal more like weeping over sinners, than blaming them. I replied that I did not wonder, if he believed that they had a sinful nature, and that sin was entailed upon them, and they could not help it.[85]

But even these criticisms were nothing new to the Hopkinsian past, and the very things had once been said of Emmons, and with perhaps the same savage retort. Indeed, Finney's most heavily criticized innovation—calling convicted sinners to come forward to an "anxious bench"—was itself merely Finney's way of calling attention to the fact that the sinner had full natural ability to perform any of the duties of repentance.

Those innovations irritated Asahel Nettleton, and when Nettleton met Finney in Albany in 1826, he was appalled not only by Finney's loudmouthed mannerisms but also that Finney had been using Nettleton's name as sanction for them. Incensed, Nettleton called on Beecher to join him in denouncing Finney as an enthusiastic fraud; Beecher, knowing of Finney only from what Nettleton told him, and not wishing to see his condominium with the Hopkinsians wrecked by an upstart New Divinity fireball, joined Nettleton in issuing a booklet containing several letters condemning Finney's "new measures." Finney's lieutenants (and probably Finney himself, though he later denied it) were alarmed at this damaging rebuff. They approached Beecher to achieve a compromise (which says something about perceptions of the relationship of Beecher and Nettleton), and a meeting of New Englanders and New Yorkers was arranged for New Lebanon, New York, in June 1827.[86]

It has to be emphasized that the New Lebanon Conference, much as it has been misdescribed by Perry Miller and others, was not a doctrinal confrontation between young, anti-intellectual, Jacksonian semi-Pelagians and old, crabbed, Tory Calvinists. Calvinism in fact never came up for debate, principally because all in attendance—including Finney—considered themselves in one way or another Calvinists.[87] It was basically an argument about methods in revivals, and it cannot be said even to have accomplished much about that, since the conference broke up with Beecher threatening Finney,

Finney, I know your plan, and you know I do; you mean to come to Connecticut, and carry a streak of fire to Boston. But if you attempt it, as the Lord liveth, I'll meet you at the state line, and call out all the artillery men, and fight every inch of the way to Boston, and then I'll fight you there.[88]

The real significance of the conference lies in what happened to Nettleton. He had been prostrated by typhus in 1822, a disease that terminated his active career and left him a semi-invalid until his death in 1844. He had not wanted to come to the New Lebanon Conference, regarding advice as a mercy wasted on the likes of Finney. At Beecher's urging, he attended anyway, and regretted it, for he must have made a poor comparison to the vigor of Finney. Was that comparison apparent to Beecher? Something close to it must have been, for a year later Beecher hurried to Philadelphia to make his peace with Finney, and in 1831, far from stopping Finney at the state line, Beecher invited him to Boston to preach in his own pulpit.

The conclusion is obvious but unpleasant: Nettleton's enfeebled constitution left Beecher without a reliable revivalist to employ; Finney, although rough around the edges, was no less Hopkinsian than Nettleton, no less successful, and considerably more healthy; ergo, Beecher shelved Nettleton (and it is noticeable how in Nettleton's papers the references to Beecher grow chillier and more bitter from now on) and, after reflecting on his extravagant threatenings, embraced Finney. And it is true not only that Finney afterwards operated under Beecher's management, and even went west to Ohio when Beecher went there, but that Finney's whole manner changed after these events. Finney's great Rochester revival of 1831 was noted for its "phenomenal dignity," and his lectures on revivals in New York City in 1835 were full of Old Calvinistlike utterances about the need for Christian activity in politics and the suspension of Sabbath mails.[89] But all the same, he never completely set aside his Hopkinsianism. His notorious definition of revivals, in those New York City lectures, as "not a miracle, nor dependent on a miracle" but "a purely philosophical result of the right use of the constituted means" was not a profession of Arminianism, but merely Finney's way of reinforcing the old Edwardsean conviction that "sinners are not bound to repent because they have the Spirit's influence, or because they can obtain it, but because they are moral agents, and have the powers which God requires them to exercise."[90]

Much as Beecher strove to take over the revival tactics and the revivalists of the New Divinity, he was noticeably more eager to absorb the second of those two quantities than the first. Beecher was not captured by New Divinity revivalism—he captured it. For one thing, he never stopped preaching that telltale mark of Old Calvinism, the "use of means," something which set him dramatically apart from Finney and Nettleton. After moving to Boston in 1828 to deal face to face with the Unitarians, Beecher preached,

Do you say, "What shall I do?" One thing I will tell you, that if you do not do something more than you have, you will be lost. . . . Will you go to some solitary place to-night, and there kneel down and pray? You are conscious you can do it. Will you do it? Will you open your Bible and read a chapter? and lest you should not know where to look I will tell you. Read the first chapter of Proverbs, and then kneel, confess your sins, and try to give yourself up to God for the rest of your life. Then seek the instruction of your minister or Christian friends; break off all outward and known sins; put yourself in the way of all religious influences, and I will venture to say you can not pursue this course a fortnight, a week, without finding a new and blessed life dawning within you.[91]

More important, Beecher preached up revivals, not for the purpose of calling the saints out of the world, but rather to thrust them back into it to Christianize it—not to better identify the pure, but to energize the orthodox to combat public infidelity. Although Beecher believed in the establishment as firmly as Dwight, he had seen as early as his arrival in Litchfield that the handwriting of secularism was on the wall. To cope with the termination of the establishment, and, along with it, the reality of a church-in-society, Beecher resorted to the creation of those myriad voluntary societies with which his name has so often been associated, thereby creating a kind of ad hoc establishment that, while it could no longer exercise the direct power of the old church, could nevertheless still exert considerable influence in Connecticut life.

The word *influence* is of enormous significance here, for the truth is that the entire movement of theological vocabulary in both the Old Calvinists and the latter-day New Divinity men—from necessity to certainty—from motives that cause the will to motives that influence it—is a sort of code, measuring the onset of disestablishment by measuring the degree to which the power and place of the church and clergy had slipped from being the monitor of a moral society to being an agency for private religious exercise. In one sense, Edwards himself was acknowledging this by abandoning any notion of justifying Calvinism on the grounds of natural necessity and deploying the concept of moral necessity. What was not clear in his time, however, was whether the recourse to occasional causality glorified the power of God (by denying that the minister is the efficient of salvation in awakenings), or whether it was instead a recognition of the power of the congregations (to sack ministers at will). As Beecher and his compatriots perceived matters (and it was irrelevant whether that perception had ever approximated reality), it had once been a necessity that the citizen stand in awe of the "queues and shoebuckles, and cocked hats, and gold-headed canes" of the ministers; after 1818 in Connecticut, the best one could hope for was the certainty of social respect.[92] The clergy were disabled now from being causes; they could only be influences. Much as Beecher railed against disestablishment, after 1818 he could only accept, with as much grace as possible, that the role of the clergy in Connecticut would henceforth remain passive.[93]

The organization of the voluntary societies was for Beecher and the others a symbol of their helpless acceptance of the demolition of the church-in-society. At the same time, though, Beecher strove to make the most of this acceptance. If the voluntary societies were limited only to the exercise of influence, very well then, it would be an influence of such a degree as would come as close as possible to the necessity once exerted by the old establishment. And yet, precisely because these organizations were voluntary, they were also sterile: one could be born into the church, but not into the American Tract Society. Casting about for a means to populate the societies, Beecher found it expedient to hit upon the revivals, and upon New Divinity men to conduct them. It might have been only bluff that caused Beecher to describe this process as *"the best thing that ever happened to the State of Connecticut,"* or maybe it was his own conviction, after all, that cutting the ministers loose from the establishment would force them to work all the harder. "They say ministers have lost their influence," Beecher said to his daughter, Catharine; "the fact is, they have gained."[94] That may have been true—if everything in the past and present were measured by the yardstick of *influence*. The ministers had actually lost something more than influence; they had lost necessity, and if Old Calvinism demonstrated anywhere its wonted penchant for resourcefulness and adaptability, it is in how they appropriated Edwardsean ideas, practices, and even reputations to shore up their loss and try to make it good. Dwight and Beecher had begun that process of cooptation. Nathaniel William Taylor would finish it.[95]

CHAPTER 8

Silencing the Ghost

Nathaniel William Taylor and the
New Haven Theology

I

Nathaniel William Taylor's lineage to Old Calvinism was what Timothy Dwight's had been to Edwardseanism. Born in 1786, he was a grandson of old Nathaniel Taylor of New Milford, Connecticut, who had maintained the Half-Way Covenant and Old Calvinism in the teeth of the hottest blasts of Connecticut New Light enthusiasm. He was ordained in 1812 after graduation from Yale in 1808, and succeeded to the pulpit of Center Church on the New Haven Green, the embattled citadel of Old Calvinism previously held by arch-Old Lights like James Noyes, Chauncey Wittlesey, and James Dana. A feeble Dana, then just a few months from his death, delivered the ordination charge (while no one less than Timothy Dwight delivered the sermon). Ten years later, in 1822, when Connecticut's Old Calvinism moved to imitate its Massachusetts counterpart at Andover by organizing a divinity school at Yale, Taylor was selected to be the first professor of Didactic Theology. A self-confident Taylor, not a little arrogant, and the handsomest man in Yale College, assumed the post with a consciousness of his great intellectual powers and of his inherited authority. It is not too much to say that Nathaniel William Taylor was the virtual embodiment of Old Calvinism carried into the new generation.[1]

Taylor manifested that heritage in other specific ways. He embraced the solutions and formulae of the Scottish philosophers, especially their incessant appeals to intuition and self-evident fact as the best cure for skepticism. He feared that unless "the competent unperverted reason

of the human mind" could be allowed to "know *some things* beyond
the possibility of mistake . . . there is an end to all knowledge and all
faith" and "universal skepticism [is] authorized."[2] But if such testimony were allowed, then harmony and goodness would reign.

Take, for instance, the matter of moral responsibility, so important
to any theory of will: a priori ethical theorizing can end only in sterility,
but an empirical inspection of "human consciousness attests human
accountability." Like James Dana before him, Taylor found in his own
consciousness indubitable proof that human beings are "intelligent,
voluntary agents; and from this fact, the conviction of right and wrong
is inseparable."[3]

Taylor longed for the church-in-society. To the churches he uttered
persistent warnings against barring their doors to all in the community
but the visibly pious few.

In the admission of members into the Christian church, we proceed not on the
principle that we can pronounce or even form a confident judgment of the
personal piety of the individuals, but on the ground that they propose to
perform an act appropriate to real Christians, and that we have no evidence
that such is *not* their character.[4]

The churches' task was not to shut out the unregenerate, but to help
them in—predictably, by the "use of means." To the surrounding society he declared an established church indispensable to the moral
health of the body politic. Even after disestablishment became a fact
in Connecticut, Taylor continued to insist that "the great ends of government must fail in every nation, without national morality" and "the
whole influence of religion in a community." In his view, come-outer
sectarianism had not only emptied churches of their covenant offspring,
but had provided the pretext for emptying society of Christianity itself.
Disestablishment, he angrily told the Connecticut legislature in 1823,
"was considered by many, not only as a release from the obligation to
support religious institutions, but as a public sanction of the sentiment,
that these institutions are unworthy of support."[5]

Taylor's wrath was especially directed at two sects. He was particularly disturbed by the Unitarians, both by their capture of the Hollis
professorship at Harvard in 1805 and by the Dedham parish case, in
which a Massachusetts judge awarded to an overwhelmingly heterodox
parish membership the right to install a Unitarian minister in the town
church over the protests of the overwhelmingly orthodox church membership. Taylor mocked the Unitarians, as serving a "monstrous in-

congruity" of a God so perfectly benevolent that he sent everyone to heaven, without conceding "the highest approbation of right, and the highest disapprobation of wrong moral action."[6] In 1820 Taylor so successfully outraged the Unitarian Andrews Norton that Norton lost his customary serenity and blasted back—which only allowed Taylor to assume the role of the persecuted victim of reactionary bigotry.[7] But Taylor was even more disturbed by the Edwardseans, whose brand of divine benevolence applauded a God whose benevolence was manifest in sending almost everyone to hell. The wisdom of Hopkins's God in permitting the existence of sin was a small consolation to Taylor, who could see little of wisdom or benevolence in a God "who on the whole prefers vice to virtue—sin to holiness," and who differed from the Unitarian Deity only in that Hopkins's God displayed his wisdom by making everyone undeservedly miserable instead of undeservedly happy. Taylor remained unimpressed by the long skeins of the New Divinity's reasoning that individuals had a natural ability to be happy if they willed. "Is it said that he has power to love God if he will, i.e. *can will morally right if he will*? This is plain nonsense in every possible meaning of the language."[8]

In his judgments of Edwardseanism, Taylor was doing little more than echoing James Dana and also Timothy Dwight (whose star pupil and private secretary Taylor had been from 1808 till 1812—Dwight had delivered Taylor's ordination sermon in Center Church). Like them, he was committed to coopting Edwardseanism, and to that end he sought, by any means possible, to stress continuities between the person of Edwards and Old Calvinism. He denied any notion of the atonement that imputed to righteousness inconsistency with "common sense." He preached as surely as any Hopkinsian that "*Christ died for all men*" to maintain the authority of God's moral government.[9] And, more important, he lauded the great works of the revivals. Converted in one of Timothy Dwight's sedate awakenings at Yale as he had been, and a preacher of no inconsiderable revivalistic fire himself, he agreed with Beecher that "with that series of religious revivals which has blessed our country, in their power and extent, there is nothing to be compared in any other portion of Christendom."[10] Whether Beecher and Taylor valued the revivals for the blessing or for the power was another matter, and precisely the point at which Beecher and Dwight had diverged from Edwardseanism. But Taylor was aware that something more than Dana's negative critique, or Dwight's cooptation of the reputation of

Edwards, or Beecher's revivalism, was needed to confront the challenges offered to Calvinism in the early nineteenth century.

In 1770 Dana had suspected that Edwardseanism would hurt Calvinism more than help it in its conflict with unbelief; he was more
afraid of atheistic skepticism à la Hume than of the atheistic materialism that so concerned Edwards (Edwards, for his part, would probably have replied in just the same terms, only adding that Dana had
underestimated the threat of atheistic materialism). Dana knew for
certain that Edwardseanism was hurting New England church practice
(Edwards would probably have said *purging*). What Dana doubtless
wanted was a defense of Calvinism aimed at the right enemy and producing the right side effects, but he could only say what was wrong
with Edwards. He failed to provide a workable alternative to *Freedom
of the Will* as an apologetic for Calvinism, and the Edwardseans took
that failure for intellectual and spiritual weakness.

Dwight and Beecher, by coopting parts of the Edwardsean image,
helped break the New Divinity's claim to be the sole heirs of Edwards
(aided by concessions made by the third-generation New Divinity men
themselves), and they helped underscore the increasing ineffectiveness
of *Freedom of the Will* in speaking to the threatening specters of Unitarianism and French skepticism. It remained for Old Calvinism to
produce an apologist for Calvinism who could respond to these challenges with all the devastating force with which Edwards had spoken
to Arminianism in *Freedom of the Will,* and contrive to do it without
threatening the church-in-society, the use of the means, or the preaching of the wisdom of God in the permission of sin. Only then could
Edwardseanism finally be rendered a dead letter and New England
made safe for Old Calvinism. Nathaniel William Taylor was that apologist.

That Taylor was thoroughly conscious of the need to finish the work
begun almost half a century before by Dana is clear from a letter Taylor
left for Beecher in 1819; it contained in capsule the script Taylor would
follow at Yale over the next four decades. Ostensibly, Taylor intended
nothing more than to supplement the theories on the will that Edwards
had put forward. He did believe, however, that because the times and
the opponents had changed from Edwards's day, questions Edwards
had never envisioned had been raised. It was now the time to replace
Freedom of the Will with an apologetic that would confront newer
menaces like the Unitarians. "I am well satisfied that something should

and may be done toward settling points which Edwards did not aim to settle," Taylor proposed, with the modest expectation that he could "to some extent, change the current of theological sentiments" (i.e. fight Unitarianism).[11] And, true to his promise, Taylor actually outlined not a supplement to Edwards, but a complete rewriting.

For Beecher's enlightenment, Taylor laid out his proposed alterations of Edwards along three lines: *causality, volition,* and *psychology.* In the first place, Taylor interpreted Edwards's occasionalist causality as a posture, a philosophical decoy to confuse the materialists. This occasionalism had also allowed Emmons and the Exercisers to make God the *cause* of all sin without being its *author*; it had allowed the Tasters to make God the author of sinful human beings without being the cause of sin itself. On both scores the Unitarians had had a field day. However, Taylor went so far as to claim that Edwards had really had no notion of cause and had intentionally shied away from adopting one:

Perhaps Edwards was wiser than we should be. He evidently felt himself obliged to go no farther than he has done. For example, he thought it to be enough to show that certainty of conduct and moral agency did coexist in fact, without venturing any hypothesis concerning the *quo modo*. Leaving this untouched, he left the loophole for Emmonsism. Emmons goes farther than Edwards by attempting to show what causes certainty of action. And so the *tasters*.[12]

In the second place, Taylor criticized Edwards's basic definition of the will more severely, especially his classic reconciliationist distinction between varieties of freedom. Taylor, like so many others, found reconciliationism to be a linguistic game that depended largely on how much one thought words could capture realities. Taylor did not have much confidence in words. "If language has any meaning, a free will is a will which is free, and to say that free will is a power to do as we please or as we will is saying nothing to the purpose."[13] And finally, he was plainly irritated at Edwards's re-construction of the psychology of volition. He rejected Edwards's soldering of perception and volition as "not sound philosophy"[14] and put a skeptical finger on the ambiguous nature of motives put forth in *Freedom of the Will.* He was convinced that a will which is *as* the greatest apparent good only throws the question back onto *why* certain things appear to the will *as* good, the kind of self-defeating question that led back only to the Taste scheme (man's depraved nature disposes him toward certain "goods") or the Exercisers (God immediately inclines men to certain "goods"). He also faulted Edwards for failing to specify how, even if one grants a necessary connection between motive and volition, this proves that *all* volitions are thus rendered necessary. For all the ingenuity of *Freedom of the Will,* Taylor advised Beecher, "the reader feels that Edwards has prostrated his antagonists, but is still at a loss what is truth."[15] In all this, Taylor had done little more than reiterate Dana, but now he proposed going beyond Dana to offer an alternative theory of volition which would "supply [Edwards's] defects" and would "give to the world that desideratum which shall show that good, sound Calvinism, or, if you please, Beecherism and Taylorism, is but another name for the truth and reality of things as they exist in the nature of God and man, and the relations arising therefrom."[16]

Over the next ten years Taylor refined and developed his reworking of Edwards. The results may be seen especially in the classroom lectures he wrote for use at Yale, which are mostly an elaboration of the three principal objections he raised in the letter to Beecher.

CAUSALITY

On causality, Taylor agreed with Edwards in one respect: in regard to human moral behavior, causality can really only be described as connection. He differed utterly from Edwards in his disbelief that connections can ever be said to be so full and fixed as to be *necessary.* For Taylor, *necessity* is the result of efficient, or (in Edwards's terms) relational, causes. *Connection,* precisely because it can never be equated with necessity, can only induce *certainty.* Just as he had implied to Beecher, Taylor was unwilling to grant that one could create moral necessities merely by establishing that certain words are *connected.* Taylor denied that terms can ever carry the kind of a priori objective weight that Edwards had made them carry in his crucial distinction between philosophical and relative necessity.

Words are the signs of the ideas or conceptions of things. . . . Here then a very important question arises, what are the ideas or conceptions which the Lawgiver intends to excite in our minds by this language? In other words, *what* and *how* much meaning belongs to these words in the intention of him who uses them? In respect to the word of *God,* the design is to not to convey to our minds that vast and comprehensive conception in all its fulness, which the infinite Being forms of himself. Here is necessary some limitation. So in respect to the words *heart* and *love*; and the design is not to send the mass of mankind to the schools of philosophy,—to the subtle metaphysician, the profound analyst of mental properties and mental phenomena—to learn what things are meant by these words of the divine law.[17]

In a nutshell, Taylor could not believe, and could not believe that anyone else could believe, in a connection made necessary merely by the terms involved.[18]

Indeed, for Taylor there were no moral *causes* that can make results necessary, but only moral circumstances that make results likely. *Why do persons choose?* Only because their circumstances, or *motives,* create an objective certainty that they will so do. Taylor hastened to add, even if certainty is not up to the level of necessity, it is just as reliable. As he had once told the Connecticut legislature, the proper political circumstances can guarantee a moral society just as readily as the penalties and threats of the old establishment. "It is precisely in these circumstances that a sound public opinion holds a check on human selfishness, for which we might look in vain to the combined strength of nations," Taylor explained. And surely the Connecticut legislature could not have minded being told by Nathaniel William Taylor that he was willing to regard the indirect influence of circumstances as an acceptable substitute for the immediate force of law, since only five years before they had stripped the clergy of the force of law. They had compelled Taylor to be content with the influence he could exert through circumstances. Taylor's election sermon of 1823 was a grudging acceptance of a demotion from necessity to certainty; his Yale lectures simply embodied the unhappy fact that Old Calvinism could now only erect circumstances around human morality and hope for the best.[19]

Secondary to the question of *why* people choose is the question of *how* they go about choosing, and Taylor's response to that was that they choose through a natural principle of self-love. Alas, that in turn only provoked a second pair of why/how questions: First, if people love themselves so naturally, *why do they choose sin?* To that, he replied that Adam's fall had created a certainty of subsequent sinful behavior in the human race; or one might say, Adam's fall was a circumstance connected to the moral actions of every one of his descendants. But at that point the *how* appears, the same old question dressed up in the same puzzling garb that had perplexed Hopkins and Bellamy and Emmons and all the others: *How* does Adam's sin create a certainty of everyone else's depraved behavior? Is it by the immediate exercise of God, determining to treat all of Adam's progeny according to Adam's faults? For Taylor, that alternative was repugnant beyond expression. For one thing, it called up again the spirit of Emmons's dread deity, making people sin as they do by divine action and restoring the hard element of necessary causality that Taylor was striving to banish from his account of human behavior. "The theory of direct divine efficiency," Taylor warned, "is both unphilosophical and contrary to the decisions of common sense."[20]

Taylor's penchant for appealing to common sense also persuaded him that the universal dictate of human reason declared that an individual is more than a bundle of ideas upheld by divine energy. "The notion of being formed by mankind generally in all ages and countries, and evinced clearly in all human languages and all human conduct" is that of "*one substance with a phenomenal nature.*"[21] Of course, Taylor acknowledged that empirical inspection of the consciousness yields little or no direct evidence of such a substance, but he simply treated that as an opportunity for humility before the Creator's wisdom. He exclaimed piously, "How many more things may be true of both the substance and of the phenomenal nature of the substance, than enter into our merely phenomenal conception of either!"[22]

Taylor also rejected the Exercisers, not only because his common sense had discovered spiritual substance where the Exercisers had not, but because his political sense feared that demons would be let loose if human consciousness were restricted to an awareness of its exercises. To deny as Emmons did the existence of complex dispositions and substance underlying human personality was to call into question the possibility that a common substance underlies the divine personalities of God the Father, God the Son, and God the Holy Spirit. Trinitarianism had for centuries been predicated on the assumption of a shared divine nature binding the personalities of the Godhead together and identifying each as "very God of very God." When the Exercisers denied the reality of substance, Taylor saw them as playing directly into the hands of the Unitarians, who were only too happy to confine God's divine nature to a single conscious personality, and not three. In that respect, the "FIRST AND GRAND ERROR OF THE UNITARIAN IN ALL HIS REASONING " was little different from that of the Exerciser scheme, since the Exercisers would be compelled to agree with the Unitarian that human reason necessarily decides that a being having one absolute substance and one phenomenal nature, qualifying him for one form of phenomenal action, cannot in the nature of things, either by any peculiarity of his substance or of his phenomenal nature, or of both, or in any mode of subsistence whatever, be qualified for three distinct personal forms of phenomenal action.[23]

But what then accounts for the certainty with which individuals manifest old Adam's sin? Is it a depraved taste? Again, Taylor demurred. Much as he thoroughly believed in the existence of an underlying nature, he shared the deep moral imperative of the Exercisers that put moral blame squarely on the conscious performer of evil, and not on something or someone else. "Nothing can be moral acts, but moral powers in exercise," Taylor reaffirmed, and to blame one's substance for tainting one's will with evil was an attempt to dodge responsibility.

I ask for an instance, in which, according to popular use, the word *disposition, temper, affection of mind,* or any synonymous term, is used to denote that which is moral and is the cause or source of moral actions, and in which it does not denote a mental preference? . . . It is then a mental act,—as really an act of the agent as are the acts which it dictates. It is therefore *not* a constitutional property of the soul.[24]

Ultimately, the Taste scheme offered little real refuge from the immediate efficiency of the Exercisers. Suppose that a depraved nature can indeed be said to cause sinful exercises: from whence comes this nature but from the immediate creating hand of God? The person "becomes a subject of sin, as the mere passive recipient of it by the act of his Maker," and that led Taylor to protest:

And what a view of God is this! Allowing that sin, guilt, really pertains to the created property of the soul, to what agent does the guilt of it belong? That the question may be truly answered, I ask, who designed it,—who produced it? Not man, but his Maker. Why? From a direct and unqualified preference of sin.[25]

It seemed illogical to Taylor to explain the cause of sin by pointing to what is already sinful. It failed to trace sinning back to its cause, and contented itself with identifying the cause as something that is really only another effect of sin. That, in turn, seemed to make sin both excusable and necessary.

And this left Taylor in something of a dilemma. He had weighed both schemes, the Tasters' and the Exercisers', in the balance and found them wanting; he could not resort, as Edwards had, to a dual notion

of causality, since he had already confined causality to the single mode
of certainty. Taylor had nowhere else to turn but to the re-construction
of the Edwardsean psychology.

In an effort to escape the Charybdis of the Exercisers and the Scylla
of the Tasters, Taylor proposed a remarkable psychology all his own.[26]
Taylor had suggested that the means which impelled people to choose
was self-love—a regard for one's own happiness and well-being. Unlike
Hopkins, Taylor could find nothing horribly sinful in a little enlightened
self-interest.

> There is another philosophy [Taylor remarked], which maintains that the high-
> est happiness of the individual may come into competition, and so be incon-
> sistent with, the highest happiness of the whole, and that therefore the
> individual may be bound to sacrifice his own to the general good. This phi-
> losophy, endorsed as it is by great names, I regard as absurd and self-contra-
> dictory. . . . To suppose a being *voluntarily* to sacrifice *absolutely all his own
> happiness* for the sake of the general good, is to suppose him to act without
> a motive, that is, to act with a motive and without a motive at the same time,
> which is a contradiction and an absurdity.[27]

Of course, it is true that the principle of self-love could lead someone
to sin, but the innate disposition to love and regard oneself was not
itself sinful. "There is an obvious difference," Taylor reasoned, "between a *disposition, propensity, or tendency to sin* which is prior to
all sin, and a *sinful disposition*."

> There are in fact both. There is what may be truly and properly called a
> disposition, or tendency, or propensity to sin, which is prior to and the cause
> of *all* sin in man. And there is also, as a *consequence* of this disposition or
> propensity to sin, what with equal propriety may be called a *sinful disposition,*
> which is the true cause of all *other* sins *itself* excepted. . . . Now of the former
> disposition or propensity to sin which is the cause of the latter, i.e., of the
> *sinful* disposition, I say it is not sinful; all the sin pertains to the latter.[28]

Functionally, then, Taylor was prepared to describe the human soul
as consisting primarily of an innate principle of self-love which, because
it is innate and placed directly by God, cannot be sinful (cannot, that
is, unless one is prepared to say that God creates each individual with
a natural necessity of sinning) and which is hence without moral quality. It is a certainty, however, in the circumstances in which the human
race lives, circumstances established by the fall of Adam, that this principle of self-love will prompt and agitate the will to go out and sin at

the earliest possible moment. Self-love can hardly do otherwise. Next, Taylor wrote, this movement of the will toward sin *creates* the beginnings of a genuinely sinful tendency that, like the beginnings of a rut in a road, forms an inclination to sin to which self-love and the will are bound to conform. "Once formed" by the will's performance of sin, this new disposition "never changes, nor can change, unless the mind changes *de novo* between the two great objects of moral choice," good and evil, and this "the mind is exceedingly unapt to do, chiefly because the preference of an object as supreme has a peculiar tendency to perpetuate itself, by confining thought and feeling to its object, and engrossing the whole mind with it."[29]

Both the Tasters and the Exercisers canceled each other out. Just as the Tasters had said, disposition determines actions; but at the same time, as the Exercisers maintained, action determines disposition. The innocent disposition to self-love prompts the will to actions that harden the self into a fully depraved nature which is thereafter the agent responsible for dragooning the self into sin. And since this unhappy condition befalls human beings not by the immediate agency of God but through "the physical constitution and the circumstances of men," sinners ought to be held to blame for their own dilemma.

No less remarkable was Taylor's account of how mankind can escape from this bondage. Taylor had said that the sinful disposition can not change, a judgment which sounds Calvinistically determined enough until one recalls that, for Taylor, determination involves certainty and not necessity. "Unless the mind changes *de novo*," Taylor wrote, man remains trapped in sin, and the likelihood of spontaneous de novo changes smacked so un-Edwardseanly of the contingency Edwards had impaled in *Freedom of the Will* that it seemed impossible that minds could ever do so. But Taylor would only say that such changes are "exceedingly unapt,"—in a psychology undergirded only by certainties and likelihoods, capable of meaning more than one thing, especially since Taylor now proposed to reveal the one degree of uncertainty that could scale the walls of sinful certainties, the one display of aptness capable of exceeding the exceedingly unapt.[30] Taylor proposed that the same *self-love* that has led people into sin, and has lain in the bonds of the sinful disposition it helped to create, now spontaneously re-awakens, throws off (or at least temporarily suspends) the sinful disposition, gives individuals a chance to consider carefully that their sinful career is leading them to hell, and then impels their will to holy actions, and thus creates a holy disposition.[31]

Of course, Taylor soon rushed in to affirm that "the change is never brought to pass in the human mind without the supernatural influence of the Spirit of God," but by this time the word *influence* had been kneaded into meaninglessness; and anyway, in the earlier versions of this doctrine, Taylor had frankly said that "the change in the mind is no other than the change, by a sinful moral being, of his own moral character."[32] Self-determination raised its head at last: "It is, thus viewed, the change which takes place, by changing as his own act that *governing principle*—that controlling disposition—which is no other than an elective preference of God to Mammon, and which alone constitutes a good or holy heart."[33]

VOLITION

The general advantages of Taylorism (for so we may call it) for Taylor are twofold. First, it renders human conduct certain. "Still there is a cause, ground or reason of the certainty of wrong moral action on the part of all men under the present system," Taylor insisted.[34] Given self-love, the will acts under its promptings, and given a set of circumstances in which self-love operates, the outcome of the will's choosing is predictable. But (and this is the second point) only predictable; merely certain. "The mere certainty of human action forces no one, compels no one," Taylor explained. "It leaves freedom, the power of choice, power to the opposite action, unimpaired."[35] The will lies only under the promptings of a principle of self-love at the beginning, not under the heavy hand of disposition or taste, and it is "exceedingly unapt" that it will not obey those promptings. According to his own dictum, Taylor offered human beings *certainty, with power to the contrary.* Although it will always be certain that willing will accord with disposition, disposition itself is a creation of willing, and the will is ever likely, de novo, to create a new, contrary disposition. "He not only *can*, if he will," wrote one of Taylor's students, "but Dr. Taylor uttered his protest against what he considered a necessitarian evasion, by affirming that '*he can if he won't*.'"[36]

II

One further question remained for Taylor to explore, and though it touched only tangentially on his theory of will, his conclusion turned out to be his most explosive one. Just what purpose does sin serve in the world, if it is indeed so certain and yet, at the same time, so spontaneously avoidable? Taylor needed to be careful, for if he said that sin does indeed serve a purpose in the world, he implied that there was a reason for its being there and thus it must be decreed by God, whereupon Taylor's scheme would fall through and sin would become the result of God's initiative, not of humankind's circumstances or volition. This train of reasoning had led the Hopkinsians to concede that, misery and evil notwithstanding, sin must be the necessary means of the greatest good and an evidence of God's wisdom. God has obviously decreed so much sin, as so many poor, that it was hard to believe he did not love it.

And that, Taylor acknowledged, although logical, was a horrendous conclusion. If sin is "the necessary means of the greatest good, there can be no sincerity, truth, or benevolence, and of course no authority in a lawgiver who should forbid it." Yet God has repeatedly told human beings not to sin. That put Hopkins in the unhappy position of having to portray God as telling his creatures how much he wants them to do good while all the while really preferring that they do the evil he has secretly decreed that they do. That contradiction incensed Taylor:

God give a law and not prefer that his subjects should obey rather than disobey! He would rather, so they tell us, that men, all things considered, should do wrong than do right! God himself the minister of sin! No. God prefers, all things considered, that men should do right; fully obey his perfect law rather than sin once.[37]

Defender that he was of a way of community fast dying among the dark Satanic mills of Jacksonian America, Taylor repeatedly lashed out at the New Divinity's idea of a distant, governing God whose wisdom in the permission of sin resembles nothing so much as an Adam Smith-like "invisible hand" that manages to bring more good out of more suffering. But, on the other side of the matter, if sin serves no purpose whatever in the world, and if no good at all can come of suffering, then it is time to say that God could not have put it there, since God is a God of purpose and not random disorder. In consequence, God cannot be blamed for it. Yet the nagging fact of its overwhelming presence implies that God was either morally arbitrary in tossing it in, or a bad planner in letting it in.

Taylor's solution was again instinctively to reject both of the two horns of the dilemma. He began with the ringing affirmation that God did not decree sin for its own sake. "If he has established moral government, the law of which requires right moral action, then he has no such preference, and has done nothing to gratify it."[38] Sin, then, is not necessary in this world; but manifestly, as every war, murder, and theft testify, sin is *certain*. And since *certainty* is the product of circumstances, Taylor saw his solution in saying that in the sort of world God has made, with all the circumstances he created in it, sin is simply incidental to its operations.[39] Specifically, the circumstances God created for this world are those of a "moral system," and within a "moral system" one must expect sin as an inescapable by-product of the system itself.

... that there should be that which gives the certainty of wrong moral action, is not necessarily inconsistent with the Creator's preference of right to wrong moral action under the present system. He may purpose this cause of the certainty of wrong moral action, not as good in itself, or, as the means of good, but solely as an evil incidental in the very nature of things to the best possible system.[40]

This is not to say that God lacks the power to eliminate sin from the world entirely; the problem is that he would have to eliminate moral government along with it. The "nature of a moral system ... includes the existence of moral beings"; but "sin or moral evil cannot be prevented in moral beings, by any power or influence which destroys their moral agency"[41]; ergo, to have a moral system of moral beings, God must tolerate their moral evil as an unhappy excrescence of the circumstances, and "God, if he adopts it, is restricted by its nature and its principles as truly as man is."[42]

For one who had all along eschewed mistaking terminological connections for reality, Taylor's "moral system" argument was an unusual departure but was excusable in his eyes for the opportunity it offered. It was now possible to say categorically that God prefers holiness to sin under all circumstances; the fact he does not always get the holiness he prefers is no longer a concession of weakness but a demonstration of God's patience with our moral system. There need be no further intricate rationalizations of the wisdom of God in the permission of sin, designed to persuade us to rejoice in the smoke arising from hell; we are now allowed to resent sin, knowing that in so doing we are mourning, along with God, for what is still, after all, a certainty.

I affirm [said Taylor] that in view of the nature of moral agency, it is impossible to prove that God could prevent sin in the best moral system. Moral agents can act morally wrong under every possible influence from God. To suppose him to prevent all wrong moral action on their part in all cases may, for aught that can be shown to the contrary, be supposing him to do what in certain cases he cannot do.[43]

But is this Calvinism? It is true, as George Park Fisher remarked, that this is not Pelagianism.[44] For Taylor sinful actions are not without connection with each other; he did insist that "no event takes place which God had not purposed shall take place" and that "not a human being will comply with the terms of life without divine grace"[45]; and his 1823 election sermon is proof that he really believed that "a moral influence, as it operates only on the reason and the conscience, is of mighty efficacy."[46] In his rejection of the Taste scheme, and in his insistence on defining sin strictly in Exerciser terms as "the transgression of God's law," Taylor laid out some remarkable parallels to Emmons.[47] And above all, his ultimate conclusion was the same as that arrived at by the New Divinity: all human beings have the ability and obligation to submit to God's government.

But it is also true that this is not Edwardseanism. The point is important because Taylor's defenders would later try to extend the tactics of cooptation to cover Taylor by insisting he was a restatement of Edwards, rather than a replacement for him. Emmons in 1838 was ready in his crackling old age to "go about half with the Taylorites," but only the half that seemed to echo the Exercise scheme's line; he would then, as he told Edwards Amasa Park, "stop and turn against them with all my might."[48] He turned because, whatever he thought about depraved nature, he could not concede spontaneous changes in volition or the reduction of God's agency to an influence. In the most obvious terms, Taylor dismissed out of hand Edwards's most crucial distinction in *Freedom of the Will*, that between moral and natural necessity. "The *natural ability of man* to obey God, as defined by Edwards and others, has no existence and can have none," Taylor declared. "It is an essential nothing."

According to this Edwardian theory, while there is not the shadow of *ability* or of power on the part of man to obey God, the *moral inability* of the theory, the inability to love and hate the same object at the same time, though undeniable, is unchangeable either by man or his Maker. Nor is this all. Such an *inability* furnishes not the slightest evidence, that when one wills morally wrong, he has not in the proper and true sense of language, power, or ability to will morally right; nor that when he has willed morally wrong, he has not power or ability to will morally right the next moment.[49]

The vehemence of Taylor's denunciation has a number of sources, not the least of which is his not-always-consistent impatience with linguistic precisionists. But underlying them all was surely Taylor's carefully sized notion of causality. Edwards, as a reconciliationist, had attributed all events to God's causal efficacy, but he nonetheless extorted freedom from causality (as reconciliationists routinely do) by hairsplitting the meaning of freedom. Taylor, by attaching only one meaning to both freedom and causality, was compelled to grant that while all events have a cause (more properly, in Taylor's terms, they have circumstances), those causes do not entirely account for all the results, such as those unapt suspensions of depravity. Taylor could claim on other occasions that he and Edwards were at one in their belief that things went the way that pleased God—but Arminius had also claimed to be Reformed on precisely the same grounds. What separated Edwards from Taylor was that for Taylor God's pleasure was not always the sufficient cause of why things happened the way they did.[50] Taylor substituted a theistic libertarianism for Edwards's reconciliationism. "In this view," Taylor would say candidly, "free agency is the grand, not to say the most momentous element in the nature of a moral being."[51]

One might argue that Taylor, in his psychology of volition, maintained at least a continuity of sorts with Edwards's Augustinian voluntarism. Taylor did insist that "every act of will not only implies the prior existence of affections toward at least two objects, but the *present* existence of such affections." If one is willing to accept Taylor's principle of self-love as the "sensibility," or the heart, it is evident that Taylor treats the will and the affections as very closely knit.[52] Taylor's colleague and disciple at Yale, Eleazar Fitch, denied in well-nigh Exerciser terms that "the heart" could be "altogether distinct from the will. . . . The only heart which the law acknowledges is the will itself of the agent, or his actual preferences."[53] But Taylor does not give us much to go on: his discussions of religious psychology are disappointing, and his implication that the soul intermittently switches from the depraved to the nondepraved admits a notion of psychological duality quite foreign to Edwards's absolutism.

But Taylor did succeed as an Edwardsean in one sense: he was able to produce an apologetic for New England Calvinism that absolved Calvinism of the most damaging criticisms the Unitarians could make against it. It is no wonder that, in that sense, his contemporaries interpreted his teachings as a redaction of *Freedom of the Will* and not a destruction. And he did it in terms that as in *Freedom of the Will* were also aimed at forcing a recalcitrant segment of the Calvinist community (this time the Edwardseans) to admit the ineffectiveness of their apologetic. This time, though, there was the glorification of sin, through divine intervention, as an advantage to the universe.

III

That Nathaniel William Taylor was at least more creative than the genuine Edwardseans is obvious from the feebleness of their response when he finally went public with his views in 1828. Actually, a number of people had had some inkling earlier of Taylor's intention to rewrite Edwardseanism. One of them was Lyman Beecher. Beecher rejoiced that Taylor was going to prove that "GOD GOVERNS MIND BY MOTIVE AND NOT BY FORCE," and do it in such a way as to show that "Edwards did not come up to that fair and square, Bellamy did not, and, in fact, nobody did until Taylor and I did."[54] Another who heard of Taylor's experiments was Asahel Nettleton, who had met Taylor in his student days at Yale when Taylor was still Timothy Dwight's secretary.

We then differed in regard to the nature of the doings of the unregenerate. He also read me a dissertation on the doctrine of the divine decrees, and the free agency of man, which I then regarded as a virtual denial of the former, and an avowal of the self-determining power of the will.[55]

Taylor (to Beecher's annoyance) had kept indiscreetly dropping hints in the hearing of Yale students that he was up to something. In 1820, watching Leonard Woods try to explain to Henry Ware how men can still be held responsible for sins committed under the influence of a depraved taste, Taylor despairingly remarked that "Dr. Ware had the better of the argument, and . . . Dr. Woods had put back the controversy with Unitarians fifty years."[56]

Then on December 15, 1821, Chauncey Goodrich, another schoolfellow and then-parishioner of Taylor's at Center Church, opened up the subject of original sin in the course of his theological-system lectures at Yale College. He proceeded to drop a bombshell. "Although there is in the human constitution some *permanent* and *adequate* cause of the great fact that every individual of our race sins from the moment that he *can* sin," nevertheless, "previous to the *first* act of moral agency, there is nothing in the mind which can *strictly* and *properly* be called sin." But if sin comes not from a depraved nature, nor God's immediate agency, then from where? Goodrich would only say, "there must be a *reason* or *cause* in the structure of our constitution," which left his students to conclude (and they did) that the cause of sin was a self-determining will. It did not help matters when, among his conclusions, Goodrich added that infants, lacking either naturally sinful dispositions or functioning wills prior to birth, can not be born sinners. Goodrich's students "thought the views exhibited in this lecture bore a striking resemblance to those of Dr. Ware," but Beecher and Nettleton knew better.[57] "The minute I heard of that I saw the end," Beecher moaned at this premature exposé. "I never felt so bad." And promptly Beecher wrote to Goodrich—and Taylor—telling them "they must take that back."[58] Nettleton likewise suspected the real influence behind Goodrich, and after Nettleton and Beecher together had examined a copy of Goodrich's lecture, Nettleton wrote directly to Taylor, warning him to disavow Goodrich. "You may speculate better than I can; but I know one thing better than you do, and I forewarn you that whenever you come out, our best Christians will revolt."[59]

Taylor chose prudence as the better part of valor: Goodrich delivered no further lectures on original sin, and the tempest blew over. In 1822 the divinity school was organized as an independent department at Yale, with Taylor moving over from Center Church to serve as professor of Didactic Theology, Goodrich as professor of rhetoric, and Eleazar T. Fitch (a classmate of Goodrich's and the college's Livingston Professor of Divinity) as instructor in systematic theology. For the most part their energies were devoted to baiting the Unitarians.[60] But even as Taylor quietly developed his thoughts, confining them to the protective circle of his classroom, ominous hints continued to leak out. Nettleton complained to Beecher that Taylor's students were becoming suspiciously evasive during their ordination examinations:

When interrogated by Ecclesiastical bodies, "Have infants souls," they answer, "I don't know." "Regeneration?" "I don't know." "Is it proper to pray for them?" "I don't know." "What is the meaning of such and such texts?" "I don't know." Now I do not wonder that ministers are alarmed at N[ew] H[aven] Theology. Interrogations like those above will always be put to his students whenever examined by Ecclesiastical bodies.[61]

Nettleton complained to Bennet Tyler that Taylor's students, when not in front of ecclesiastical councils, boasted of "the wonderful discoveries which had recently been made by Dr. Taylor of N. Haven."

As the story was going he had discovered the *essence of sin*—which was likely to make as great a revolution in the systems of theology, as was in the science of chemistry on the discovery of the *basis of potash* by Sir Humphrey Davy.[62]

Taylor wanted only time before openly challenging the Edwardseans, and he got four years of it, until in July of 1826 "a battery" was "opened in Connecticut, and a standard raised, and a campaign begun" by Taylor and his two coadjutors that would eliminate the burden of *Freedom of the Will* for good from New England theology.[63]

Typically, it was not Taylor who chose to fire the first shot, but Fitch, acting as Taylor's skirmisher. In *Two Discourses on the Nature of Sin*, preached on July 30, 1826, to the entire student body of Yale College, Fitch dramatically proposed to answer the fundamental moral question of Edwardseanism: *Why do men will to sin?* Fitch observed that Calvinists agree that men sin *because of Adam*; the only genuinely contested aspect of the question lay in the nature of the relationship between Adam and his posterity, and here Fitch called down a pox on all the houses and camps of the Edwardseans. The relationship can not be through the inheritance of a sinful nature, because sin is a moral quality that attaches itself only to sinful actions.

Many entertain confused notions respecting the real nature of a sinful heart; as though it were some physical, uncontrollable, source of sin, existing apart from the active agency of his being or his determinations. . . . Nothing in Adam, or in his descendants, is itself sin, or recognized of God to be such, in any form or instance, except those acts in which each personally violated known law. . . . They who affirm that moral disposition, moral affection, moral quality, in an agent . . . is not, in its nature, an act of will, a choice or preference of the agent, but an essential property or part of his created constitution, maintain the doctrine of physical depravity which is opposed in these discourses.[64]

On the other hand, Fitch did not want to be mistaken for an Exerciser. The fact that he did not believe in a sinful nature did not mean that he disbelieved in a nature, or that he was about to attribute the choice of sin to immediate divine agency.

The distinction between the constitutional powers and susceptibilities of a moral agent and his actual preferences, which is overlooked or disregarded by those who make moral disposition commence previous to moral action, is, nevertheless, a distinction always made in common life. . . . Nor can this dis-

tinction between the constitution of a moral being and his moral determinations, possibly be avoided except by directly denying the very existence of any
being who acts; or indirectly by denying it, by analyzing such being into a bare
succession of mental phenomena. And if any will so far reason themselves out
of their own natural convictions as to deny the existence of any created sub-
jectum with its powers which is called the soul . . . they must be left to carry
on the war of their philosophy with their own minds.[65]

Having eliminated as the cause of sin both a passive inheritance of
Adam's nature and the incensed intervention of an angry God, Fitch
now had to say just how Adam's sin *did* act on his descendants. And
Fitch candidly conceded that he had obviated anything that looked like
a causal relationship—a concession that at once allowed him to suggest
that the problem might best be solved by forgetting the notion of cause
altogether and describing the relationship as a "connection." By substituting "connection" for "cause," Fitch, like Taylor, deliberately sac-
rificed necessity for certainty. Fitch was confident that nothing of any
importance would be lost, especially compared to the apologetical
ground to be gained. "If Adam by his sin created in any way the
grounds of moral certainty that his posterity in the first responsible
determinations of will should sin," Fitch assured his students, "then
all the connection exists which is requisite to account for the fact of
the sinfulness of his posterity."[66]

If Adam did not *cause* sin, but if his fall only provided circumstances
that make it certain that we, too, will sin, then two conclusions will
appear. First, the initial immediate choice of sin is an act determined,
at least in part, by the will itself. Granted, sinful volition occurs in
response to circumstances, but circumstances are a ground only of
certainty, not necessity. "Let what may, be the causes that influence an
agent to such determination," Fitch declared; "whether any previous
determination of the will or any thing else, they do not render the given
determination of the will, any other than a determination of which the
sinner is the immediate author, and in which he violates obligations."[67]
Circumstances and influences do not entirely account for the observed
effects of volition; hence the will must determine in some part its own
choice. Second, all subsequent choices of sin are the product of the
habit established by the first-sin-in-its-circumstances. One's first sin,
made certain by its Adamic circumstances, creates a circumstance of
its own, a sinful disposition, and from then on one continues to sin
more and more. "There may be created by the first sinful volition of
a moral agent, a ground of certainty respecting all the future sins of

his being," Fitch explained, "which original determination of will or moral purpose, operates, in addition to his original susceptibilities, as a ground of his succeeding acts being sinful."[68]

It goes without saying that Fitch's *Discourses* were virtually a distillation of Taylorism, with the revival-oriented intent of assuring "us of the certainty of evil" while clearing God "from the aspersion of creating and countenancing it, and to throw the aspersion, as He does, on a revolting world."[69] But it is also tempting to see Fitch's *Discourses* as a trial balloon for Taylor, replete with easily retractable suggestions that the answer "may" lie in these directions, and sent aloft to see what fire it might draw. Far away in Princeton, Ashbel Green and Archibald Alexander read the *Discourses* and produced a withering attack on Fitch's notion of a sinless nature that, among other things, meticulously pointed out Fitch's deviations from Edwards. In New Haven itself, Gardiner Spring (there to fill a preaching engagement) delivered an Edwardsean response by attacking Fitch for putting in sinners' heads the idea that they had power to save themselves.[70]

The wonder is that Fitch's *Discourse* did not arouse far greater criticism. One reason may be that in 1827 Nettleton was consumed with the debacle at New Lebanon, and with Finney's "new measures," and Bennet Tyler was preoccupied with resigning the presidency of Dartmouth College and moving to the Second Church of Portland, Maine.[71] Moreover, recalled Tyler, "those who were dissatisfied dreaded an explosion which should hazard the peace of the churches, and refrained from publishing their views."[72] In any case, either because he felt compelled to rescue Fitch from the critics or because he was pleasantly surprised that the critics had not done worse to him, Taylor proceeded to enter the fray himself. A suitable opportunity was presented in the fall of 1828 when the General Association of Connecticut invited him to preach before the assembled dignitaries of the association and the student body of Yale College, in the college chapel on the evening of commencement, September 10. Taylor cast his sermon in the form of the customary *Concio ad Clerum* ("declaration to the clergy"). Standing in the high round pulpit of the college chapel, with the faculty sitting in box pews ranged beside and below him, and the mixed congregation of students and ministers packing the long pews below and the galleries above, he now prepared to sound the death knell of *Freedom of the Will*.

His text was Ephesians 2:3: "*And were by nature the children of wrath even as others."* As with Fitch, the question was once again, *Why do men will to sin?* Taylor's answer was, predictably, not all that different from Fitch's: We sin because we are depraved by nature. But what, for Taylor, was depravity? It was not any "essential attribute or property of the soul," nor was it some continuously created oneness with Adam, nor was it the desires of any natural faculty, nor even *"any disposition or tendency* to sin, which is *the cause of all sin,"* since there was no point in looking for depravity—the cause of sinful volition— in a disposition already sinful.[73] Depravity, he concluded, *"is man's own act, consisting in a free choice of some object rather than God, as his chief good—or a free preference of the world and of worldly good, to the will and glory of God."*[74] The emphasis here is upon the *act*: the cause of our sinfulness is something we do, not something we are. We are depraved, then, because we sin, and not sinners because we are in some prior and passive fashion depraved. Depravity is selfish choosing, just as Emmons had once replied when asked in what sin consisted, *in sinning.* Depravity is not a quality that inheres originally in a nature; it is a primal action of the soul.

It is not entirely clear from the *Concio ad Clerum* whether Taylor conceived of this primal sinful preference of the world as a single oc- currence, which, like the missetting of a saw at the beginning of a run of lumber, guarantees the perverting of all subsequent action; or whether he looked upon all volitions as containing two aspects, a fun- damental selfish preference which is manifested in turn in a particular act of sin. Either way (and both can be adduced from the *Concio* and from his lectures), however, *"this—this* is man's depravity," a volition and not a substance.

This is that evil treasure of the heart from which proceed evil things; this is the fountain, the source of all other abominations—man's free, voluntary pref- erence of the world as his chief good, amid the revealed glories of a perfect God.[75]

It is worth noting that here, as before, Taylor occasionally displayed an Edwardslike penchant for the a priori explanation. Why do people sin? Because, by Taylor's definition of depravity, they are sinning beings. In the same fashion, one may as well ask why people in a race run: Taylor's answer would be that there is, of course, no such thing as a latent runful disposition in people. They are runners, quite simply, because they run—what else do you expect to find in a race?

But in putting his answers in those terms, Taylor implied that a context had made sinning possible in the first place. One expects people to run because they are runners, but one only expects them to be runners in the context of a race; likewise, to say that people sin because they are sinning beings confesses that there is some linkage between being and sinning. And indeed, for Taylor there was, and that linkage was what he called *nature*. Granted, he did not believe, as the Tasters had, in a sinful disposition; but he did not believe, whatever superficial resemblances Taylor's "depravity" had to Emmons, as the Exercisers did that the only context for human action and even human consciousness was the divine energy.

Humankind was, Taylor declared, "depraved *by nature*." But what was nature? It is, Taylor said, an "occasion," a *something* which he preferred to analyze in terms of what it allows rather than what it is or does. Nature is so constituted that human beings "will sin and only sin in all the appropriate circumstances of their being."[76] Taylor was at pains to make clear that he did not believe that circumstances cause people to sin—he was not a behaviorist. But he did not believe, either, that this nature "is the *physical* or *efficient* cause of their sinning."[77] Rather, he thought of nature as a quantity, *whatever* it is, which in the "appropriate circumstances" guarantees that humans "will sin and only sin." Placed in the context of "appropriate circumstances," human nature guarantees sinful action, and in this case, the implication is that the sinful action in question is the predominant preference for the world, which in turn produces all those other abominations.

This, in sum, was Taylor's explanation of depravity by nature: We commit sin because we first sin in loving the world rather than God, and we sin like that at first because, given the circumstances of the human context, our nature (*whatever* it is) induces us to do so.

But was this new-model Calvinism believable? That is a better question to ask than whether it is true, if only because the care and art of its construction underscores the fact that Taylor was playing to what his hearers wanted to, or could, believe. In some ways it must have seemed outlandishly farfetched. One has the uneasy feeling in reading the *Concio* that Taylor was playing with words rather than substance. Throughout the sermon, human beings operate in a vague alembic called "appropriate circumstances," which influences in an unspecified way the activity of a nature he defined only as an occasion—and not even an occasional *cause*—of behavior. It is strange not that Taylor seemed to be contradicting the Edwardsean psychology of volition, but that he never offered any concrete or even terminological example of an alternative.

One has the equally unsettling feeling that Taylor was forever taking one step backward for every two forward, simply to forestall potential critics. By his theory, he claimed, infants dying as infants need not be considered automatically damned: infants, lacking a knowledge of good and evil, lack the circumstances of a moral system that will trigger their natures into sin. And with their natures not in themselves sinful, there can be no grounds upon which to condemn them. But then, to avoid any overt resemblance to the Arminians, he promptly added that it is just as likely that they may become sinful very quickly. "They sin *as soon as they can . . . ; so early* that the literal interval, if there be such an interval, between birth and the commencement of sin, is either so short or so unimportant, that the Spirit of inspiration has not thought it worthy of particular notice."[78] What was given with one hand was taken away by the other—but not completely, for the burden of proof had now subtly shifted onto those who damned infants, forcing them to show first how the infants had *become* guilty, rather than by challenging the unbelievers to show how they could logically be innocent.

More startling for his hearers, and subsequent readers, was the introduction of his notion of the place of sin in the best possible moral system. It was plain from the *Concio* that, although he never addressed how it is that humans become holy (and so Taylor never had to expose where his libertarianism was most obvious), Taylor did not believe that people have to be depraved. Their natures do not make them that way, nor does God's immediate agency. But if depravity is not *necessary,* then why does God allow it to be there? What purpose does sin serve if it is theoretically dispensable, apart from making miserable the lives of people who would be better off without it?

The New Divinity had answered that by discovering that sin *was* the necessary means of the greatest good, and that God preferred sin because, on the whole and on Bellamy's calculus, more holiness turned up in the general result. Taylor's answer, which he consigned only to a lengthy footnote in the printed edition of the *Concio,* was to suggest that though sin is *theoretically* dispensable, and that God prefers holiness to sin in all circumstances, yet God tolerates sin as something incidental to a moral system (those "appropriate circumstances"). Morality is the judgment one makes about choice: to eliminate sin would leave only good to be chosen, and thus would leave nothing that really deserves the name of choice. To preserve choice, and with it a "moral system," God endures sin, and so it may be that sin exists not because God enjoys it and finds it the only way to bring good to pass, but because he really has no other option. Prefer holiness as he might, God has to accept the presence of sin in a moral system.[79]

But having aroused his hearers with a proposition so radical that it seemed literally to say that human sin is as great a problem for God as for men, Taylor dropped quietly back to say that this was merely a suggestion put forward in the interest of debate. God may—and *may* was the maddening word—"really purpose sin, though wholly an evil, considered as *incidental,* so far as his power of prevention is concerned, to the best moral system, as purpose it, considered as so excellent in its nature and relation, as to be the necessary means of the greatest good."[80] Having suggested one outrage, he shielded himself by urging what his audience—most of them anyway—could not disagree with, that it was no worse than Hopkins's outrages.

And yet, although once again there is the sense of a shell game, it is in these shifts back and forth that the real believability of the *Concio* lay—just as it had, ironically, in *Freedom of the Will.* For the *Concio* preserved the rhetoric of necessity without once resorting to the term *necessary,* and instead allowed the phrase "will sin and only sin" to create an illusion of necessity in the hearer's imagination. In short, Taylor had maintained all the effects of Calvinism, without any of the unpalatable Calvinist causes, and all the gloss and glitter of Edwardsean rhetoric on the will while simultaneously retiring *Freedom of the Will.* How many of Taylor's listeners understood him that night? Some must have comprehended at once what Taylor was doing; one minister showed to Bennet Tyler some doggerel verse he had penciled while listening to an earlier version of Taylor's theories at an association meeting:

> Immortal Edwards, whom religion hails
> Her favorite son, a Taylor overthrew;
> A Taylor now the great man's ghost assails,
> His doctrine doubts, and error vamps anew.[81]

But few beyond Taylor's students could have know that what Taylor meant by "circumstances" was the notion of "moral system" until Taylor, in the printed version of the *Concio,* added an explanation: that our "first sin" is committed under the influence of an amoral principle of self-love that prompts the will to make the sinner's heart what it is; that the Edwardseanlike evocation of "occasion" was a cover for an escape from causality; and that the connection of "nature" with the fact that man "will sin and only sin" (and it is remarkable how carefully Taylor worded his definition of depravity to avoid saying *how* circumstances operate on nature) amounted to no more than the certainty exerted by an influence.

Even those who would have taken instant offense at these conclusions (had they been put baldly) must have been lulled by Taylor's skill at presenting them, for Taylor had learned from Dwight and Beecher much about the necessity of coopting the Edwardsean vocabulary. How, for instance, is this statement to be taken?

> Not a human being does or can become thus sinful or depraved but by his own choice. God does not compel him to sin by the *nature* he gives him. Nor is his sin, although a consequence of Adam's sin, in such a sense its consequence as not to be a free voluntary act of his own. He sins freely, voluntarily.[82]

Taylor's lectures and papers make it a matter of record that he thought Edwards's mind was "all confusion" on the subject of necessity, and yet here is an utterance so carefully worded that it could be argued that it is Edwards's own.[83] It was certainly the same conclusion; and it was placed at just the point of Taylor's appeal in the *Concio* for purer revival preaching. Of course, it was also true that Taylor's appeal included no calls for elaborate reconciliations of natural ability and moral inability; and though Taylor invoked the "Spirit of all grace" to save the sinner, to the sinner he said in very un-Edwardsean accents, "His sin is his own. He yields himself by his own free act, by his own free choice, to those propensities of his nature, which under the weight of God's authority he *ought to govern*."[84] Here at last is a will, free of necessity and free of nature, and free at last to will what it wills. But it was all put forth on the authority of no one less than Edwards, and Taylor's citations of Edwards and Bellamy are the largest proofs he offers for the orthodoxy of his theory of depravity. And even though this would open Taylor to the charge of intellectual dishonesty, it was precisely Taylor's skill in manipulating and deploying the Edwardsean legacy that permitted him to make his libertarianism palatable; or rather, that allowed New England divines to think they could claim Edwards as their own while preaching certainty with power to the contrary.[85]

IV

Of course, not all New England divines thought that way, and certainly not Tyler, Nettleton, Woods, or Griffin. Beecher estimated that only as many as one-tenth of the Connecticut clergy could be counted upon to sympathize with Taylor; Ebenezer Porter of Andover thought only "a few men say 'Dr. Taylor is right, and Calvinism wrong'" and "not one tenth of the New England ministers, and not one hundredth of those that are thirty-five years old" could agree that Taylor and Calvinism could be reconciled.[86] Nettleton, scandalized by the *Concio ad Clerum,* immediately began urging Woods to reply to it; Ebenezer Porter warned Lyman Beecher that Gardiner Spring, David Porter, Alvan Hyde, James Richards, and Edward Dorr Griffin were all preparing to pounce on Taylor. But the first shot was fired by a relatively unknown parson from Westchester, Connecticut, named James Harvey. Harvey published a major attack on Taylor in the spring of 1829.

Evidently, Taylor had anticipated trouble. In the summer of 1828 Goodrich and Beecher had bought the magazine *Christian Spectator* to turn it into a quarterly organ for the Yale theological faculty, since Beecher and Taylor realized that the case would not be decided by who controlled the clergy but by who controlled the distribution of information and argument. Events soon proved the wisdom of the decision. Taylor initiated a flurry of reprisals and counterreprisals in print, denouncing Harvey in the June 1829 *Spectator,* and from that point on, Taylor used the *Spectator* to dominate all subsequent discussion.

Nettleton tried the personable and persuasive tactics that had served him so well in his revivals. He visited Taylor in New Haven in July, and vainly tried to reason with him. Nettleton came away conceding that Taylor's overall motive in the *Concio* was not a wrongheaded one. "The object of Br. T's note [the footnote in the *Concio* on the best possible moral system] seems to be to vindicate the character of God in the sincerity of the calls & offers of the gospel," Nettleton reported to Woods; the problem was with Taylor's method, for Nettleton complained to Woods that Taylor had done so on libertarian grounds. "The general impression, however, is, I think, a bad one—that the government of the Universe of moral agents depends primarily, if not wholly, on themselves."[87] Failing with the direct approach, Nettleton next appealed to Beecher, warning him that New Haven would have to be considered as "at war with Edwards," and suggested that Beecher (who had by then removed to Boston's Hanover Street Church) organize a forum in which Taylor could confront his critics and perhaps mend his ways.[88] A meeting was finally arranged at Andover on September 23, 1829, including Taylor, Goodrich, Gardiner Spring, and the Andover faculty, but Taylor showed no sign of budging. Far from it, both Beecher and Taylor assumed a new aggressiveness, and in October, when Nettleton visited Beecher in Boston, Beecher threatened, "Taylor & I made you what you are & now if you do not behave yourself, we will have you down."[89]

Taylor's increased intransigence attracted increased fire. Between December 1829 and May 1833 Bennet Tyler (who had only just come across a copy of the *Concio* while traveling from Maine through Connecticut) began to publish a series of criticisms of Taylor. Taylor responded with a mixture of annoyance and evasiveness. In the spring of 1830 Leonard Woods published *Letters to Rev. Nathaniel W. Taylor, D.D.*, a series of polite but unfriendly public letters urging Taylor to be candid about his heresies. And in 1833 Edward Dorr Griffin published an even more careful and thoughtful assault on Taylor, *The Doctrine of Divine Efficiency*. It can hardly be said that Woods or Griffin refuted Taylor; it cannot even be said they pinned him down. Rather than be boxed in theologically, Taylor preferred to resort to the tactics of cooptation. He got his former students to assure the local associations that Tyler and his allies were arguing over nonessentials, and that there was really "no difference" between Tyler and Taylor.[90] Samuel Rogers Andrew assured the South Association of Litchfield County that, viewed from the right perspective, Tyler and Taylor were really saying the same thing about sinfulness of the human will.

Now, what is the real amount of difference on this point between the contending parties? Not (as has sometimes been said) that one of the parties supposes mankind to be *born holy*. This sentiment is equally discarded by both parties. Not that mankind are born without any *foundation* of moral character, and that they become possessed of such a foundation at some period subsequent to their birth. Not that there is any want of *certainty* as to what men's moral character will be, as soon as they have a moral character, be that time when it may,—for both parties alike hold that that character will be sinful, and only sinful.[91]

Tyler, who had been prepared to play Samuel Hopkins all over again, was driven frantic by this tactic and repeatedly tried to draw Taylor out into the open in the *Christian Spectator*. But Taylor refused to be drawn, and when he finally grew weary of publishing notices of Tyler's articles, he simply closed the pages of the *Spectator* to any further comment on the subject. He persuaded Beecher to do likewise in the periodicals he controlled.

In frustration, in September 1833, Tyler eventually called upon the anti–New Haven ministers of Connecticut to form their own Pastoral Association, calling in effect for the first schism in Connecticut Congregationalism since the days of James Davenport and Timothy Allen. Funded in large measure by Nettleton (who had acquired a considerable fortune from the royalties of a hymnal he had compiled in his retirement), a Theological Institute was formed as a counterseminary to Yale. It was located in East Windsor, the birthplace of Jonathan Edwards, and its cornerstone was a stone step from the old Edwards homestead. In the long run, this was precisely the schism to which Ezra Stiles had predicted the New Divinity would lead—from their point of view, the problem was that it was too little, too late.

Nevertheless, the criticisms they leveled showed that Taylor by no means had a monopoly on perspicuity. Leonard Woods grasped one of the central problems when he questioned whether Taylor had any right to use language in such a vague, half-formed manner. "You think there is in moral agency itself, a power so resistless, that it is impossible for God himself, however strong may be his desire, to prevent the existence, or even the present degree of sin," Woods complained, wanting to know who or what had authorized Taylor to talk of "moral system" as though it were a generally agreed-upon universal:

Your theory, my dear Brother, supposes, that there is something in moral agency, which renders it impossible for divine power to control it. But what this something is, you have no where told so. ... I could not adopt your language, or the theory which in my view it evidently implies, without denying what the Bible everywhere teaches.[92]

Joseph Harvey was similarly suspicious of Taylor's reiterated promise that men will sin and only sin. "The question instantly arises, what is the ground of this certainty," Harvey demanded, "for this certainty is all the partition, between the sentiment of this sermon [*Concio ad Clerum*], and downright Arminianism."[93]

Their bafflement over Taylor's language struck out in several directions. Woods protested Taylor's vocabulary again on the best-possible-moral-system business, since he believed that Taylor's argument implied a peculiarly cocky confidence that Taylor knew enough about God's moral character to build his argument on how that divine moral character would react to sin in the "present moral system." "No man can urge the moral character of God as an argument against the doctrine of man's depravity," Woods protested, "except upon the supposition, that we are competent to determine, by our own reason, in what manner God's moral perfection will be developed."[94] Tyler objected on the grounds of simple logic: given Taylor's proposal in the footnote to the *Concio*—that God must endure the sinfulness of the "present moral system" because he cannot avoid tolerating sin if he wants to have a "moral system" on earth—this would mean that God must have somehow "for his own glory . . . foreordained that which is not for his glory, and which he cannot over rule for his glory." Or, Tyler continued, putting an Edwardsean barb on his question, how can God prefer that which can never be (by Taylor's reasoning) a greatest apparent good?

[Has] any being ever purposed or chose that a thing should exist, when he preferred, all things considered, that something else should exist in its stead? . . . How is it possible for him to prefer, on any account, the existence of sin, if, all things considered,—that is, on all accounts,—he prefers something else in its stead, in all instances?[95]

They objected even more deeply to Taylor's new psychology. Tyler, of course, as a Taster, did not deny that "the transgression of known law is sin," but "to affirm that there is no other sin, is to affirm that no man ever sins without knowing it at the time, which is evidently contrary to fact"[96]; on the other hand, Edward Dorr Griffin the Exerciser did not mind confining sin to sinful actions, but he did revolt at Taylor's unwillingness to account for those actions by divine efficiency. "Dr. T. holds that God can create a being constitutionally qualified to act," Griffin complained, "without being acted upon."[97] Both joined, however, in protesting Taylor's award to the principle of self-love the power to prompt the will to make a new heart, holy or otherwise. Nettleton joined the argument at precisely this point when he declared that it was absurd to have an actor create a disposition when a disposition was first required in order to act. "No sinner ever did, or ever will make a holy choice, prior to an inclination, bias, or tendency to holiness."[98] But by the same token, Tyler added, if "every moral act is either sinful or holy," then to say that sinners, out of self-love, make themselves holy is ludicrous. Not only is self-love to be subordinated to benevolence, but Taylor makes it into the unholy means whereby an unholy person somehow produces holy actions. "Consequently," Tyler concluded, conjuring up for the last time the rusty catapult of Edwards's infinite-regress argument, Taylor's psychology of conversion makes the sinner begin "to be holy before he is born again," an "absurdity" which is the same as saying "the sinner begins to be holy before he begins to be holy."[99]

Taylor's notion of will excited the anti–New Havenites' greatest fear, both in terms of self-definition and in terms of the divine decree. They were determined to understand him only as an apostate from Edwards, and not as a fellow-Calvinist looking for ways to stave off the Unitarian menace. Tyler, as early as his first blast at Taylor in 1829, noted that, in a formal way, Taylor did indeed acknowledge divine sovereignty over human volition, but his departures from Edwards on the will obviated that acknowledgment. "He does indeed maintain that regeneration is produced by the power of God, or by the agency of the Holy Spirit; and yet," Tyler complained, "he makes no distinction between the act of God who is the author of this change, and the act of the sinner who is the subject of it."[100] And Taylor's doctrine of "certainty, with power to the contrary," only confirmed Tyler's suspicions that Taylor was promoting the self-determining will of the Arminians. Tested by Edwards's logic in *Freedom of the Will*, Taylor manifested precisely the inconsistencies Edwards had described in the Arminians. What is liberty? It is the power to act as we please. Then, asked Tyler, "*Does Liberty, or free agency, imply power to act contrary to our prevailing inclination?*" Obviously, no: "to act thus would be directly the opposite of freedom."[101] Woods was similarly puzzled by what Taylor meant by a power of contrary choice. Is choice ever more than the willing of one thing? Can one ever have the power of literally contrary choice? Woods wrote in amazement, "however great our power of choosing differently from what we do, we never, in any instance whatever exercise it."

Let it be that we have such a power. I say that we cannot *use* it, except by choosing at the very same time differently from what we do choose. But how can this be? At the very same time that we choose to speak the truth, how can we use the power of a contrary choice, and choose to speak falsehood? Now how strange it is, that any one should represent free agency as consisting in a power, which, if it should exist, would never be used, and the use of which would imply a contradiction.[102]

For that reason, nothing struck more personally at these latter-day Edwardseans than Taylor's claim to Edwards's authority. "Is your theory of moral agency the same as that which Edwards maintained in his treatise on the Will?" Woods demanded of Taylor, and the answer he saw in Taylor's writings was no assurance that it was.[103] Instead, Woods complained, "we find you, on several interesting points, siding against the Orthodox and siding with Dr. John Taylor [Edwards's opponent in *Original Sin*] against Edwards on some of the main questions at issue between them."[104] That did nothing to deter Taylor and Fitch from claiming that Edwardsean mantle Samuel Hopkins had long ago feared was passing out of New England; it did not stop them from putting Edwards's imprimatur on the pages of the *Christian Spectator*. "It is common practice with writers of this school to make confident appeals to Edwards," Griffin wailed, "when they are as far from these divines as Arminianism is from Calvinism."[105] What Griffin did not understand was Taylor's motive: "Why dress up palpable Arminianism in such Calvinistic drapery?" he wondered.[106] Why indeed, unless by coopting the Edwardsean image one not only eliminated the Edwardsean competition but deceived those likely to be impressed by it. Nettleton, who understood better what was going on, wearily uttered to Samuel Miller what may be taken as the epitaph of the Edwardsean–New Divinity–Hopkinsian family:

It is not the first, nor the thousandth time that Edwards has been claimed as vindicating the measures & doctrines which every man who is acquainted with his works knows he did most sadly deplore & publicly condemn. . . . The phrase "New Divinity," too, is liable to be misunderstood in like manner by all Eng. & Scotland, & nine-tenths of the Presbyterian church & this misunderstanding is what has given such advantage to the New Haven divines. They love to have it so.[107]

Epilogue
The Unanswered Question

By the time Bennet Tyler organized the Theological Institute of Connecticut, the sun had already set on Edwardseanism in New England. Taylor and Beecher and their students and allies had converted all the major Connecticut periodicals into mouthpieces for Taylor's new-style Old Calvinism, and the Yale Divinity School belonged clearly to Taylor. And with that, Taylor controlled all that he needed to control: by the 1830s American theological discourse had moved out of the realm of the pamphlet and printed sermon (where the New Divinity had flourished) and away from the book-length treatise (such as *Freedom of the Will* or *True Religion Delineated*) and onto the pages of the quarterly periodical, where professors of theology rather than country parsons assumed the role of oracle in fifty-page reviews patterned after German theological writers. By controlling Yale and monopolizing the legitimacy which a seminary now conferred, Taylor could (like Archibald Alexander) dictate who would be admitted to the company of Connecticut divines; by controlling the periodicals, he could determine what they would continue to think after they joined that company. Such a determination was, of course, far from air-tight, but then again it did not have to be for the New Haven theology to exercise a predominant influence in Connecticut Congregationalism.

The New Divinity, by contrast, could not learn the new tricks—it was, by then, anything but new itself. Tyler, Nettleton, and Woods were never quite at home in the new realm of discourse laid out by the periodical, and the Theological Institute of Connecticut never mounted any serious challenge to Yale's hegemony over Connecticut Congregationalism. Far from stemming Taylor's tide, Nettleton was reduced to writing ferocious letters to Samuel Miller and Charles Hodge, warning them against the Yale graduates who were spilling over into the Presbyterian church.[1] Embittered, Nettleton died in 1844, after a final visit from Taylor in which Nettleton adamantly refused reconciliation and breathed out his last defiance.[2] He might have saved those breathings for all the good they accomplished. The Yale review, *The New Englander*, marked Nettleton's death by blithely insisting that between Nettleton and Taylor there was really "no difference."[3] Tyler died in 1858, the same year as Taylor, while the broken remains of the Edwardseans quarreled amongst themselves and with Tyler over who was or was not truly loyal to the Edwardsean legacy. He left behind him a Theological Institute hardly more significant than when it had begun, and shortly thereafter the school left the Edwardsean atmosphere of East Windsor for Hartford, where it eventually sent Asahel Nettleton's portrait up to the attic to gather dust.[4]

Things were no better for the Edwardseans in Massachusetts. By the 1830s Edwardseanism had vanished even from the Berkshires, as the rural parishes turned to the more respectable graduates of the Yale Divinity School, Andover Theological Seminary, and Andover's seedling school, Bangor Theological Seminary.[5] Leonard Woods of Andover and Enoch Pond of Bangor remained two last lonely guardians of Edwardseanism, but Pond's *Lectures on Christian Theology* (dedicated to the memory of Nathanael Emmons) dropped stillborn from their author's pen in 1867, while Woods's Edwardseanism grew more and more attenuated as the years passed. Woods's colleague at Andover, Moses Stuart, made no secret of his admiration for Taylor, and published his own repudiation of *Freedom of the Will* in the *Christian Spectator*.

One may say (as it has often been said) the will always acts from motives, and is decided by them. . . . But is there not something in free agency, which takes a higher position still, and has within its control even the very motives to good and evil which are presented? I cannot philosophize about it, nor make a verbal diagram of it, nor draw it out in propositions exposed to the eye; but *I can and do feel it,* every conscious moment of my life. My soul is sovereign over all the objects which surround it. . . . My present belief is that the very essence of sin lies in yielding to sinful excitement, when we have physical and metaphysical power to resist it.[6]

Outside New England, the legacy of *Freedom of the Will* would continue to find partisans. In the academic world of the seminaries, Henry Boynton Smith at Union Seminary in New York City and W. G. T. Shedd, first of Andover and then of Union, continued to embody many of the central concerns of Edwardseanism, and Smith wrote perhaps the most cogent essay ever written on Nathanael Emmons. A much more popular figure, who ensured that the shibboleths of Edwardseanism would become institutionalized in the development of American evangelicalism, was Charles Grandison Finney. Nettleton had been rightly suspicious that Finney's revivalism had elements of strange, un-Edwardsean fire in it; and Beecher's influence in the early 1830s brought Finney at least temporarily into the New Haven orbit. But the Princetonian Albert B. Dod shrewdly observed that Finney's relationship to New Haven was ambivalent: "The new measures, we believe were in full action before the theology of New Haven shed its light upon the world." Rather, Dod thought that Finney's meteoric rise to popular notice was produced by a conjunction "between the coarse, bustling fanaticism of the New Measures, and the refined, intellectual abstractions of the New Divinity."[7] And after 1835, when Finney left New York to take the presidency of Oberlin College, both Beecher and Taylor fade completely out of the view of his *Memoirs,* as does Finney out of the *Autobiography* of Beecher. Though he was free to work out his own conclusions in the Ohio wilderness, Finney's debt to Edwardseanism reasserted itself in the development of his ethics, his doctrine of perfectionism, and his revival techniques.[8] Through Finney, Mark Hopkins, J. H. Fairchild, and even Dwight L. Moody, the torch of Edwardsean immediacy was passed on to yet further generations, although in successively watered-down forms.

Princeton Seminary, however, remained impervious to the insinuations of the New Haven theology. Alexander, Hodge, and Miller proved as remarkably successful in winnowing Edwardsean influence out of Princeton as Taylor had at Yale, and they might have been just as effective in keeping Taylorism out of the Presbyterian church entirely— had it not been for the Plan of Union. The "Presbygational" Plan of Union had long been the Achilles heel of Old Side Presbyterianism, for its terms had permitted a constant seepage of Edwardsean ministers, principally from Connecticut, into the synods of upstate New York and the old Western Reserve of Ohio. But this had been tolerable—though only barely so—so long as the migrants had been genuine Edwardseans. When Yale began pumping Taylorite graduates westward, a crisis ensued that shattered Presbyterian unity.

The crisis centered around one major figure, Albert Barnes, a Yale graduate who occupied the pulpit of the First Presbyterian Church in

Philadelphia and whose biblical commentaries retailed a number of obnoxious Taylorisms. The problem that Barnes presented to the Old Side, or Old School, Presbyterians was not so much himself or even his writings, but the discovery that, due to the weight of the New York synods in the General Assembly, the Old Schoolers could do nothing to touch him. Twice, Barnes was tried for heresy; twice, sweet and smiling, he was acquitted. Barnes's immunity from prosecution was further aggravated by Lyman Beecher, who accepted a call in 1832 to become president of the new Lane Seminary in Cincinnati. Old Schoolers tried first to block him from entering the Presbyterian church at all; he circumvented them by obtaining a transfer into a friendly New York synod. They tried next to try him for heresy in Cincinnati; they failed again, and had to listen to Beecher's son Edward boast about how they would now erect a "Yale of the West" in Illinois to propagate their doctrines.[9]

At the eleventh hour the Old Schoolers, rallied by Archibald Alexander and Samuel Miller, summoned their forces to the 1837 General Assembly and proceeded to abrogate the Plan of Union and declare the "New School" synods organized under the plan null and void. Old School Presbyterianism thus saved itself from Taylorism, but only by a drastic amputation, and only for a limited time. In the 1860s the unchastened New School Presbyterians were reunited to the Old School majority in a compromise that, by the 1920s, would prove fatal to Old School orthodoxy.

This fatality is often laid at Edwards's doorstep, and that may be true, but only if we regard Edwards and *Freedom of the Will* as the cause of the New Haven agitation. Of course it must be conceded that this makes for a neat, tidy intellectual genealogy, sending the line of ideas straight from Edwards to Hopkins to Emmons to Taylor, and from thence to Finney and the rest of American revivalism and evangelicalism, and thus proving again what New England's sons have always suspected to be true, that the American mind has always been a New England one. But the fact remains that Taylor was not an Edwardsean, and in order to get that neat progression from Edwards to Taylor, one must obscure the connection that stands between Taylor and Old Calvinism, and the irreconcilable differences that lay between Old Calvinism and *Freedom of the Will*.

For all their protests about their fealty to Edwards, Edwards had become for Beecher and Taylor what the doctrines of grace had been to Moses Mather and Moses Hemmenway, an *icon*, a kind of philosophical Gray Champion. And even while parading their New England icon around, they frankly muttered their skepticism about his ideas to themselves. "God saw the error which lay at the bottom of the New England philosophy of free agency, depravity, and regeneration, both the Taste and Exercise schemes," Beecher told Taylor in 1835; both had been predicated on *Freedom of the Will,* and that "demanded a convulsion to root them up."[10] And Taylor as much as admitted his distance from Edwardseanism when he said that "the theory of Dr. Tyler though embraced by others, is uniformly adopted by no theological sect or class except the high Hopkinsians"—meaning, of course, that *he* owned no kinship to them.[11] This hostility to Edwardseanism resounds even louder in Taylor's pupils. Zebulon Crocker threw *Freedom of the Will* to the winds in his defense of the New Haven theology in 1838:

The New Haven divines regard man as a complete agent in himself, and the author or efficient cause of his own moral acts. He is a cause of action out of God, created and upheld by him, but free in his volitions, though always acting in view of motives, and under the influences which God is pleased to exert upon him. They regard not merely *the exercise of the will* in voluntary acts, but *the power of choosing and refusing,* under all circumstances, essential to moral agency.[12]

But, just as important, Horace Bushnell laid his finger on the applications of *Freedom of the Will* as the things the New Havenites loathed in Edwards:

The attention he had bestowed on the will gave a still more intense form of individualism, probably to his teachings. . . . It makes nothing of the family, and the church, and the organic powers God has constituted as vehicles of grace. It takes every man as if he had existed *alone,* presumes that he is unreconciled to God until he has undergone some sudden and explosive experience, in adult years, or after the age of reason; demands that experience, and only when it is reached, allows the subject to be an heir of life.[13]

This latter as much as anything else was the engine that drove the New Haven theology. Perhaps it is true that Taylor's critique drew its strength from pure philosophical resentment of Edwardseanism; and it is probably true that Taylor was responding to the demand of the Jacksonian era for a place for the autonomous hero in the universe. But it is hard not to think that Taylor was looking backward, rather than forward, to the comfortable covenantal unity that Edwards had tried to force New England to sacrifice in his struggle with an earlier Zeitgeist.

In that sense, Taylor finished the job James Dana had set out to do, to eliminate *Freedom of the Will* not just as a misguided apologetic that worried about atheistic materialism when it should have been worrying about atheistic skepticism, but as an ominous black question pointed at the heart of the New England Way. For, whatever they thought about the merits of Edwards's philosophical assumptions, both Taylor and Dana had found *Freedom of the Will* standing obstinately in the way of their idea of national community, because it demanded they confront the problem of free will in such a way as to jeopardize New England community. The *Concio* successfully spoke to fears of those who had come to share both of those anxieties, and it offered to them a workable apologetical substitute to *Freedom of the Will* that would not simultaneously call for an end to their ecclesiastical worlds. The *Concio,* therefore, means the end of *Freedom of the Will* as a living force in American thought, and the confident burial of freedom of will as a serious theological problem.

But only as a theological problem. Although by 1828 the ghost of Hobbes had faded far enough over the horizon for Americans, and the Scottish philosophy of intuited freedom now seemed so secure that Calvinists need no longer worry themselves with troubling apologetics for divine sovereignty, the New Haven divines celebrated the end of the Edwardsean embarrassment a little too prematurely. For, in the end, it turned out that Edwards had been right: the real threat to Christian orthodoxy did not come from the Humean skeptics but from the materialists, after all. In thirty years, Charles Darwin would publish the *Origin of Species,* trampling under its feet any divinity erected on Scottish intuitionism and reawakening the nightmare of hard, materialistic determinism. This time, there was no Edwards to rally the forces of theism against materialism and drive the skulkers out to battle.

From thence, the question of free will moved into a new and overwhelmingly secular context. But this would happen only because Nathaniel Taylor had knowingly prevailed on his peers to ignore *Freedom of the Will* and substitute in its place a different kind of apologetic that, in the event, turned out to be just as fruitless as Edwards had all along insisted such apologetics would be. To some degree that explains why Nathaniel William Taylor was fast becoming a forgotten man by the time of his death in 1858, one hundred years after Edwards's death

("... built in such a logical way / That it ran a hundred years to a day") and one year before the publication of *The Origin of Species*. And perhaps that also means that the whole legitimacy of Edwards's bid to force the settlement of issue, which had become even in his time a secular one, into an exclusively theological framework remains an open, but an unanswered, question.

Notes

Introduction

1. Alexander Viets Griswold Allen, *Jonathan Edwards* (Boston: Houghton Mifflin, 1889), 283–285.
2. Paul Oskar Kristeller, "The Moral Thought of Renaissance Humanism," in *Renaissance Thought II: Papers on Humanism and the Arts* (New York: Harper & Row, 1965), 56; Michael J. O'Brien, *The Socratic Paradoxes and the Greek Mind* (Chapel Hill: University of North Carolina Press, 1967), 40, 211; Norman Fiering, *Moral Philosophy at Seventeenth-Century Harvard* (Chapel Hill: University of North Carolina Press, 1981), 80.
3. Peter Brown, *Augustine of Hippo* (Berkeley: University of California Press, 1969), 168, 172–173.
4. St. Augustine, *Confessions,* VII.3, VIII.9, ed. R. S. Pyne-Coffin (London: Penguin Books, 1961), 136, 164, 172; St. Augustine, "On Grace and Free Will" V, in *The Nicene and Post Nicene Fathers* [Second Series], ed. Philip Schaff (1887; Grand Rapids, MI: William B. Eerdmans, 1976), 5:446; see also Robert Cushman, "Faith and Reason," in *A Companion to the Study of St. Augustine,* ed. R. W. Battenhouse (1955; Grand Rapids, MI: Baker Book House, 1981), 289–290.
5. Norman Fiering, "Will and Intellect in the New England Mind," *William and Mary Quarterly* 29 (1972), 525.
6. John Calvin, *Institutes of the Christian Religion* I.15.7, eds. F. L. Battles, H. Bettenson, and J. T. McNeill (Philadelphia: Westminster Press, 1960), 1:194.
7. John Calvin, *Commentary on Romans* [12:2], trans. R. Mackenzie (Grand Rapids, MI: William B. Eerdmans, 1973), 265; John Calvin, *Commentary on Ephesians* [4:17], trans. T. H. L. Parker (Grand Rapids, MI: William B. Eerdmans, 1965), 186.
8. Vernon K. Bourke, *Will in Western Thought: An Historico-Critical Study* (New York: Sheed & Ward, 1964), 129–142.
9. Etienne Gilson, *History of Christian Philosophy in the Middle Ages* (New York: Random House, 1955), 463–464.
10. William Ames, *The Marrow of Theology* I.3, trans. John D. Eusden (1968; Durham, NC: Labyrinth Press, 1983), 80.
11. Bourke, *Will in Western Thought,* 129; St. Augustine, *Confessions* X.38, XIII.9, ed. Pyne-Coffin, 247, 317.
12. St. Augustine, "Against Two Letters of the Pelagians," I.5, in *Nicene and Post Nicene Fathers,* 5:379.
13. Terrence Erdt, *Jonathan Edwards: Art and the Sense of the Heart* (Amherst: University of Massachusetts Press, 1980), 15.
14. John Winthrop, *Winthrop Papers* (Boston: Massachusetts Historical Society, 1943), 3:339, 343.

15. John Cotton, *The Way of Life* (London, 1641), 127–133, 134.
16. Ibid., 200–201, 206.
17. For a more complete outline of these concepts of volitional freedom than space allows here, see Bourke, *Will in Western Thought,* and the opening chapters of the dissertation which gave rise to this book, "The Unanswered Question: The Legacy of Jonathan Edwards's *Freedom of the Will* in Early American Religious Philosophy," (Ph.D. dissertation, University of Pennsylvania, 1986).
18. Brand Blandshard, "The Case for Determinism," in *Determinism and Freedom in the Age of Modern Science,* ed. Sidney Hook (New York: New York University Press, 1958), 3–4.
19. Paul Edwards, "Hard and Soft Determinism," in *Determinism and Freedom,* 106; Moritz Schlick, "When Is a Man Responsible?" in *Free Will and Determinism,* ed. Bernard Berofsky (New York: Harper and Row, 1966), 59.
20. R. E. Hobart, "Free Will as Involving Determinism and Inconceivable Without It," in *Free Will and Determinism,* 78, 87.
21. Wesley C. Salmon, "Determinism and Indeterminism in Modern Science," in *Reason and Responsibility: Readings in Some Basic Problems in Philosophy* (Belmont, CA: Wadsworth, 1981), 355.
22. John Calvin, *Concerning the Eternal Predestination of God,* trans. J. K. S. Reid (London: James Clarke, 1961), 162.
23. Jacobus Arminius, "A Declaration of the Sentiments of Arminius" and "Nine Questions" in *The Writings of James Arminius,* ed. W. R. Bagnall (Grand Rapids, MI: Baker Book House, 1977), 1:231–232, 380.
24. Alister McGrath, *Iustitia Dei: A History of the Christian Doctrine of Justification* (Oxford: Oxford University Press, 1986), 1:27.
25. Martin Luther, *The Bondage of the Will,* eds. J. I. Packer and O. R. Johnston (London: James Clarke, 1957), 81, 102.
26. Calvin, *Institutes* II.3.5, 294–296.
27. John Norton, *The Orthodox Evangelist* (London: J. Macock, 1654), 199.
28. Calvin, *Institutes* II.2.7, 264.
29. Luther, *Bondage of the Will,* 313–314.
30. Richard Baxter, *The Reasons of the Christian Religion* (1667), in Richard Westfall, *Science and Religion in Seventeenth-Century England* (New Haven: Yale University Press, 1958), 22–23.
31. Thomas Hobbes, "Of Liberty and Necessity," in *British Moralists, 1650–1860,* ed. D. D. Raphael (Oxford: Oxford University Press, 1969), 1:67.
32. Thomas Hobbes, *Leviathan,* ed. W. G. Pogson Smith (1909; Clarendon Press, 1967), 161.
33. Daniel Whitby, *A Discourse concerning the true import of the words Election and Reprobation* (London, 1817), 34.
34. Samuel Clarke, *Demonstration of the Being and Attributes of God* (London, 1711), 163; Norman Fiering, *Jonathan Edwards's Moral Thought and Its British Context* (Chapel Hill: University of North Carolina Press, 1981), 279–282; for Clarke's celebrated debate with Leibniz, in which the ontological status of freedom is thoroughly debated, see *The Leibniz-Clark Correspondence,* ed. H. G. Alexander (Manchester: Manchester University Press, 1956) and Chapter XI of Alexander Koyre, *From the Closed World to the Infinite Universe* (Baltimore: Johns Hopkins University Press, 1957).

35. R. F. Stalley, "The Will in Hume's Treatise," *Journal of the History of Philosophy* 24 (1986), 41–53; John Redwood, *Reason, Ridicule, and Religion: The Age of Enlightenment in England, 1660–1750* (Cambridge: Harvard University Press, 1976), 208–209.

36. Thomas Reid, *Essays on the Active Powers of the Mind*, ed. Baruch Brody (Cambridge: Harvard University Press, 1969), 259, 283; Selwyn A. Grave, *The Scottish Philosophy of Common Sense* (Oxford: Oxford University Press, 1960), 206–207.

1. The New England Dilemma

1. *Sibley's Harvard Graduates: Biographical Sketches of Those Who Attended Harvard College*, ed. Clifford K. Shipton (Cambridge: Harvard University Press, 1873–1970), 4:94, 98.

2. Michael Walzer, *The Revolution of the Saints: A Study in the Origins of Radical Politics* (London: Weidenfeld & Nicolson, 1966), 313.

3. Sir Charles Firth, *Oliver Cromwell and the Rule of the Puritans in England* (London: Oxford University Press, 1900, 1972), 123; Christopher Hill, *Oliver Cromwell, 1658–1958* (London: The Historical Association, Pamphlet no. 38, 1958, 1973), 25–27.

4. John Winthrop, "A Modell of Christian Charity," in *The Puritans: A Sourcebook of Their Writings*, eds. Perry Miller and Thomas H. Johnson (New York: Harper & Row, 1938, 1963), 1:198.

5. Michael Zuckerman, "The Fabrication of Identity in Early America," in *William and Mary Quarterly*, 37 (1980), 194.

6. Paul R. Lucas, *Valley of Discord: Church and Society Along the Connecticut River, 1636–1725* (Hanover, NH: University Press of New England, 1976), 155.

7. Ralph Coffman, *Solomon Stoddard* (Boston: Twayne Publishers, 1978), 69, 101.

8. Patricia J. Tracy, *Jonathan Edwards, Pastor: Religion and Society in Eighteenth-Century Northampton* (New York: Hill & Wang, 1980), 24–26.

9. Stoddard, "Defects of Preachers Reproved," in *The Great Awakening: Documents on the Revival of Religion, 1740–1745*, ed. Richard Bushman (New York: Atheneum, 1970), 13.

10. Tracy, *Jonathan Edwards, Pastor*, 32; Coffman, *Solomon Stoddard*, 84.

11. Harry S. Stout, *The New England Soul: Preaching and Religious Culture in Colonial New England* (New York: Oxford University Press, 1986), 176, 180.

12. Edwards, "Personal Narrative," in *Jonathan Edwards: Representative Selections*, eds. Clarence Faust and Thomas H. Johnson (New York: Hill and Wang, 1935, 1962), 57.

13. Ola Elizabeth Winslow, *Jonathan Edwards, 1703–1758: A Biography* (New York: Macmillan, 1940), 49–50.

14. Iain Murray, *Jonathan Edwards: A New Biography* (London: Banner of Truth Trust, 1987), 26.

15. Jonathan Edwards, "Natural Philosophy," in *WJE: Scientific and Philosophical Writings*, ed. Wallace E. Anderson (New Haven: Yale University Press, 1980), 192.

16. Clyde Holbrook, *Jonathan Edwards: The Valley and Nature* (Lewisburg, PA: Bucknell University Press, 1987), 54; Edwards, "Things to be Con-

sidered," in *WJE: Scientific and Philosophical Writings,* ed. Anderson, 242.

17. Edwards, "Personal Narrative," in *Representative Selections,* eds. Faust and Johnson, 58–60.

18. On the ambiguities in determining exactly what constituted a charge of "Arminianism," see Gerald J. Goodwin, "The Myth of 'Arminian-Calvinism' in Eighteenth-Century New England," in *New England Quarterly,* 41 (1968), 225.

19. Edwards, "Diary," in *Representative Selections,* eds. Faust and Johnson, 51.

20. James Warch, *School of the Prophets: Yale College, 1701–1740* (New Haven: Yale University Press, 1973), 170.

21. Murray, *Jonathan Edwards,* 283; Joseph Ellis, *The New England Mind in Transition: Samuel Johnson of Connecticut, 1696–1772* (New Haven: Yale University Press, 1973), 113.

22. Edwards, "Diary," in *Representative Selections,* eds. Faust and Johnson, 53.

23. Edwards, "A Faithful Narrative of the Surprising Work of God," in *WJE: The Great Awakening,* ed. C. C. Goen (New Haven: Yale University Press, 1972), 113.

24. Edwards, "Faithful Narrative," in *WJE: The Great Awakening,* ed. Goen, 148.

25. Conrad Wright, *The Beginnings of Unitarianism in America* (Boston: Starr King Press, 1955), 21–22.

26. John Bass, *A True Narative of an Unhappy Contention* (Boston: Gookin, 1751), 26–27.

27. Experience Mayhew, *Grace Defined in a Modest Plea for an Important Truth* (Boston: Green, 1744), 156.

28. Edwards, "Miscellaneous Remarks," in *The Works of Jonathan Edwards* ed. Edward Hickman (1834; rept. London: Banner of Truth Trust, 1976), 2:534.

29. Edwards, "Diary," in *Representative Selections,* eds. Faust and Johnson, 42, 53; Edwards, "Outline of 'A Rational Account,'" in *WJE: Scientific and Philosophical Writings,* ed. Anderson, 397.

30. Sereno Edwards Dwight, "Memoirs of Jonathan Edwards," in *Works of Jonathan Edwards,* ed. Hickman, 1:clxxxii.

31. Louis E. Loeb, *From Descartes to Hume: Continental Metaphysics and the Development of Modern Philosophy* (Ithica, NY: Cornell University Press, 1981), 36–62.

32. Richard I. Aaron, *John Locke* (Oxford: Oxford University Press, 1955), 30, 95–98, 102, 111; John Yolton, *Thinking Matter: Materialism in Eighteenth-Century Britian* (Minneapolis: University of Minnesota Press, 1983), 139–140.

33. Paul Helm, "John Locke and Jonathan Edwards," in *Journal of the History of Philosophy* 7 (1969), 54; Murray Murphey, "Jonathan Edwards," in Elizabeth Flower and Murray Murphey, *A History of Philosophy in America* (New York, G. P. Putnam, 1977), 1:144–145.

34. Charles McCracken, "Stages on a Cartesian Road to Immaterialism," *Journal of the History of Philosophy* 24 (1986), 39–40; Norman Fiering, *Jonathan Edwards's Moral Thought and Its British Context* (Chapel Hill: University of North Carolina Press, 1981), 38–47.

35. Fiering, *Edwards's Moral Thought*, 135–137; Helm, "John Locke and Jonathan Edwards," 61.
36. See Wallace Anderson's introduction and notes in *WJE: Scientific and Philosophical Writings*, 186, 203, for calculations of the date of composition.
37. Edwards, "Of Atoms," in *WJE: Scientific and Philosophical Writings*, ed. Anderson, 208.
38. Holbrook, *Jonathan Edwards: The Valley and Nature*, 25.
39. On Newton's and More's influence, see Wallace E. Anderson, "Immaterialism in Jonathan Edwards," *Journal of the History of Ideas* 25 (1964), 182, and "Editor's Introduction" to *WJE: Scientific and Philosophical Writings*, 23–24, 60–63; on More's relation to Newton, see Richard Westfall, *Never at Rest: A Biography of Isaac Newton* (Cambridge: Cambridge University Press, 1980), 97, 301–304.
40. Anderson, "Immaterialism," 183, 189; George Rupp, "The 'Idealism' of Jonathan Edwards," in *Harvard Theological Review* 62 (1969), 215.
41. Paul R. Conkin, *Puritans and Pragmatists: Eight Eminent American Thinkers* (New York: Dodd, Mead, 1968), 52; James Hoopes, "Jonathan Edwards's Religious Psychology," *Journal of American History* 69 (1983), 853.
42. Edwards, "Of Atoms," in *WJE: Scientific and Philosophical Writings*, ed. Anderson, 215.
43. Edwards, "Miscellanies no. 880" and "no. 1208", in *The Philosophy of Jonathan Edwards from His Private Notebooks*, ed. Harvey G. Townsend (1955; Westport, CT: Greenwood Press, 1972), 87, 142; Rupp, "Idealism," 217.
44. Edwards, "Of Atoms," in *WJE: Scientific and Philosophical Writings*, ed. Anderson, 215, 235; in the same volume, see also "The Mind no. 61," 376–380.
45. Edwards, "God Glorified in Man's Dependence," in *Works*, ed. Hickman, 2:3.
46. Norman Fiering, "The Rationalist Foundations of Jonathan Edwards's Metaphysics," *Jonathan Edwards and the American Experience*, eds. Nathan O. Hatch and Harry S. Stout (New York: Oxford University Press, 1988), 88–90; Anderson, "Immaterialism," 199–200; Anderson, "Editor's Introduction," in *WJE: Scientific and Philosophical Writings*, 53.
47. Edwards, "Of Being," in *WJE: Scientific and Philosophical Writings*, ed. Anderson, 205–206.
48. Rupp, "Idealism," 220–221; Bruce Kuklick, *Churchmen and Philosophers: From Jonathan Edwards to John Dewey* (New Haven: Yale University Press, 1985), 30.
49. Edwards, "Of Being," in *WJE: Scientific and Philosophical Writings*, ed. Anderson, 204, 206.
50. Edwards, "The Mind no. 40," in Ibid., 359.
51. Edwards, "The Mind no. 15" and "Notes on Knowledge and Existence," in Ibid., 344–345, 398.
52. Edwards, "The Mind no. 40," in Ibid., 355.
53. Edwards, "The Mind no. 40," in Ibid., 358–359; Murphey, "Jonathan Edwards," 1:167–168.

54. Edwards, "Miscellany no. 782," in *Philosophy of Jonathan Edwards,* ed. Townsend, 113–114.

55. Ibid., 119.

56. Edwards, "A Divine and Supernatural Light," in *Works,* ed. Hickman, 2:17; Edwards, "Miscellanies no. 782," in *Philosophy of Jonathan Edwards,* ed. Townsend, 125.

57. Edwards, "Miscellanies no. 782," in *Philosophy of Jonathan Edwards,* ed. Townsend, 120.

58. Helm, "John Locke and Jonathan Edwards," 56–60; Terrence Erdt, *Jonathan Edwards: Art and the Sense of the Heart* (Amherst: University of Massachusetts Press, 1980), 22–24.

59. Jonathan Edwards, *WJE: Religious Affections,* ed. John E. Smith (New Haven, CT: Yale University Press, 1959, 1976), 206.

60. Edwards, *WJE: Religious Affections,* ed. Smith, 259–260; Hoopes, "Edwards's Religious Psychology," 862; Kuklick, *Churchmen and Philosophers,* 40–41.

61. Edwards, "Miscellanies no. 782," in *Philosophy of Jonathan Edwards,* ed. Townsend, 124.

62. Edwards, "Personal Narrative," in *Representative Selections,* eds. Faust and Johnson, 61–62.

63. Edwards, "A Divine and Supernatural Light," in *Works,* ed. Hickman, 2:14.

64. Erdt, *Jonathan Edwards,* 35, 55.

65. Clyde Holbrook, *The Ethics of Jonathan Edwards: Morality and Aesthetics* (Ann Arbor: University of Michigan Press, 1973), 28, 38; Erdt, *Jonathan Edwards,* 28–29.

66. Holbrook, *Ethics of Jonathan Edwards,* 28.

67. Edwards, *WJE: Religious Affections,* ed. Smith, 266.

68. Edwards, "Some Thoughts Concerning the Revival," in *WJE: The Great Awakening,* ed. Goen, 297–298.

69. Edwards, *WJE: Religious Affections,* ed. Smith, 97.

70. Ibid., 99.

71. Ibid., 95.

72. Edwards, "Faithful Narrative," in *WJE: The Great Awakening,* ed. Goen, 164, 168.

73. Nathan Cole, "Spiritual Travels," in *The Great Awakening,* ed. Bushman, 40, 68.

74. Edwards, "Some Thoughts Concerning the Revival," in *WJE: The Great Awakening,* ed. Goen, 503.

75. Patricia Tracy is doubtless correct in *Jonathan Edwards, Pastor,* that Perry Miller erred in setting up the communion controversy as a struggle between Edwards's "pure" Calvinism and "the Williams clan's ideological Arminianism." But the accuracy of her observation extends only so far as the word *ideological* will take it. Edwards, even if he never went so far as public accusation, probably believed that the Williamses ought to have been Arminians even if they weren't in strict terms. In Edwards's mind, he had finally persuaded himself that the intricate schemes of preparationism and half-way covenants devised by New England divines like his cousin Solomon Williams to protect their churches contained within them notions of natural inability which were fatal to consistent Calvinism, even if the perpetrators of them insisted they were still loyal to Calvinist the-

ology. While Miller falls off on the one side trying to pin *ideological* Arminianism on Edwards's relations, Tracy falls off on the other by assuming that no *ideological* Arminianism means no Arminianism at all, and Edwards certainly knew better than that.

76. Edwards to John Erskine, July 5, 1750, in Dwight, "Memoirs of Jonathan Edwards," in *Works,* ed. Hickman, 1:cxx.
77. Edwards, "Farewell Sermon," in *Representative Selections,* eds. Faust and Johnson, 199–200.
78. Edwards to John Erskine, August 3, 1757, in *WJE: Freedom of the Will,* ed. Paul Ramsey (New Haven: Yale University Press, 1957, 1979), 466.
79. Edwards, "The Mind no. 70," in *WJE: Scientific and Philosophical Writings,* ed. Anderson, 385.
80. Edwards, "Six Letters of Jonathan Edwards to Joseph Bellamy," *New England Quarterly* 3 (1928), 230–231; Winslow, *Jonathan Edwards,* 370.
81. Edwards to John Erskine, in Dwight, "Memoirs of Jonathan Edwards," in *Works,* ed. Hickman, 1:xciv.
82. Edwards to John Erskine, July 5, 1750, in Dwight, "Memoirs of Jonathan Edwards," in *Works,* ed. Hickman, 1:cxviii.
83. Winslow, *Jonathan Edwards,* 370.
84. Edwards to John Erskine, July 7, 1752, in Dwight, "Memoirs of Jonathan Edwards," in *Works,* ed. Hickman, 1:cxlv; Murray, *Jonathan Edwards,* 425.
85. Winslow, *Jonathan Edwards,* 320.
86. Edwards to John Erskine, April 15, 1755, in Dwight, "Memoirs of Jonathan Edwards," in *Works,* ed. Hickman, 1:clxv.
87. Murray, *Jonathan Edwards,* 388.
88. Ibid., 425.
89. Charles Chauncy, *Seasonable Thoughts on the State of Religion* (Boston: Samuel Eliot, 1743), 398–399.
90. Edwards, "Author's Preface," in *WJE: Freedom of the Will,* ed. Ramsey, 130.
91. See Alexander V. G. Allen, *Jonathan Edwards* (Boston: Houghton Mifflin, 1889), 281, and Rem B. Edwards, *A Return to Moral and Religious Philosophy in Early America* (Washington, DC: University Press of America, 1982), 25.
92. Edwards, "Author's Preface," in *WJE: Freedom of the Will,* ed. Ramsey, 133.
93. Ibid., 137.
94. Edwards, "The Mind no. 60," in *WJE: Scientific and Philosophical Writings,* ed. Anderson, 376.
95. Edwards, *WJE: Freedom of the Will,* ed. Ramsey, 141.
96. Holbrook, *Ethics of Jonathan Edwards,* 41.
97. Edwards, *WJE: Freedom of the Will,* ed. Ramsey, 148.
98. Edwards, "The Mind no. 60," in *WJE: Scientific and Philosophical Writings,* ed. Anderson, 376.
99. Edwards, *WJE: Freedom of the Will,* ed. Ramsey, 146–147.
100. Conrad Cherry, *The Theology of Jonathan Edwards* (1966; rept. Gloucester, MA: Peter Smith, 1974), 132.
101. Edwards to Joseph Bellamy, January 15, 1750, in *Representative Selections,* eds. Faust and Johnson, 390–391.

102. Edwards, "The Mind no. 60," in *WJE: Scientific and Philosophical Writings*, ed. Anderson, 376.
103. Edwards, "Miscellanies no. 782," in *Philosophy of Jonathan Edwards*, ed. Townsend, 121.
104. Edwards, "Miscellaneous Remarks," in *Works*, ed. Hickman, 2:532–533.
105. Edwards, *WJE: Freedom of the Will*, ed. Ramsey, 172; see Edwards's original sketches for these arguments in "Miscellanies no. 1153" and "no. 1155," in *Philosophy of Jonathan Edwards*, ed. Townsend, 165–180, 182–183.
106. Edwards, *WJE: Freedom of the Will*, ed. Ramsey, 345–346.
107. Ibid., 149–150.   108. Ibid., 151–152.
109. Ibid., 152–153.
110. Ibid., 156; Arnold S. Kaufman and William K. Frankena, "Introduction," to Edwards, *Freedom of the Will* (Indianapolis: Bobbs-Merrill, 1969), xxv.
111. Edwards, *WJE: Freedom of the Will*, ed. Ramsey, 156–157.
112. Ibid., 156.   113. Ibid., 157.
114. Ibid., 160.   115. Ibid., 159.
116. Ibid., 160; Holbrook, *Ethics of Jonathan Edwards*, 42–43; see also Edwards's illustration of this in relation to the idea of *power* in "Miscellanies no. 71," in *Philosophy of Jonathan Edwards*, ed. Townsend, 155.
117. Edwards, "Miscellanies no. 71" in *Philosophy of Jonathan Edwards*, ed. Townsend, 156; *Freedom of the Will*, ed. Ramsey, 162.
118. Ibid., 181; see also "The Justice of God in the Damnation of Sinners," in *Works*, ed. Hickman, 1:675, and Carl Bogue, *Jonathan Edwards and the Covenant of Grace* (Cherry Hill, NJ: Mack Publishing, 1975), 221.
119. Edwards, *Freedom of the Will*, ed. Ramsey, 164.
120. Edwards, "Miscellanies no. 573," in *Philosophy of Jonathan Edwards*, ed. Townsend, 161.
121. Ibid.
122. Edwards, *Freedom of the Will*, ed. Ramsey, 360–361; see also Edwards's original sketch of this line of reasoning in "Miscellanies no. 830," in *Philosophy of Jonathan Edwards*, ed. Townsend, 162–163.
123. Ibid., 205.   124. Ibid.
125. Ibid., 322.   126. Ibid., 331.   127. Ibid., 326.
128. Edwards, *Freedom of the Will*, ed. Ramsey, 278.
129. Ibid., 291.   130. Ibid., 296.
131. Edwards, "Miscellanies no. 31," in *Philosophy of Jonathan Edwards*, ed. Townsend, 154.
132. Edwards, *Freedom of the Will*, ed. Ramsey, 304.

2. Jonathan Edwards

1. Jonathan Edwards, *WJE: Freedom of the Will*, ed. Paul Ramsey (New Haven: Yale University Press, 1957, 1979), 131–132.
2. T. H. Bushell, *The Sage of Salisbury: Thomas Chubb, 1679–1747* (New York, 1967), 6–7, 9, 11–12.
3. Thomas Chubb, "Tract 29," in *A Collection of Tracts on Various Subjects* (London, 1754), 2:306.
4. Ibid., 307.

5. Chubb, "Tract 20," in ibid., 19.
6. Ibid., 27.   7. Ibid., 27.
8. Ibid., 28.   9. Ibid., 27.
10. Chubb, "Tract 28," in ibid., 269–270.
11. Chubb, "Tract 20," in ibid., 35.
12. Chubb, "Tract 28," in ibid., 264–265.
13. Chubb, "Tract 20," in ibid., 74.
14. Chubb, "Tract 23," in ibid., 131.
15. Edwards, *WJE: Freedom of the Will*, ed. Ramsey, 225–226.
16. Ibid., 226–227.   17. Ibid., 228–229.
18. Ibid., 232–233.
19. Chubb, "Tract 27," in *Collection of Tracts*, 2:243; Edwards, *WJE: Freedom of the Will*, ed. Ramsey, 235.
20. Edwards, *WJE: Freedom of the Will*, ed. Ramsey, 237–238.
21. Daniel Whitby, *Sermons on the Attributes of God* (London, 1710), 39.
22. John Redwood, *Reason, Ridicule and Religion: The Age of Enlightenment in England, 1660–1750* (Cambridge: Harvard University Press, 1976), 160.
23. Whitby, *Sermons*, 218.
24. Daniel Whitby, *A Discourse concerning the true import of the words Election and Reprobation* (London, 1817 [fourth edition]), 305. Edwards and his contemporaries referred to this work as Whitby's "Discourse on the Five Points."
25. Ibid., 34.   26. Ibid., 195.
27. Ibid., 86.   28. Ibid., 110.   29. Ibid., 223.
30. Whitby, *Sermons*, 218.
31. Whitby, *Discourse*, 193–194.
32. Ibid., 260.   33. Ibid., 262–263.
34. Ibid., 267.   35. Ibid., 284.
36. Sereno E. Dwight, "Memoirs of Jonathan Edwards," in *Works of Jonathan Edwards*, ed. Edward Hickman (1834; rept. London: Banner of Truth Trust, 1976), 1:clxii.
37. Edwards, *WJE: Freedom of the Will*, ed. Ramsey, 193–194.
38. Whitby, *Discourse*, 193.
39. Edwards, *WJE: Freedom of the Will*, ed. Ramsey, 220.
40. Arthur P. Davis, *Isaac Watts: His Life and Works* (New York: Dryden Press, 1943), 11–12, 45–47, 109, 111, 118–120.
41. C. C. Goen, "Editor's Introduction," in *WJE: The Great Awakening* (New Haven: Yale University Press, 1972), 38–46.
42. Michael Watts, *The Dissenters: From the Reformation to the French Revolution* (Oxford: Oxford University Press, 1977), 1:459–460.
43. Isaac Watts, "Philosophical Essays on Various Subjects," in *Works* (London, 1750), 5:560, 613.
44. Ibid., 536.   45. Ibid., 547.
46. Ibid., 618.   47. Ibid., 507, 539.
48. Watts, "An Essay on the Freedom of Will in God and in Creatures," in *Works*, 6:376–378.
49. Watts, "Philosophical Essays," in *Works*, 5:623.
50. Watts, "An Essay on the Freedom of Will," in ibid., 379–380.
51. Ibid., 382.   52. Ibid., 385.

53. Ibid., 385. 54. Ibid., 390.
55. Ibid., 392. 56. Ibid., 395. 57. Ibid., 405.
58. Paul Ramsey, "Editor's Introduction," *WJE: Freedom of the Will*, 95.
59. Edwards, *WJE: Freedom of the Will*, ed. Ramsey, 198.
60. Ibid., 201. 61. Ibid., 198–199. 62. Ibid., 200.
63. Norman Fiering, *Jonathan Edwards's Moral Thought and Its British Context* (Chapel Hill: University of North Carolina Press, 1981), 47, 51.
64. Edwards, *WJE: Freedom of the Will*, ed. Ramsey, 377.
65. Ibid., 380. 66. Ibid., 272. 67. Ibid., 392.
68. Arnold Kaufman and William Frankena, "Introduction" to Edwards, *Freedom of the Will* (Indianapolis: Bobbs-Merrill, 1969), xxxiii–xxxiv.
69. John Calvin, *Institutes of the Christian Religion* 1.15.2, eds. F. L. Battles, H. Bettenson, and J. T. McNeill (Philadelphia: Westminster Press, 1960), 1:184–185.
70. Jonathan Edwards, "The Mind no. 67," in *WJE: Scientific and Philosophical Writings*, ed. Wallace E. Anderson (New Haven: Yale University Press, 1980), 384.
71. Edwards, "Notes on Knowledge and Existence," in *WJE: Scientific and Philosophical Writings*, ed. Anderson, 398.
72. Edwards, "The Mind no. 72," in ibid., 385–386.
73. Edwards, "The Mind no. 13," in ibid., 344.
74. Edwards, "The Mind no. 61," in ibid., 380.
75. Jonathan Edwards, *WJE: Original Sin*, ed. Clyde Holbrook (New Haven: Yale University Press, 1970), 404.
76. Ibid., 385. 77. Ibid., 389. 78. Ibid., 404.
79. Edwards, "The Mind no. 61," in *WJE: Scientific and Philosophical Writings*, ed. Anderson, 378.
80. Edwards, "The Mind no. 36," in ibid., 355.
81. Edwards, "The Mind no. 40," in ibid., 359.
82. Edwards, *WJE: Freedom of the Will*, ed. Ramsey, 156–157.
83. Edwards, "The Mind no. 6," in *WJE: Scientific and Philosophical Writings*, ed. Anderson, 340.
84. Edwards, "The Mind no. 9," in ibid., 341.
85. Edwards, "The Mind no. 10," in ibid., 342.
86. *The Ontological Argument*, eds. Alvin Platinga and Richard Taylor (Garden City, NY: Anchor Books/Doubleday, 1965), 66–67.
87. John Hospers, "What Means This Freedom?" in *Free Will and Determinism*, ed. Bernard Berofsky (New York: Harper & Row, 1966), 30–31.
88. Jonathan Edwards, "A Faithful Narrative of the Surprising Work of God," in *WJE: The Great Awakening*, ed. C. C. Goen (New Haven: Yale University Press, 1972), 195, 200.
89. Edwards, "Miscellaneous Remarks concerning Efficacious Grace," in *Works*, ed. Hickman, 2:545.
90. Ibid., 563; on Edwards's repudiation of preparationism, see also Norman Pettit, *The Heart Prepared: Grace and Conversion in Puritan New England* (New Haven: Yale University Press, 1966), 209–212.
91. Edwards, *WJE: Freedom of the Will*, ed. Ramsey, 423.
92. Edwards, "The Mind no. 36," in *WJE: Scientific and Philosophical Writings*, ed. Anderson, 355.
93. Edwards, *WJE: Freedom of the Will*, ed. Ramsey, 141, 142.

94. Edwards, *WJE: Freedom of the Will*, ed. Ramsey, 148; Arthur Murphy, "Jonathan Edwards on Free Will and Moral Agency," in *Philosophical Review* 68 (1959), 200.
95. Edwards, "Sermon on Romans 9:18," in *Works*, ed. Hickman, 2:849.
96. Fiering, *Edwards's Moral Thought*, 311.
97. Edwards, *WJE: Freedom of the Will*, ed. Ramsey, 399.
98. Jonathan Edwards, "Miscellanies no. 85," in *The Philosophy of Jonathan Edwards from His Private Notebooks*, ed. Harvey G. Townsend (Westport, CT: Greenwood Press, 1972), 157.
99. Edwards, *WJE: Freedom of the Will*, ed. Ramsey, 402, 407.
100. Ibid., 399.
101. Edwards, "A Divine and Supernatural Light," in *Works*, ed. Hickman, 2:13.
102. Edwards, "The Mind no. 26," in *Scientific and Philosophical Writings*, ed. Anderson, 350.
103. Perry Miller, *Jonathan Edwards* (New York: William Sloane, 1949), 252.
104. Bruce Kuklick, *Churchmen and Philosophers: From Jonathan Edwards to John Dewey* (New Haven: Yale University Press, 1985), 20.
105. Edwards, *WJE: Freedom of the Will*, ed. Ramsey, 143.
106. Edwards, "The Mind no. 60," in *WJE: Scientific and Philosophical Writings*, ed. Anderson, 376.
107. Edwards, *WJE: Freedom of the Will*, ed. Ramsey, 374; see the reference to Hobbes in "Miscellanies 'f'" in *Philosophy of Jonathan Edwards*, ed. Townsend, 193.
108. Edwards, "The Mind and Related Papers," in *WJE: Scientific and Philosophical Writings*, ed. Anderson, 386–393, 396.
109. Gordon Wood, "Conspiracy and the Paranoid Style: Causality and Deceit in the Eighteenth Century," *William and Mary Quarterly* 39 (July 1982), 416–420.
110. Edwards, "Distinguishing Marks of a Work of the Spirit of God," in *WJE: The Great Awakening*, ed. Goen, 256.
111. Richard L. Bushman, "Jonathan Edwards as Great Man: Identity, Conversion, and Leadership in the Great Awakening," in *Critical Essays on Jonathan Edwards*, ed. William J. Scheick (Boston: G. K. Hall, 1980), 61; see also Wilson Carey McWilliams, *The Idea of Fraternity in America* (Berkeley: University of California Press, 1973), 168–169.
112. John Winthrop, "Modell of Christian Charity," in *The Puritans: A Sourcebook of their Writings*, eds. Perry Miller and Thomas Johnson (New York: Harper & Row, 1938, 1963) 1:198.

3. Bellamy and Hopkins

1. Samuel Hopkins to Joseph Bellamy, January 19, 1758, in the Joseph Bellamy Papers, Presbyterian Historical Society, Philadelphia.
2. Alan Heimert, *Religion and the American Mind from the Great Awakening to the Revolution* (Cambridge: Harvard University Press, 1976), 7.
3. Moses Hemmenway, *Remarks on the Rev. Mr. Hopkins's Answer to a Tract* (Boston: Kneeland, 1774), 137; Ezra Stiles Ely, *A Contrast Between Hopkinsianism and Calvinism* (New York, 1811), 157.
4. Israel Holly, *Old Divinity Prefarable to Modern Divinity* (Litchfield, CT: Collier and Buel, 1795), 30.

5. Ezra Stiles, *The Literary Diary of Ezra Stiles, D.D.*, ed. F. B. Dexter (New York: Charles Scribner, 1901), 3:5.

6. Andrew Fuller to Samuel Hopkins, March 17, 1798, in the Gratz Collection, Historical Society of Pennsylvania, Philadelphia.

7. Charles Chauncy to Ezra Stiles, June 14, 1771, in *Extracts from the Itineraries and Other Miscellanies of Ezra Stiles*, ed. F. B. Dexter (New Haven: 1916), 451.

8. Joseph Haroutunian, *Piety Versus Moralism: The Passing of the New England Theology* (New York: Henry Holt, 1932), 71.

9. Stephen Berk, *Calvinism Versus Democracy: Timothy Dwight and the Origins of American Evangelical Orthodoxy* (Hamden, CT: Archon Books, 1974), 62.

10. Thomas Andros, *An Essary in which the Doctrine of a Positive Divine Efficiency . . . is Candidly Discussed* (Boston, 1820), v–vi.

11. Bellamy, in Donald Weber, "The Recovery of Jonathan Edwards," in *Jonathan Edwards and the American Experience*, eds. Nathan O. Hatch and Harry S. Stout (New York: Oxford University Press, 1988), 52–53.

12. "Nathanael Emmons," in *Annals of the American Pulpit*, ed. William B. Sprague (New York: Robert Carter and Brothers, 1857), 1:701, 704.

13. Robert L. Ferm, *A Colonial Pastor: Jonathan Edwards the Younger, 1745–1801* (Grand Rapids, MI: William B. Eerdmans, 1976), 134–157.

14. Michael P. Anderson, "The Pope of Litchfield County: An Intellectual Biography of Joseph Bellamy," Ph.D. dissertation, Claremont Graduate School, 1980, 20, 184–189; *Annals of the American Pulpit*, ed. Sprague, 2:62, 144.

15. Joseph A. Conforti, *Samuel Hopkins and the New Divinity Movement: Calvinism, the Congregational Ministry, and Reform in New England between the Great Awakenings* (Grand Rapids, MI: William B. Eerdmans, 1981), 179; *Annals of the American Pulpit*, ed. Sprague, 1:195, 2:143–144, 147, 276.

16. Charles Roy Keller, *The Second Great Awakening in Connecticut* (New Haven: Yale University Press, 1942), 33.

17. Stiles, *Literary Diary*, 3:464.

18. Edwards the Younger, in Ferm, *A Colonial Pastor*, 65.

19. Conforti, *Samuel Hopkins*, 181–183.

20. William Bentley, *The Diary of William Bentley* (Salem, MA: The Essex Institute, 1905–1914), 1:160, 4:302.

21. Nathanael Emmons, *Works*, ed. Jacob Ide (Boston: Crocker and Brewster, 1842), 3:182.

22. David Porter, *A Sermon on Divine Decrees and Moral Necessity, Reconciled with Freedom of the Will* (Catskill, NY, 1804), 5.

23. Ibid., 7.

24. Joseph Bellamy, *True Religion Delineated, or, Experimental Religion as distinguished from formality and enthusiasm* (1750; Morristown, NJ, 1804), 20.

25. Ibid., 3–11.

26. Samuel Hopkins, "An Inquiry Into the Nature of True Holiness," in *Works* (Boston: Doctrinal Tract and Book Society, 1854), 3:64.

27. Jonathan Edwards the Younger, "A Dissertation on Liberty and Necessity," in *Works*, ed. Tryon Edwards (Boston: Doctrinal Tract and Book Society, 1850), 1:333.

28. Ibid., 392.
29. John Smalley, "On the Preservation and Perseverance of the Saints," in *Sermons on a Number of Connected Subjects* (Hartford: Oliver D. Cooke, 1803), 374.
30. Josiah Sherman, *God in no sense the Author of Sin* (Hartford, 1784), 9.
31. Stephen West, *An Essay on Moral Agency* (Salem, MA: Thomas C. Cushing, 1794), 22.
32. Levi Hart, *Liberty Described and Recommended* (Hartford: E. Watson, 1775), 9.
33. Edwards the Younger, "Dissertation," in *Works,* 1:310.
34. Smalley, "On the Preservation and Perseverance of the Saints," in *Sermons* (1803), 374.
35. Hart, *Liberty Described,* 9.
36. West, *Essay,* xi.
37. Edwards the Younger, "Dissertation," in *Works,* 1:421.
38. John Smalley, *The Consistency of the Sinners Inability to Comply with the Gospel; with his inexcusable guilt in not complying* (Hartford, 1769), 16.
39. Asa Burton, *Essays on Some of the First Principles of Metaphysicks, Ethicks, and Theology* (Portland, ME: A. Shirley, 1824), 220.
40. Porter, *Divine Decrees,* 7.
41. Burton, *Essays,* 89; Porter, *Divine Decrees,* 7.
42. West, *Essay,* 29.
43. Burton, *Essays,* 138.
44. Bellamy, *True Religion,* 12.
45. Porter, *Divine Decrees,* 15.
46. Burton, *Essays,* 141.
47. Sherman, *God in no sense the Author of Sin,* 15–16.
48. Edwards the Younger, "Dissertation," in *Works,* 1:372.
49. Samuel Whitman, *A Dissertation on the Origin of Evil* (Northampton, MA, 1797), 29.
50. Burton, *Essays,* 100.
51. Edwards the Younger, "Dissertation," in *Works,* 1:344.
52. Ibid., 467.
53. Burton, *Essays,* 118.
54. West, *Essay,* 71.
55. Ibid., 66–67.
56. Ibid., 71.
57. Edwards the Younger, "Dissertation," in *Works,* 1:374–375.
58. Samuel Spring, *Moral Disquisitions and Strictures* (Newburyport, MA: John Mycall, 1789), 62.
59. Edwards the Younger, "Dissertation," in *Works,* 1:312.
60. Porter, *Divine Decrees,* 13–14.
61. Emmons, *Works,* 4:351.
62. Spring, *Moral Disquisitions,* 189.
63. Smalley, *Consistency of the Sinners Inability,* 35.
64. John Smalley, "Two Sermons," in *The Atonement: Discourses and Treatises,* ed. Edwards Amasa Park (Boston: Congregational Board of Publication, 1859), 81.
65. Burton, *Essays,* 86–87.
66. Spring, *Moral Disquisitions,* 189.

67. Hopkins, "The True State and Character of the Unregenerate," in *Works*, 3:297.
68. Smalley, *Consistency of the Sinners Inability*, 46.
69. Bellamy, *True Religion Delineated*, 192.
70. Smalley, "On Regeneration," in *Sermons* (1803), 279.
71. Smalley, *Consistency of the Sinners Inability*, 48.
72. Jacob Ide, "Additional Memoir," in Emmons, *Works*, 1:xlvii.
73. Spring, *Moral Disquisitions*, 171.
74. Emmons, *Works*, 2:420.
75. Nathan Strong, *Sermons on Various Subjects, Doctrinal, Experimental, and Practical* (Hartford: Oliver D. and I. Cooke, 1798–1800), 1:29.
76. Ibid., 2:336.
77. Bellamy, *True Religion Delineated*, 109–110.
78. Hopkins, "An Inquiry Concerning the Promises of the Gospel," in *Works*, 2:248.
79. Hopkins, "The True State and Character of the Unregenerate," in *Works*, 3:445.
80. Smalley, "On Regeneration," in *Sermons* (1803), 301.
81. Hopkins, "The True State and Character of the Unregenerate," in *Works*, 3:296.
82. Smalley, *Inconsistency of the Sinners Inability*, 65.
83. Bellamy, *True Religion Delineated*, 196, 358.
84. Emmons, *Works*, 4:514.
85. Joseph Bellamy, "The Half-Way Covenant: A Dialogue between a Minister and His Parishioner," in *Works* (New York: Stephen Dodge, 1812), 3:443.
86. Hopkins, "The True State and Character of the Unregenerate," in *Works*, 3:445.
87. Smalley, "On Repentance, Conversion, and Pardon," in *Sermons* (1803), 321.
88. Hopkins, "The True State and Character of the Unregenerate," in *Works*, 3:296.
89. Burton, *Essays*, 100, 140.
90. West, *Essay*, 59, 61–62.
91. Spring, *Moral Disquisitions*, 51–52.
92. West, *Essay*, 66–67.   93. Ibid., 69.
94. Hopkins, in Edwards Amasa Park, "Memoir," in *Works*, 1:200–202.
95. Hopkins, "An Inquiry Concerning the Promises of the Gospel," in *Works*, 3:235–236; see also "The Cause, Nature and Means of Regeneration," in *Works*, 3:563, 564, 565.
96. Burton, *Essays*, 13.
97. Ibid., 178.   98. Ibid., 131.   99. Ibid., 225.
100. Smalley, "On Original Sin," in *Sermons* (1803), 188.
101. Sherman, *God in no sense the Author of Sin*, 11, 14.
102. Burton, *Essays*, 18.
103. Gardiner Spring, *Personal Reminiscences* (New York, 1866), 2:142.
104. West, *Essay*, 34.
105. Ibid., 55.   106. Ibid., 56.   107. Ibid., 23.
108. West, *Essay*, 43.
109. Spring, *Moral Disquisitions*, 20.

110. Samuel Whitman, *The Perfection of the Divine Constitution* (Northampton, MA: William Butler, 1793), 31.
111. Emmons, "Man's Activity and Dependence Illustrated and Reconciled," in *Works,* 4:355–356.
112. Ibid., 357.
113. Emmons, "God Sovereign in Man's Formation," in *Works,* 4:397.
114. Hopkins to Levi Hart, March 23, 1785, in the Gratz Collection, Historical Society of Pennsylvania, Philadelphia.
115. Isaac Backus, *The Diary of Isaac Backus,* ed. William McLoughlin (Providence: Brown University Press, 1979), 2:1166.
116. Edwards Amasa Park, "Reflections of a Visitor," in Emmons, *Works,* 1:cxliii.
117. Edwards Amasa Park, "Memoir," in Hopkins, *Works,* 1:200.

4. The New Divinity

1. William Bentley, *The Diary of William Bentley* (Salem, MA: The Essex Institute, 1905–1914), 1:196–197.
2. Ezra Stiles, *The Literary Diary of Ezra Stiles, D.D.,* ed. F. B. Dexter (New York: Charles Scribner, 1901), 3:419.
3. Nathanael Emmons, "Man's Activity and Dependence Illustrated and Reconciled," in *Works,* ed. Jacob Ide (Boston: Crocker and Brewster, 1842) 4:360.
4. Nathan Strong, *Sermons on Various Subjects, Doctrinal, Experimental, and Practical* (Hartford: Oliver D. and I. Cooke, 1798–1800), 1:164.
5. Nathan Strong, *The Doctrine of Eternal Misery Reconcileable with the Infinite Benevolence of God* (Hartford: Hudson and Goodwin, 1796), 305.
6. Samuel Hopkins, "Inquiry Concerning the Promises of the Gospel," in *Works* (Boston: Doctrinal Tract and Book Society, 1854), 3:194–195.
7. Emmons, *Works,* 1:255.
8. Strong, *Sermons,* 2:372.
9. Strong, *Eternal Misery,* 341.
10. Hopkins, "The Knowledge of God's Law Necessary in Order to the Knowledge of Sin," in *Works,* 3:521–523.
11. Joseph Bellamy, *True Religion Delineated, or, Experimental Religion as distinguished from formality and enthusiasm* (Morristown, NJ, 1804), 54, 93–95; the *locus classicus* of the "infinity" argument is in Edwards's sermon "The Justice of God in the Damnation of Sinners" in *Works of Jonathan Edwards,* ed. Edward Hickman (1834; rept. London: Banner of Truth Trust, 1976), 1:669.
12. Bellamy, *True Religion Delineated,* 48, 200.
13. Joseph Bellamy, "The Half-Way Covenant: A Dialogue between a Minister and His Parishioner" [1769] in *Works* (New York: Stephen Dodge, 1812), 3:435.
14. Bellamy, *True Religion Delineated,* 426.
15. Strong, *Sermons,* 2:158.
16. Samuel Spring, *Moral Disquisitions and Strictures* (Newburyport, MA: John Mycall, 1789), 120, 210.
17. Hopkins, "The Knowledge of God's Law Necessary," *Works,* 3:524.

18. John Smalley, *Sermons on a Number of Connected Subjects* (Hartford: Oliver D. Cooke, 1803), 348.
19. Strong, *Sermons*, 2:185.
20. Samuel Hopkins, Ms. Journal, February 5, 1742, p. 27, in the Gratz Collection, Historical Society of Pennsylvania, Philadelphia. Edwards remarked on the same outburst of enthusiasm in a letter to Thomas Prince, December 12, 1743, in *WJE: The Great Awakening*, ed. C. C. Goen (New Haven: Yale University Press, 1972), 550.
21. Hopkins, "The Knowledge of God's Law Necessary," in *Works*, 3:540.
22. Bellamy, "A Blow at the Refined Antinomianism of the Present Age," [1769] in *Works*, 3:96.
23. Bennet Tyler, editor, *New England Revivals . . . First Published in the Connecticut Evangelical Magazine* (Boston: Massachusetts Sabbath School Society, 1846), 17–23.
24. Bellamy, "A Blow at the Root of the Refined Antinomianism of the Present Age," in *Works*, 3:79, 85–86, 88.
25. Strong, *Sermons*, 2:115.
26. Hopkins, "The True State and Character of the Unregenerate," in *Works*, 3:419.
27. Emmons, *Works*, 2:298.
28. Hopkins, "An Inquiry Concerning the Promises of the Gospel," [1765] in *Works*, 3:230–231.
29. Hopkins, "The True State and Character of the Unregenerate," [1769] in *Works*, 3:292.
30. Strong, *Sermons*, 2:23.
31. Emmons, *Works*, 2:370.
32. Hopkins, "True State and Character of the Unregenerate," in *Works*, 3:366.
33. Emmons, *Works*, 2:371.
34. John Smalley, *Sermons on Various Subjects, Doctrinal and Practical* (Middletown, CT: Hart and Lincoln, 1814), 327.
35. Hopkins, "The True State and Character of the Unregenerate," in *Works*, 3:309, 312.
36. Hopkins, "The Cause, Nature, and Means of Regeneration," in *Works*, 3:567.
37. Hopkins, "An Inquiry Concerning the Promises of the Gospel," in *Works*, 3:265.
38. Hopkins, "The True State and Character of the Unregenerate," in *Works*, 3:287.
39. Bellamy, *True Religion Delineated*, 179.
40. Hopkins, "The True State and Character of the Unregenerate," in *Works*, 3:409.
41. Hopkins, "An Inquiry Concerning the Promises of the Gospel," in *Works*, 3:244.
42. Strong, *Sermons*, 1:110.
43. Hopkins, "The True State and Character of the Unregenerate," in *Works*, 3:485–486.
44. Samuel Hopkins, Ms. sermon, July 28, 1747, in the Gratz Collection, Historical Society of Pennsylvania, Philadelphia.
45. Strong, *Sermons*, 1:110.

46. Hopkins, "The Cause, Nature, and Means of Regeneration," in *Works*, 3:569.
47. Josiah Sherman, *God in no sense the Author of Sin* (Hartford, 1784), 30.
48. Spring, *Moral Disquisitions*, 86.
49. Smalley, "On Regeneration," in *Sermons* (1803), 297.
50. Hopkins, "The True State and Character of the Unregenerate," in *Works*, 3:388.
51. John Smalley, *The Consistency of the Sinners Inability to Comply with the Gospel; with his inexcusable guilt in not complying . . . In Two Discourses* (Hartford, 1769), 47.
52. Bellamy, *True Religion Delineated*, 179.
53. Hopkins, "The True State and Character of the Unregenerate," in *Works*, 3:409.
54. Smalley, *Sermons* (1814), 328.
55. Bellamy, "The Half-Way Covenant: A Dialogue," in *Works*, 3:443.
56. Michael Watts, *The Dissenters: From the Reformation to the French Revolution* (Oxford: Oxford University Press, 1977), 1:459–460.
57. Strong, *Sermons*, 2:106–107.
58. Smalley, *Sermons* (1814), 255.
59. Bellamy, "A Blow at the Refined Antinomianism of the Present Age," in *Works*, 3:112.
60. Joseph A. Conforti, *Samuel Hopkins and the New Divinity Movement: Calvinism, the Congregational Ministry, and Reform in New England between the Great Awakenings* (Grand Rapids, MI: William B. Eerdmans, 1981), 80–82.
61. Bellamy, "The Half-Way Covenant," in *Works*, 3:443.
62. Mark Noll, "Ebenezer Devotion," in *Church History* 45 (September 1976), 298.
63. Isaac Backus, *The Diary of Isaac Backus*, ed. William McLoughlin (Providence: Brown University Press, 1979), 1:816, 889 and 2:1234, 1362, 1388.
64. Stiles, *Literary Diary*, 3:4–5, 286.
65. Samuel Hopkins, *The System of Doctrines Contained in Divine Revelation* (Boston: Isaiah Thomas, 1793), 2:262–263.
66. Ezra Stiles, *Extracts from the Itineraries and Other Miscellanies of Ezra Stiles*, ed. F. B. Dexter (New Haven, 1916), 413.
67. Mark Noll, George Marsden, and Nathan Hatch, *The Search for Christian America* (Westchester, IL, 1983), 57; for a somewhat different view of the engagement of the Edwardseans with the Revolutionary enterprise, see Donald Weber, *Rhetoric and History in Revolutionary New England* (New York: Oxford University Press, 1988).
68. Samuel Hopkins to John Erskine, December 8, 1774, in the Gratz Collection, Historical Society of Pennsylvania, Philadelphia.
69. Levi Hart, *Liberty Described and Recommended* (Hartford: E. Watson, 1775), 13–14.
70. Smalley, "Man's Native Enmity to God," in *Sermons* (1803), 231–232.
71. Smalley, "On the Desirableness and Importance of the Office and Work of a Gospel Minister," in *Sermons* (1814), 41.
72. *Annals of the American Pulpit*, ed. William B. Sprague (New York: Robert Carter and Brothers, 1857), 2:285–286; Emmons, *Works*, 2:45, 112, 228.

73. Isaac Backus, *Diary*, ed. McLoughlin, 2:1079–1080, 1237–1238.
74. James Waddel Alexander, *The Life of Archibald Alexander, D.D.* (New York: Charles Scribner, 1854), 245–246, 249.
75. Richard D. Shiels, "The Second Great Awakening in Connecticut: a Critique of the Traditional Interpretation," in *Church History* 49 (December 1980), 414.
76. Bellamy, "The Half-Way Covenant," in *Works*, 3:420.
77. Ibid., 400; see also Edwin S. Gaustad, *The Great Awakening in New England* 1957; Chicago: Quadrangle Books, 1968), 106–107.
78. Strong, *Sermons*, 1:117.
79. Smalley, "On the Sovereignty of God, In the Effectual Calling of Sinners," in *Sermons* (1803), 246.
80. Strong, *Sermons*, 2:26.
81. Nathaniel Niles, *Two Discourses on Liberty* (Newburyport, MA, 1774), 45.
82. Strong, *Sermons*, 1:117, 2:60.
83. Ibid., 1:272.
84. *Reformed Dogmatics, Set Out and Illustrated from the Sources*, ed. Heinrich Heppe (1950; Grand Rapids, MI: Baker Book House, 1978), 471–472.
85. Samuel Willard, *A Compleat Body of Divinity* (Boston: B. Green and S. Kneeland, 1729), 282, 311–312, 392.
86. *Creeds and Platforms of Congregationalism*, ed. Williston Walker (1893); Philadelphia: Pilgrim Press, 1969), 378–379.
87. Smalley, "On Original Sin," in *Sermons* (1803), 178.
88. Emmons, "The Law of Paradise," in *Works*, 4:477.
89. Emmons, "Original Sin," in *Works*, 4:490–491.
90. Hopkins, "The Knowledge of God's Law Necessary," in *Works*, 3:533.
91. Spring, *Moral Disquisitions*, 246.
92. Strong, *Eternal Misery*, 271.
93. John Smalley, "Two Sermons," in *The Atonement: Discourses and Treatises*, ed. Edwards Amasa Park (Boston: Congregational Board of Publication, 1859), 57.
94. Bellamy, "A Blow at the Root of the Refined Antinomianism of the Present Age," in *Works*, 3:88.
95. Spring, *Moral Disquisitions*, 147.
96. Smalley, "Two Sermons," in *The Atonement*, ed. Park, 56, 63.
97. Ibid., 55–56.   98. Ibid., 59.   99. Ibid., 61.
100. Smalley, "The Necessity of Man's Present Exertions, for Obtaining Salvation," in *Sermons* (1814), 327.
101. Smalley, "On Repentance, Conversion and Pardon," in *Sermons* (1803), 308.
102. Bellamy, *True Religion Delineated*, 253, 268.
103. Smalley, "Two Sermons," in *The Atonement*, ed. Park, 49.
104. Smalley, "The Sufficiency of the Atonement of Christ for All Men," in *Sermons* (1814), 273.
105. Hopkins, "Sin, Through Divine Interposition, An Advantage to the Universe," in *Works*, 2:521–522.
106. Bellamy, *True Religion Delineated*, 72.
107. Daniel Read, "Providence," in *The American Singing Book* (New Haven, 1787).

108. Joseph Bellamy, *Four Sermons on the Wisdom of God in the Permission of Sin* (Morristown, NJ, 1804), 91, 106.
109. Bellamy, *True Religion Delineated*, 332.
110. Smalley, "Two Sermons," in *The Atonement*, ed. Park, 50.
111. Smalley, "Humbleness of Mind, A Necessary Preparation for Future Glory," in *Sermons* (1814), 216.
112. Smalley, *Sermons* (1803), 244–245.
113. Bellamy, *True Religion Delineated*, 423.
114. Smalley, "Two Sermons," in *The Atonement*, ed. Park, 74.
115. Bellamy, *True Religion Delineated*, 343.
116. Conforti, *Samuel Hopkins*, 164–167.
117. Bellamy, *True Religion Delineated*, 344.
118. Edwards, "Great Guilt No Obstacle to the Pardon of the Returning Sinner," in *Works*, ed. Hickman, 2:111; see also Robert W. Jenson, *America's Theologian: A Recommendation of Jonathan Edwards* (New York: Oxford University Press, 1988), 44–45, 124–127.
119. Jonathan Edwards, *WJE: Freedom of the Will*, ed. Paul Ramsey (New Haven: Yale University Press, 1957, 1979), 435.
120. Edwards, "The Preface to True Religion," in *WJE: The Great Awakening*, ed. Goen, 572.
121. On Edwards's notions about the atonement, see Doris Paul Rudisill, *The Doctrine of the Atonement in Jonathan Edwards and His Successors* (New York: Poseidon Books, 1971).
122. Emmons, "Autobiography," in *Works*, 1:xxx–xxxii.
123. William Patten, *Reminiscences of the late Rev. Samuel Hopkins* (Boston: Crocker and Brewster, 1843), 36.
124. Jonathan Edwards, *WJE: The Religious Affections*, ed. John E. Smith (New Haven: Yale University Press, 1959, 1976), 120.

5. Old Calvinism

1. Richard Birdsall, *Berkshire County: A Cultural History* (New Haven: Yale University Press, 1959), 59–60.
2. *Annals of the American Pulpit*, ed. William B. Sprague (New York: Robert Carter and Brothers, 1857), 1:603; see also Edmund Sears Morgan, *The Gentle Puritan: A Life of Ezra Stile* (New Haven: Yale University Press, 1962), 413.
3. Joseph Huntington, *A Plea Before the Venerable Ecclesiastical Council at Stockbridge* (Norwich, CT: Coverly and Hodge, 1780), 6.
4. Ibid., 14.   5. Ibid., 12.   6. Ibid., 21.
7. The most recent attempt to give the Old Calvinists their due is Harry Stout's recognition that the dichotomy of pro-Awakening and anti-Awakening simply does not explain the sum of New England Congregationalism; Stout, however, regards Old Calvinism more in the nature of a re-union movement of chastened New Lights and Old Lights in the face of war with France, rather than a separate grouping all of its own; see Harry S. Stout, *The New England Soul: Preaching and Religious Culture in Colonial New England* (New York: Oxford University Press, 1986), 212–216.
8. Samuel Hopkins, "The Sins of Men are so under the Direction and Con-

trol of God as to Glorify Him," in *Works* (Boston: Doctrinal Tract and Book Society, 1854), 3:759.

9. Samuel Spring, *Moral Disquisitions and Strictures* (Newburyport, MA: John Mycall, 1789), 153.
10. John Smalley, *The Consistency of the Sinners Inability to Comply with the Gospel; with his inexcusable guilt in not complying . . . In Two Discourses* (Hartford, 1769).
11. Hopkins, "The Sins of Men are so under the Direction and Control of God as to Glorify Him," in *Works*, 3:762.
12. *Annals of the American Pulpit*, ed. Sprague, 1:456.
13. Ezra Stiles, *The Literary Diary of Ezra Stiles, D.D.*, ed. F. B. Dexter (New York: Charles Scribner, 1901), 2:191–192.
14. Samuel Langdon, *Remarks on the Leading Sentiments of the Rev'd Dr. Hopkins' SYSTEM OF DOCTRINES* (Exeter, MA, 1794),15–16, 28.
15. Elijah Sill [charge to Ebenezer Baldwin], in Naphtali Daggett, *The Great and Tender Concern of Faithful Ministers for the Souls of their People* (New Haven, 1770), 30.
16. Morgan, *The Gentle Puritan*, 174–175, 417.
17. *Annals of the American Pulpit*, ed. Sprague, 1:545.
18. Louis L. Tucker *Puritan Protagonist: President Thomas Clap of Yale College* (Chapel Hill: University of North Carolina Press, 1962), 47–58, 142, 186.
19. Joseph Tracy, *The Great Awakening* (1842; rept. London: Banner of Truth Trust, 1976), 302.
20. *Annals of the American Pulpit*, ed. Sprague, 1:325.
21. Christopher Hill, *The Experience of Defeat: Milton and Some Contemporaries* (New York: Viking Press, 1984), 216.
22. Moses Hemmenway, *A Discourse Concerning the Church* (Boston: Thomas and Andres, 1792), 8.
23. Langdon, *Remarks*, 48.
24. Joseph Huntington, *Letters of Friendship to those Clergymen who have lately renounced Communion with the Ministers and Churches of Christ in general* (Hartford, 1780), 18.
25. William Hart, *Brief Remarks on a Number of False Propositions* (New London, CT, 1769), 15; Moses Hemmenway, *Discourse*, 56, 96–98, and *Seven Sermons, On the Obligation and Encouragement of the Unregenerate* (Boston: Kneeland and Adams, 1767), 35.
26. Ezra Stiles, *Literary Diary*, 3:361, and in *Extracts from the Itineraries and Other Miscellanies of Ezra Stiles* ed. F. B. Dexter (New Haven, 1916), 223.
27. Norman Fiering, *Jonathan Edwards's Moral Thought and Its British Context* (Chapel Hill: University of North Carolina Press, 1981), 129–138.
28. Douglas Sloan, *The Scottish Enlightenment and the American College Ideal* (New York, 1971), 88–89; Sidney E. Ahlstrom, "The Scottish Theology and American Philosophy," in *Church History* (1955), 261.
29. Edwards Amasa Park, "New England Theology," in *Bibliotheca Sacra* 9 (January 1852), 191.
30. Landgon, *Remarks*, 48.
31. Huntington, *Plea*, 23.
32. Stiles, *Itineraries and Miscellanies*, 479.
33. Hemmenway, *Discourse*, 61.

34. Experience Mayhew, *Grace Defended in a Modest Plea* (Boston: Green, 1744), 13.
35. Ibid., 6.
36. Langdon, *Remarks*, 24.
37. James Dana, *Two Discourses* (Boston: Edes and Gill, 1767), 10.
38. Hemmenway, *Seven Sermons*, 169.
39. Hart, *Brief Remarks*, 52.
40. Hemmenway, *Seven Sermons*, 23–24.
41. Huntington, *Letters of Friendship*, 17.
42. Stiles, *Literary Diary*, 3:275.
43. Stiles, *Itineraries and Miscellanies*, 591–592.
44. Ibid., 592.
45. Tucker, *Puritan Protagonist*, 215–218; *Annals of the American Pulpit*, ed. Sprague, 1:565–566; Stiles, *Itineraries and Miscellanies*, 424.
46. James Dana, *An Examination of the late Reverend President Edwards's 'Enquiry on Freedom of Will'* (Boston: S. Kneeland, 1770), iii–iv.
47. Dana, *Examination*, 33; E. Brooks Holifield, *A History of Pastoral Care in America: From Salvation to Self-Realization* (Nashville: Abingdon Press, 1983), 100–101.
48. James Dana, *The "Examination of the late Rev'd President Edwards's Enquiry on Freedom of Will," Continued* (New Haven, 1773), 28.
49. Dana, *An Examination*, 64.
50. Ibid., v.
51. Dana, *The Examination . . . Continued*, 22.
52. Dana, *An Examination*, 4.
53. Dana, *The Examination . . . Continued*, 31.
54. Ibid., 137.   55. Ibid., 33.   56. Ibid., 39.
57. Ibid., 40.   58. Ibid., 35.   59. Ibid., 18.
60. Dana, *An Examination*, 43.
61. Ibid., 80–81.   62. Ibid., 118.   63. Ibid., 44.
64. Dana, *The Examination . . . Continued*, 48.
65. Dana, *An Examination*, 56.
66. Ibid., 55.
67. Dana, *The Examination . . . Continued* 36; Dana, *An Examination*, 119.
68. Dana, *An Examination*, 111.
69. Ibid., 117.
70. Dana, *The Examination . . . Continued*, 54.
71. Dana, *An Examination*, 103–104.
72. Dana, *The Examination . . . Continued*, 127.
73. Dana, *An Examination*, 126.
74. Ibid., 84.
75. Dana, *An Examination*, 90, 95; and *The Examination . . . Continued*, 98.
76. Dana, *Two Discourses*, 47–49.
77. Israel Holly, *Old Divinity Prefarable to Modern* (Litchfield, CT: Collier and Buel, 1795), 6.
78. Beach Newton, *A Preservative against the Doctrine of Fate: Occasioned by reading Mr. Jonathan Edwards against FREE WILL* (Boston, 1770), 26.
79. Israel Dewey, *Israel Dewey's Letters to Samuel Hopkins* (1759), 4.
80. Samuel Moody, *An Attempt to point out the fatal and pernicious Con-*

sequences of the Rev. Mr. Joseph Bellamy's Doctrines (Boston: Edes and Gill, 1759), 23–24.

81. Joseph Huntington, *A Droll, A Deist, and John Bacon, Master of Arts* (Hartford, 1781), 9.

82. Ibid., 12–13.

83. Huntington, *Letters of Friendship*, 23.

84. Ebenezer Devotion, *A Letter to the Rev'd Joseph Bellamy, D.D., Concerning Qualifications for Christian Communion* (New Haven, 1770), 20.

85. Jedidiah Mills, *An Inquiry Concerning the State of the Unregenerate under the Gospel* (New Haven, 1769), 105.

86. Newton, *A Preservative*, 25.

87. Devotion, *A Letter*, 21.

88. Huntington, *A Droll, A Deist, and John Bacon*, 5.

89. Moody, *An Attempt*, 18–19.

90. Mills, *An Inquiry*, 102–103.

91. Holly, *Old Divinity*, 19.

92. Langdon, *Remarks*, 19.

93. Ibid., 20.   94. Ibid., 24.   95. Ibid., 19.

96. Moses Hemmenway, *A Vindication of the Power, Obligation and Encouragement of the Unregenerate to attend the Means of Grace* (Boston: S. Kneeland, 1772), 18–19, 22–26, 80–81, 198–199.

97. William K. Breitenbach, "New Divinity Theology and the Idea of Moral Accountability," Ph.D. dissertation, Yale University, 1978, 202, 206.

98. Mills, *An Inquiry*, 103.

99. Hemmenway, *A Discourse*, 33.

100. Moses Mather, *The Visible Church in Covenant with God* (New York: Gaine, 1769), 54.

101. Huntington, *Letters of Friendship*, 95.

102. Hemmenway, *A Discourse*, 17, 103.

103. Ibid., 8.   104. Ibid., 64.

105. Huntington, *Letters of Friendship*, 20–21.

106. Hemmenway, *A Discourse*, 42.

107. Mather, *The Visible Church*, 6.

108. Hemmenway, *A Discourse*, 50, 70; Mather, *The Visible Church*, 9–11.

109. Hemmenway, *A Discourse*, 42.

110. Huntington, *A Plea*, 15.

111. Devotion, *A Letter*, 10.

112. Ibid., 11.

113. Mather, *The Visible Church*, 7.

114. Hemmenway, *A Discourse*, 27.

115. Mather, *The Visible Church*, 14–16.

116. Hemmenway, *A Discourse*, 27, 29; Mather, *The Visible Church*, 9.

117. Hart, *Brief Remarks*, 20.

118. Hemmenway, *Seven Sermons*, 17.

119. Ibid., 138.   120. Ibid., 162.

121. Mills, *An Inquiry*, 19.

122. Devotion, *A Letter*, 8.

123. Hart, *Brief Remarks*, 35.

124. William Hart, *A Sermon of the New Kind, Never Preached, nor ever will be* (New Haven, 1767), 24.

125. Ibid., 27–28.
126. Mills, *An Inquiry*, 90.
127. Devotion, *A Letter*, 20–21.
128. Hemmenway, *Seven Sermons*, 123.

6. Presbyterianism

1. Ezra Stiles, *The Literary Diary of Ezra Stiles, D.D.*, ed. F. B. Dexter (New York: Charles Scribner, 1901), 1:337.
2. John Tennent, *The Nature of Regeneration Opened* (Boston, 1735), 6, 8, 11–12.
3. Charles Grandison Finney, *Autobiography* (1876; rept. Old Tappan, NJ: Fleming Revell, 1908), 264; see also Samuel Davies, *Sermons* (New York: Robert Carter, 1857), 2:502.
4. Marilyn J. Westerkamp, *Triumph of the Laity: Scots-Irish Piety and the Great Awakening, 1625–1760* (New York: Oxford University Press, 1988), 146–147.
5. Nevin, in Theodore Appel, *The Life and Work of John Williamson Nevin* (Philadelphia: Reformed Church Publication House, 1889), 30–31.
6. Frederick L. Weis, *The Colonial Clergy of the Middle Colonies: New York, New Jersey, and Pennsylvania, 1628–1776* (Worcester, MA, 1957); see also Elwyn A. Smith, *The Presbyterian Ministry in American Culture: A Study in Changing Concepts, 1700–1900* (Philadelphia: Westminster Press, 1962), 32.
7. John Thomas, "The Government of the Church of Christ," in *The Great Awakening*, eds. Alan Heimert and Perry Miller (Indianapolis: Bobbs-Merrill, 1967), 126.
8. Thomas Brainerd, *The Life of John Brainerd* (Philadelphia: Presbyterian Publication Committee, 1865), 56.
9. Davies to Bellamy, March, 1757, in Joseph Bellamy Papers, The Presbyterian Historical Society, Philadelphia; see also Cedric Cowing, *The Great Awakening and the American Revolution: Colonial Thought in the 18th Century* (Chicago: Rand, McNally, 1972), 181.
10. Michael Anderson, "The Pope of Litchfield County: An Intellectual Biography of Joseph Bellamy," Ph.D. dissertation, Claremont Graduate School, 1980, 166–168, 173.
11. Brainerd, *Life of John Brainerd*, 56.
12. Keith J. Hardman, "Jonathan Dickinson and the Course of American Presbyterianism, 1717–1740," unpublished Ph.D. dissertation, University of Pennsylvania, 1971, 14; *Annals of the American Pulpit*, ed. William B. Sprague (New York: Robert Carter and Brothers, 1857), 3:15–16; Leonard J. Trinterud, *The Forming of an American Tradition: A Re-examination of Colonial Presbyterianism* (Philadelphia: Westminster Press, 1949), 94, 116, 123.
13. Dickinson to Thomas Foxcroft, August 23, 1743, in Archibald Alexander, *The Log College: Biographical Sketches of William Tennent and his Students, together with an Account of the Revivals under their Ministries* (1851; rept. London: Banner of Truth Trust, 1968), 242.
14. Jonathan Dickinson, *The True Scripture-Doctrine concerning some important points of Christian Faith* (1741; Philadelphia: Presbyterian Board of Publication, 1835), 144.

15. Jonathan Dickinson, *A Display of God's Special Grace* (Boston: Rogers and Fowle, 1742), 11.
16. E. Brooks Holifield, *A History of Pastoral Care in America: From Salvation to Self-Realization* (Nashville: Abingdon Press, 1983), 77.
17. Dickinson, *True Scripture-Doctrine*, 166.
18. Ibid., 39.   19. Ibid., 17, 61.   20. Ibid., 61.
21. Ibid., 103, 110.   22. Ibid., 93.
23. Ibid., 111.   24. Ibid., 112.
25. Hardman, "Jonathan Dickinson," 12, 250.
26. Dickinson, *True Scripture-Doctrine,* 60.
27. Ibid., 39.   28. Ibid., 11.   29. Ibid., 39.
30. *Annals of the American Pulpit*, ed. Sprague, 3:15–16.
31. John Blair, "Observations on Regeneration," in *Sermons and Essays by the Tennents and Their Contemporaries,* ed. Archibald Alexander (Philadelphia, 1855), 190–191.
32. Ibid., 195.   33. Ibid., 197–198.   34. Ibid., 201.
35. Ibid., 192.   36. Ibid., 190.
37. John Blair, *The New Creature Delineated* (Philadelphia: Bradfords, 1767), 16.
38. Blair, "Observations on Regeneration," in *Sermons and Essays,* ed. Alexander, 196.
39. Ibid., 194.   40. Ibid., 190.
41. John Blair, "An Essay on the Nature, Uses, and Subjects of the Sacraments," in *Essays* (New York: Holt, 1771), 13, 33.
42. Blair, "An Essay on the Means of Grace," in *Sermons and Essays,* ed. Alexander, 217.
43. Samuel Buell, *Intricate and Mysterious Events of Providence design'd to display Divine Glory* (New London, CT, 1770), 19.
44. James Patriot Wilson, *Sin Destitute of the Apology of Inability* (Philadelphia, 1820), 18.
45. Ibid., 19, 27.
46. James Patriot Wilson, *Moral Agency, or, Natural Ability Consistent with Moral Inability* (Philadelphia, 1819), 8, 11.
47. James Patriot Wilson, "Theological Essays," Manuscript commonplace book, Presbyterian Historical Society, Philadelphia, 90, 176.
48. Jacob Green, *Sinners Faultiness and Spiritual Inability* (New York: Gaine, 1767), 15.
49. Ibid., 12–13.
50. Gardiner Spring, *The Doctrine of Election Illustrated and Established* (Richmond, 1828), 14, 16.
51. Green, *Sinners Faultiness,* 35.
52. Davies, *Sermons,* 2:396.
53. Wilson, *Sin Destitute,* 27.
54. Wilson, "Theological Essays," 3.
55. Ibid., 109.
56. Gardiner Spring, *A Dissertation on Native Depravity* (New York, 1833), 8, 37.
57. Gardiner Spring, *Personal Reminiscences of the Life and Times of Gardiner Spring* (New York, 1866), 1:157.
58. Wilson, "Theological Essays," 110, 197.
59. Spring, *Doctrine of Election Illustrated,* 8.

60. Gilbert Tennent, *The Substance and Scope of Both Testaments* (Philadelphia, n.d.), 10; see also H. Shelton Smith, *Changing Conceptions of Original Sin: A Study in American Theology since 1750* (New York: Charles Scribner, 1955), 8.

61. William Sprague, *Lectures on Revivals of Religion* (1832; rept. London: Banner of Truth Trust, 1978), 180–181.

62. Gardiner Spring, *A Dissertation on the Means of Regeneration* (New York, 1827), 14–15.

63. Ibid., 44.   64. Ibid., 45, 47.

65. Spring, *Personal Reminiscences,* 1:124–125.

66. Fred J. Hood, *Reformed America: The Middle and Southern States, 1783–1837* (University, AL: University of Alabama Press, 1980), 111–112.

67. Jonathan French, *Discourses Delivered in the South Parish in Andover* (Newburyport, MA, 1804), 17.

68. Ned Landsman, "Revivalism and Nativism in the Middle Colonies: The Great Awakening and the Scots Community in East New Jersey," in *American Quarterly* 34 (Summer 1982), 161–164.

69. Boudinot, in Alexander, *Log College,* 130.

70. William Tennent, *God's Sovereignty, no Objection to the Sinner's Striving* (New York, 1765), 5, 6, 11.

71. Trinterud, *Forming of an American Tradition,* 213–227; Smith, *Presbyterian Ministry,* 78–79; Joseph A. Conforti, *Samuel Hopkins and the New Divinity Movement: Calvinism, the Congregational Ministry, and Reform in New England between the Great Awakenings* (Grand Rapids, MI: William B. Eerdmans, 1981), 73–74.

72. Jack Scott, "Introduction" to *An Annotated Edition of Lectures on Moral Philosophy by John Witherspoon* (Newark, NJ, 1982), 32.

73. Bradford to Bellamy, April 1772, in Joseph Bellamy Papers, Presbyterian Historical Society, Philadelphia.

74. Henry F. May, *The Enlightenment in America* (New York: Oxford University Press, 1976), 62–63.

75. *Minutes of the Presbyterian Church in America, 1706–1788,* ed. Guy S. Klett (Philadelphia: Presbyterian Historical Society, 1976), 538, 571.

76. Ernest Trice Thompson, *Presbyterians in the South* (Richmond: John Knox Press, 1963), 1:353–355.

77. George Marsden, *The Evangelical Mind and the New School Presbyterian Experience: A Case Study of Thought and Theology in Nineteenth-Century America* (New Haven: Yale University Press, 1970), 40–41.

78. Spring, *Personal Reminiscences,* 1:102–103; Robert Hastings Nichols, *Presbyterians in New York State* (Philadelphia: Westminster Press, 1963), 110–112; Lefferts A. Loetscher, *Facing the Enlightenment and Pietism: Archibald Alexander and the Founding of Princeton Theological Seminary* (Westport, CT: Greenwood Press, 1983), 133.

79. Ezra Stiles Ely, *A Contrast Between Calvinism and Hopkinsianism* (New York, 1811), 255.

80. Ibid., 104, 115.   81. Ibid., 217, 219, 220, 131.

82. Ibid., 131.   83. Ibid., 244–245.   84. Ibid., 163.

85. Alfred Nevin, *History of the Presbytery of Philadelphia* (Philadelphia: W. S. Fortescue, 1888), 188–189.

86. James Waddel Alexander, *The Life of Archibald Alexander, D.D.* (New York: Charles Scribner, 1854), 108–109.

87. Alexander, in Loetscher, *Facing the Enlightenment and Pietism,* 45.
88. Archibald Alexander, "God to be Glorified by Those Bought with a Price," in *Practical Sermons; to be Read in Families and Social Meetings* (Philadelphia: Presbyterian Board of Publications, 1850), 294.
89. Alexander, in Loetscher, *Facing the Enlightenment and Pietism,* 46.
90. Alexander, "The Misery of Impenitent Sinners," in *Practical Sermons,* 484.
91. Loetscher, *Facing the Enlightenment and Pietism,* 58.
92. Alexander, "The Knowledge of Sin By the Law," in *Practical Sermons,* 34.
93. J. W. Alexander, *Life of Archibald Alexander,* 238–241, 245.
94. Alexander, *Thoughts on Religous Experience* (1844; rept. London: Banner of Truth Trust, 1967), 25.
95. J. W. Alexander, *Life of Archibald Alexander,* 248.
96. Archibald Alexander, *Outlines of Moral Science* (New York: Charles Scribner, 1860), 148–149.
97. Alexander, *Thoughts on Religious Experience,* 62.
98. Ibid., 10, 145.
99. Alexander, "The New Creation," in *Practical Sermons,* 112.
100. Alexander, "Privileges of the Sons of God," in *Practical Sermons,* 153–154.
101. Alexander, "The New Creation," in *Practical Sermons,* 114.
102. Alexander, *Thoughts on Religious Experience,* 63.
103. Alexander, *Thoughts on Religious Experience,* 27.
104. Alexander, "Difficulty of Knowing our Faults," in *Practical Sermons,* 515.
105. Alexander, "The New Creation," in *Practial Sermons,* 110.
106. Alexander, *Moral Science,* 125.
107. Loetscher, *Facing the Enlightenment and Pietism,* 197.
108. Alexander, *Moral Science,* 125.
109. Archibald Alexander, *A Sermon Delivered at the Opening of the General Assembly* (Philadelphia, 1808), 11–12.
110. Alexander, "The Misery of Impenitent Sinners," in *Practical Sermons,* 482–483.
111. J. W. Alexander, *Life of Archibald Alexander,* 424–425; Mark A. Noll, "Introduction" to *The Princeton Theology* (Grand Rapids, MI: Baker Book House, 1984), 19.
112. Alexander, *Thoughts on Religious Experience,* 27.
113. Alexander, "Inaugural Address," in *The Princeton Theology,* ed. Mark Noll, 86.
114. Appel, *Life and Work of John Williamson Nevin,* 48.

7. The Waning of Edwardseanism

1. There was bound to be disagreement about the actual numbers of thoroughgoing Edwardseans, ranging from the estimate of Joel Hawes, who thought that Connecticut was substantially dominated by Old Calvinists, to Heman Humphrey, who claimed that all of Connecticut was Hopkinsian; see Leonard Woods, *History of Andover Theological Seminary* (Boston, 1885), 29–30.
2. James Hoopes, "Calvinism and Consciousness from Edwards to Beecher,"

in *Jonathan Edwards and the American Experience* (New York: Oxford University Press, 1988), 217–218.

3. Asa Burton, *The Life of Asa Burton Written by Himself* (Thetford, VT, 1973), 62.

4. Asa Burton, *Essays on Some of the First Principles of Metaphysicks, Ethicks, and Theology* (Portland, ME: A. Shirley, 1824), 15.

5. Ibid., 17.   6. Ibid., 53.   7. Ibid., 70.

8. Ibid., 100.   9. Ibid., 84.

10. Bruce Kuklick, *Churchmen and Philosophers: From Jonathan Edwards to John Dewey* (New Haven: Yale University Press, 1985), 57–58.

11. Ezra Stiles, *The Literary Diary of Ezra Stiles, D.D.*, ed. F. B. Dexter (New York: Charles Scribner, 1901), 3:274–275.

12. Bennet Tyler, *The Life and Labours of Asahel Nettleton*, ed. Andrew Bonar (1854; rept. London: Banner of Truth Trust, 1975), 19; "Leonard Woods" and "Edwards Dorr Griffin" in *DAB*; Tyler, *Lectures in Theology*, ed. Nahum Gale (Boston, 1859), 128. For discussions in conventional Edwardsean terms of the standard *loci* of New Divinity theology, see Leonard Woods, *Works* (Boston: John P. Jewett, 1851), 3:555, and Nettleton, *Remains of the Late Rev. Asahel Nettleton, D.D.*, ed. Bennet Tyler (Hartford: Robins and Smith, 1845), 356–357 on natural ability; Woods, *Works*, 3:23, Heman Humphrey, *Revival Sketches and Manual* (New York, 1859), 431, and W. B. Sprague, *Lectures on Revivals of Religion* (1852; rept. London: Banner of Truth Trust, 1978), 47–48, 52, 68–69 on the use of means; and Tyler, *Lectures*, 337–338; Tyler, *Memoir of the Life and Character of the Rev. Asahel Nettleton* (Boston: Doctrinal Tract and Book Society, 1844), 216; Richard Chipman, *A Discourse on the Nature and Means of Ecclesiastical Prosperity* (Hartford, CT: 1839), and Edward Dorr Griffin, *The Life and Sermons of Edward Dorr Griffin*, ed. W. B. Sprague (1839; rept. London: Banner of Truth Trust, 1987), 1:474–478, and also Griffin, *Sermons, Not Before Published* (New York: M. W. Dodd, 1844), 28–29 for moral absolutism.

13. Tyler, *Lectures*, 256, 270, 281.

14. Woods, *Works*, 2:114–115, 131.

15. Leonard Woods, *An Essay on Native Depravity* (Boston, 1835), 64.

16. Woods, "Remarks on Cause and Effect," in *Works*, 5:106.

17. Ibid., 2:97–98.

18. Woods, *Native Depravity*, 155.

19. Tyler, *Lectures*, 298–299.

20. Ibid., 315, 358.

21. Woods, "Letters to Young Ministers," in *Works*, 5:23.

22. Ibid., 2:70, 143.

23. Woods, *Native Depravity*, 190–191.

24. Griffin, *Sermons* (1844), 152–153.

25. Edward Dorr Griffin, *The Doctrine of Divine Efficiency* (New York, 1833), 65.

26. Ibid., 91.   27. Ibid., 168.

28. Tyler, *Memoir of Nettleton*, 124.

29. Ibid., 357; Gardiner Spring, *Personal Reminiscences of the Life and Times of Gardiner Spring* (New York, 1866), 2:16.

30. *Historical Statistics of the United States, Colonial Times to 1970* (Washington, DC: U.S. Government Printing Office, 1975), 1:76.

31. Bruce Kuklick, *Churchmen and Philosophers: From Jonathan Edwards to John Dewey* (New Haven: Yale University Press, 1985), 86.
32. Basic discussion of the founding of Andover can be found in Conrad Wright, *The Beginnings of Unitarianism* (Boston: Starr King Press, 1955), 274–280; Woods, *History of the Andover Theological Seminary*, 72–94; Joseph W. Phillips, *Jedidiah Morse and New England Congregationalism* (New Brunswick, NJ: Rutgers University Press, 1983), 138–140; Spring, *Personal Reminiscences*, 1:303–328.
33. Stephen Berk, *Calvinism versus Democracy: Timothy Dwight and the Origins of American Evangelical Orthodoxy* (Hamden, CT: Archon Books, 1974), 178–183.
34. Phillips, *Morse*, 144–146; see also H. B. Stowe in *The Autobiography of Lyman Beecher* (New York: Harper and Brothers, 1865), 2:280, and Daniel T. Fiske, "New England Theology," in *Bibliotheca Sacra* 22 (July 1865), 476.
35. Leon Howard, *The Connecticut Wits* (Chicago: University of Chicago Press, 1943), 214–215; Stiles, *Literary Diary*, 3:274.
36. Edmund S. Morgan, *The Gentle Puritan: A Life of Ezra Stiles* (New Haven: Yale University Press, 1962), 417.
37. Timothy Dwight, *Theology Explained and Defended In a Series of Sermons* (Middletown, CT, 1818–1819), 2:18; Berk, *Calvinism Versus Democracy*, 45–46; Howard, *Connecticut Wits*, 354.
38. Kenneth Silverman, *Timothy Dwight* (New York: Twayne Publishers, 1969), 105.
39. Timothy Dwight, *Decisions of Questions Discussed by the Senior Class in Yale College in 1813 and 1814* (New York, 1833), 84.
40. Ibid., 88.
41. Dwight, *Theology*, 4:133; Charles Roy Keller, *The Second Great Awakening in Connecticut* (New Haven: Yale University Press, 1942), 62–65.
42. Silverman, *Timothy Dwight*, 102.
43. James Waddel Alexander, *The Life of Archibald Alexander, D.D.* (New York: Charles Scribner, 1854), 241.
44. Berk, *Calvinism versus Democracy*, 72.
45. J. W. Alexander, *Life of Archibald Alexander*, 240.
46. Dwight, *Theology*, 1:255.
47. Ibid., 4:530–531.   48. Ibid., 4:520, 528.
49. Nettleton to Philader Parmele, c. 1809, in Nettleton Manuscript Collection, Hartford Theological Seminary, Hartford; see also Tyler, *Memoir of Nettleton*, 36–37.
50. Timothy Dwight, *Sermons* (New Haven: Hezekiah Howe, 1828), 1:327.
51. Dwight, *Theology*, 1:4, 6, 246.
52. Ibid., 1:245–246.   53. Ibid., 1:387.
54. Ibid., 1:457.   55. Ibid., 3:39.
56. Howard, *Connecticut Wits*, 356.
57. Dwight, *Theology*, 4:463.
58. Dwight, "Secret Things Belong to God," in *Sermons*, 1:20.
59. Dwight, "Man Cannot Find Out a Religion Which Will Render Him Acceptable to God," in ibid., 1:72–73.
60. Dwight, *Theology*, 1:248–249.
61. Ibid., 1:410–411.   62. Ibid., 3:45.   63. Ibid., 3:166.
64. Ralph H. Gabriel, *Religion and Learning at Yale* (New Haven: Yale Uni-

versity Press, 1958), 70–77; Roland Bainton, *Yale and the Ministry* (New York: Harpers, 1957), 115.

65. Stuart C. Henry, *Unvanquished Puritan: A Portrait of Lyman Beecher* (Grand Rapids, MI: William B. Eerdmans, 1973), 42.
66. Beecher, *Autobiography,* 1:44.
67. Ibid., 2:52, 53, 56.   68. Ibid., 1:344.
69. Ibid., 1:69; Lyman Beecher, *Views in Theology* (Cincinnati: Truman and Smith, 1836), 59.
70. Beecher, *Autobiography,* 1:509.
71. Lyman Beecher, *Dependence and Free Agency* (Boston, 1832), 10.
72. Beecher, *Autobiography,* 1:472.
73. Ibid., 2:26.   74. Ibid., 2:175.
75. Beecher, *Views in Theology,* 42–43, 45.
76. Beecher, *Autobiography,* 2:578.
77. Beecher, "The Bible a Code of Laws," in *Sermons Delivered on Various Occasions* (Boston, 1828), 140, 141.
78. Beecher, "The Government of God Desirable," in *Sermons* (1828) 18–19.
79. Beecher, *Dependence and Free Agency,* 32–33.
80. Beecher, *Autobiography,* 2:581–582.
81. Mann, in Ann Douglas, *The Feminization of American Culture* (New York: Alfred Knopf, 1977), 42.
82. Charles Grandison Finney, *Memoirs of Charles G. Finney* (1876; Old Tappan, NJ: Fleming Revell, 1908), 42–43.
83. Ibid., 189.
84. Finney, "Sinners Bound to Change Their Own Hearts," in *Notions of Americans, 1820–1860,* ed. David Grimstead (New York: George Braziller, 1970), 78.
85. Finney, *Memoirs,* 83; see also Whitney R. Cross, *The Burned-Over District: The Social and Intellectual History of Enthusiastic Religion in Western New York, 1800–1850* (1950; rept. New York: Harper & Row, 1965), 151–164.
86. John F. Thornbury, *God Sent Revival: The Story of Asahel Nettleton and the Second Great Awakening* (Grand Rapids, MI: Evangelical Press, 1977), 158–173; George Hugh Birney, "The Life and Letters of Asahel Nettleton, 1783–1844," Ph.D. dissertation, Hartford Theological Seminary, 1943, 114–137.
87. Thornbury, *God Sent Revival,* 174–179; Birney, "Life and Letters of Nettleton," 151; the minutes of the New Lebanon Conference were surreptitiously printed in the Unitarian magazine *Christian Examiner and Theological Review* 4 (1827), 357–370.
88. Beecher, *Autobiography,* 2:101; Finney, *Memoirs,* 220.
89. Cross, *Burned-Over District,* 155, 164–168.
90. Charles Grandison Finney, *Lectures on the Revival of Religion* (Old Tappan, NJ: Fleming Revell, n.d.), 5, 116.
91. Beecher, *Autobiography,* 2:116–117.
92. Beecher, *Autobiography,* 1:344.
93. David L. Weddle, "The Law and the Revival: A 'New Divinity' for the Settlements," in *Church History* 47 (June 1978), 196, 199; Conrad Cherry, *Nature and Religious Imagination from Edwards to Bushnell* (Philadelphia: Fortress Press, 1980), 126–127.

94. Beecher, *Autobiography*, 1:344.
95. One of the great confusions about the motives of those who participated in the Second Great Awakening and those who organized the voluntary societies which sprang to life at virtually the same time concerns the degree to which the revivalists hoped to use the awakening to feed the societies and thus recover whatever measure of social control they thought they had lost. Some, such as Clifford Griffin, Charles Cole, and Timothy L. Smith, argued for a direct linkage, and with various degrees of moral comment on the appropriateness of such a connection. Others, such as Lois Banner, Richard Shiels, and Richard Birdsall, have insisted that the revivalists of the Second Great Awakening had no ulterior manipulative motives, and that the revivals were individualistic in orientation, with little connection to the organization of voluntary societies. I am suggesting that, in fact, both arguments may be true—depending on the area and the people concerned. Shiels, for instance, comes to his conclusion—that the revivals were not intended to recover lost political ground for the clergy—by lumping both old-line Edwardseans like Charles Backus in with Beecher and Dwight, and then taking Backus's disavowals of politics as coverage for the likes of Beecher. In that sense, Shiels does just what Beecher hoped people would do—mistake him for an Edwardsean. I am quite sure that Backus meant every word he said about the clergy needing to disassociate themselves from politics, but he said that because he was a New Divinity man, and therefore in a different league from Beecher. When Beecher, and every other Old Calvinist, talked revival, he meant something entirely different, which perhaps explains Fred J. Hood's point that the voluntary societies were top-heavy with Calvinists of the "old side" persuasion. Edwardsean revivalism, it is true, had little interest in saving the world as it was; but Edwardseans were not the only people who had learned how to play the revival game. Hence, the necessity for careful distinctions between New Divinity Calvinists and Old Calvinists, even up through the nineteenth century. See Richard D. Shiels, "The Second Great Awakening in Connecticut: Critique of the Traditional Interpretation," in *Church History* 49 (December 1980); 411–414, and Richard D. Birdsall, "The Second Great Awakening and the New England Social Order," in *Church History* 39 (1970) 358; also, Douglas, *Feminization of American Culture*, 35–49.

8. Silencing the Ghost

1. Sidney E. Mead, *Nathaniel William Taylor, 1786–1858: A Connecticut Liberal* (Chicago: University of Chicago Press, 1942), 16–37, 192, Bainton, *Yale and the Ministry* (New York: Harpers, 1957), 81–83.
2. Nathaniel William Taylor, *Essays, Lectures, Etc. Upon Select Topics* (New York, 1859), 221.
3. Ibid., 465; Mead, *Nathaniel William Taylor*, 108–109, 110–112, 159–162; Mark A. Noll, "Common Sense Traditions and American Evangelical Thought," in *American Quarterly* 37 (Summer 1985), 225–226; Ralph Gabriel, *Religion and Learning at Yale* (New Haven: Yale University Press, 1958), 135; Bruce Kuklick, *Churchmen and Philosophers: From Jonathan Edwards to John Dewey* (New Haven: Yale University Press, 1985), 97.
4. Taylor, *Essays . . . Upon Select Topics*, 154.

5. Nathaniel William Taylor, *A Sermon Addressed to the Legislature of the State of Connecticut* (New Haven, 1823), 22, 34.
6. Nathaniel William Taylor, *Lectures on the Moral Government of God* (New York, 1859), 1:158–159.
7. Mead, *Nathaniel William Taylor*, 180–186.
8. Taylor, *Lectures on the Moral Government of God*, 2:21.
9. Taylor, *Sermon Addressed to the Legislature*, 19; on the atonement, see also *Lectures on the Moral Government of God*, 1:82–126, 2:17–20.
10. Taylor, *Essays . . . Upon Select Topics*, 376.
11. Taylor to Beecher, January 14, 1819, in Lyman Beecher, *The Autobiography of Lyman Beecher* (New York: Harper and Brothers, 1865), 1:384; Stuart Henry, *Unvanquished Puritan: A Portrait of Lyman Beecher* (Grand Rapids, MI: William B. Eerdmans, 1973), 134–135.
12. Taylor, in Beecher, *Autobiography*, 1:385.
13. Ibid., 1:386.   14. Ibid., 1:387.
15. Ibid., 1:385.   16. Ibid., 1:385.
17. Taylor, *Essays . . . Upon Select Topics*, 224.
18. George Park Fisher, "The System of Dr. N. W. Taylor in its Connection with Prior New England Theology," in *Discussions in History and Theology* (New York: Scribners, 1880), 308–309.
19. Taylor, *Sermon Addressed to the Legislature*, 9.
20. Taylor, *Essays . . . Upon Select Topics*, 12.
21. Ibid., 34–35.   22. Ibid., 180.
23. Ibid., 48; James Hoopes, "Calvinism and Consciousness from Edwards to Beecher," in *Jonathan Edwards and the American Experience*, eds. Nathan O. Hatch and Harry S. Stout (New York: Oxford University Press, 1988), 219.
24. Taylor, *Essays . . . Upon Select Topics*, 183–185.
25. Ibid., 392.
26. Fisher, "System of N. W. Taylor," in *Discussions in History and Theology*, 310–311, and George Nye Boardman, *A History of the New England Theology* (New York, 1899), 257.
27. Taylor, *Lectures on the Moral Government of God*, 1:186.
28. Taylor, *Essays . . . Upon Select Topics*, 194.
29. Taylor, *Lectures on the Moral Government of God*, 1:26–27; James Hoopes, "Calvinism, Consciousness, and Personal Identity from Edwards to Taylor" (unpublished ms., 1984), 26–28.
30. Taylor, *Essays . . . Upon Select Topics*, 192.
31. Fisher, "System of N. W. Taylor," in *Discussions in History and Theology*, 313–314; Boardman, *New England Theology*, 272.
32. Taylor, *Lectures on the Moral Government of God*, 2:23.
33. Taylor, *Essays . . . Upon Select Topics*, 204.
34. Ibid., 423.
35. Taylor, *Lectures on the Moral Government of God*, 1:195.
36. Fisher, "System of N. W. Taylor," in *Discussions in History and Theology*, 312; see also Kuklick, *Churchmen and Philosophers*, 99.
37. Taylor, *Essays . . . Upon Select Topics*, 380.
38. Taylor, *Lectures on the Moral Government of God*, 2:300.
39. Fisher, "System of N. W. Taylor," in *Discussions in History and Theology*, 329; see also the explanations offered by Taylor's student Edward R. Tyler in his pamphlet *Holiness Preferable to Sin* (New Haven, 1829), 4–5, and

by Taylor's colleague Eleazar Fitch in his article "Divine Permission of Sin," in *Quarterly Christian Spectator* 4 (December 1832), 622–635.
40. Taylor, *Lectures on the Moral Government of God,* 1:196.
41. Ibid., 1:306.
42. Taylor, *Essays . . . Upon Select Topics,* 383.
43. Taylor, *Lectures on the Moral Government of God,* 1:179.
44. Fisher, "System of N. W. Taylor," in *Discussions in History and Theology,* 329.
45. Ibid., 2:305.
46. Taylor, *Sermon Addressed to the Legislature,* 15–16.
47. Taylor, *Essays . . . Upon Select Topics,* 379.
48. Emmons to Park, August 7, 1838, in Robert L. Ferm, *A Colonial Pastor: Jonathan Edwards the Younger, 1745–1801* (Grand Rapids, MI: William B. Eerdmans, 1976), 178.
49. Taylor, *Lectures on the Moral Government of God,* 2:134.
50. For two opposing views on Taylor's intellectual relationship to Edwards, see Mead, *Nathaniel William Taylor,* 102–114, 123–124, and Kuklick, *Churchmen and Philosophers,* 102–105; it would be well, also, on this point to take into account James Hoopes's review of *Churchmen and Philosophers* in *American Quarterly* (Spring 1986), 140–145.
51. Taylor, *Lectures on the Moral Government of God,* 1:25.
52. Taylor, *Lectures on the Moral Government of God,* 2:197–198.
53. Eleazar T. Fitch, *Two Discourses on the Nature of Sin* (New Haven: Treadway and Adams, 1826), 9.
54. Beecher, *Autobiography,* 2:157.
55. Nettleton, in George Hugh Birney, "The Life and Letters of Asahel Nettleton, 1783–1844," Ph.D. dissertation, Hartford Theological Seminary, 1943, 155.
56. Bennet Tyler, *Letters on the Origin and Progress of the New Haven Theology* (New York: Robert Carter, 1837), 6.
57. Ibid., 6–7, 8–9.
58. Beecher, *Autobiography,* 2:157; Goodrich defended his views to Lyman Beecher in a letter of January 6, 1822, in Beecher, *Autobiography,* 1:469.
59. Nettleton, in J. F. Thornbury, *God Sent Revival: The Story of Asahel Nettleton and the Second Great Awakening* (Grand Rapids, MI: Evangelical Press, 1977), 191.
60. Mead, *Nathaniel William Taylor,* 186–188.
61. Nettleton to Beecher, September 18, 1829, in Birney, "Life and Letters of Asahel Nettleton," 342.
62. Nettleton to Tyler, February 4, 1836, in ibid., 389.
63. Ebenezer Porter to Lyman Beecher, May 22, 1829, in Beecher, *Autobiography,* 1:165; see also Tyler, *Letters on the New Haven Theology,* 102.
64. Fitch, *Two Discourses on the Nature of Sin,* 3–4, 19, 35–36.
65. Ibid., 37.   66. Ibid., 24.   67. Ibid., 16.
68. Ibid.   69. Ibid., 32.
70. Boardman, *History of New England Theology,* 255; Birney, "Life and Letters of Asahel Nettleton," 159; Tyler, *Letters on the New Haven Theology,* 10–11.
71. Birney, "Life and Letters of Nettleton," 160.
72. Tyler, *Letters on the New Haven Theology,* 11.
73. Nathaniel William Taylor, *Concio ad Clerum: A Sermon Delivered in the*

Chapel of Yale College, September 10, 1828 (New Haven: Hezekiah Howe, 1828), 5, 6.

74. Ibid., 8.   75. Ibid., 13.   76. Ibid., 13–14.
77. Ibid., 14.   78. Ibid., 24.
79. Fisher, "System of N. W. Taylor," in *Discussions in History and Theology*, 321–322.
80. Taylor, *Concio ad Clerum*, 34.
81. Tyler, *Letters on the New Haven Theology*, 7.
82. Taylor, *Concio ad Clerum*, 28.
83. James Hoopes, "Calvinism, Consciousness, and Personal Identity," 25.
84. Taylor, *Concio ad Clerum*, 38.
85. Goodrich and Fitch, Taylor's colleagues, proved equally adept at this maneuver: see Fitch's invocation of "Puritan principles" and "a Puritan ancestry" in *National Prosperity Perpetuated* (New Haven, 1828), 15, and Goodrich's attempt to make Bellamy appear as a proto-Taylorite in his "Review of Bellamy on the Permission of Sin," in *Quarterly Christian Spectator* 2 (September 1830), 531–533.
86. Tyler, *Letters on the New Haven Theology*, 99.
87. Nettleton to Leonard Woods, May 6, 1829, in Birney, "Life and Letters of Asahel Nettleton," 334–335.
88. Nettleton, in Tyler, *Letters on the New Haven Theology*, 17.
89. Nettleton to Charles Hodge, December 9, 1837, in Rare Books & Manuscripts Collection, Firestone Library, Princeton University, Princeton, NJ.
90. Tyler, *Letters on the New Haven Theology*, 77.
91. Samuel Rogers Andrew, "What is the Real Difference Between the New-Haven Divines and Those Who Oppose Them?" in *Quarterly Christian Spectator* (February 1834), 7.
92. Leonard Woods, *Letters to Rev. Nathaniel W. Taylor, D.D.* (Andover, MA. 1830), 40–41, 57.
93. Joseph Harvey, *A Review of a Sermon* (Hartford, 1829), 27.
94. Leonard Woods, *An Essay on Native Depravity* (Boston, 1835), 10–11.
95. Tyler, *Lectures on Theology*, ed. Nahum Gale (Boston, 1859), 220–221.
96. Tyler, *Lectures in Theology*, 197, 346.
97. Edward Dorr Griffin, *The Doctrine of Divine Efficiency* (New York, 1833), 43.
98. Nettleton, in Bennet Tyler, *Memoir of the Life and Character of Rev. Asahel Nettleton* (Boston: Doctrinal Tract and Book Society, 1844), 293.
99. Bennet Tyler, *Strictures on the Review of Dr. Spring's Dissertation* (Portland, ME, 1829), 57.
100. Ibid., 11.
101. Tyler, *Lectures on Theology*, 265.
102. Leonard Woods, "Remarks on Cause and Effect," in *Works* (Boston: John P. Jewett, 1851), 5:124, 128–129.
103. Leonard Woods, *Letters to Rev. Nathaniel W. Taylor* (Andover, MA, 1830), 105.
104. Ibid., 99–100.
105. Griffin, *Doctrine of Divine Efficiency*, 47.
106. Ibid., 59.
107. Nettleton to Samuel Miller, August 21, 1835, in Rare Books & Manuscripts Room, Firestone Library, Princeton University, Princeton, NJ.

Epilogue

1. Whitney Cross, *The Burned-Over District: The Social and Intellectual History of Enthusiastic Religion in Western New York, 1800–1850* (1950; rept. New York: Harper and Row, 1965), 164.
2. Bennet Tyler, *Memoir of the Life and Character of Rev. Asahel Nettleton* (Boston: Doctrinal Tract and Book Society, 1844), 300–301.
3. "Life and Character of Rev. Dr. Nettleton," in *The New Englander* 3 (January 1845), 88–89.
4. John F. Thornbury, *God Sent Revival: The Story of Asahel Nettleton and the Second Great Awakening* (Grand Rapids, MI: Evangelical Press, 1977), 229.
5. Richard Birdsall, *Berkshire County: A Cultural History* (New Haven: Yale University Press, 1959), 120.
6. Moses Stuart, "Hints on Sin and Free Agency," in *Quarterly Christian Spectator* 6 (April 1834), 180.
7. Albert Baldwin Dod, "On Revivals of Religion," in *Essays, Theological and Miscellaneous reprinted from the Princeton Review* (New York: Robert Carter, 1847), 137.
8. James Hamilton and Edward H. Madden, "Edwards, Finney, and Mahan on the Derivation of Duty," in *Journal of the History of Philosophy* 13 (1975), 347–350; for a more hostile analysis of this connection, see B. B. Warfield, *Perfectionism,* ed. Samuel G. Craig (Philadelphia: Presbyterian and Reformed, 1967), 46–47.
9. George Marsden, *The Evangelical Mind and the New School Presbyterian Experience: A Case Study of Thought and Theology in Nineteenth-Century America* (New Haven: Yale University Press, 1970), 27–28, 56–57, 63; Stuart C. Henry, *Unvanquished Puritan: A Portrait of Lyman Beecher* (Grand Rapids, MI: William B. Eerdmans, 1973), 209–222.
10. Beecher to Taylor, April 25, 1835, in Lyman Beecher, *The Autobiography of Lyman Beecher* (New York: Harper and Brothers, 1865), 2:344.
11. Nathanial William Taylor, *Dr. Taylor's Reply to Dr. Tyler's Examination* (New Haven, 1832), 3–4.
12. Zebulon Crocker, *The Catastrophe of the Presbyterian Church in 1837* (New Haven, 1838), 212.
13. Horace Bushnell, *An Argument for "Discourses on Christian Nurture"* (Hartford: Edwin Hunt, 1847), 14, 15–16.

Bibliography

I. Primary Sources

1. Manuscript Collections

The most significant collections of papers used in composing this book are the Joseph Bellamy Papers at the Presbyterian Historical Society, Philadelphia, and the letters and manuscript "Journal" of Samuel Hopkins in the Gratz Collection of the Historical Society of Pennsylvania, also in Philadelphia. Extensive use was also made of the Asahel Nettleton Papers in the Case Memorial Library of the Hartford Theological Seminary, Hartford, CT. The "Commonplace Book" of James Patriot Wilson, in the Presbyterian Historical Society in Philadelphia, yielded information on the Presbyterian Edwardseans, as did the letters written by Nettleton and Bennet Tyler to Samuel Miller and Charles Hodge, which are in the Charles Hodge Papers, Rare Book Room of the Firestone Library, Princeton University, Princeton, NJ.

2. Published Works of Jonathan Edwards

The basic Edwardsean texts used for this book are Yale University Press editions (cited in the notes as "WJE," for *Works of Jonathan Edwards*) as follows:

Freedom of the Will. Ed. Paul Ramsey. New Haven: Yale University Press, 1957, 1979.

Religious Affections. Ed. John E. Smith. New Haven: Yale University Press, 1959, 1976.

Original Sin. Ed. Clyde A. Holbrook. New Haven: Yale University Press, 1970.

The Great Awakening. Ed. C. C. Goen. New Haven: Yale University Press, 1972.

Apocalyptic Writings. Ed. Stephen J. Stein. New Haven: Yale University Press, 1977.

Scientific and Philosophical Writings. Ed. Wallace E. Anderson. New Haven: Yale University Press, 1980.

The Life of David Brainerd. Ed. Norman Pettit. New Haven: Yale University Press, 1985.

Other editions of Edwards's works that were extensively used:

Faust, Clarence, and Johnson, Thomas H., editors. *Jonathan Edwards: Representative Selections.* New York: Hill and Wang, 1962.

Frankena, William K., editor. *The Nature of True Virtue.* Ann Arbor, MI: University of Michigan Press, 1979.

Hickman, Edward, editor. *The Works of Jonathan Edwards* (two volumes). 1834; rept. London: Banner of Truth Trust, 1976.

Kaufman, Arnold S., and Frankena, William K., editors. *Freedom of the Will*. Indianapolis: Bobbs-Merrill, 1969.

Miller, Perry, editor. *Images or Shadows of Divine Things*. Westport, CT: Greenwood Press, 1977.

Townsend, Harvey G., editor. *The Philosophy of Jonathan Edwards from His Private Notebooks*. Westport, CT: Greenwood Press, 1972.

3. Other Primary Sources

Alexander, Archibald. *A Sermon Delivered at the Opening of the General Assembly . . . May 1808*. Philadelphia, 1808.

———. *Evidences of the Authenticity, Inspiration, and Canonical Authority of the Holy Scriptures*. Philadelphia: Presbyterian Board of Publication, 1836.

———. *Outlines of Moral Science*. New York: Charles Scribner, 1860.

———. *Practical Sermons; to be read in Families and Social Meetings*. Philadelphia: Presbyterian Board of Publication, 1850.

———. *The Log College: Biographical Sketches of William Tennent and His Students*. 1851; rept. London: Banner of Truth Trust, 1968.

———. *Thoughts on Religious Experience*. 1844; rept. London: Banner of Truth Trust, 1967.

———, editor. *Sermons and Essays by the Tennents and their Contemporaries*. Philadelphia, 1855.

Alexander, H. G., editor. *The Leibniz-Clarke Correspondence*. Manchester: Manchester University Press, 1956.

Alexander, James Waddel. *Correspondence of J. W. Alexander* (two volumes). New York: Charles Scribner, 1860.

———. *The Life of Archibald Alexander, D.D.* New York: Charles Scribner, 1854.

Ames, William. *The Marrow of Theology*, John D. Eusden, translator. 1955; rept. Durham, NC: Labyrinth Press, 1983.

Andrew, Samuel Roger. "What is the Real Difference Between the New-Haven Divines and Those who Oppose Them?" in *Christian Spectator* 6 (February 1834).

Andros, Thomas. *An Essay in Which the Doctrine of a Positive Divine Efficiency exciting the Will of Men to Sin . . . is Candidly Discussed*. Boston, 1820.

Arminius, Jacobus. *The Writings of James Arminius* (three volumes). Grand Rapids, MI: Baker Book House, 1977.

Augustine. *The City of God*. Eds. H. Bettenson and D. Knowles. Baltimore: Penguin Books, 1972.

Backus, Isaac. *The Diary of Isaac Backus* (two volumes). Ed. William McLoughlin. Providence: Brown University Press, 1979.

Bass, John. *A True Narrative of an Unhappy Contention*. Boston: Gookin, 1751.

Beecher, Lyman. *The Autobiography of Lyman Beecher* (two volumes). New York: Harper and Brothers, 1865.

———. *Dependence and Free Agency*. Boston, 1832.

———. *Sermons Delivered on Various Occasions*. Boston, 1828.

———. *Views in Theology*. Cincinnati: Truman and Smith, 1836.

Bellamy, Joseph. *True Religion Delineated, or, Experimental Religion as distinguished from formality and enthusiasm*. Morristown, NJ, 1804.

————. *Four Sermons on the Wisdom of God in the Permission of Sin.* Morristown, NJ, May 1804.

————. *That there is But One Covenant.* New Haven: T. and S. Green, 1769.

————. *The Works of Joseph Bellamy* (three volumes). New York: Stephen Dodge, 1812.

Bentley, William. *The Diary of William Bentley* (four volumes). Salem, MA: The Essex Institute, 1905–1914.

Berkeley, George. *A Treatise Concerning the Principles of Human Knowledge.* Ed. Philip Wheelwright. New York: Doubleday, Doran, 1935.

————. *Three Dialogues Between Hylas and Philonous.* Ed. C. M. Turbayne. Indianapolis: Bobbs-Merrill, 1954.

Blair, John. *Essays.* New York: Holt, 1771.

————. *The New Creature Delineated.* Philadelphia: Bradfords, 1767.

Blair, John D. *Sermons.* Richmond, VA, 1825.

Briant, Lemuel. *The Absurdity and Blasphemy of depreciating Moral Virtue.* Boston: Gookin, 1749.

Buell, Samuel. *Intricate and Mysterious Events of Providence, design'd to display Divine Glory.* New London, CT, 1770.

Burton, Asa. *Essays on Some of the First Principles of Metaphysicks, Ethicks, and Theology.* Portland, ME: A. Shirley, 1824.

————. *The Life of Asa Burton Written by Himself.* Thetford, VT, 1973.

Bushman, Richard, editor. *The Great Awakening: Documents on the Revival of Religion.* New York: Atheneum, 1970.

Bushnell, Horace. *An Argument for "Discourses on Christian Nurture."* Hartford: Edwin Hunt, 1847.

————. *Christian Nurture.* Ed. John Mulder. 1861 ed.; rept. Grand Rapids, MI: Baker Book House, 1979.

Calvin, John. *Concerning the Eternal Predestination of God.* Trans. J. K. S. Reid. London: James Clarke, 1961.

————. *Institutes of the Christian Religion.* Eds. F. L. Battles, H. Bettenson, and J. McNeill (two volumes). Philadelphia: Westminster Press, 1960.

Camp, Ichabod. *Men Have Freedom of Will and Power.* New Haven, 1760.

Chauncy, Charles. *Seasonable Thoughts on the State of Religion.* Boston: Samuel Eliot, 1743.

Chipman, Richard. *A Discourse on the Nature and Means of Ecclesiastical Prosperity.* Hartford, 1839.

Chubb, Thomas. *A Collection of Tracts on Various Subjects.* London, 1754.

Clap, Thomas. *An Essay on the Nature and Foundation of Moral Virtue and Obligation . . . For the Use of the Students of Yale College.* New Haven, 1765.

Cohen, I. Bernard, editor. *Isaac Newton's Papers and Letters on Natural Philosophy.* Cambridge: Harvard University Press, 1978.

Cole, M. "Stuart on the Romans," in *Christian Spectator* 4 (December 1832).

Collins, Anthony. *A Philosophical Inquiry Concerning Human Liberty.* Ed. James O'Higgins. London, 1717; rept. The Hague: Martinus Nijhoff, 1976.

Cotton, John. *A Treatise on Faith.* Boston, 1713.

————. *The Way of Life.* London, 1641.

Crocker, Zebulon. *The Catastrophe of the Presbyterian Church in 1837.* New Haven, 1838.

Daggett, Naphtali. *The Great and Tender Concern of Faithful Ministers for the Souls of their People.* New Haven, 1770.

————. *The great Importance of Speaking in the most intelligible Manner in the Christian Church*. New Haven, 1768.

————. *The excellency of a Good Name, A Sermon . . . occasioned by the death of Mr. Job Lane*. New Haven, 1768.

Dana, James. *Two Discourses*. Boston: Edes and Gill, 1767.

————. *Men's sins not chargeable on God but on themselves*. New Haven, 1782.

————. *An Examination of the late Reverend President Edwards's 'Enquiry on Freedom of Will.'* Boston: S. Kneeland, 1770.

————. *The "Examination of the late Rev'd President Edwards's Enquiry on Freedom of Will," Continued*. New Haven, 1773.

Davies, Samuel. *Sermons* (three volumes). New York: Robert Carter, 1857.

————. *Sermons on Important Subjects* (two volumes). New York, 1845.

Day, Jeremiah. *An Inquiry Respecting the Self-Determining Power of the Will*. New Haven: Herrick and Noyes, 1838.

Devotion, Ebenezer. *A Letter to the Rev'd Joseph Bellamy, D.D., Concerning Qualifications for Christian Communion*. New Haven, 1770.

Dewey, Israel. *Israel Dewey's Letters to Samuel Hopkins*. n.p., 1759.

Dickinson, Jonathan. *A Display of God's Special Grace*. Boston: Rogers and Fowle, 1742.

————. *The True Scripture-Doctrine concerning some important points of Christian Faith*. Philadelphia: Presbyterian Board of Publication, 1835.

Dow, Daniel. *New Haven Theology, alias Taylorism, alias Neology*. Thompson, CT, 1834.

Dwight, Timothy. *Decisions of Questions Discussed by the Senior Class in Yale College in 1813 and 1814*. New York, 1833.

————. *Sermons* (two volumes). New Haven: Hezekiah Howe, 1828.

————. *Theology Explained and Defended In a Series of Sermons* (four volumes). Middletown, CT, 1818–1819.

Edwards, Jonathan (the Younger). *The Works of Edwards the Younger*. Ed. Tryon Edwards (two volumes). Boston: Doctrinal Tract and Book Society, 1850.

Ely, Ezra Stiles. *A Contrast Between Calvinism and Hopkinsianism*. New York, 1811.

Emmons, Nathanael. *The Works of Nathanael Emmons*. Ed. Jacob Ide (seven volumes). Boston: Crocker and Brewster, 1842.

Finney, Charles Grandison. *Autobiography*. Old Tappan, NJ: Fleming Revell, 1908.

————. *Lectures on the Revival of Religion*. Old Tappen, NJ: Fleming Revell, n.d.

Fitch, Eleazar T. *An Inquiry into the Nature of Sin*. New Haven, 1827.

————. "Divine Permission of Sin," in *Christian Spectator* 4 (December 1832).

————. *National Prosperity Perpetuated*. New Haven, 1828.

————. "Review of Bellamy on the Permission of Sin," in *Christian Spectator* 2 (September 1830).

————. *Two Discourses on the Nature of Sin*. New Haven: Treadway and Adams, 1826.

French, Jonathan. *Discourse Delivered in the South Parish in Andover*. Newburyport, MA, 1804.

Goodrich, Chauncey. "Review of Bellamy on the Permission of Sin," in *Christian Spectator* 2 (September 1830).

Green, Jacob. *Sinners Faultiness and Spiritual Inability.* New York: Gaine, 1767.

Griffin, Edward Dorr. *The Life and Sermons of Edward Dorr Griffin* (two volumes). Ed. W. B. Sprague. 1839; rept. London: Banner of Truth Trust, 1987.

———. *Sermons, Not Before Published.* New York: M. W. Dodd, 1844.

———. *The Doctrine of Divine Efficiency.* New York, 1833.

Hart, Levi. *Liberty Described and Recommended.* Hartford: E. Watson, 1775.

Hart, William. *A Sermon of the New Kind, Never Preached, nor ever will be; Containing a Collection of Doctrines, belonging to the Hopkintonian Scheme of Orthodoxy; or the Marrow of the most Modern Divinity.* New Haven, 1767.

———. *Brief Remarks on a Number of False Propositions.* New London, CT, 1769.

Harvey, Joseph. *A Review of a Sermon, Delivered in the Chapel of Yale College, September 28, 1828, by Nathaniel W. Taylor, D.D.* Hartford, 1829.

Hemmenway, Moses. *A Discourse Concerning the Church.* Boston: Thomas and Andrews, 1792.

———. *A Vindication of the Power, Obligation and Encouragement of the Unregenerate to attend the Means of Grace.* Boston: S. Kneeland, 1772.

———. *Remarks on the Rev. Mr. Hopkins's Answer to a Tract.* Boston: Kneeland, 1774.

———. *Seven Sermons, on the Obligation and Encouragement of the Unregenerate.* Boston: Kneeland and Adams, 1767.

Hobbes, Thomas. *Leviathan.* Ed. W. G. Pogson Smith. Oxford: Clarendon Press, 1967.

Hodge, Charles. *The Constitutional History of the Presbyterian Church in the United States of America* (two volumes). Philadelphia: Presbyterian Board of Publication, 1851.

Holly, Israel. *Old Divinity Prefarable to Modern Novelty.* Litchfield, CT: Collier and Buel, 1795.

Hopkins, Samuel. *The Works of Samuel Hopkins* (three volumes). Boston: Doctrinal Tract and Book Society, 1854.

———. *The System of Doctrines Contained in Divine Revelation.* Boston: Isaiah Thomas, 1793.

Humphrey, Heman. *Revival Sketches and Manual.* New York, 1859.

Huntington, Joseph. *A Droll, a Deist, and John Bacon, Master of Arts.* Hartford, 1781.

———. *A Plea Before the Venerable Ecclesiastical Council at Stockbridge.* Norwich, CT: Coverly and Hodge, 1780.

———. *Letters of Friendship to those Clergymen who have lately renounced Communion with the Ministers and Churches of Christ in general.* Hartford, 1780.

———. *The Vanity and Mischief of Presuming on Things Beyond our Measure.* Norwich, CT, 1774.

Hutcheson, Francis. *Illustrations of the Moral Sense.* Ed. Bernard Peach. Cambridge: Harvard University Press, 1971.

Inaugural Address on Laying the Cornerstone of the Theological Institute of Connecticut, May 14, 1834. Hartford, 1834.

Klett, Guy S. *Presbyterians in Colonial Pennsylvania.* Philadelphia: University of Pennsylvania Press, 1937.

————, editor. *Minutes of the Presbyterian Church in America, 1706–1788.* Philadelphia: Presbyterian Historical Society, 1976.

Langdon, Samuel. *Remarks on the Leading Sentiments in the Rev'd Dr. Hopkins' SYSTEM OF DOCTRINES.* Exeter, MA, 1794.

Locke, John. *An Essay Concerning Humane Understanding.* London, 1690.

————. *An Essay Concerning Humane Understanding.* London, 1693.

————. *Two Treatises on Government.* Ed. Peter Laslett. New York: New American Library, 1965.

Luther, Martin. *The Bondage of the Will.* Eds. J. I. Packer and O. R. Johnson. London: James Clarke, 1957.

Malebranche, Nicholas. *The Search After Truth.* Eds. Thomas M. Lennon and Paul J. Olscamp. Columbus, OH, 1980.

Mather, Moses. *Divine Sovereignty displayed by Predestination.* New Haven, 1763.

————. *The Visible Church in Covenant with God.* New York: Gaine, 1769.

Mayhew, Experience. *Grace Defended in a Modest Plea for an Important Truth.* Boston: Green, 1744.

Mayhew, Jonathan. *Sermons.* Boston: Draper, 1755.

Mills, Jedidiah. *An Inquiry Concerning the State of the Unregenerate under the Gospel.* New Haven, 1769.

————. *A Vindication of Gospel-Truth.* Boston: Rogers and Fowle, 1747.

Minutes of the General Assembly of the Presbyterian Church, 1836. Philadelphia, 1836.

Moody, Samuel. *An Attempt to point out the fatal and pernicious Consequences of The Rev. Mr. Joseph Bellamy's Doctrines.* Boston: Edes and Gill, 1759.

Nettleton, Asahel. *Remains of the Late Rev. Asahel Nettleton, D.D.* Ed. Bennet Tyler, Hartford: Robins and Smith, 1845.

Newton, Beach. *A Preservative against the Doctrine of Fate: Occasioned by reading Mr. Jonathan Edwards against FREE WILL.* Boston, 1770.

Niles, Nathaniel. *Two Discourses on Liberty.* Newburyport, MA, 1774.

————. *The American Hero, Made on the Battle of Bunker Hill, and the Burning of Charlestown.* Boston, 1775.

Norton, Andrews. *Views of Calvinism.* 1822.

Norton, John. *The Orthodox Evangelist.* London: J. Macock, 1654.

Park, Edwards Amasa, editor. *The Atonement: Discourses and Treatises.* Boston: Congregational Board of Publication, 1859.

Pond, Enoch. *The Autobiography of the Rev. Enoch Pond.* Ed. E. P. Parker. Boston: Congregational Publishing and Sunday School Society, 1883.

Porter, David. *A Sermon on Divine Decrees and Moral Necessity, Reconciled with Freedom of the Will.* Catskill, NY, 1804.

Preston, John. *The Breastplate of Faith and Love.* London: Nicholas Bourne, 1634.

Raphael, D. D., editor. *British Moralists, 1650–1860.* Oxford: Oxford University Press, 1969.

Reid, Thomas. *Essays on the Active Powers of the Mind.* Ed. Baruch Brody. Cambridge: Harvard University Press, 1969.

————. *Inquiry and Essays.* Eds. R. E. Beanblossom and Keith Lehrer. Indianapolis: Hackett Publishing, 1983.

Riddel, William. *Christian Doctrines Stated and False Teachers Discovered.* Wiscasset, ME: Hoskins, 1800.

Sherman, Josiah. *God in no sense the Author of Sin*. Hartford, 1784.
Smalley, John. *Sermons on a Number of Connected Subjects*. Hartford: Oliver D. Cooke, 1803.
———. *Sermons on Various Subjects, Doctrinal and Practical*. Middletown, CT: Hart and Lincoln, 1814.
———. *The Consistency of the Sinners Inability to Comply with the Gospel; with his inexcusable guilt in not complying . . . In Two Discourses*. Hartford, 1769.
Sprague, William B. *Lectures on Revivals of Religion*. 1832; rept. London: Banner of Truth Trust, 1978.
Spring, Gardiner. *A Dissertation on Native Depravity*. New York, 1833.
———. *A Dissertation on the Means of Regeneration*. New York, 1827.
———. *Personal Reminiscences of the Life and Times of Gardiner Spring* (two volumes). New York, 1866.
———. *The Doctrine of Election Illustrated and Established*. Richmond, 1828.
Spring, Samuel. *Moral Disquisitions and Strictures*. Newburyport, MA: John Mycall, 1789.
Stiles, Ezra. *Extracts from the Itineraries and Other Miscellanies of Ezra Stiles*. Ed. F. B. Dexter. New Haven, 1916.
———. *The Literary Diary of Ezra Stiles, D.D.* (two volumes). Ed. F. B. Dexter. New York: Charles Scribner, 1901.
Strong, Nathan. *Sermons on Various Subjects, Doctrinal, Experimental, and Practical* (two volumes). Hartford: Oliver D. and I. Cooke, 1798–1800.
———. *The Doctrine of Eternal Misery Reconcileable with the Infinite Benevolence of God*. Hartford: Hudson and Goodwin, 1796.
Stuart, Moses. "Hints on Sin and Free Agency," in *Christian Spectator* 6 (April 1834).
Taylor, Nathaniel William. *A Sermon Addressed to the Legislature of the State of Connecticut*. New Haven, 1823.
———. *Concio ad Clerum. A Sermon Delivered in the Chapel of Yale College, September 10, 1828*. New Haven: Hezekiah Howe, 1828.
———. *Dr. Taylor's Reply to Dr. Tyler's Examination*. New Haven, 1832.
———. *Essays, Lectures, Etc. Upon Select Topics*. New York, 1859.
———. *Lectures on the Moral Government of God* (two volumes). New York, 1859.
Tennent, Gilbert. *A Persuasive to the Right Use of the Passions in Religion*. Philadelphia, 1760.
———. *The Substance and Scope of Both Testaments*. Philadelphia, 1749.
Tennent, John. *The Nature of Regeneration Opened*. Boston, 1735.
Tennent, William. *God's Sovereignty, no Objection to the Sinner's Striving*. New York, 1765.
Thayer, H. S., editor. *Newton's Philosophy of Nature*. New York: Hafner Press, 1974.
Tyler, Bennet. *Lectures in Theology*. Ed. Nahum Gale. Boston, 1859.
———. *Letters on the Origin and Progress of the New Haven Theology*. New York: Robert Carter, 1837.
———. *Memoir of the Life and Character of Rev. Asahel Nettleton*. Boston: Doctrinal Tract and Book Society, 1844.
———. *Strictures on the Review of Dr. Spring's Dissertation on the Means of Regeneration*. Portland, ME, 1829.

―――. *The Life and Labours of Asahel Nettleton*. Ed. Andrew Bonar. 1859; rept. London: Banner of Truth Trust, 1975.

―――, editor. *New England Revivals ... First Published in the Connecticut Evangelical Magazine*. Boston: Massachusetts Sabbath School Society, 1846.

Walker, Williston, editor. *Creeds and Platforms of Congregationalism*. 1893; rept. Philadelphia: Pilgrim Press, 1960.

Watts, Isaac. *The Works of Isaac Watts* (six volumes). London, 1750.

West, Samuel. *Essays on Liberty and Necessity*. Boston, 1793.

―――. *Essays on Liberty and Necessity* (Second Series). New Bedford, MA, 1794.

West, Stephen. *An Essay on Moral Agency*. Salem, MA: Thomas C. Cushing, 1794.

Whitby, Daniel. *A Discourse concerning the true import of the words Election and Reprobation*. London, 1817.

―――. *Sermons on the Attributes of God*. London, 1710.

Whitman, Samuel. *A Dissertation on the Origin of Evil*. Northampton, MA, 1797.

―――. *The Perfection of the Divine Constitution*. Northampton, MA, 1793.

Whittlesey, Chauncey. *A Sermon preach'd at New Haven on the Sabbath preceding the Publick Commencement, Sept. 9, 1744*. New London, CT, 1744.

―――. *The importance of religion in the civil Ruler, considered*. New Haven, 1778.

Willard, Samuel. *A Compleat Body of Divinity*. Boston: B. Green and S. Kneeland, 1729.

Wilson, James Patriot. *Moral Agency; or, Natural Ability Consistent with Moral Inability*. Philadelphia, 1819.

―――. *Sin Destitute of the Apology of Inability*. Philadelphia, 1820.

Woods, Leonard. *An Essay on Native Depravity*. Boston, 1835.

―――. *History of the Andover Theological Seminary*. Boston, 1885.

―――. *Letters to Rev. Nathaniel W. Taylor, D.D.* Andover, MA, 1830.

―――. *The Works of Leonard Woods, D.D.* (six volumes). Boston: John P. Jewett, 1851.

II. Secondary Sources

1. Published Works

Aaron, Richard I. *John Locke*. Oxford: Oxford University Press, 1955.

Adler, Mortimer. *The Idea of Freedom* (two volumes). Garden City, NY: Doubleday, 1958–61.

Ahlstrom, Sidney. "The Scottish Philosophy and American Theology," in *Church History* 24 (1955).

―――, editor. *Theology in America: The Major Protestant Voices from Puritanism to Neo-Orthodoxy*. Indianapolis: Bobbs-Merrill, 1967.

Anderson, Wallace E. "Immaterialism in Jonathan Edwards' Early Philosophical Notes," in *Journal of the History of Ideas* 25 (1964).

Appel, Theodore. *The Life and Work of John Williamson Nevin*. Philadelphia: Reformed Church Publication House, 1889.

Bainton, Roland. *Yale and the Ministry*. New York: Harpers, 1957.

Berk, Stephen. *Calvinism Versus Democracy: Timothy Dwight and the Origins of American Evangelical Orthodoxy*. Hamden, CT: Archon Books, 1974.

Berofsky, Bernard, editor. *Free Will and Determinism.* New York: Harper and Row, 1966.

Birdsall, Richard. *Berkshire County: A Cultural History.* New Haven: Yale University Press, 1959.

——. "The Second Great Awakening and the New England Social Order," in *Church History* 39 (1970).

Boardman, George Nye. *A History of New England Theology.* New York, 1899.

Bogue, Carl. *Jonathan Edwards and the Covenant of Grace.* Cherry Hill, NJ: Mack Publishing, 1975.

Bourke, Vernon K. *Will in Western Thought: An Historico-Critical Survey.* New York: Sheed and Ward, 1964.

Bozeman, Theodore Dwight. *Protestants in an Age of Science: The Baconian Ideal and Antebellum Religious Thought.* Chapel Hill, NC: University of North Carolina Press, 1973.

Brainerd, Thomas. *The Life of John Brainerd.* Philadelphia: Presbyterian Publication Committee, 1865.

Breen, T. H. *Puritans and Adventurers: Change and Persistence in Early America.* New York: Oxford University Press, 1980.

Bushell, T. H. *The Sage of Salisbury: Thomas Chubb, 1679–1747.* New York, 1967.

Bushman, Richard L. "Jonathan Edwards as Great Man: Identity, Conversion, and Leadership in the Great Awakening," in *Critical Essays on Jonathan Edwards.* Ed. William J. Scheick. Boston: G. K. Hall, 1980.

Butler, Jon. "Enthusiasm Descried and Decried: The Great Awakening as Interpretive Fiction," in *Journal of American History* 69 (September 1983).

Buxbaum, Melvin. *Benjamin Franklin and the Zealous Presbyterians.* University Park, PA: Pennsylvania State University Press, 1975.

Cecil, Anthony C. *The Theological Development of Edwards Amasa Park: Last of the "Consistent Calvinists."* Missoula, MT: Scholars Press, 1974.

Cherry, Conrad. *Nature and Religious Imagination from Edwards to Bushnell.* Philadelphia: Fortress Press, 1980.

——. *The Theology of Jonathan Edwards: A Reappraisal.* Gloucester, MA: Peter Smith, 1974.

Church, R. W. *A Study in the Philosophy of Malebranche.* London, 1937.

Cochrane, Charles Norris. *Christianity and Classical Civilization.* London: Oxford University Press, 1957.

Colman, John. *John Locke's Moral Philosophy.* Edinburgh: Edinburgh University Press, 1983.

Conforti, Joseph A. *Samuel Hopkins and the New Divinity Movement: Calvinism, the Congregational Ministry, and Reform in New England between the Great Awakenings.* Grand Rapids, MI: William B. Eerdmans, 1981.

Conkin, Paul R. *Puritans and Pragmatists: Eight Eminent American Thinkers.* New York: Dodd, Mead, 1968.

Copleston, F. C. *A History of Medieval Philosophy.* London, 1972.

Cowing, Cedric. *The Great Awakening and the American Revolution: Colonial Thought in the 18th Century.* Chicago: Rand, McNally, 1972.

Cross, Whitney R. *The Burned-Over District: The Social and Intellectual History of Enthusiastic Religion in Western New York, 1800–1850.* 1950; rept. New York: Harper & Row, 1965.

Davidson, Edward H. *Jonathan Edwards: The Narrative of a Puritan Mind.* Cambridge: Harvard University Press, 1966.

Davis, Arthur P. *Isaac Watts: His Life and Works.* New York: Dryden Press, 1943.

Douglas, Ann. *The Feminization of American Culture.* New York: Alfred Knopf, 1977.

Dwight, Timothy. *Memories of Yale Life and Men, 1845–1899.* New York: Dodd, Mead, 1903.

Ellis, Joseph. *The New England Mind in Transition: Samuel Johnson of Connecticut, 1696–1772.* New Haven: Yale University Press, 1973.

Erdt, Terrence. *Jonathan Edwards: Art and the Sense of the Heart.* Amherst, MA: University of Massachusetts Press, 1980.

Ferm, Robert L. *A Colonial Pastor: Jonathan Edwards the Younger, 1745–1801.* Grand Rapids, MI: William B. Eerdmans, 1976.

Fiering, Norman. *Jonathan Edwards's Moral Thought and Its British Context.* Chapel Hill, NC: University of North Carolina Press, 1981.

———. *Moral Philosophy at Seventeenth-Century Harvard: A Discipline in Transition.* Chapel Hill, NC: University of North Carolina Press, 1981.

Fisher, George Park. *Discussions in History and Theology.* New York: Charles Scribner, 1880.

Fiske, Daniel T. "New England Theology," in *Bibliotheca Sacra* 22 (July 1865).

Flower, Elizabeth, and Murphey, Murray. *A History of Philosophy in America* (two volumes). New York: G. P. Putnam, 1977.

Foster, Frank Hugh. *A Genetic History of the New England Theology.* Chicago: University of Chicago Press, 1907.

Fritz, Anita. "Berkeley's Self—Its Origins in Malebranche," in *Journal of the History of Ideas* 15 (1954).

Gabriel, Ralph H. *Religion and Learning at Yale.* New Haven: Yale University Press, 1958.

Gaustad, Edwin S. *The Great Awakening in New England.* Chicago: Quadrangle Books, 1968.

Gay, John H. "Matter and Freedom in the Thought of Samuel Clarke," in *Journal of the History of Ideas* 24 (1963).

George, Charles and Katharine. *The Protestant Mind of the English Reformation.* Princeton, NJ: Princeton University Press, 1961.

Gilby, Thomas, editor. *Thomas Aquinas: Philosophical Texts.* London, 1952; rept. Durham, NC: Labyrinth Press, 1983.

Gilson, Etienne. *History of Christian Philosophy in the Middle Ages.* New York: Random House, 1955.

———. *The Christian Philosophy of St. Augustine.* New York: Random House, 1960.

Goodwin, Gerald J. "The Myth of 'Arminian-Calvinism' in Eighteenth-Century New England," in *New England Quarterly* 41 (June 1968).

Grave, Selwyn A. *The Scottish Philosophy of Common Sense.* Oxford: Oxford University Press, 1960.

Greven, Philip. *The Protestant Temperament: Patterns of Child-Rearing, Religious Experience, and the Self in Early America.* New York: Alfred Knopf, 1977.

Griffin, Edward M. *Old Brick: Charles Chauncy of Boston, 1705–1787.* Minneapolis: University of Minnesota Press, 1980.

Hamilton, James, and Madden, Edward H. "Edwards, Finney, and Mahan on the Derivation of Duty," in *Journal of the History of Philosophy* 13 (1975).

Haroutunian, Joseph. *Piety Versus Moralism: The Passing of New England Theology.* New York: Henry Holt, 1932.

Hatch, Nathan O., and Stout, Harry S., editors. *Jonathan Edwards and the American Experience.* New York: Oxford University Press, 1988.

Heimert, Alan. *Religion and the American Mind from the Great Awakening to the Revolution.* Cambridge: Harvard University Press, 1966.

Helm, Paul. "John Locke and Jonathan Edwards: A Reconsideration," in *Journal of the History of Philosophy* 7 (1969).

Henry, Stuart C. *Unvanquished Puritan: A Portrait of Lyman Beecher.* Grand Rapids, MI: William B. Eerdmans, 1973.

Hershbell, Jackson. "Berkeley and the Problem of Evil," in *Journal of the History of Ideas* 31 (1970).

Hoeveler, J. David. *James McCosh and the Scottish Intellectual Tradition.* Princeton, NJ: Princeton University Press, 1981.

Hoffecker, Andrew. *Piety and the Princeton Theologians.* Philipsburg, NJ: Presbyterian and Reformed, 1981.

Holbrook, Clyde A. *Jonathan Edwards: The Valley and Nature.* Lewisburg, PA: Bucknell University Press, 1987.

———. *The Ethics of Jonathan Edwards: Morality and Aesthetics.* Ann Arbor: University of Michigan Press, 1973.

Holifield, E. Brooks. *A History of Pastoral Care in America: From Salvation to Self-Realization.* Nashville: Abingdon Press, 1983.

Hood, Fred J. *Reformed America: The Middle and Southern States, 1783–1837.* University, AL: University of Alabama Press, 1980.

Hook, Sidney, editor. *Determinism and Freedom in the Age of Modern Science.* New York: New York University Press, 1958.

Hoopes, James. "Art as History: Perry Miller's *New England Mind,*" in *American Quarterly* 34 (Spring 1982).

———. "Jonathan Edwards's Religious Philosophy," in *Journal of American History* 69 (1983).

Howard, Leon. *The Connecticut Wits.* Chicago: University of Chicago Press, 1943.

Jedrey, Christopher. *The World of John Cleaveland: Family and Community in Eighteenth-Century New England.* New York: W. W. Norton, 1979.

Keller, Charles Roy. *The Second Great Awakening in Connecticut.* New Haven: Yale University Press, 1942.

Kendall, R. T. *Calvin and English Calvinism to 1649.* Oxford: Oxford University Press, 1979.

Koyre, Alexander. *From the Closed World to the Infinite Universe.* Baltimore: Johns Hopkins University Press, 1956.

Kristeller, Paul Oskar. *Renaissance Thought II: Papers on Humanism and the Arts.* New York: Harper and Row, 1965.

Kuklick, Bruce. *Churchmen and Philosophers: From Jonathan Edwards to John Dewey.* New Haven: Yale University Press, 1985.

Landsman, Ned. "Revivalism and Nativism in the Middle Colonies: The Great Awakening and the Scots Community in East New Jersey," in *American Quarterly* 34 (Summer 1982).

Lodge, Martin S. "The Crisis of the Churches in the Middle Colonies, 1720–1750," in *Pennsylvania Magazine of History and Biography* 95 (April 1971).

Loeb, Louis E. *From Descartes to Hume: Continental Metaphysics and the Development of Modern Philosophy.* Ithaca, NY: Cornell University Press, 1981.

Loetscher, Lefferts A. *Facing the Enlightenment and Pietism: Archibald Alexander and the Founding of Princeton Theological Seminary.* Westport, CT: Greenwood Press, 1983.

Long, A. A. *Hellenistic Philosophy: Stoics, Epicureans, Sceptics.* London: Duckworth, 1974.

Lowrie, Ernest Benson. *The Shape of the Puritan Mind: The Thought of Samuel Willard.* New Haven: Yale University Press, 1974.

Luce, A. A. *Berkeley and Malebranche: A Study in the Origins of Berkeley's Thought.* Oxford: Oxford University Press, 1934.

Manuel, Frank E. *A Portrait of Isaac Newton.* Cambridge: Belknap Press/ Harvard University Press, 1968.

———. *The Religion of Isaac Newton.* Oxford: Clarendon Press, 1974.

Marini, Stephen A. *Radical Sects of Revolutionary New England.* Cambridge: Harvard University Press, 1982.

Marsden, George M. *The Evangelical Mind and the New School Presbyterian Experience: A Case Study of Thought and Theology in Nineteenth-Century America.* New Haven: Yale University Press, 1970.

May, Henry F. *The Enlightenment in America.* New York: Oxford University Press, 1976.

McCosh, James. *The Scottish Philosophy, Biographical, Expository, Critical, from Hutcheson to Hamilton.* New York: Robert Carter, 1875.

McCracken, Charles. *Malebranche and British Philosophy.* Oxford: Oxford University Press, 1983.

———. "Stages on a Cartesian Road to Immaterialism," in *Journal of the History of Philosophy,* 24 (1986), 19–40.

Mead, Sidney E. *Nathaniel William Taylor, 1786–1858: A Connecticut Liberal.* Chicago: University of Chicago Press, 1942.

Meyer, D. H. *The Instructed Conscience: The Shaping of the American National Ethic.* Philadelphia: University of Pennsylvania Press, 1972.

Middlekauff, Robert. *The Mathers: Three Generations of Puritan Intellectuals, 1596–1728.* New York: Oxford University Press, 1971.

Miller, Perry. *Jonathan Edwards.* New York: William Sloane, 1949.

Miller, Perry, and Heimert, Alan, editors. *The Great Awakening.* Indianapolis: Bobbs-Merrill, 1967.

Miller, Perry, and Johnson, Thomas J., editors. *The Puritans: A Sourcebook of their Writings* (two volumes). New York: Harper and Row, 1963.

More, Paul Elmer. *Platonism.* 3rd ed., Princeton: Princeton University Press.

Morgan, Edmund Sears. *The Gentle Puritan: A Life of Ezra Stiles.* New Haven: Yale University Press, 1962.

Morris, William S. "The Genius of Jonathan Edwards," in *Reinterpretation in American Church History,* Jerald S. Brauer, editor. Chicago: University of Chicago Press, 1968.

Murphy, Arthur. "Jonathan Edwards on Free Will and Moral Agency," in *Philosophical Review* 68 (1959).

Murray, Iain. *Jonathan Edwards: A New Biography.* London: Banner of Truth Trust, 1987.

Nevin, Alfred. *History of the Presbytery of Philadelphia.* Philadelphia: W. S. Fortescue, 1888.

Newlin, Claude M. *Philosophy and Religion in Colonial America*. New York: Philosophical Library, 1962.

Nichols, Robert Hastings. *Presbyterianism in New York State*. Philadelphia: Westminster Press, 1963.

Noll, Mark. "Common Sense Traditions and American Evangelical Thought," in *American Quarterly* 37 (Summer 1985).

———. "Ebenezer Devotion," in *Church History* 45 (September 1976).

———, editor. *The Princeton Theology*. Grand Rapids, MI: Baker Book House, 1983.

Nozick, Robert. *Philosophical Explanations*. Cambridge: Harvard University Press, 1981.

O'Brien, Michael J. *The Socratic Paradoxes and the Greek Mind*. Chapel Hill: University of North Carolina Press, 1967.

O'Higgins, James. *Anthony Collins: The Man and His Works*. The Hague: Martinus Nijhoff, 1970.

Patten, William, *Reminiscences of the late Rev. Samuel Hopkins, D.D.* Boston: Crocker and Brewster, 1843.

Pettit, Norman. *The Heart Prepared: Grace and Conversion in Puritan New England*. New Haven: Yale University Press, 1966.

Phillips, Joseph W. *Jedidiah Morse and New England Congregationalism*. New Brunswick, NJ: Rutgers University Press, 1983.

Redwood, John. *Reason, Ridicule, and Religion: The Age of Enlightenment in England*. Cambridge: Harvard University Press, 1976.

Rist, John M. *Stoic Philosophy*. Cambridge: Cambridge University Press, 1969.

Rome, Beatrice K. *The Philosophy of Malebranche: A Study of His Integration of Faith, Reason, and Experimental Observation*. Chicago: Henry Regnery, 1963.

Rudisill, Doris Paul. *The Doctrine of the Atonement in Edwards and His Successors*. New York: Poseidon Books, 1971.

Rupp, Gordon. "The 'Idealism' of Jonathan Edwards," in *Harvard Theological Review* 62 (1969).

Scott, Douglas M. *From Office to Profession: The New England Ministry, 1750–1850*. Philadelphia: University of Pennsylvania Press, 1978.

Shiels, Richard D. "The Second Great Awakening: A Critique of the Traditional Interpretation," in *Church History* 49 (December 1980).

Silverman, Kenneth. *Timothy Dwight*. New York: Twayne Publishers, 1969.

Simonson, Harold P. *Jonathan Edwards: Theologian of the Heart*. Grand Rapids, MI: William B. Eerdmans, 1974.

Smith, Elwyn A. *The Presbyterian Ministry in American Culture: A Study in Changing Concepts, 1700–1900*. Philadelphia: Westminster Press, 1962.

Smith, H. Shelton. *Changing Conceptions of Original Sin: A Study in American Theology since 1850*. New York: Charles Scribner, 1955.

Smith, John Holland. *The Death of Classical Paganism*. London: G. Chapman, 1976.

Spicer, E. E. *Aristotle's Conception of the Soul*. London, 1934.

Sprague, William B., editor. *Annals of the American Pulpit* (eight volumes). New York: Robert Carter and Brothers, 1857.

Sprunger, Keith L. *The Learned Doctor William Ames: Dutch Backgrounds of English and American Puritanism*. Urbana: University of Illinois Press, 1972.

Stout, Harry S. *The New England Soul: Preaching and Religious Culture in Colonial New England.* New York: Oxford University Press, 1986.

Strong, E. W. "Newton and God," in *Journal of the History of Ideas* 13 (1952).

Thompson, Ernest Trice. *Presbyterians in the South* (two volumes). Richmond: John Knox Press, 1963.

Thornbury, John F. *God Sent Revival: The Story of Asahel Nettleton and the Second Great Awakening.* Grand Rapids, MI: Evangelical Press, 1977.

Tracy, Joseph. *The Great Awakening: A History of the Revival of Religion in the Time of Edwards and Whitefield.* 1841; rept. London: Banner of Truth Trust, 1976.

Tracy, Patricia J. *Jonathan Edwards, Pastor: Religion and Society in Eighteenth-Century Northampton.* New York: Hill and Wang, 1980.

Trinterud, Leonard J. *The Forming of an American Tradition: A Re-examination of Colonial Presbyterianism.* Philadelphia: Westminster Press, 1949.

Tucker, Louis L. *Puritan Protagonist: President Thomas Clap of Yale College.* Chapel Hill, NC: University of North Carolina Press, 1962.

Turner, James. *Without God, Without Creed: The Origins of Unbelief in America.* Baltimore: Johns Hopkins University Press, 1985.

Walton, Craig. "Malebranche's Ontology," in *Journal of the History of Philosophy* 7 (1969).

Warfield, Benjamin B. *Calvin and Augustine.* Philadelphia: Presbyterian and Reformed, 1956.

———. *Perfectionism.* Ed. Samuel G. Craig. Philadelphia: Presbyterian and Reformed, 1967.

Weber, Donald. *Rhetoric and History in Revolutionary New England.* New York: Oxford University Press, 1988.

Westerkamp, Marilyn J. *The Triumph of the Laity: Scots-Irish Piety and the Great Awakening.* New York: Oxford University Press, 1988.

Westfall, Richard. *Never at Rest: A Biography of Isaac Newton.* Cambridge: Cambridge University Press, 1980.

———. *Science and Religion in Seventeenth-Century England.* New Haven: Yale University Press, 1958.

Williams, Daniel Day. *The Andover Liberals: A Study in American Theology.* New York: King's Crown Press, 1941.

Winslow, Ola Elizabeth. *Jonathan Edwards, 1703–1758.* New York: Macmillan, 1940.

Wood, Gordon. "Conspiracy and the Paranoid Style: Causality and Deceit in the Eighteenth Century," in *William and Mary Quarterly* 39 (July 1982).

Wood, M. H. *Plato's Psychology.* New York, 1907.

Wright, Conrad. *The Beginnings of Unitarianism in America.* Boston: Starr King Press, 1955.

Yolton, John. *John Locke and the Way of Ideas.* Oxford: Oxford University Press, 1956.

———. *Locke and the Compass of Human Understanding: A Selective Commentary on the Essay.* Cambridge: Cambridge University Press, 1970.

———. *Thinking Matter: Materialism in Eighteenth-Century Britain.* Minneapolis: University of Minnesota Press, 1983.

———, editor. *John Locke: Problems and Perspectives.* Cambridge: Cambridge University Press, 1969.

Zuckerman, Michael. *Peaceable Kingdoms: New England Towns in the Eighteenth Century.* New York: Vintage-Knopf, 1970.

2. *Unpublished Works and Articles*

Anderson, Michael P. "The Pope of Litchfield County: An Intellectual Biography of Joseph Bellamy," Ph.D. dissertation, Claremont Graduate School, 1980.

Birney, George Hugh. "The Life and Letters of Asahel Nettleton, 1783–1844," Ph.D. dissertation, Hartford Theological Seminary, 1943.

Breitenbach, William K. "New Divinity Theology and the Idea of Moral Accountability," Ph.D. dissertation, Yale University, 1978.

Hardman, Keith J. "Jonathan Dickinson and the Course of American Presbyterianism, 1717–1740," Ph.D. dissertation, University of Pennsylvania, 1971.

Hoopes, James. "Calvinism, Consciousness, and Personal Identity from Edwards to Taylor," unpublished manuscript, July 1984.

Morris, William S. "The Young Jonathan Edwards: A Reconstruction," Ph.D. dissertation, University of Chicago, 1955.

Index

church
  disestablishment of, 224, 230, 238–
    239, 241, 246
  purpose of (Hemmenway), 148
  purpose of (Old Calvinism vs. New
    Divinity), 170
Church of England, Old Calvinists
    threatened by, 147
church establishment
  Dwight for, 223–224
  Presbyterians for, 194
  Taylor for, 241
church membership
  Alexander on, 205–206
  under Congregational Way, 19
  Old Calvinism vs. New Divinity on,
    169–175
  and preparationism, 105, 138 (see also
    preparationism)
  self-experience as basis for, 20, 124,
    169, 170, 171, 205–206
  under Stoddard, 20
  see also separatism; use of means of
    grace
church-in-society, 148
  Beecher for, 229–230
  and Dwight, 223
  and Edwards on choosing, 15
  Edwards's individualism against, 276
  New Divinity repudiation of, 124–
    125, 126, 128–129
  and Old Calvinism, 207, 219
  and Presbyterianism, 178, 194–195,
    207
  and Stockbridge excommunication
    case, 142, 143
  Taylor for, 241
Clap, Thomas, 146, 147, 150, 181
Clarke, Samuel, 13, 23, 35
  and Edwards, 71, 136
  and Leibniz, 67, 68, 70, 185
  and two-stage process of volition, 40–
    41
  and Watts, 64
Cleaveland brothers, 146
Cole, Nathan, 35
Colebrook, Connecticut, Edwards the
    Younger in, 92
College of New Jersey at Princeton. See
    Princeton, College of New Jersey at
Collins, Anthony, and Freedom of the
    Will quotes, 162
Columbia Theological Seminary, 218
common sense
  Edwards's appeal to, 50, 73–74
  moralism of, 215–216

Scottish philosophy of, 13, 150–151,
    152–153, 162 (see also Scottish
    common-sense philosophy)
  Taylor for, 247
community
  of being vs. doing or willing, 148–
    149, 175
  and church (Huntington), 142
  and emigration to New England, 149
  and Freedom of the Will, 15, 86
  Presbyterian conception of, 179
  and Taylor/Dana vs. Freedom of the
    Will, 277
  see also church-in-society
Compleat Body of Divinity, A (Willard),
    179
compulsion
  Hospers on, 78–79
  vs. necessity (Emmons), 100
Concio ad Clerum ("declaration to the
    clergy") of Taylor, 260–266, 267,
    268, 269, 277
Confessions (Augustine), 3
Congregationalism, 19
  and Presbyterianism, 179–180
  resistance to, 20
  seminaries for, 218
  and separatism, 124
Congregationalism, English, 179
Congregationalism, New England, 144,
    163
Congregational Way, 19, 124, 149
Connecticut, disestablishment in, 224,
    238, 241, 246
connection
  causality as (Taylor), 245–246
  in Edwards's view of necessity, 45–46,
    49
  and Fitch on sin, 259
  in New Divinity view of sin, 130
consciousness. See experience; personal
    identity
Contrast Between Hopkinsianism and
    Calvinism (Ely), 88, 198
conversion
  and Bellamy on Great Awakening, 116
  in Blair's view, 187
  and Dickinson's theory, 183
  and Edwards's "ideal apprehension,"
    32, 33, 34
  Edwards's Narrative on, 64
  and Great Awakening confessions, 35,
    79–80 (see also Great Awakening)
  "morphologies" of, 79, 105
  New Divinity on, 101–102, 108

About the Author

Allen C. Guelzo was born in Yokohama, the only child of service parents then stationed in occupied Japan. He was educated in the United States, receiving an M.A. (1979) and Ph.D. (1986) from the University of Pennsylvania. A professor of church history at the Theological Seminary of the Reformed Episcopal Church, Guelzo is also an assistant adjunct professor of history at Drexel University Evening College in Philadelphia and an ordained presbyter in the Reformed Episcopal Church. He has published numerous articles. His home is in Philadelphia.

About the Book

Edwards on the Will was composed on the Mergenthaler Linotron 202 in Sabon, a contemporary typeface designed by the late Swiss typographer, teacher, scholar, book designer, and type designer Jan Tschichold.

The book was composed by Brevis Press, Bethany, Connecticut, and designed by Kachergis Book Design, Pittsboro, North Carolina.

WESLEYAN UNIVERSITY PRESS, 1989